Essential
Food and Beverage Service

for levels 1 and 2

John Cousins • Dennis Lillicrap

Orders: please contact Bookpoint Ltd, 130 Milton Park, Abingdon, Oxon OX14 4SB. Telephone: (44) 01235 827720. Fax: (44) 01235 400454. Lines are open from 9.00 to 5.00, Monday to Saturday, with a 24-hour message answering service. You can also order through our website **www.hoddereducation.co.uk**

If you have any comments to make about this, or any of our other titles, please send them to educationenquiries@hodder.co.uk

British Library Cataloguing in Publication Data
A catalogue record for this title is available from the British Library.

ISBN: 978 1444 11252 8

First edition published 2010
Impression number 10 9 8 7 6 5 4 3 2 1
Year 2014, 2013, 2012, 2011, 2010

Cover photo © Corbis.
Typeset by Fakenham Photosetting.
Printed in Italy for Hodder Education, an Hachette UK Company, 338 Euston Road, London NW1 3BH

Contents

Introduction to the book

The aim of the book

Essential Food and Beverage Service covers the foundation of knowledge and skills necessary for those studying and/or working in food and beverage service. The book has been specifically prepared to support the studies of those working towards the City and Guilds Certificate and Diploma in Professional Food and Beverage Service and those wishing to be assessed at NVQ/SVQ Levels 1 to 2 in Food and Beverage Service. In addition, the book will support the broader-based study requirements of a range of other qualifications and especially in-company training programmes.

Requirements for professionalism in food and beverage service

Foodservice operations are continuing to improve and develop, together with advances in quality. The demand for food and beverages away from the home has increased and, with a broader spectrum of the population eating out, customer needs are continuing to diversify.

Food and restaurant styles are also continuing to diversify to meet the challenges of the demands being made by increasingly knowledgeable and value-conscious customers. Menu and beverage list contents are constantly being influenced by trends, fads and fashions, the relationship between health and eating, dietary requirements, cultural and religious influences, the advance of vegetarianism, and customer acceptance, or otherwise, of irradiation and genetically modified foods. Expansion of the industry has generally meant greater choice. This, together with potential skill shortages and drives for efficiency, has seen a streamlining of foodservice operations.

Good food and beverage service in any sector is achieved where customers' needs are met and where management consistently reinforce and support service staff in the maintenance of clearly identified technical standards and service goals.

The primary aspect of a meal that enhances the customer's enjoyment and appreciation of it is where members of the food and beverage service staff have the confidence to provide a professional level of service that is also genuinely welcoming. But this is not something just anyone can do well. Although there is less emphasis on sophisticated service techniques in some sectors, there is now a far greater emphasis throughout the industry on the need for professional food and beverage service personal that have:

- sound product knowledge
- well-developed interpersonal skills
- technical competence
- the ability to work as part of a team.

However, food and beverage service also represents the ultimate paradox: the better it is, the less it is noticed.

John Cousins and Dennis Lillicrap
April 2010

Acknowledgements

The preparation of this book has drawn upon a variety of experience and literature. We especially want to thank Suzanne Weekes of Thames Valley University, who was the editing consultant for this book. We would also like to express our sincere thanks to all the organisations and individuals who gave assistance and support in the revision of this text. In particular we would like to thank:

Academy of Culinary Arts, UK; Academy of Food and Wine Service, UK; Mathew Alexander, Lecturer, University of Strathclyde, Glasgow; City and Guilds of London Institute; Croners Catering, Croners Publications; Dunk Ink; Andrew Durkan, author and consultant, formerly of Ealing College, London; Elia International Ltd, Middlesex; Euroservice UK, Welford, Northants; Foodservice Consultants Society International, UK; Professor David Foskett, author, consultant and Dean at the London School of Hospitality and Tourism, Ealing, the Operations Team at the School, and students from the School; German Wine Information Service, London; Simon Girling, Restaurant Manager, The Ritz Hotel, London; The Glasgow Hilton Hotel; Gleneagles Hotel, Auchterarder, Scotland; IFS Publications; The International Coffee Organisation; International Standards Organisation; Le Columbier Restaurant, London; Louvet Turner Coombe Marketing; Meiko UK Ltd; National Checking Co UK; Kevin O'Gorman, University of Strathclyde, Glasgow; PalmTEQ Limited UK; The Restaurant Association of Great Britain; Six Continents Hotels, London; Snap-Drape Europe Limited; Steelite International; The Tea Council; Uniwell Systems (UK) Ltd; The Westbury Hotel, London; Linden Wilkie, Managing Director, The Fine Wine Experience Ltd, London; and Williams Refrigeration, UK.

New photographs for this book were taken by Andrew Callaghan at Thames Valley University. The authors and publishers are grateful to everyone involved, particularly the students who appear in the book:

- Nickeisha Carter
- Jennifer Copp
- Pablo Antonio Flores
- Will Miles.

Illustrations are by Barking Dog Art. Photos from *Food and Beverage Service*, seventh edition, are by Carl Drury, except where stated. We would also like to thank the following for permission to reproduce copyright photos: page 1 © Christian Michel/View Pictures/Rex Features; fig. 1.1 © Stockbyte/Getty Images; fig. 1.2 © Imagestate Media; figs 1.3, 1.4 © Ingram Publishing Ltd; fig. 1.5 © Clover/Amana Images/Photolibrary; figs 1.6–8 © Photodisc/Getty Images; page 45 © Chris Gascoigne/View Pictures/Rex Features; fig. 6.8 © Thomas Perkins/iStockphoto.com; fig. 6.12 © xyno/istockphoto.com; p.125 © Wilfried Krecichwost/Photographer's Choice RF/Getty Images; p.207 © Jonathan Player/Rex Features.

The Academy of Food and Wine

The Academy of Food and Wine is the professional body for Front of House Service Personnel. We focus on helping to provide the hospitality industry with well-trained and qualified employees and on improving the status of Front of House Service as a rewarding and meaningful career choice.

The academy is nationally recognised as the industry's leading voice for raising standards in the delivery of food and in service skills. Affiliated to the Association de la Sommellerie Internationale, the Academy is also the official professional body for Sommeliers working in the UK.

The academy is delighted to endorse *Essential Food and Beverage Service for Levels 1 and 2* as a high-quality resource supporting students and tutors in the delivery of the new Diplomas in Professional Food and Beverage Service.

The United Kingdom Bartenders' Guild

The United Kingdom Bartenders' Guild came into being in 1933 and is a trade association with the prime aim of advancing the professional skills of bar men and women throughout the country.

The Guild promotes a high standard of workmanship and encourages the development of creative new cocktails through rewarding competitions both at home and abroad. The Guild also maintains a strict code of ethics within the bartending business.

The Guild is very pleased to support the publication of this invaluable resource for students.

UKBG UNITED KINGDOM BARTENDERS' GUILD

The structure of the book and how to use it

Structure of the book

The content of the book has been structured to follow a logical progression from exploring the hospitality industry, underpinning knowledge and skills of food and beverage operations, service areas and equipment, product knowledge of food and beverages, through to interpersonal and technical service skills and their application.

The book is presented in four parts:

Part A The industry: provides an overview of the hospitality industry and also identifies the types of operation, sectors, the reasons for eating out, production and service methods and service staff roles.

Part B Underpinning knowledge and skills: provides foundation knowledge of service areas and equipment, workplace skills, legislation in food and beverage service, and customer service and customer relations.

Part C Product knowledge: covers knowledge of menus and wine and drink lists, essential menu knowledge, non-alcoholic and alcoholic beverages.

Part D Service skills: begins by identifying basic technical skills and food and beverage service conventions followed by a description of the full service sequence from taking bookings to clearing after service. The last chapter covers bookings, billing and revenue control. Finally, a list of cocktail and mixed drink recipes and methods is provided in **Annex A**.

The content of the book, while having its origins in classic cuisine and service (the context and the body of knowledge on which modern foodservice operations are based) is also intended to reflect current practice within the industry. Therefore, while the book gives information and describes various aspects of food and beverage service, it is not intended to be a prescriptive book. Clearly the actual operation of the service will be substantially affected by the style and business needs of the individual operation.

Throughout the book we have referred to job titles and job categories such as manager, waiter, supervisor, bar tender, servers and catering assistants. In all cases these terms, in line with general trends within the industry, refer to both male and female personnel.

How to use this book

The information in the book can be found in three ways:

- Using the detailed contents list at the front of the book (pages iii–vi)
- Using the learning outcomes identified at the beginning of each chapter
- Using the index at the back of the book (pages 327–352.)

The detailed contents list takes account of the various examining and awarding body recommendations and assessment requirements, especially the City and Guilds Professional Certificate and Diploma in Food and Beverage Service together with the National Vocational Qualifications. Because of the wide variety of hospitality operations, the contents list indicates the broad range of knowledge and skills that will be relevant to a range of food service operations.

At the beginning of each chapter there is a list of the learning outcomes covered by that chapter.

The index at the back of the book provides a list of key words from the text together with their relevant page numbers.

PART A

The Industry

CHAPTER 1

The hospitality industry

This chapter will help you to learn about:

1 The international hospitality industry
2 The UK hospitality industry
3 Sectors of the hospitality industry
4 The foodservice industry
5 Employment in the hospitality industry

1.1 The international hospitality industry

Wherever there are groups of people there is likely to be some kind of hospitality provision, in other words, somewhere where people can get food, drink and accommodation.

The word 'hospitality' encompasses all aspects of the hotel and catering (or foodservice) industry. It is a relatively modern word, meaning the friendly and generous treatment of guests and strangers. The word 'catering' refers to offering facilities to people, especially the provision of food and beverages. There is also the more internationally understood term 'foodservice' which is the same as catering in the UK and is now becoming used more often.

An international industry

Businesses today find themselves competing in a world economy for survival, growth and profitability. Managers working in the industry have to learn to adjust to change in line with market demands for quality and value for money, and increased organisational attention must be devoted to profitability and professionalism.

The globalisation of the hospitality and tourism industries has advanced under the pressures of increased technology, communication, transportation, deregulation, elimination of political barriers, socio-cultural changes and global economic development, together with growing competition in a global economy. An international hospitality company must perform successfully in the *world's* business environment.

Travel, tourism and hospitality together make up the world's largest industry. According to the World Travel and Tourism Council (WTTC), the annual gross output of the industry is greater than the gross national product (GNP) of all countries except the USA and Japan. Worldwide, the industry employs over 112 million people.

In many countries, especially in emerging tourist destinations, the hospitality and tourism industry plays a very important role in the national economy, being the major foreign currency earner.

Travel, tourism and hospitality – the world's largest industry

As the world economy continues to become more interdependent, this will give rise to increasing amounts of business travel. With this in mind, it is clear that the global economic environment plays a significant role in the internationalisation opportunities available to hospitality and tourism companies, and that global economic policies and developments play a critical role in the hospitality and tourism industry.

Key influences affecting the hospitality industry

- Social trends/lifestyle
- Amount of disposable income people have to spend
- Inflation
- Available credit
- Cultural factors – people using hospitality to celebrate occasions such as birthdays, weddings, etc.
- Regulation – taxation, VAT, tourism
- Media – television, advertising, magazines, celebrity chefs

The hospitality product

The hospitality product consists of elements of food, drink and accommodation, together with the service, atmosphere and image that surround and contribute to the product.

The hospitality industry contains many of the characteristics of other service industries but with the added complications of the production process. It is the production process that is the difficult element as it focuses on production and delivery, often within a set period of time.

The need to provide a specialist environment within which hospitality can be delivered means that most hospitality businesses must invest a substantial amount in plant and premises. This creates a high fixed cost/low variable cost structure. Fixed costs are those that remain the same or similar regardless of how much business is being carried out, such as rent and salaries. Variable costs, on the other hand, are those that change depending on the volume of business, such as food costs. The variable costs in servicing a room are minimal, although the hotel itself – particularly in the luxury hotel market – has a high fixed cost. In general, the financial break-even point for hospitality businesses is fairly high. The break-even point is the point when the total expenditure (the amount the business is spending to operate) matches the income from the sales. Exceeding this level will result in high profits, but when income is below the break-even point, the low volumes will result in substantial losses.

There are four main characteristics of the hospitality industry that make it a unique operation.

1 Hospitality cannot be delivered without customers. The customer is directly involved in many aspects of the delivery of the hospitality service, and is the judge of the quality of the hospitality provided.
2 Achieving a satisfactory balance between demand patterns, resource scheduling and operations is a particularly difficult task in the hospitality industry.
3 All hospitality operations require a combination of manufacturing expertise and service skill, in many cases 24 hours a day. To deliver a consistent product to each individual customer requires teams of people well trained to deliver to a set standard every time.
4 No matter how well planned the operation, how good the design and the environment, if the interaction between customer and service provider is not right this will have a detrimental effect on the customer experience of the total product. It will be a missed opportunity to sell future products. Good interaction between customers and service providers can also increase current sales – for example, waiting staff can use positive selling techniques to suggest additions to the meal, perhaps items the customer may not have considered but which they are delighted to have recommended.

Importance of professionalism

The ability to deliver a consistent product to every customer is also an important consideration and in order to do this staff must be trained in teams to deliver a consistent standard of product and service. This means being able to cater not just for individual customers, but also to the needs of many different groups of customers, all with slightly different requirements. The success of any customer experience will be determined at the interaction point between the customer and the service provider.

The service staff have an additional part to play in serving the customer: they are important in the future selling process, in other words, if they provide the customer with a good experience the customer is more likely to return in the future. Service staff should, therefore, be trained to use such opportunities to generate additional revenue.

The need for forecasting

Demand for hospitality services fluctuates over time and by type of customer. Because of the mixture of patterns and variables that can affect demand, forecasting is often difficult, thus making planning, resourcing and scheduling difficult. Hospitality cannot be delivered without customers. Achieving a satisfactory balance between demand patterns, resource scheduling and operational capacity is a difficult task for managers in hospitality.

Scheduling of resources is also difficult. If too many staff are on duty to cover the forecast demand, then profitability suffers as too many people are being paid for too little work. Insufficient staffing creates problems with servicing and staff morale – there is too much work to do and too few people to do it. Forecasting is therefore a crucial function, which contributes to the successful operation of the hospitality business.

Definitions

Fluctuations in demand: when demand for a product or service varies from time to time. This could be day to day, month to month or at certain times of the year. For example, January is not usually a good time of the year for hotels and restaurants as many people do not have the money to spend straight after Christmas, so business may go down.

Variables: other changes that may affect business, such as changes in people's income, higher taxation so people have less money to spend or changes in the weather which can affect whether people decide to go out or stay at home. Competition from supermarkets producing restaurant-style food at a reasonable price may mean that more people choose to eat at home rather than go out.

Resourcing: providing the food, labour and equipment to do the job.

Demand patterns: patterns of customer behaviour, for example, when the weather is bad people tend to stay at home; at the weekend more people go out to eat; at certain times of the year restaurants get very busy, for instance, during the Christmas period.

Resource scheduling: planning and making sure that all the resources are in place when they are needed, such as the food, staff and equipment.

Operational capacity: how much work (number of customers/orders/functions) the operation is able to cope with to deliver a product at the required standard to satisfy the customer.

1.2 The UK hospitality industry

The hospitality industry in the UK employs around 1.7 million people and is growing all the time. It provides excellent opportunities for training and employment.

Figure 1.1 **Golf courses usually have bars, serve food and offer a range of other hospitality services**

Like all leisure markets, hospitality and catering benefits from improving economic conditions. For many people, real disposable income has grown over the last 20 years, and forecasts suggest that it will continue to grow. In wealthy markets, the leisure and pleasure sectors generally outperform the economy. As people become wealthier, their extra income tends not to be spent on upgrading the essentials but on pleasure and luxury items. However, whenever there is a downturn in the economy, the leisure sectors suffer disproportionately.

Number of businesses

The leisure sector includes hospitality, travel and tourism and employs in the region of two million people. Around seven per cent of all jobs in the UK are in the leisure sector or, put another way, the sector accounts for about one in every 14 UK jobs.

There are approximately 142,000 hospitality, leisure, travel and tourism businesses in the UK that operate from 192,100 outlets. The restaurant industry is the largest within the sector (both in terms of the number of outlets and size of the workforce), followed by pubs, bars and nightclubs and the hotel industry.

Table 1.1 Number of businesses (enterprises) by industry

Industry	Number of businesses	%
Restaurants	63,600	45
Pubs, bars and nightclubs	49,150	35
Hotels	10,050	7
Travel and tourist services	6,750	5
Food and service management (contract catering)	6,350	4
Holiday centres and self-catering accommodation	3,650	3
Gambling	1,850	1
Visitor attractions	450	*
Youth and backpacker hostels	150	*
Hospitality, leisure, travel and tourism total	142,050	100

* Negligible

The UK leisure industry (tourism and hospitality) is estimated by the government to have been worth £85 billion in 2009, but including all business expenditure the total market is worth much more than this. Expenditure on accommodation is difficult to pin down, but it is estimated that it contributes £10.3 billion (excluding categories such as camp sites and youth hostels) to the total leisure market.

Size of the hospitality industry

- 1.7 million people employed
- £85 billion to the UK economy
- £7.5 billion on accommodation

The hospitality industry consists of all those business operations that provide for their customers any combination of the three core services of food, drink and accommodation. While there is a clear overlap with tourism, there are a number of sectors within the hospitality industry that are sometimes regarded as separate from tourism, for example, industrial catering and those aspects of hospitality that attract only the local community.

Hotels, restaurants, bars, pubs and clubs are all part of what is known as the commercial sector. Businesses in the commercial sector need to make a profit so that the business can survive and grow. Catering provided in places like hospitals, schools, colleges, prisons and the armed services also provides thousands of meals each day. This sort of catering is part of what is known as the public sector (also known as the secondary service sector). Businesses in the public sector do not need to make a profit and are often called cost provision sectors, but these days many catering services in the public sector are run by profit-making contract caterers.

Despite its complexity, catering represents one of the largest sectors of the UK economy and is fifth in size behind retail food, cars, insurance and clothing. It is also an essential support to tourism, another major part of the economy, and one of the largest employers in the UK.

Main types of businesses

There are three main types of business: small to medium-sized business enterprises (SMEs), public limited companies and private companies.

SMEs

These have up to 250 employees. In the UK as a whole, SMEs account for over half of all employment (58.7 per cent). These are usually private companies that may become public limited companies if they become very large.

Public limited companies and private companies

The key difference between public and private companies is that a public company can sell its shares to the public, while private companies cannot. A share is a certificate representing one unit of ownership in a company, so the more shares a person has, the more of the company they own.

Before it can start in business or borrow money, a public company must prove to Companies House (the department where all companies in the UK must be registered) that at least £50,000 worth of shares have been issued and that each share has been paid up to at least a quarter of its nominal value (so 25 per cent of £50,000). It will then receive authorisation to start business and borrow money.

Other types of businesses

The types of business in operation in the catering and hospitality industry can be further divided into sole traders, self-employed, partnership and limited liability companies. These are usually private companies.

Sole trader

A sole trader is the simplest form of setting up and running a business. It is suited to the smallest of businesses. The sole trader owns the business, takes all the risks, is liable for any losses and keeps any profits. The advantage of operating in business as a sole trader is that very little formality is needed. The only official records required are those for HM Revenue and Customs (HMRC), National Insurance and VAT. The accounts are not available to the public.

Self-employed

There is no precise definition of self-employment, although guidance is offered by HMRC. It is important to note that a mere agreement with an individual that he or she will be regarded as self-employed is insufficient for the purposes of HMRC and the Contributions Agency.

In order to determine whether an individual is truly self-employed, the whole circumstances of his or her work need to be considered. This may include whether he or she:

- is in control of their own time, the amount of work they take on and the decision-making

- has no guarantee of regular work
- receives no pay for periods of holiday or sickness
- is responsible for all the risks of the business
- attends the premises of the person giving him or her the work
- generally uses his or her own equipment and materials
- has the right to send someone else to do the work.

Partnership

A partnership consists of two or more people working together as the proprietors of a business. Unlike limited liability companies (see below), there are no legal requirements in setting up as a partnership. A partnership can be set up without the partners necessarily being fully aware that they have done so.

The partnership is similar to a sole trader in law, in that the partners own the business, take all the risks, stand any losses and keep any profits. Each partner individually is responsible for all the debts of the partnership. So, if the business fails, each partner's personal assets are fully at risk. It is possible, though not very common, to have partners with limited liability. In this case the partner with limited liability must not play any active part in the management or conduct of the business. In effect, he or she has merely invested a limited sum of money in the partnership.

The advantages of operating a business as a partnership can be very similar to those of the sole trader. Very little formality is needed, although those contemplating entering into a partnership should consider taking legal advice and having a partnership agreement drawn up.

The main official records that are required are records for HM Revenue and Customs (HMRC), National Insurance and VAT. The accounts are not available to the public. There may be important tax advantages, too, when compared with a limited company. For example, partners might be able to pay the tax they owe at a later date, or treat deductible expenses more generously. These are business expenses that can be claimed against tax, in other words, taken away from the business's income, so the amount of money taxed is less, which means the amount of tax owed is less.

Limited liability companies

These are companies that are incorporated under the Companies Acts. This means that the liability of their owners (the amount they will have to pay to cover the business's debts if it fails, or if it is sued) is limited to the value of the shares each shareholder (owner) owns.

Limited liability companies are much more complex than sole traders and partnerships because the owners can limit their liability. As a consequence it is vital that people investing in them or doing business with them are aware of the financial standing of the company. Company documents are open to inspection by the public. These documents are:

- the **Constitution:** this comprises two documents – the memorandum of association and the articles of association
- the **Memorandum of Association:** this is the 'outer face' of the company, informing the outside world of its name and purpose
- the **Articles of Association:** this is the 'inner face' of the company and is concerned with the detailed conduct of the company, including rules about general meetings, the powers of the directors, accounts, and so on.

Franchising

Many operations in the hospitality industry are also run under a franchise agreement. A franchise is an agreement where a person or group of people pay a fee and some set-up costs to use an established name or brand that is well known and is therefore likely to attract more customers than an unknown or start-up brand.

An example of this is where the contract caterer, Compass Group, buys a franchise in the Burger King brand from Burger King's owner. It pays a fee plus a proportion of the turnover (the amount of money it makes). The franchisor (the branded company franchise provider) will normally lay down strict guidelines or 'brand standards' that the franchisee (franchise user) has to meet. In this example these will affect things like which ingredients and raw materials are used and where they come from, as well as portion sizes and the general product and service. The franchisor will use mystery shopping services to regularly check on the brand standards to ensure that the brand reputation is not being put at risk. The franchisor will normally also provide advertising and marketing support, accounting services, help with staff training and development and designs for merchandising and display materials.

1.3 Sectors of the hospitality industry

A summary of the hospitality sectors is given in Table 1.2, page 21.

Hotels and other tourist accommodation

Hotels provide accommodation in private bedrooms. Many also offer other services such as restaurants, bars and room service, as well as reception, porters and housekeepers.

Hotels are rated from five star down to one star. A luxury hotel will have five stars while a more basic hotel will have one star.

What a hotel offers will depend on the type of hotel it is and how many stars it has.

The hotel sector is predominantly independently owned. The properties come in all shapes, sizes and locations. More than three quarters of them have fewer than 20 rooms and are invariably family run. There are many international hotel chains, such as the Hilton, Radisson, Mandarin Oriental and Intercontinental in the five-star hotel market. There are also budget hotels, guesthouses and bed and breakfast accommodation.

Figure 1.2 The Savoy Hotel, London

To attract as many guests as possible, many hotels now offer even more services. These may include office and IT services (e.g. internet access, fax machines, a quiet area to work in), gym and sports facilities, swimming pool, spa, therapy treatments, hair and beauty treatments, and so on.

The hotel sector, despite its disparate nature, can be divided into distinct categories, such as luxury, business, resort, townhouse and budget properties. Each category has its own characteristics. Business hotels, as the name suggests, are geared to the corporate traveller; the emphasis therefore tends to be on functionality. These hotels will usually have a dedicated business centre, up-to-date communications technology in the bedrooms, and ample conference and meeting facilities. Business hotels are more likely to be chain operated, often with a strong brand element. Townhouses, meanwhile, are notable for their individuality, intimacy and emphasis on service. These hotels are invariably small and, as the name suggests, located in converted townhouses with a domestic feel that is emphasised by their decor. The fastest-growing sector is budget hotels (e.g. Travelodge, Premier Inn), where the accommodation units are co-located with a food source operation such as Little Chef.

Marketing consortia

'Consortia' is the plural of 'consortium'. A consortium is a group of independent hotels that make an agreement to buy products and services together. For example, they might all pay a specialist company to do their marketing (advertising and so on). This might mean, for example, that the members of the consortium could then use international reservation systems and compete against the larger hotel chains.

Food and beverage provision

The provision of food and beverage services varies greatly between establishments. Again, some general differences can be discerned between the various hotel categories. Upmarket hotels are likely to provide a full range of services, usually with at least one à la carte restaurant, 24-hour room service and a well-stocked bar. Townhouse properties, by contrast, generally provide little or no food, while budget hotels are characterised by the presence of a family restaurant. This is often a stand-alone, branded outlet that also draws custom from the surrounding area.

Recently, many hotels have been re-examining the place of food and beverage in their operations. While many townhouses open with no restaurant at all, other hotels believe that food and beverage provision is an essential guest service. This has led them to consider alternative methods of running a restaurant, such as contracting out to a third party or introducing a franchise operation.

Some hotels have speciality restaurants. For example, a high-profile or celebrity chef may run a restaurant, or it may specialise in steaks, sushi or seafood.

The contracting-out of food and beverage services to third parties will continue to be a major trend in the hotel catering sector over the next few years, although this will be much stronger in London than in the provinces. As many hotels continue to remain sluggish in response to evolving consumer demand for food and beverages and intense competition from the high street, the attraction of outsourcing food and beverage services will become increasingly appealing.

Outsourcing is not always a straightforward option for hotels, however. To attract walk-in dining customers, a hotel ideally needs to be located where there is easy access to the restaurant and the location of the hotel itself (city centre, countryside, etc.) needs to fit with the clientele that are being targeted – that is, the product must be attractive to the passing trade. Despite these constraints, the number of outsourced restaurants is expected to increase considerably, for example, Gordon Ramsey at Claridges and Gary Rhodes at the Cumberland.

With increased consumer interest in food and eating out, hotels are becoming more focused on developing attractive food and beverage facilities in-house. The success of in-house catering development will depend on the willingness of hotels to deliver a product that will be attractive to the outside market, and to maintain this product so that it evolves with changing consumer tastes and trends. According to human resource specialists within the hotel sector, key factors holding back further development are that food and beverage managers in hotels tend to be hoteliers rather than restaurateurs, as well as a shortage of experienced culinary and service staff.

Country house hotels

Country house hotels are mostly in attractive old buildings, such as stately homes or manor houses, in tourist and rural areas. They normally have a reputation for good food and wine and a high standard of service. They may also offer the additional services mentioned above.

Budget hotels

Budget hotels like motels and Travelodges are built near motorways, railway stations and airports. They are aimed at business people and tourists who need somewhere inexpensive to stay overnight. The rooms are reasonably priced and have tea- and coffee-making facilities. No other food or drink is included in the price. There are not many members of staff and there is no restaurant. However, usually there will be shops, cafés, restaurants or pubs close by, which are often run by the same company as the hotel.

Guesthouses and bed and breakfasts

There are guesthouses and bed and breakfast establishments all over the UK. They are small, privately owned businesses. The owners usually live on the premises and let bedrooms to paying customers, many of whom are regular customers. Some guesthouses offer lunch and an evening meal as well as breakfast.

Farms

The rural tourism industry is important in the UK. Farmers understand this and have formed a national organisation called the Farm Holiday Bureau. The farms in the organisation usually offer bed and breakfast and holiday cottages. Most members of the organisation have invested money to improve their bedrooms to meet the standards required by the National Tourist Board. The accommodation is usually on or near a working farm.

Youth hostels

The Youth Hostels Association runs hostels in various locations in England and Wales. These establishments cater for single people, families and groups travelling on a limited budget. They mainly provide dormitory accommodation, but some also have a few private rooms. In some locations they include a number of sports and leisure facilities. Basic, wholesome meals are provided at a low cost in some hostels and they all have a kitchen that can be used by visitors to store and prepare their own food.

Restaurants

Restaurants in the UK have approximately 40 per cent of the commercial hospitality market, and small establishments employing fewer than 10 staff make up the majority of the industry. The south-east of England has the highest concentration of catering and hospitality outlets.

Figure 1.3

The restaurant sector has become the largest in the UK hospitality industry. It includes exclusive restaurants and fine-dining establishments, as well as a wide variety of mainstream restaurants, fast-food outlets, coffee shops and cafés.

Many restaurants specialise in regional or ethnic food styles, such as Asian and Oriental, Mexican and Caribbean, as well as a wide range of European-style restaurants. New restaurants and cooking styles are appearing and becoming popular all the time.

Moderately priced speciality restaurants are very popular. In order for them to succeed, the manager must understand what customers want and plan a menu that will attract enough customers to make a good profit. A successful caterer is one who gives customers what they want; they will be aware of changing trends and adapt to them. The most successful catering establishments are those that are able to keep selling plenty of food over a long service period and throughout the year.

Chain organisations

There are many restaurant chains, coffee shops, chain stores and shops with restaurants in. Many of these chains are spread over wide areas and, in some cases, overseas. These are usually well-known companies that advertise widely. They often serve morning coffee, lunches and teas, or may be in the style of snack bars and cafeterias.

Fast food and takeaways

Many customers now want the option of popular foods at a reasonable price, with little or no waiting time. Fast-food establishments offer a limited menu that can be consumed on the premises or taken away. Menu items are quick to cook and have often been partly or fully prepared beforehand at a central production point.

Drive-ins and Drive-thrus

The concept of Drive-ins and Drive-thrus came from America. In Drive-ins, the customer enters a parking area and the servers come to the car to deliver the order. At present there are none of these in the UK. There are now many Drive-thrus across the UK. The most well known are the Drive-thrus at McDonald's fast-food restaurants. Customers stay in their vehicles and drive up to a microphone where they place their order. As the car moves forward in a queue, the order is prepared and is ready for them to pick up at the service window when they get there.

Figure 1.4

Delicatessens and salad bars

These offer a wide selection of salads and sandwich fillings to go in a variety of breads and rolls at a 'made-to-order' sandwich counter. The choice of breads might include panini, focaccia, pitta, baguette and tortilla wraps. Fresh salads, homemade soups, chilled foods and a hot 'chef's dish of the day' may also be available, along with ever-popular baked jacket potatoes with a good variety of fillings. With such a wide variety of choices these establishments can stay busy all day long, often serving breakfast as well.

Retail

Many retail operations offer catering services alongside the retail operation. This can range from vending machines to take-away services, through to full service restaurants in prestigious stores. Some retail operations also include a branch of well-known coffee chains or other popular catering restaurant brands. Independent foodservice operations are located within shopping centres and retail parks.

Event catering

Many hospitality operations have separate event planning departments. There are also a number of organisations that specialise in providing event management services. Event management is when a person or company plans and organises events, such as parties, dinners and conferences, for other people or companies. This will include such tasks as hiring the venue, organising the staff, the food and drink, music, entertainment and any other requests the host may have.

Corporate hospitality

Corporate hospitality is hospitality provided by businesses, usually for its clients or potential clients. The purpose of corporate hospitality is to build business relationships and to raise awareness of the company. Corporate entertaining is also used as a way to thank or reward loyal customers.

Leisure

The leisure sector covers a variety of types of establishment, including cinemas, theatres and sporting events. Catering services are always to be found at these premises.

Timeshare villas and apartments

A timeshare owner buys a particular amount of time (usually a few weeks) per year in a particular self-catering apartment, room or suite in a hotel or a leisure club. The arrangement may be for a period of years or indefinite. There will usually be a number of restaurants, bars and other leisure facilities within the same complex for timeshare owners to use.

Holiday centres

Holiday centres around the UK provide leisure and hospitality facilities all together in the same place, on a single site. They cater for families, single people and groups of people. Many holiday centres have invested large amounts of money to improve the quality of the holiday experience. Center Parcs, for example, have developed sub-tropical pools and other sporting and leisure activities that can be used even if the weather is bad. The holiday centres (sometimes called complexes) include a range of different restaurants and food courts, bars and coffee shops. These are examples of year-round holiday centres that encourage people to take holidays and weekend breaks from home.

Figure 1.5

Health clubs and spas

These are often luxury establishments or hotels where the client can have a number of specialist health treatments. The number of these has increased rapidly over recent years and they have become very popular. They usually offer healthy food, therapies and activities that fit in with people's modern-day lifestyles and their interest in being fit, healthy and contented.

Theme parks

Theme parks are now extremely popular venues for a family day out or even a full holiday. The larger theme parks include several different eating options ranging from fast food to fine dining. Some include branded restaurants (such as McDonald's and Burger King), which the visitor will already know. Theme parks are also used for corporate hospitality and conferences and many have conference and banqueting suites for this purpose, while larger theme parks may even have their own hotels.

Museums

Nowadays, museums provide much more than just interesting exhibits. For example, many museums have one or more cafés and restaurants for visitors. Some run events such as lunch lectures, family events and children's discovery days where food is provided as part of the event. Museums can even be used as an interesting venue for private events and banqueting during the hours they are closed to the general public. Sometimes outside caterers are employed for the occasion, but many museums employ their own catering team to provide a wide range of food.

Figure 1.6 **Hampton Court**

Historical buildings and visitor attractions

Numerous historical buildings and places of interest have food outlets such as cafés and restaurants. Many in the UK specialise in light lunches and afternoon tea for the general public. Some are also used as venues to host large private or corporate events.

Places like Hampton Court and Kew Gardens can be categorised as visitor attractions. They will usually have refreshments outlets serving a variety of food and drinks. Some, like Kew Gardens, are also used to stage large theatrical events or concerts in the summer.

Motorway service stations

Now sometimes also referred to as roadside services, motorway service stations provide a variety of services for motorists and other travellers. These include fuel, car washing and maintenance facilities and convenience shops. Many are becoming more sophisticated, with baby changing, infant and pet feeding facilities, bathrooms and showers, a variety of branded food outlets (such as Burger King and M&S Simply Food) and sometimes accommodation. The catering usually consists of food courts offering travellers a wide range of meals 24 hours, seven days a week. MOTO is an example of a company that provides these sorts of services nationwide.

Industrial catering

Catering for business and industry

The provision of staff dining rooms and restaurants in industrial and business settings has provided employment for many catering workers outside traditional hotel and restaurant catering. Working conditions in these settings are often very good. Apart from the main task of providing meals, these services may also include retail shops, franchise outlets and vending machines. It will also include catering for meetings and conferences as well as for larger special functions.

In some cases a 24-hour, seven-days-a-week service is necessary, but usually the hours are more streamlined than in other areas of the hospitality industry. Food and drink is provided for all employees, often in high-quality restaurants and dining rooms. The catering departments in these organisations are keen to retain and develop their staff, so there is good potential for training and career development in this sector.

Many industries have realised that satisfied employees work more efficiently and produce better work, so have spent a great deal of money on providing first-class kitchens and dining rooms. In some cases companies will subsidise (i.e. pay a proportion of) the cost of the meals so that employees can buy the food at a price lower than it costs to produce.

The contract foodservice sector

The contract foodservice sector, which has already been mentioned several times in relation to other sectors of the hospitality industry, consists of companies that provide catering services to other organisations. This sector has grown a lot in recent years.

Contract food service management provides food for a wide variety of people, such as those at work in business and industry, those in schools, colleges and universities, private and public healthcare establishments, public and local authorities and other non-profit-making outlets such as the armed forces, police or ambulance services.

It also includes more commercial areas, such as corporate hospitality events and the executive dining rooms of many corporations, special events, sporting fixtures and places of entertainment, and outlets such as leisure centres, galleries, museums, department stores and DIY stores, supermarket restaurants and cafés, airports and railway stations. Some contractors also provide other support services such as housekeeping and maintenance, reception, security, laundry, bars and retail shops.

Welfare catering

Public sector organisations that need catering services include hospitals, universities, colleges, schools, prisons, the armed forces, police and ambulance services, local authorities and many more.

While the aim of catering in hotels, restaurants and other areas of the leisure and travel industry (known as the private sector) is to make a profit, the aim of public sector catering is to keep costs down by working efficiently. However, these days the business of catering for public sector organisations is tendered for. This means that different companies will compete to win a contract to provide the catering for these organisations. Many public sector catering tenders have been won by contract caterers (contract food service providers) which have introduced new ideas and more commercialism (promoting business for profit) into the public sector. Because much of the public sector is now operated by profit-making contractors, it is sometimes referred to as the secondary service sector.

For a variety of reasons, the types of menu in the public sector may be different from those in the private sector. For example, school children, hospital patients and soldiers have particular nutritional needs (they may need more energy from their food or more of particular vitamins and minerals), so their menus should match their needs. Menus may also reflect the need to keep costs down.

Prisons

Catering in prisons may be carried out by contract caterers or by the Prison Service itself. The food is usually prepared by prison officers and inmates. The kitchens are also used to train inmates in food production. They can gain a recognised qualification to encourage them to find work when they are released. In addition to catering facilities for the inmates, there are also staff catering facilities for all the personnel (staff) who work in a prison, such as administrative staff and prison officers.

Armed forces

Catering in the armed forces includes providing meals for staff in barracks, in the field and on ships. Catering for the armed forces is specialised, especially when they are in the field, and they have their own well-established cookery training programmes. However, like every other part of the public sector, the forces need to keep costs down and increase efficiency. Consequently, they also have competitive tendering for their catering services. The Ministry of Defence contracts food service providers to cater for many of their service operations.

National Health Service

Hospital caterers need to provide well-cooked, nutritious and appetising meals for hospital patients and must maintain strict hygiene standards. High standards of food in hospitals can contribute to the recovery of patients.

The scale of catering services in the NHS is enormous. Over 300 million meals are served each year in approximately 1,200 hospitals. NHS trusts must ensure that they get the best value for money within their catering budget.

As well as providing nutritious meals for patients in hospital (many of whom need special diets), provision must also be made for out-patients (people who come into hospital for treatment and leave again the same day), visitors and staff. This service may be provided by the hospital catering team, but is sometimes allocated to commercial food outlets, or there may be a combination of in-house hospital catering and commercial catering.

The education sector school meals service

School meals play an important part in the lives of many children, often providing them with the only hot meal of the day. In April 2001, for the first time in over 20 years, minimum nutritional standards were reintroduced by the government. These standards are designed to bring all schools up to a measurable standard set down in law. Since this date, local education authorities (LEAs) have been responsible for ensuring that the minimum nutritional standards for school lunches are met. Schools also have to provide a paid-for meal, where parents request one, except where children are under five years old and only go to school part time. This does not affect the LEA's or the school's duty to provide a free meal to those children who qualify for one. In 2006 the government announced new standards for school food, consisting of three parts to be phased in by September 2009. Together the new standards cover all food sold or served in schools – breakfast, lunch and after-school meals, tuck shops, vending machines, mid-morning break snacks and anything sold or served at after-school clubs.

Residential establishments

Residential establishments include schools, colleges, university halls of residence, nursing homes, homes for the elderly, children's homes and hostels where all the meals are provided. The food and beverages provided have to satisfy all the residents' nutritional needs, as the people eating these meals may have no other food provision. Many of these establishments cater for children who may lead energetic lives and will be growing fast, so the food should be well prepared from good ingredients and nutritious, varied and attractive.

Licensed trade

Licensed house (pub) catering

There are tens of thousands of licensed public houses (pubs) in the UK and almost all offer food of some sort or another. The type of food they serve is ideal for many people as it is usually quite simple, inexpensive and quickly served in a comfortable atmosphere. In recent times many pubs have moved into selling food, revisiting their product offer (i.e. what they have to offer the customer) and the total pub experience for their customers in order to stay in business, for example, by adding restaurants, offering more bar snacks and putting on live entertainment.

Figure 1.7

There is now a great variety of food available in pubs, from those that serve ham and cheese rolls to those that have exclusive à la carte restaurants.

Clubs and casinos

Private clubs are usually run by managers who are appointed by club members. People pay to become members of private clubs and what most members want from a club in Britain, particularly in the fashionable areas of London, are good food and drink and informal service.

Most nightclubs and casinos are open to the public rather than to members only. As well as selling drinks to their customers, many now also provide food services, such as restaurants.

Transport catering

In addition to providing foodservice operations at ports, airport terminals and railway stations, there is considerable provision for people on the move, including marine, airline and on-train services.

Marine

There is a variety of types of sea-going vessels on which catering is required for both passengers and crew. Catering for passengers on ferries and cruise liners is becoming increasingly important in today's competitive markets.

Sea ferries

There are several ferry ports in the UK. Ferries leave from these every day, making a variety of sea crossings to Ireland and mainland Europe. As well as carrying passengers, many ferries also carry the passengers' cars and freight lorries. In addition to competing against each other, ferry companies also compete against airlines and, in the case of English Channel crossings, Eurostar and Eurotunnel.

In order to win customers they have invested in improving their passenger services, with most ferries having several shops, bars, cafés and lounges on board. Some also have very good restaurant and leisure facilities, fast-food restaurants and branded food outlets. These can also be run by contract caterers on behalf of the ferry operator. More recently, well-known chefs have become involved in providing top-quality restaurants on popular ferry routes.

Cruise liners

Cruise ships are floating luxury hotels and more and more people are becoming interested in cruising as a holiday. The food provision on a large cruise liner is of a similar standard to the food provided in a five-star hotel and is usually high-quality, banquet-style cuisine. Many shipping companies are known for the excellence of their cuisine.

Figure 1.8

As cruising becomes more popular, cruise companies are investing in increasing numbers of ever larger cruise liners. On cruises where the quality of the food is of paramount importance, other factors such as the dining room's ambience of refinement and elegance are also of great significance. Ship designers generally wish to avoid Las Vegas-type glittery dining rooms, but also those that are too austere. Ships must also be designed with easy access to the galley so waiters are able to get food quickly and with as little traffic as possible.

Dining is one of the most important selling points for cruise liners. People who take cruises want to dine well and generally they do, though cooking dinner for 800 people per sitting and giving people what they want takes skill and good management.

Many modern cruise liners are giant ships that have many different dining rooms. On such ships passengers can eat in the dining room of their choice, more or less whenever they want, at tables of various sizes, giving passengers maximum freedom.

Other vessels

As well as luxury liners, catering at sea includes smaller cargo and passenger ships and the giant cargo tankers. The food provision for crew and passengers on these ships will vary from good restaurants and cafeterias to more industrial-style catering on the tankers. On all types of ship, extra precautions have to be taken in the kitchen in rough weather.

Airline services

With increased air travel, the opportunities and need for food services catering to the industry have also increased. The food provision varies greatly both from airport to airport and airline to airline.

Airports offer a range of hospitality services catering for millions of people every year. They operate 24 hours a day, 365 days a year. Services include a wide variety of shops along with bars, themed restaurants, speciality restaurants, coffee bars and food courts.

In-flight catering is a specialist service. The catering companies are usually located at or near airports in the UK and around the world. The meals provided vary from snacks and basic meals to luxury meals for first-class passengers. Menus are chosen carefully to make sure that the food can safely be chilled and then reheated on board the aircraft.

The price of some airline tickets includes a meal served at your seat. The budget airlines usually have an at-seat trolley service from which passengers can buy snacks and drinks.

Rail services

Snacks can be bought in the buffet car on a train and some train operators also offer a trolley service so that passengers can buy snacks without leaving their seats. Main meals are often served in a restaurant car. However, there is not much space in a restaurant car kitchen, and there is a lot of movement of the train, so it can be quite difficult to provide anything other than simple meals.

Two train services run by separate companies run through the Channel tunnel. One is Eurotunnel's Le Shuttle train, which transports drivers and their vehicles between Folkestone and Calais in 35 minutes. Passengers have to buy food and drink for their journey before they board the train. Eurostar is a passenger-only service that operates between London St Pancras and Paris or Brussels. Eurostar is in direct competition with the airlines, so it provides catering to airline standards for first- and premier-class passengers. Meals are served by uniformed stewards in a similar service to an airline's business class. The food and beverages are included in the ticket price. Economy travellers usually buy their food separately from buffet cars or trolley services.

Outside catering (ODC)

When events are held at venues where there is no catering available, or where the level of catering required is more than the normal caterers can manage, then a catering company may take over the management of the event. This type of function will include garden parties, agricultural and horticultural shows, the opening of new buildings, banquets, parties in private houses, military pageants and tattoos, sporting fixtures such as horse racing, motor racing, football and rugby, and so on.

There is a lot of variety in this sort of outside catering work, but the standards are very high and people employed in this area need to be adaptable and creative. Sometimes specialist equipment will be required, especially for outdoor jobs, and employees need to be flexible as the work often involves a lot of travel, remote locations and outdoor venues.

1.4 The foodservice industry

The foodservice (or catering) industry provides millions of meals a day in a wide variety of types of foodservice operation.

- **Food** can include a wide range of styles and cuisine types. These can be classified by country, for example, traditional British or Italian; by type of cuisine, for example, oriental; or a particular speciality such as fish, vegetarian or health food.
- **Beverages** include all alcoholic and non-alcoholic drinks. Alcoholic beverages include wines and all other types of alcoholic drink such as cocktails, beers and cider, spirits and liqueurs. Non-alcoholic beverages include bar beverages such as mineral waters, juices, squashes and aerated waters, as well as tea, coffee, chocolate, milk and milk drinks and also proprietary drinks such as Bovril.

Figure 1.9 **Multiple food outlets at the Trafford Centre, Manchester (image courtesy of FCSI, UK)**

Within the hospitality industry there are a number of different industrial sectors. These are categorised according to the type of customer demand being met. To help identify the nature of demand being met within each sector, Table 1.2 provides a summary of the hospitality industry sectors already identified in this chapter and identifies the prime purpose of the foodservice operations within them. An historical summary is also given, together with an identification of both UK and international terminology. This identification of sectors also provides a framework for those studying the food and beverage service industry to which further studies and experience may be related.

Each section in Table 1.2 may be further analysed by reference to a set of variables that exist in the different sectors (Table 1.3). These variables represent elements that vary in particular sectors and thus provide a basis for examining the operation of different types of foodservice operation within specific sectors. They enable a comprehensive picture of industrial sectors to be compiled, and also provide the basis for the comparison of the different sectors.

Table 1.2 Sectors of the hospitality industry

Industry sector – UK terminology	Purpose of the foodservice operation	Historical summary	Industry sector – international terminology
Hotels and other tourist accommodation	Provision of food and drink together with accommodation services	Supported by developments in transport and increases in business and leisure-related tourism	*Hotel, motel and other tourist accommodation* Often now referred to as the *lodging industry*
Restaurants including conventional and specialist operations	Provision of food and drink, generally at a high price with high levels of service	Grew out of hotel restaurants (which were originally highly formal) through chefs wishing to start their own businesses	*Separate eating and drinking places* Categories usually defined by reference to three criteria: • level of service, e.g. quick service to full service or fine dining • extent of menu, e.g. limited to full • price range, e.g. low to high
Popular catering including cafés, pizza, grills, specialist coffee shops, roadside restaurants and steak houses	Provision of food and drink, generally at low/medium price with limited levels of service and often high customer throughput	Has gone through various phases. More recently highly influenced by the USA	
Fast food including McDonald's and Burger King	Provision of food and drink in highly specialised environment, characterised by high investment, high labour costs and vast customer throughput	Grew from combination of popular catering and takeaway, heavily influenced by US concepts; highly sophisticated meal packaging and marketing	
Takeaway including ethnic, KFC, snacks, fish and chips, sandwich bars, kiosks	Fast provision of food and drink	Developed from a variety of concepts. More recently, influenced by USA and trends in food tastes	
Retail stores	Provision of food and drink as an adjunct to retail provision	Developed originally from prestigious stores wishing to provide food and drink as part of the retailing experience	*Retail market*
Events/banqueting/ conferencing/ exhibitions	Provision of large-scale food and drink for events	Originally associated with hotels but has now become major sector in its own right	*Event market*
Leisure attractions such as theme parks, museums, galleries, cinemas and theatres	Provision of food and drink to people engaged in another pursuit	Increases in leisure have made profit from food and drink attractive to leisure and amenity providers	*Leisure market*

Motorway service stations	Provision of food and drink, together with petrol and other retail services, often in isolated locations	Developed in the 1960s with the advent of motorways. Influenced by USA and became specialised because of government regulations on provision of foodservice operations, retail services and fuel as well as location	*Highway (interstate) market*
Industrial catering either in-house operations or through catering/ foodservice contractors	Provision of food and drink to people at work	Developed out of recognition that well-fed workers are more productive. Given substantial boost during First and Second World Wars. Further developed by worker unions wanting to preserve conditions and the emergence of professional contract caterers/foodservice operators	*Business/industry markets*
Welfare catering	Provision of food and drink to people in colleges, universities, the armed forces and to people through established social need	Highly regulated and maintained now through public social conscience	*Social caterer/ foodservice* (student, healthcare, institutional and military)
Licensed trade including public houses, wine bars, licensed clubs and members' clubs	Provision of food and drink in an environment dominated by licensing requirements	Developed from bars and other drinking places with increased regulation and liquor licensing requirements	*Separate drinking places* But also some units included in *Separate eating and drinking places* shown above
Transport catering including railways, airlines and marine	Provision of food and drink to people on the move	Grew out of the need to meet the demands of the travelling public. Originally services were of high level, reflecting the type of traveller. Eventually changed to meet the needs of a wide range of travellers	*Transportation market*
Outdoor catering (ODC) (also known as off-premises catering or event catering)	Provision of food and drink away from home base; suppliers usually associated with a major event	Developed through the need to provide services at special events. The term ODC is misleading as little of this catering actually takes place outside	*Catering market*

Table 1.3 Variables in foodservice sectors

• Historical background • Reasons for customer demand • Size of sector: – in terms of outlets – in terms of turnover • Policies: – financial – marketing – catering	• Interpretation of demand/catering concept • Technological development • Influences • State of sector development • Primary/secondary activity • Types of outlets • Profit orientation/cost provision • Public/private ownership

There are many different industry sectors such as hotels, independent and chain restaurants, popular catering, pubs and wine bars, fast food, leisure attractions and banqueting. There are also sectors where food and beverages are provided as part of another business. These include transport catering, welfare, clubs, education, industrial feeding and the armed forces.

Some sectors provide food and beverages for profit, while others work within the constraints of a given budget, often called **cost provision** (for example, welfare and industrial). In addition, some sectors provide services to the general public whereas others provide them for restricted groups of people.

It is useful to define these different types of market as follows:

- General market
  - Non-captive: customers have a full choice.
- Restricted market
  - Captive: customers have no choice, e.g. welfare.
  - Semi-captive: customers have a choice before entering, e.g. marine, airline, trains, some hotels and some leisure activities. The customers could have chosen alternatives to these but, once chosen, have little choice of food and drink other than that on offer.

Taking these definitions into account, a general summary of sectors may be drawn up as shown in Table 1.4 although recent developments, such as the contracting out of catering and other services have blurred the division between profit- and cost-orientated establishments. However, defining the nature of the market in this way helps us to understand why different methods of organisation may be in operation. For example, in captive markets customers might be asked to clear their own tables, whereas in non-captive markets this is unlikely to be successful.

Table 1.4 Summary of sectors in the foodservice industry

Profit orientated (public or private ownership) (foodservice as main or secondary activity)		Cost provision
Restricted market	General market	Restricted market
Transport catering	Hotels/restaurants	Institutional catering
Clubs	Popular catering	Schools
Industrial (contract)	Fast food/takeaway	Universities and colleges
Private welfare	Retail stores	Hospitals
	Events/conferences/exhibitions	Armed forces
	Leisure attractions	Prisons
	Motorway service stations	Industrial (in-house)
	Pubs and wine bars	
	ODC (off-premises catering)	

1.5 Employment in the hospitality industry

Staffing and organisation structure

Hospitality companies need to have a structure for their staff in order for the business to run efficiently and effectively. Different members of staff have different jobs and roles to perform as part of the team so that the business is successful.

In smaller organisations, some employees have to become multi-skilled so that they can carry out a variety of duties. Some managers may have to take on a supervisory role at certain times.

A hospitality team will consist of operational staff, supervisory staff, management staff and, in large organisations, senior management. These roles are explained below.

Operational staff

These are usually practical, hands-on staff and include the chefs de partie, (section chefs), commis chefs, waiters, apprentices, reception staff and accommodation staff.

Supervisory staff

Generally the supervisors oversee the work of the operational staff. In some establishments the supervisors will be the managers for some of the operational staff.

Management staff

Managers are responsible for making sure the operation runs smoothly and within budget. They are accountable to the owners to make sure that the products and services on offer are what the customer expects and wants, and provide value for

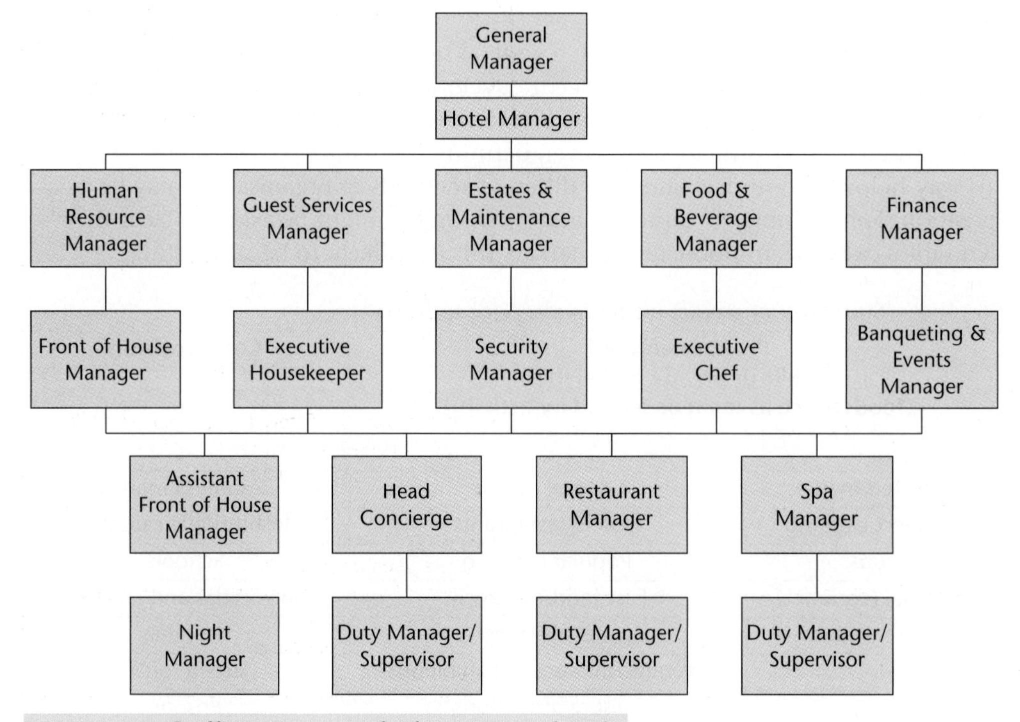

Figure 1.10 **Staffing structure of a four-star spa hotel**

money. Managers may also be responsible for planning for the future. They will be required to make sure that all the health and safety policies are in place and that health and safety legislation is followed. In smaller establishments they may also act as the human resources manager.

A hotel will normally have a manager, assistant managers, an accommodation manager, a restaurant manager and a reception manager. Within each section of the hotel there could be a manager with departmental responsibilities; a head chef is a manager, for example.

Employment rights and responsibilities

Those employed in the hospitality industry need to understand that there is a considerable amount of legislation that regulates both the industry itself and employment in the industry. Employers who contravene (break) the law or attempt to undermine the statutory (legal) rights of their workers, for example, by paying less than the national minimum wage or denying them their right to paid annual holidays, are not only liable to prosecution and fines but could be ordered by a tribunal and the court system to pay substantial amounts of compensation.

Both employers and employees have employment rights.

Employers must provide the employee with:

- a detailed job description
- a contract of employment that gives details of the job itself, working hours, the amount of annual holiday the employee will have and the notice period.

Job description: Restaurant Waiter

Purpose of job: To provide a quality food and beverage service to meet our customers' expectations and to enhance and maintain the reputation of the company.

Reporting to: Restaurant Supervisor

Skills, experience and qualifications required

- Good communication, presentation, time management and social skills
- One year's similar experience
- Wine knowledge useful but not essential as training will be given
- Current Food Handlers' Certificate desirable but full training will be provided

Main duties

- Preparation of the restaurant area ready for service in accordance with the establishment daily duties list
- Service of food and beverages to customers in accordance with the service specification
- Ensuring correct charges are made and payment received
- Clearing of restaurant area in accordance with service specification
- Ensuring compliance with control procedures for equipment and other stocks
- Following correct health and safety procedures to ensure welfare of both staff and customers
- Being able to explain for customers the content, preparation and presentation of all menu and beverage items, and promoting sales through positive selling techniques
- Additional food and beverage service duties as required in order to meet the business demands

Training requirements

- Induction and company policy as contained in the Staff Handbook
- Menu and beverage list content and updates as required
- Customer care programme
- Basic food hygiene
- Basic fire training at induction and further training every six months
- Basic Health and Safety at induction and full COSHH every six months
- Manual handling at induction

Performance measures

- Customer feedback
- Management feedback
- Regular knowledge test on foods, wine and other services offered
- Six monthly appraisals with restaurant supervisor

Figure 1.11 Example of a job description

An essential feature of a contract of employment is the 'mutuality of obligation'. This means that the employer will provide the employee with work on specified days of the week for specified hours and, if employed under a limited-term contract, for an agreed number of weeks or months. In return, the employee agrees to carry out the work for an agreed wage or salary.

Employers must adhere to laws relating to employment of staff, health and safety and food safety.

Employees must work in the way that has been agreed to in the contract and job description and follow all the organisation's policies and practices.

Workers and employees

An employee is a person who is employed directly by the company under a contract of employment or service.

A worker is someone who works for another company (a sub-contractor) that has won a contract to carry out work or provide services, i.e. they are not actually an employee of the company itself.

Workers who are not employees are still protected by:

- Health & Safety legislation
- Working Time Regulations (1998)
- Anti-discriminatory laws
- Public Interest Disclosure Act (1998)
- National Minimum Wage Act (1998)
- Part-time Workers (Prevention of Less Favourable Treatment) Regulations.

Recruitment and selection

When advertising for new staff it is important to be aware of the relevant legislation:

- Children and Young Persons Act (1933)
- Licensing Act (1964)
- Rehabilitation of Offenders Act (1974)
- Data Protection Act (1988)
- Asylum and Immigration Act (1996)
- National Minimum Wage Act (1998)
- Working Time Regulations (1998)
- Sex Discrimination Act (1975)
- Race Relations Act (1976)
- Disability Discrimination Act (1995)
- Human Rights Act (1998)

Job advertisements

It is unlawful to discriminate against job applicants on grounds of:

- sex, marital status or gender
- colour, race, nationality or national or ethnic origins
- disability
- sexual orientation
- religion or beliefs
- trades union membership or non-membership.

The following words and phrases should be avoided in a job advertisement as they could be construed (understood) or misconstrued as indicating an intention to discriminate on grounds of sex, race or disability:

- pleasing appearance
- strong personality
- energetic
- articulate
- dynamic
- no family commitments.

Use of job titles with a sexual connotation (e.g. 'waiter', 'barmaid', 'manageress') will also be taken to indicate an intention to discriminate on the grounds of a person's sex, unless the advertisement contains an indication or an illustration to the contrary.

Job applications

Job application forms must be designed with care. If sensitive personal information is needed, such as a health record or disability disclosure, the reason for this should be explained, and the candidate reassured that the data will remain confidential and will be used and stored in accordance with the provisions of the Data Protection Act 1998.

Human Rights Act

Candidates must be informed when the application is sent out, and again at interview, if they have to wear a uniform or protective clothing when on duty. Any surveillance monitoring the company is likely to carry out must also be disclosed to applicants.

Asylum and Immigration Act

It is an offence under the Asylum and Immigration Act (1996) to employ a foreign national subject to immigration control (i.e. a person who needs a visa or work permit, for example) who does not have the right to enter or remain in the UK, or to take up employment while in the UK. Job application forms should caution future employees that they will be required, if shortlisted, to produce documents confirming their right to be in, and to take up employment in, the UK.

Job interviews

The purpose of the job interview is to assess the suitability of a particular applicant for the vacancy. The interviewer should ask questions designed to test the applicant's suitability for the job, covering their qualifications, training and experience, and to find out about the individual's personal qualities, character, development, motivation, strengths and weaknesses.

If a job applicant resigned or was dismissed from previous employment, the interviewer may need to know why. Any health problems, injuries or disabilities the candidate has admitted to may also need to be discussed in order to determine the applicant's suitability for employment – for example, in a high-risk working environment.

Employers may lawfully ask a job applicant if he or she has been convicted of any criminal offence, but must be aware of the right of job applicants, under the Rehabilitation of Offenders Act (1974), not to disclose details of any criminal convictions that have since become 'spent' (i.e. those that occurred so long ago that they have been dealt with and are no longer an issue).

The interviewer should not ask questions about sexuality or religion. However, questions on religion may be asked if, for example, aspects of the job may directly affect the beliefs of an individual – an example would be the handling of alcoholic drinks.

Job offers

An offer of employment should be made or confirmed in writing and is often conditional on the receipt of satisfactory references from former employers. Withdrawing an offer of employment once it has been accepted could result in a civil action for damages by the prospective employee.

Statutory sick pay

Employers in the UK are liable to pay up to 28 weeks' statutory sick pay to any qualified employee who is unable to work because of illness of injury. Employers who operate their own occupational sick pay schemes may opt out of the statutory sick pay scheme, as long as the payments available to their employees under such schemes are equal to or greater than payments they would be entitled to under statutory sick pay, and so long as these employees are not required to contribute towards the cost of funding such a scheme. Payments made under statutory sick pay may be offset against contractual sick pay and vice versa.

Working Time Regulations

The Working Time Regulations apply not only to employees but also to every worker (part-time, temporary, seasonal or casual) who undertakes to do work or carry out a service for an employer. The 1998 Regulations are policed and enforced by employment tribunals (in relation to a worker's statutory rights to rest breaks, rest periods and paid annual holidays) and by local authority environmental health officers.

Learning and qualifications

The hospitality industry provides many opportunities to learn because of its complexity and diversity. There are many different sectors, trends and themes, and there are new developments in training all the time.

Qualifications show that a person has studied a subject successfully and a certificate is usually awarded as proof of the qualification. Successfully achieving a qualification usually involves some sort of assessment, either in the form of examinations, coursework, observation by an assessor, or a combination of these things. The assessor decides whether the student has learned what they were supposed to and whether they have performed the skills to the required standard. Courses without assessment are not viewed very highly by potential employers.

Qualifications inform employers of what you should be able to do. They indicate to the employer whether you have the skills required to do the job. Qualifications differ all over the world and it is often difficult to make comparisons between qualifications in different countries.

Even in the UK there are many different qualifications and that is why some employers ask job applicants to do a practical test before they have an interview. Some employers ask chef applicants to do a trial day or more of work.

Despite this, it is important to obtain qualifications as they provide better career prospects and opportunities for personal development. Qualifications also help to boost confidence and self-esteem. There are a number of college-based courses that will help you to develop a range of practical and theoretical skills such as numeracy, language and information technology.

Apprenticeships are a way to learn skills within a workplace setting while also getting a qualification. An apprenticeship can be through a day-release course at college or may be completely work-based, where an assessor monitors your learning and development.

Whichever type of learning you choose, it is important to understand that learning is for life. In order to ensure that you have a job throughout your life you must continue to learn and develop your skills. You can improve your knowledge by reading hospitality journals, books and food magazines and by searching the internet for food sites. Electronic learning (by using CDs, DVDs and the internet) can help you to learn in the way that suits you best and to work at your own pace, testing yourself when you are ready to be tested.

Assessment will help you to understand what you have achieved and what you must do to improve, and provides the building blocks for further learning and achievement.

CHAPTER 2

Food and beverage operations

This chapter will help you to learn about:

1 Foodservice operations
2 Food production methods
3 Food and beverage service methods
4 Food and beverage service personnel

2.1 Foodservice operations

Food and beverage (or foodservice) operations in the hospitality industry are concerned with the provision of food and drink ready for immediate consumption (but excluding retailing and food manufacturing).

Foodservice operations are concerned with:

1. The *consumer needs and market potential* in the various sectors of the foodservice industry.
2. The *formulation of policy and business objectives* that will guide the choice of operational methods that will be used.
3. The *interpretation of demand* in order to make decisions on the range and type of food and beverages to be provided, as well as other services, and the service levels and prices to be charged.
4. The *planning and design of facilities* required for the food and beverage operations and the plant and equipment required.
5. The *organisation of provisioning* for food and beverages and other purchasing requirements to meet the needs of the food production, beverage provision and the service methods being used.
6. Knowledge of the operational and management requirements for the *food production, beverage provision and service processes and methods*, and decision-making on the appropriateness of the various processes and methods, together with the management and staffing needs in order to meet the requirements of the operation.
7. *Control of costs* of materials and other costs, such as labour and overheads, associated with the operation of food production, beverage provision and other services, and the *control of revenue*.
8. The *monitoring of customer satisfaction* to continually check on the extent to which the operation is meeting customer needs and achieving customer satisfaction.

The eight elements of this sequence may be referred to as the *foodservice cycle* as represented in Figure 2.1. This summarises what food and beverage (or foodservice) operations are concerned with and illustrates that it is not simply about food production, beverage provision or food and beverage service.

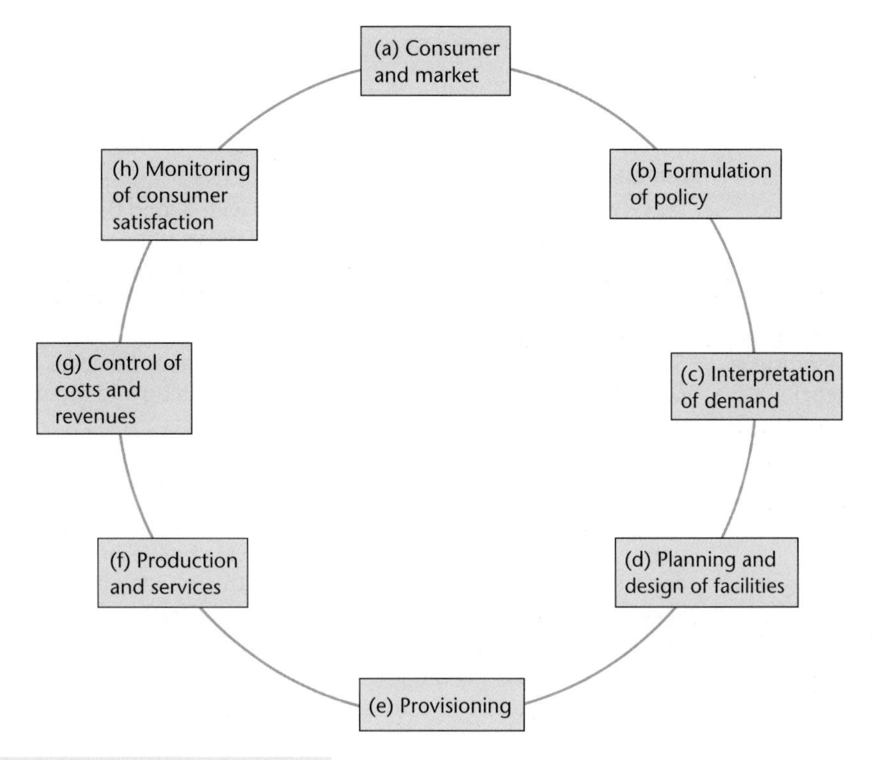

Figure 2.1 **The foodservice cycle**

The foodservice cycle can be used as a basis to analyse and compare how different foodservice operations work. It provides a standard template or checklist so that information about a specific operation can be collected and organised in a specific way. This can then be compared with the same information collected on other foodservice operations.

The foodservice cycle is also a dynamic model in that it can be used to help understand how an individual operation works. Difficulties in one element of the cycle will cause difficulties in the elements of the cycle that follow. For example, difficulties with purchasing will have effects on food production and service and control. Similarly, difficulties experienced under one element of the cycle will have their causes in preceding elements. For example, difficulties experienced in food and beverage service are often caused by factors such as poor purchasing, inadequate stock control, equipment shortages, poor room layouts or staffing problems.

Types of foodservice operations

Food and beverage (or foodservice) operations include various types of restaurants (bistros, brasseries, coffee shops, first-class/fine dining, ethnic, themed), cafés, cafeterias, takeaways, canteens, function rooms, tray service operations, lounge service operations, home delivery operations and room service operations for hotel guests. Examples of the types of operation are given in Table 2.1.

Table 2.1 **Examples of types of food and beverage operations**

Type of operation	Description
Bistro	Often a smaller establishment, with check tablecloths, bentwood chairs, cluttered decor and friendly, informal staff. Tends to offer honest, basic and robust cooking
Brasserie	This is generally a fairly large, styled room with a long bar, normally serving one-plate items rather than formal meals (though some offer both). Often it is possible just to have a drink, coffee or snack. Service provided by waiters, often in traditional style of long aprons and black waistcoats
New-wave brasserie (gastrodome)	Slick modern interior design, coupled with similar approaches to contemporary cuisine and service. Busy and bustling and often large and multilevel
Coffee shop	Similar to brasserie-style operations, often themed. May be open all day and serve all meal types from breakfast through to supper
First-class restaurant	Usually formal fine dining restaurants with classical preparation and presentation of food and offering a high level of table (silver, gueridon and/or plated) service. Often associated with classic/haute cuisine
Restaurant	Term used to cover a wide variety of operations. Price, level and type of service, decor, styles, cuisines and degree of choice varies enormously across the range of types of operation. Service ranges from full table service to assisted service such as carvery-style operations
International restaurant	Indian, Oriental, Asian, Spanish, Greek, Italian, Creole and Cajun are just some of the many types of cuisine available, with establishments tending to reflect specific ethnic origins. Many of the standard dishes are now appearing within a range of other menu types
Themed restaurant	Often international in orientation, e.g. Icelandic hot rock with food prepared and cooked at the table, 'Beni-hana' oriental theme, again with food prepared and cooked at table. Also includes themes such as jungle, rainforest or music/opera, where waiting staff perform as well as serve
International destination restaurant	Often Michelin-starred fine dining restaurants, offering a distinctive personality, cuisine, ambiance, beverages and service. Usually table service at various levels but mostly personal and highly attentive. Generally considered as the home of gastronomy. Expensive but also value-laden
Health food and vegetarian restaurants	Increasing specialisation of operations into vegetarianism and/or health foods (though vegetarian food is not necessarily healthy), to meet lifestyle needs as well as dietary requirements
Cafeteria	Primarily self-service with customer choosing selection from a counter or counters in varying designs and layouts. Originally developed for the industrial feeding market but now seen in a variety of sectors
Popular catering and fast-food outlets	Developed from table service teashops and cafés through to steakhouses, and now incorporating snack bars, kiosks, diners, takeaways and cafeterias, with modern-day burger, chicken and fish concepts, and with ethnic foods also being incorporated. Meeting the needs of all-day meal-taking (grazing) and also the need for 'grab and go' service, especially for the leisure, industrial and travelling markets
Public houses	Licensed environment primarily for drinking alcoholic beverages. May be simply a serving bar with standing room for customers or may have more plush surroundings incorporating the offer of a variety of foods. These can range from simple plated dishes through to establishments offering full restaurant service (sometimes called gastropubs)
Wine bars	Often a mixture of bar and brasserie-style operation, commonly wine themed, serving a variety of foods

The list of operations given in Table 2.1 identifies types of operations but not necessarily the type of customer demand being met. For example, cafeterias may be found in motorway service stations, in airline terminals, at railway stations, in retail catering and in industrial or welfare catering. This is also true for a variety of other foodservice operations. Therefore, throughout the hospitality industry similar types of foodservice operation are found in different types of industry sector.

Variables in foodservice operations

The list of types of operations in Table 2.1 (see above) by itself indicates very little in terms of methods of organisation adopted and the management of them. In a similar way to the identifying variables for sectors described in Table 1.3 (Chapter 1, page 23), variables can also be identified for different foodservice operations. These variables have been identified from a variety of published sources as well as from experience. They can be separated into three groups:

1. Organisational
2. Customer experience
3. Performance measures.

These different groups of variables enable the systematic examination and comparison of types of food and beverage operations. Profiles of differing types of operations can be drawn, based upon the examples of variables identified in Table 2.2. The foodservice cycle also provides a useful framework or checklist when gathering information about a foodservice operation. It helps to organise the information as it is collected and also helps to identify where there are gaps in the information being collected.

Table 2.2 Variables in foodservice operations

Organisational variables	
• Nature of market being met	• Capacity
• Legislative controls	• Staff working hours
• Scale of operation	• Staff organisation
• Marketing/merchandising	• Staff capability
• Style of menu and drinks list	• Number of staff
• Range of choice	• Specialised service requirements
• Opening times/service period	• Provisioning and storage methods
• Production methods	• Billing methods
• Type and capability of equipment	• Checking (order-taking) methods
• Service methods	• Clearing methods
• Dining arrangements	• Dishwashing methods
• Seating time	• Control method costs/revenue
• Number of covers available	

Customer experience variables	
• Food and drink available	• Atmosphere (including decor, lighting, air conditioning, acoustics, noise, size and shape of room, other customers, attitude of staff)
• Level of service and other services	
• Price range/value for money	
• Cleanliness and hygiene	

Performance measure variables	
• Seat turnover/customer throughput	• Sales analysis
• Customer spend/average check	• Departmental profit
• Revenue per member of staff	• Stock turnover
• Productivity index	• Stock holding
• Ratio of food and beverage sales to total sales	• Complaint levels
• Sales/profit per sq m (or ft)/per seat	• Level of repeat business

2.2 Food production methods

For a foodservice operation, the production system has to be organised to produce the right quantity of food at the correct standard, for the required number of people, on time, using the resources of staff, equipment and materials effectively and efficiently.

As costs of space, equipment, fuel, maintenance and labour continue to rise, more thought and time have to be given to the planning of a production system and to kitchen design. The requirements of the production system have to be clearly matched to the type of food that is to be prepared, cooked and served, to the required market at the correct price. All allocation of space and the purchase of the different types of equipment have to be justified, and the organisation of the kitchen personnel also has to be planned at the same time.

Many modern food production operations are based on the process approach, as opposed to the 'partie' (product approach) system. The process approach concentrates on the specific techniques and processes of food production. This system places importance on the identification of these common techniques and processes across the full range of required dishes. In developing the production system, groupings are not then based on the types of dishes or foods, which is the basis of the 'partie' system, but on the clustering of similar production techniques and processes which apply a range of common skills and encourage flexible open-endedness.

Food production is an operating system and can be managed through the application of the systems approach. A whole range of different cuisines are able to fit more neatly into this approach, because the key elements focus on the process, the way the food is prepared, processed (cooked), stored and served. Using this approach, food production systems may be identified using the input/process/output model of systems. Developing this approach further, nine standard production methods can be identified and these are shown in Table 2.3.

Table 2.3 Food production methods

Method	Description
Conventional	Term used to describe production utilising mainly fresh foods and traditional cooking methods
Convenience	Method of production utilising mainly convenience foods
Call order	Method where food is cooked to order either from customer (as in cafeterias) or from waiter. Production area is often open to customer area
Continuous flow	Method involving production line approach where different parts of the production process may be separated (e.g. fast food)
Centralised	Production not directly linked to service. Foods are 'held' and distributed to separate service areas
Cook-chill	Food production storage and regeneration method utilising principle of low temperature control to preserve qualities of processed foods
Cook-freeze	Production, storage and regeneration method utilising principle of freezing to control and preserve qualities of processed foods. Requires special processes to assist freezing
Sous-vide	Method of production, storage and regeneration utilising principle of sealed vacuum to control and preserve the quality of processed foods
Assembly kitchen	A system based on accepting and incorporating the latest technological development in manufacturing and conservation of food products

In reality, many foodservice operations combine a number of these food production methods to meet the needs of the operation.

2.3 Food and beverage service methods

The service of food and beverages may be carried out in many ways depending on the following factors:

- type of establishment
- time available for the meal
- type of customer to be served
- turnover of custom expected
- type of menu presented
- site of the establishment
- cost of the meal served

The customer is central to the process and also an active participant within it. Consequently, understanding the customers' involvement in the process, and identifying the experience they are likely to have and should expect, has become critical to the business success of foodservice operations.

It is also now recognised that food and beverage service actually consists of two separate sub-systems, operating at the same time:

1 The **service sequence** – which is primarily concerned with the delivery of the food and beverages to the customer.
2 The **customer process** – which is concerned with the experience the customer undertakes to be able to order, be served, consume and have the area cleared.

This modern view of a foodservice operation can be summarised in a simple model as shown in Figure 2.2.

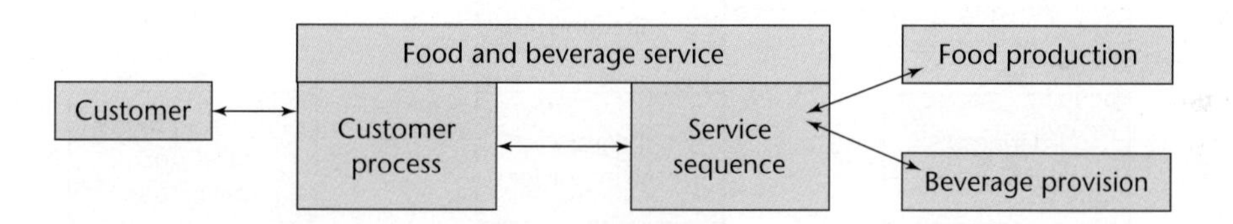

Figure 2.2 **Simple model of a foodservice operation**

The service sequence

The service sequence is essentially the bridge between the production system, beverage provision and the customer process (or customer experience). The service sequence may consist of 11 or more stages as summarised in Table 2.4.

Table 2.4 **Food and beverage service sequence**

1 Preparation for service	7 Clearing during service
2 Taking bookings	8 Billing
3 Greeting and seating/directing	9 Dealing with payments
4 Taking food and beverage orders	10 Dishwashing
5 Serving of food	11 Clearing following service
6 Serving beverages	

Each of these stages of the service sequence may be carried out by a variety of methods and these different methods are described throughout the book. The choice of method for the individual stage depends on the factors listed at the start of this section and the process that the customer is to experience.

The customer process

The customer receiving the food and beverage product is required to undertake or observe certain requirements: this is the customer process. Essentially, a customer enters a food service area, orders or selects his or her choice and then is served (the customer may pay either at this point or later). Food and beverages are then consumed, following which the area is cleared.

Bringing these approaches together, it is possible to summarise the relationship between the various systems within a foodservice operation, as shown in Figure 2.3. This model identifies the key stages of a foodservice operation: for the customer, for the food and beverage service staff and for those involved in food production and beverage provision. It also reinforces the existence of the two sub-systems within food and beverage service that have to be managed at the same time.

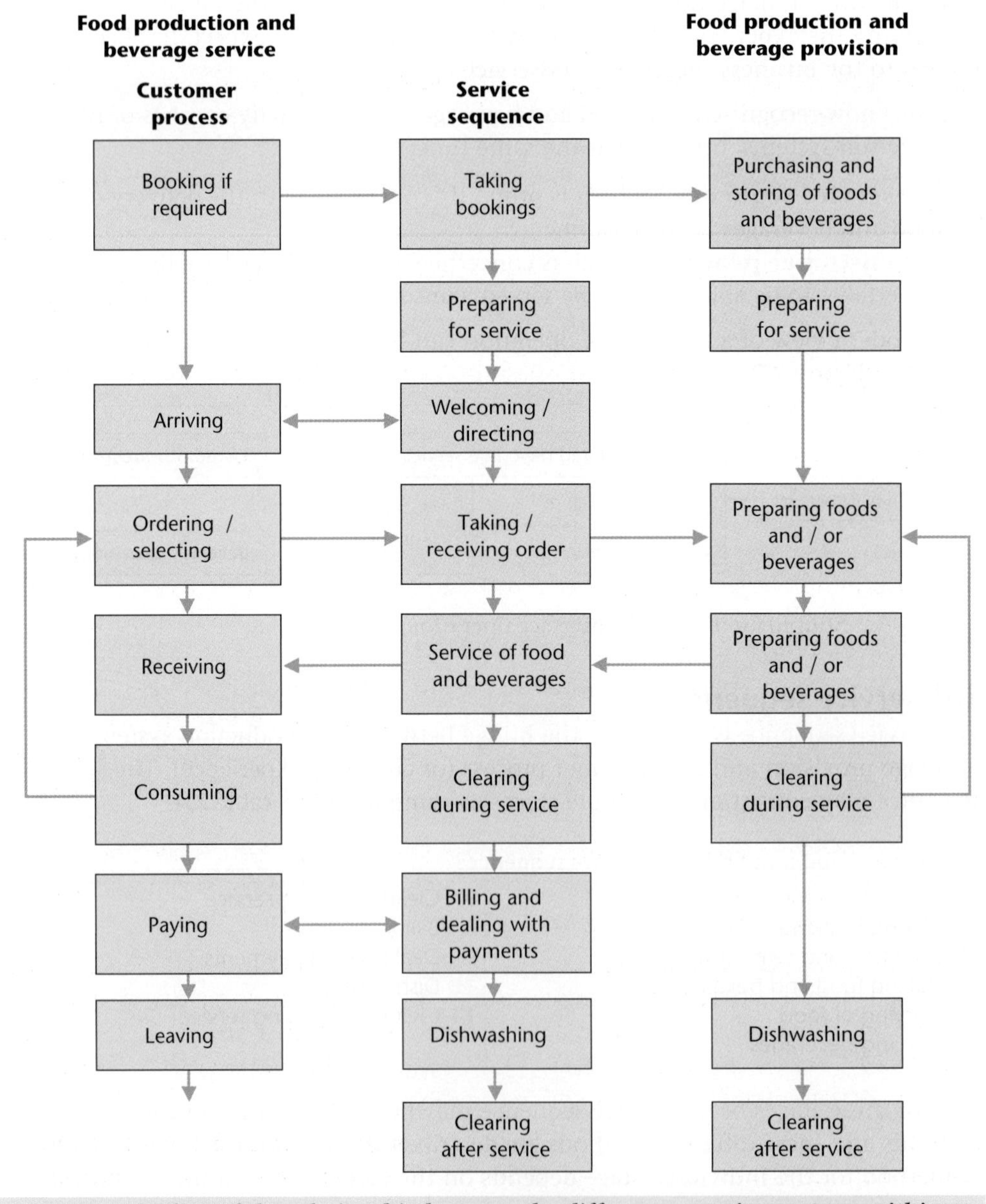

Figure 2.3 **Outline of the relationship between the different operating systems within a foodservice operation**

Categorising the different service methods

When considering food and beverage service from a *customer process* perspective, rather then considering it purely as a set of delivery methods, five basic types of customer process can be identified as indicated in Table 2.5.

Table 2.5 **Simple categorisation of the customer processes in food and beverage service**

Service method	Service area	Ordering/ Selection	Service	Dining/ Consumption	Clearing
Table service	Customer enters and is seated	From menu	By staff to customer	At laid cover	By staff
Assisted service	Customer enters and is usually seated	From menu, buffet or passed trays	Combination of both staff and customer	Usually at laid cover	By staff
Self-service	Customer enters	Customer selects items onto a tray	Customer carries	Dining area or takeaway	Various
Single-point service	Customer enters	Orders at single point	Customer carries	Dining area or takeaway	Various
Specialised or in situ service	Where the customer is located	From menu or predetermined	Brought to the customer	Served where the customer is located	By staff or customer clearing

All modern food and beverage service methods can then be grouped or categorised under the five customer processes summarised in Table 2.5 as follows.

A **Table service:** the customer is served at a laid table. This type of service, which includes plated service or silver service, is found in many types of restaurant, cafés and in banqueting.

B **Assisted service:** the customer is served part of the meal at a table and is required to obtain part through self-service from some form of display or buffet. This type of service is found in carvery-type operations and is often used for meals such as breakfast in hotels. It may also be used for functions.

C **Self-service:** the customer is required to help him or herself from a buffet or counter. This type of service can be found in cafeterias and canteens.

D **Single point service:** the customer orders, pays and receives the food and beverages, for instance at a counter, at a bar in licensed premises, in a fast-food operation or at a vending machine.

E **Specialised service (or service in situ):** the food and drink is taken to where the customer is. This includes tray service in hospitals or aircraft, trolley service, home delivery, lounge and room service.

In groups A–D of the customer processes, the customer comes to where the food and beverage service is offered and the service is provided in areas primarily designed for that purpose, such as a restaurant or takeaway. In customer process E, the service is provided in another location, where the area is not primarily designed for the purpose, for example, in a guest room, lounge or hospital ward.

A detailed listing of all the modern food and beverage service methods is given in Table 2.6 (pages 38–39) and listed under each of the groups A to D. For a particular service method, such as waiter service, a number of tasks and duties are undertaken during the actual service of food and beverages. However, there are other tasks and duties that contribute to the service. These may be identified using the service sequence (see Table 2.4, page 39). Additionally, the level of complexity of food and beverage service in terms of staff skills, tasks and duties reduces from Group A (the most complex) to Group D. Group E contains specialised forms of service, which require an additional range of service skills.

Note: With the exception of fast-food operations, there is no particular link between a specific service method and a specific food production method. It is also possible that the production and service may be separated by distance or time, or both, as, for example, in off-premises catering.

2.4 Food and beverage service personnel

The various types of job roles in food and beverage service are identified below. In some smaller operations a number of these job roles may be combined.

Table 2.6 **Food and beverage service methods**

Group A: Table service		
Service to customers at a laid cover		
1 Waiter	a) Silver/English	Presentation and service of food by waiting staff, using a spoon and fork, onto a customer's plate, from food flats or dishes
	b) Family	Main courses plated (but may be silver served) with vegetables placed in multi-portion dishes on tables for customers to help themselves; sauces offered separately
	c) Plate/ American	Service of pre-plated foods to customers. Now also widely used for banqueting
	d) Butler/ French	Presentation of food serving dishes individually to customers by food service staff for customers to serve themselves
	e) Russian	Table laid with food for customers to help themselves (this is a modern interpretation and may also sometimes be used to indicate gueridon or butler service)
	f) Gueridon	Food served onto customer's plate at a side table or trolley; may also include carving, jointing and fish filleting, the preparation of foods such as salads and dressings and flambage
2 Bar counter	Service to customers seated at bar counter (often U-shaped) on stools	
Group B: Assisted service		
Combination of table service and self-service		
3 Assisted	a) Carvery	Some parts of the meal are served to seated customers; other parts are collected by the customers from the buffet. Also used for breakfast service and for banqueting
	b) Buffets	Customers select food and drink from displays or passed trays; consumption is either at tables, standing or in lounge area

Group C: Self-service		
Self-service of customers		
4 Cafeteria	a) Counter	Customers queue in line formation past a service counter and choose their menu requirements in stages before loading them onto a tray (may include a 'carousel' – a revolving stacked counter, saving space)
	b) Free-flow	Selection as in counter (above) but in food service area where customers move at will to random service points; customers usually exit area via a till point
	c) Echelon	Series of counters at angles to the customer flow within a free-flow area, thus saving space
	d) Supermarket	Island service points within a free-flow area

Note: Some 'call order' production may be included in cafeterias.

Group D: Single-point service		
Service of customers at single point – consumed on premises or taken away		
5 Takeaway	a) Takeaway	Customer orders and is served from single point, at a counter, hatch or snack stand; customer consumes off the premises; some takeaway establishments provide dining areas
	b) Drive-thru	Form of takeaway where customer drives vehicle past order, payment and collection points
	c) Fast food	Term originally used to describe service at a counter or hatch where customers receive a complete meal or dish in exchange for cash or ticket; commonly used nowadays to describe type of establishment offering limited-range menu, fast service with dining area and takeaway facility
6 Vending	Provision of food service and beverage service by means of automatic retailing	
7 Kiosks	Outstation used to provide service for peak demand or in specific location; may be open for customers to order and be served or used for dispensing to staff only	
8 Food court	Series of autonomous counters where customers may either order and eat (as in Bar counter described above) or buy from a number of counters and eat in separate eating area or takeaway	
9 Bar	Term used to describe order, service and payment point and consumption area in licensed premises	
Group E: Specialised (or in situ) service		
Service to customers in areas not primarily designed for service		
10 Tray	Method of service of whole or part of meal on tray to customer in situ, e.g. at hospital beds, aircraft seats and train seats; also used in ODC	
11 Trolley	Service of food and beverages from a trolley, away from dining areas, e.g. for office workers at their desks; for customers at aircraft seats; at train seats	
12 Home delivery	Food delivered to customer's home or place of work, e.g. 'meals on wheels', pizza home delivery, or sandwiches to offices	
13 Lounge	Service of variety of foods and beverages in lounge area, e.g. hotel lounge	
14 Room	Service of variety of foods and beverages in guest bedrooms or in meeting rooms	
15 Drive-in	Customers park their motor vehicle and are served at their vehicles	

Note: Banquet/function is a term used to describe catering for specific numbers of people at specific times in a variety of dining layouts. Service methods also vary. In these cases banquet/function catering refers to the organisation of service rather than a specific service method.

Food and beverage manager

Depending on the size of the establishment, the food and beverage manager is either responsible for the implementation of agreed policies or for contributing to the setting of the food and beverage policies. The larger the organisation, the less likely the manager is to be involved in policy setting. In general, food and beverage managers are responsible for:

- ensuring that the required profit margins are achieved for each food and beverage service area, in each financial period
- updating and compiling new wine lists according to availability of stock, current trends and customer needs
- compiling, in liaison with the kitchen, menus for the various food service areas and for special occasions
- purchasing of all materials, both food and drink
- ensuring that quality in relation to the price paid is maintained
- determining portion size in relation to selling price
- ensuring staff training, sales promotions and maintenance of the highest professional standards
- employing and dismissing staff
- holding regular meetings with section heads to ensure all areas are working effectively, efficiently and are well coordinated.

Restaurant manager/supervisor

The restaurant manager or supervisor has overall responsibility for the organisation and administration of particular food and beverage service areas. These may include the lounges, room service (in hotels), restaurants and possibly some of the private function suites. It is the restaurant manager who sets the standards for service and is responsible for any staff training that may be required, either on or off the job. They may make out duty rotas, holiday lists and hours on and off duty, and contribute to operational duties (depending on the size of the establishment) so that all the service areas run efficiently and smoothly.

Reception headwaiter

The reception headwaiter is responsible for accepting any bookings and for keeping the booking diary up to date. They will reserve tables and allocate these reservations to particular stations. The reception headwaiter greets guests on arrival and takes them to the table and seats them.

Headwaiter/maître d'hôtel/supervisor

The headwaiter has overall charge of the staff team and is responsible for seeing that all the pre-preparation duties necessary for service are efficiently carried out and that nothing is forgotten. The headwaiter will aid the reception headwaiter during the service and will possibly take some orders if the station waiter is busy. The headwaiter also helps with the compilation of duty rotas and holiday lists and may relieve the restaurant manager or reception headwaiter on their days off.

Station headwaiter/section supervisor

For larger establishments the restaurant area is broken down into sections. The station headwaiter has the overall responsibility for a team of staff serving a number of stations within a section of the restaurant area. Each of the sets of tables (which may be anything from four to eight in number) within the section of the restaurant area is called a **station**.

The station headwaiter must have a good knowledge of food and wine and its correct service and be able to instruct other members of staff. He or she will take the food and beverage orders (usually from the host) and carry out service at the table with the help of the chef de rang, who is in command of one of the stations within the section.

Station waiter/chef de rang

The chef de rang or station waiter provides service to one set of tables (between about four and eight) known as a station within the restaurant area. The chef de rang will normally have had less experience than a station headwaiter.

Assistant station waiter/demi-chef de rang

The assistant station waiter or demi-chef de rang is the person next in seniority to the station waiter and assists as directed by the station waiter.

Waiter/server/commis de rang

The waiter or commis de rang acts by instruction from the chef de rang. This person mainly fetches and carries, may do some of the service of either vegetables or sauces, offers rolls, places plates upon the table and so on, and also helps to clear the tables after each course. During the pre-preparation period much of the cleaning and preparatory tasks will be carried out by the commis de rang.

Trainee/commis/debarrasseur/apprentice

The trainee commis or debarrasseur is the apprentice or learner, having just joined the food and beverage service staff, and who wishes to take up food service as a career. During the service this person will keep the sideboard well stocked with equipment and may help to fetch and carry items as required. The debarrasseur will carry out some of the cleaning tasks during the pre-preparation periods. They may also be given the responsibility of looking after and serving hors-d'oeuvre, cold sweets and assorted cheeses from the appropriate trolleys.

Carver/trancheur

The carver or trancheur is responsible for the carving trolley and the carving of joints at the table as required. The carver will plate up each portion and serve with accompaniments as appropriate.

Floor or room service staff/chef d'étage/floor or room waiter

The floor or room service staff are often responsible for a complete floor in an establishment or, depending on the size of the establishment, a number of rooms or suites. Room service of all meals and beverages throughout the day is normally only offered by a first-class establishment. In smaller establishments room service may be limited to early morning teas and breakfasts with the provision of in-room mini bars and tea and coffee facilities.

If full floor service is in operation, the staff will consist of a head floor waiter with the appropriate number of floor waiters working for them. This team of staff are then responsible for the service of all meals and beverages (alcoholic and non-alcoholic) in guest rooms. A thorough knowledge of food and drink and their correct service is therefore essential. The importance of good liaison and cooperation with the housekeeping staff cannot be over-emphasised here. The floor service staff will normally work from a floor pantry or central kitchen with all food and drink reaching the appropriate floor and the required room by lift and in a heated trolley.

Lounge staff/chef de salle

Lounge service staff may be employed only for lounge service within larger establishments. In a smaller establishment it is usual for members of the food service staff to take over these duties on a rota basis. The lounge staff are responsible for the service of morning coffee, afternoon teas, aperitifs and liqueurs before and after both lunch and dinner, and any coffee required after meals. They are responsible for setting up the lounge in the morning and maintaining its cleanliness and presentation throughout the day.

Wine butler/wine waiter/sommelier

The sommelier is responsible for the service of all alcoholic drinks and non-alcoholic bar drinks during the service of meals. The sommelier must also be a sales person. This employee should have a thorough knowledge of all drink to be served, of the best wines and drinks to go with certain foods, and of the liquor licensing laws in respect of the particular establishment and area.

Bar staff/bar tender/mixologist

The people working within bar areas must be responsible and competent in preparing and serving a variety of wine, drinks and cocktails. They should have a thorough knowledge of all alcoholic and non-alcoholic drinks being offered within the establishment, the ingredients necessary for the making of cocktails, and have knowledge of the requirements of the liquor licensing laws to ensure legal compliance. A mixologist is an employee who mixes and serves alcoholic beverages at a bar and is also often used as a name for people who are creators of new mixed drinks. Can also mean a cocktail maker or cocktail bar person or simply bartender. Mixology is the art of making mixed drinks.

Barista

The word 'barista' is of Italian origin. In Italian, a *barista* is a male or female bartender who typically works behind a counter, serving both hot and cold beverages as well as alcoholic beverages. Barista does not mean specifically a coffee maker although it is now often used as such. The plural in English is baristas.

Buffet assistant/buffet chef/chef de buffet

The chef de buffet is in charge of the buffet in the room, its presentation, the carving and portioning of food and its service. This staff member will normally be a member of the kitchen team.

Cashier

The cashier is responsible for billing and taking payments or making ledger account entries for a food and beverage operation. This may include making up bills from food and drink checks or, in a cafeteria for example, charging customers for their selection of items on a tray.

Counter assistants

Counter assistants are found in cafeterias where they will stock the counter and sometimes serve or portion food for customers. Duties may also include some cooking of call order items.

Table clearers

Again, table clearers can be found in seating areas where the service is not waiter service. These people are responsible for clearing tables using trolleys specially designed for the stacking of crockery, glassware, cutlery, etc.

Function catering/banqueting staff/events staff

In establishments with function catering facilities there will normally be a certain number of permanent staff. These will include the banqueting and conferencing manager, one or two assistant managers, one or two headwaiters, a dispense bar person and a secretary to the banqueting and conferencing manager. All other banqueting, conferencing and events staff are normally engaged as required on a casual basis. In small establishments, where there are fewer events, the manager, the assistant manager and the headwaiter will undertake the necessary administrative and organisational work.

Staffing requirements

The staffing requirements in various establishments will differ for a number of reasons. Table 2.7 gives examples of the food and beverage staffing that might be found in different types of operation.

Table 2.7 **Examples of staffing requirements for different types of foodservice operation**

Medium-class hotel	**Cafeteria**
Hotel manager	Catering manager
Assistant manager	Supervisors
Head waiter	Assistant supervisors
Waiters	Counter service hands
Wine waiter	Clearers
Cashier	Cashier
Popular price restaurant	**Industrial foodservice/welfare catering**
Restaurant manager/supervisor	Catering manager
Waiting staff	Assistant catering manager
Dispense bar assistant	Supervisors
	Assistant supervisors
	Waiter
	Steward/butler
	Counter service staff
	Clearers
	Cashiers

PART B

Underpinning Knowledge and Skills

CHAPTER 3

Service areas and equipment

This chapter will help you to learn about:

1. The importance of design and purchasing factors
2. The stillroom
3. The hotplate
4. The wash-up
5. The bar
6. Furniture
7. Linen
8. Crockery
9. Tableware *(flatware, cutlery and hollow-ware)*
10. Glassware
11. Disposables
12. Automatic vending

3.1 The importance of design and purchasing factors

In any establishment a customer's first impressions on entering the service areas are of great importance: a customer may be gained or lost on these impressions alone. Atmosphere, decor, furnishings and equipment are major factors that contribute to the success of the foodservice operation. Careful selection of items in terms of shape, design and colour will enhance the overall decor or theme. The choice of furniture and its layout and choice of linen, tableware, small equipment and glassware will be determined by considering such factors as:

- the type of clientele expected
- the site or location of the establishment
- the layout of the food and beverage service area
- the type of service offered
- the funds available.

The general points to be considered when purchasing equipment for a food and beverage service areas are:

- flexibility of use
- type of service being offered
- type of customer
- design
- colour
- durability
- ease of maintenance
- stackability

- availability in the future – replacements
- storage
- rate of breakage, i.e. crockery
- shape
- psychological effect on customers
- delivery time
- costs and funds available.

It is important that the front-of-house areas are well designed for operational purposes as these are the busiest areas of a food service establishment and that department heads ensure that all members of staff know exactly how to carry out their duties efficiently and effectively.

The back-of-house areas include the stillroom, hotplate (or pass) area and the wash-up. They are usually situated between the kitchen and food and beverage service, or front-of-house areas. They are important parts of the design of a foodservice operation, acting as the link between kitchen or food preparation areas and the restaurant or food and beverage service areas. Well designed layout of these areas is essential to ensure an even flow of work by the various members of staff. These areas need to be well organised, efficient, stocked with well-designed equipment and supervised.

3.2 The still room

The still room provides items of food and beverages required for the service of a meal that are not catered for by the other major departments in a foodservice operation, such as the kitchen, larder and pastry. The duties performed in this service area will vary according to the type of meals offered and the size of establishment concerned.

Because of the number of hours that the still room has to remain open and to ensure it is run efficiently, staff may work on a shift basis.

Figure 3.1 Example of a still room

Equipment

The following are examples of items that might be needed in the still room:

- refrigerator for storage of milk, cream, butter, fruit juices, etc.
- hot and cold beverage-making facilities
- large double sink and draining board for washing-up purposes

- dishwasher of a size suitable for the still room but large enough to ensure efficient turnover of equipment
- salamander or toasters
- bread-slicing machine
- worktop and cutting board
- storage space for small equipment such as crockery, glassware, cutlery and tableware
- storage cupboard for all dry goods held in stock and for such paper items as doilies, kitchen papers, napkins, etc.
- coffee-grinding machine to ensure the correct grind of coffee for the brewing method to be used
- ice maker.

Provisions

As a basic guide, the following food items would normally be dispensed from the still room:

- all beverages such as coffee, tea, chocolate, tisanes, Bovril, Horlicks, Ovaltine and other drinks
- assorted fruit juices: orange, tomato, pineapple and grapefruit
- milk, cream and alternatives
- sugars: loose, pre-wrapped portions, brown coffee crystals, demerara, etc., and alternatives
- preserves: marmalade, cherry, plum, raspberry, strawberry, apricot and honey. For the purpose of control and to reduce wastage, many establishments now offer pre-portioned jars or pots of jams or preserves at breakfast and for afternoon tea, rather than a preserve dish
- butter: either passed through a butter pat machine, curled or pre-wrapped portions and also butter alternatives
- sliced and buttered brown, white and malt bread
- rolls, brioche and croissants
- bread substitute items: gluten-free, rye, rice crackers, etc.
- dry cracker, digestive and water biscuits for service with cheese; sweet biscuits for service with early morning and afternoon teas and coffees
- assorted breakfast cereals: cornflakes, Weetabix, muesli, etc. In many establishments cereals of all types are offered in pre-wrapped, portion-controlled packets
- toasted scones and teacakes
- pastries, gateaux and sandwiches.

Control

There are two main ways of controlling goods to be issued from the still room:

- If a foodservice area requires items such as butter, sugar, preserves, etc. in bulk, a requisition signed by a supervisor is required before the still room will issue the items.
- Upon receipt of a waiter's check, tea, coffee or any other beverage required in the necessary portions will be dispensed.

3.3 The hotplate

The hotplate or pass is the meeting point between the service staff and the food preparation staff. Active cooperation and a good relationship between the members of staff of these two areas help to ensure that the customer receives an efficient and quick service of the meal.

The hotplate itself should be stocked with all the crockery necessary for the service of a meal. This may include some or all of the following items:

- soup plates/soup cups/consommé cups
- fish/joint/sweet plates
- platters.

Food flats and serving dishes are placed on the top of the hotplate and it should be lit/switched on well in advance of the service to ensure all items are sufficiently heated before the service.

Figure 3.2 **Example of a hotplate area**

Aboyeur or barker

The aboyeur, or barker, is in charge of and controls the hotplate (pass) during the service period. The aboyeur will receive the clearly written food check from the waiter. The aboyeur checks that none of the dishes ordered are off the menu. The order to the various 'parties' or 'sections' of the kitchen is then called out.

With the modern use of an EPOS (electronic point of sale) system the electronic order can be sent directly from the restaurant to each section of the kitchen and the aboyeur would be the coordinator for the dishes to arrive on the pass at the same time, checking for quality before releasing the dishes to the waiting staff. The control department would then use the EPOS information to control sales and revenue. (For an example of a radio-controlled electronic system for order-taking and communication, see Figure 14.4, page 258.)

3.4 The wash-up

Servers should stack trays of dirties correctly within the wash-up area, stack all the same sized plates together and place cutlery into a plastic bowl filled with hot, soapy water or wire baskets or containers in readiness for washing. The server must place any debris into the bin or bowl provided. All used paper, such as napkins, doilies or kitchen paper should be placed in separate waste bins to ensure proper recycling. Glassware that has not had grease or fat in it should be taken to a separate glass wash-up point, usually in the bar.

Dishwashing methods

There are four main methods of dishwashing for foodservice operations and a summary of these is shown in Table 3.1.

Table 3.1 **Summary of dishwashing methods (based on a chart from Croner's Catering)**

Method	Description
Manual	Soiled ware washed by hand or brush machine
Automatic conveyor	Soiled ware loaded in racks, mounted on a conveyor, by operators for automatic transportation through a dishwashing machine
Flight conveyor	Soiled ware loaded within pegs mounted on a conveyor, by operators for automatic transportation through a dishwashing machine
Deferred wash	Soiled ware collected together, stripped, sorted and stacked by operators for transportation through a dishwashing machine at a later stage

Manual

The dirty crockery is placed into a tank of hot water containing a soap detergent. After washing, the plates are placed into wire racks and dipped into a second sterilising tank containing clean hot water at a temperature of approximately 75°C (179°F). The racks are left for two minutes and then lifted out and the crockery left to drain. If sterilised in water at this temperature the crockery will dry by itself without the use of drying-up cloths. This is more hygienic. After drying, the crockery is stacked into piles of the correct size and placed on shelves until required for further use.

Automatic

Many larger establishments have dishwashing machines. These are necessary because of the high usage of crockery.

Figure 3.3 **Automatic conveyor dishwasher with stand for loading the racks at the right of the picture and a trolley for collection of completed racks on the left (image courtesy of Maidaid – Halcyon)**

Debris should be removed from the crockery before it is placed into the wire racks. The racks are then passed through the machine, the crockery being washed, rinsed, and then sterilised in turn. Having passed through the machine the crockery is left to drain for two to three minutes and is then stacked and placed on shelves until required for further use. As with the tank method, the plates do not require drying with tea cloths.

3.5 The bar

The bar may be situated within a food and beverage service area and dispense wine or other alcoholic drinks to be served to a customer consuming a meal or using a lounge area. Wine and other alcoholic drinks are sometimes obtained from bars situated outside the food and beverage service area itself, from one of the public bars. All drinks dispensed must be checked for and controlled (see page 55 and Section 14.4 (page 257)).

Equipment

For efficient service of all forms of wine and drink, the bar should have available all the necessary equipment for making cocktails, decanting wine, serving wine and preparing any other drinks ordered correctly. The equipment should include the items described below.

Main items

- **Cocktail shaker:** the ideal utensil for mixing ingredients that will not normally blend together well by stirring. A three-part utensil.
- **Boston shaker:** consists of two cones, one of which overlaps the other to seal in the mix. Made of stainless steel, glass or plated silver. The mix is strained using a Hawthorn strainer.
- **Mixing glass:** like a glass jug without a handle, but has a lip. Used for mixing clear drinks which do not contain juices or cream.
- **Strainer:** there are many types, the most popular being the Hawthorn. This is a flat spoon-shaped utensil with a spring coiled round its edge. It is used in conjunction with the cocktail shaker and mixing glass to hold back the ice after the drink is prepared. A special design is available for use with liquidisers and blenders.
- **Bar spoon:** for use with the mixing glass when stirring cocktails. The flat 'muddler' end is used for crushing sugar and mint in certain drinks.
- **Bar liquidiser** *or* **blender:** used for making drinks that require puréed fruit.
- **Drink mixer:** used for drinks that do not need liquidising, especially those containing cream or ice cream. If ice is required, use only crushed ice.

Other items

Examples include:

- assorted glasses
- ice buckets and stands
- wine baskets
- water jugs
- assorted bitters: peach, orange, Angostura
- cutting board and knife
- coasters
- cork extractor
- ice pick
- small ice buckets and tongs
- ice-crushing machine
- drinking straws
- cocktail sticks

- carafes
- wine and cocktail/drinks lists
- coloured sugars
- glass cloths, napkins and service cloths
- sink unit
- refrigerator
- ice-making machine
- glass-washing machine
- optics/spirit measures
- wine measures
- cooling trays
- bottle opener
- muslin and funnel
- lemon-squeezing machine
- swizzle sticks
- strainer and funnel
- service salvers
- wine knife and cigar cutter (where legislation allows smoking)
- bin
- hot beverage maker
- juice press
- mini whisk.

Food items

Examples include:

- olives
- Worcestershire sauce
- salt and pepper
- nutmeg
- Angostura bitters
- caster sugar
- eggs
- mint
- orange
- coconut cream
- maraschino cherries
- Tabasco sauce
- cinnamon
- cloves
- cube sugar
- demerara sugar
- cream
- cucumber
- lemon
- lime
- salted nuts/crisps
- gherkins.

Safety and hygiene

Great care must be observed to ensure that the materials used in the make-up of the bar are hygienic and safe. Flooring must be non-slip. The bar top should be of a material suited to the general decor that is hard-wearing, easily wiped down and has no sharp edges.

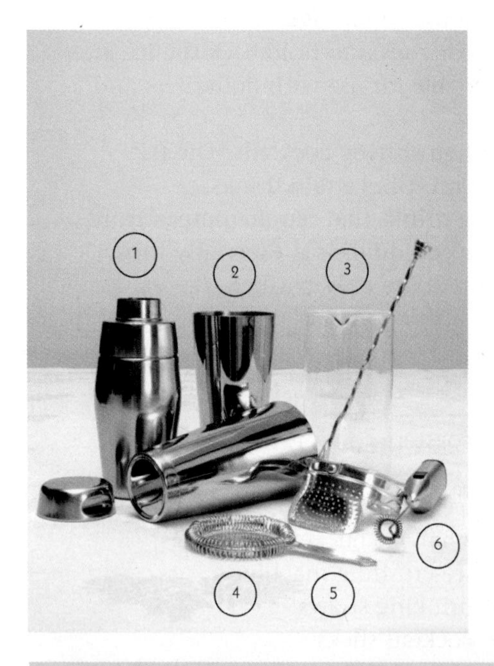

Figure 3.4(a) **Examples of cocktail bar equipment: (1) cocktail shaker, (2) Boston shaker, (3) mixing glass with bar spoon, (4) Hawthorn strainer, (5) jug strainer insert, (6) mini whisk, (7) straws, (8) ice crusher, (9) juice press, (10) ice bucket and tongs**

Figure 3.4(b) **Examples of bar equipment: (1) bottle coaster, (2) Champagne star cork grip, (3) wine bottle holder, (4) vacu-pump, (5, 7, 9, 12) wine bottle openers, (6, 10) Champagne bottle stoppers, (8) wine funnel, (11) wine bottle foil cutter, (13) Champagne cork grip, (14) wine cork extractor, (15) appetiser bowls and cocktail stick holder, (16) measures on drip tray, (17) cutting board and knife, (18) cigar cutters, (19, 21) bottle stoppers, (20) bottle pourers, (22) crown cork opener, (23) mini juice press**

The bar area should be cleaned after each service, paying attention to all surfaces, fridges, preparation and dispense equipment and waste removal. Sinks and glass washers should be emptied and cleaned as required throughout service.

Any perishable items should be correctly covered and refrigerated as necessary. Good stock rotation will avoid unnecessary wastage.

Cellar storage

For beverages the cellar is the focal point for the storage of alcoholic and non-alcoholic liquor.

Beers

The factors that determine good beer cellar management are:

- good ventilation
- cleanliness
- even temperatures of 13–15°C (55–58°F)
- avoidance of strong draughts and wide ranges of temperatures
- on delivery, all casks should be placed immediately upon the stillions
- casks remaining on the floor should be bung uppermost to better withstand the pressure
- spiling should take place to reduce any excess pressure in the cask
- tappings should be carried out 24 hours before a cask is required
- pipes and engines should be cleaned at regular intervals
- all beer lines should be cleaned weekly with a diluted pipe-cleaning fluid and the cellar floor washed down weekly with a weak solution of chloride and lime (mild bleach)
- beer left in pipes after closing time should be drawn off
- returned beer should be filtered back into the cask from which it came
- care should be taken that the cellar is not overstocked
- all spiles removed during service should be replaced after closing time
- all cellar equipment should be kept scrupulously clean
- any ullage should be returned to the brewery as soon as possible
- re-ordering should be carried out on one set day every week after checking the bottle stocks of beers, wines, minerals, etc.
- strict rotation of stock must be exercised, with new bottle crates or cases being placed at the rear and old stock pulled to the front for first issue.

Wine

Wines should ideally be stored in a subterranean cellar, which has a northerly aspect and is free from vibrations, excessive dampness, draughts and odours. The cellar should be absolutely clean and well ventilated, with only subdued lighting and a constant cool temperature of 12.5°C (55°F) to help the wine develop gradually.

Wines should be stored on their sides in bins so that the wine remains in contact with the cork. This keeps the cork expanded and prevents air from entering the wine – a process that quickly turns wine to vinegar. The wines are also stored on their sides with the labels uppermost. This ensures that the wines can be easily identified, the protection of the label (away from the base surface of the bin) and ensures that any sediment is always located on the side of the bottle away from the label. This approach is also used for wines with alternative stoppers such as screw tops. White, sparkling and rosé wines are kept in the coolest part of the cellar and in bins nearest the ground (because warm air rises). Red wines are best stored in the upper bins. Commercial establishments usually have special refrigerators or cooling cabinets for keeping their sparkling, white and rosé wines at serving temperature.

Other drinks

Spirits, liqueurs, squashes, juices and mineral waters are stored upright in their containers, as are fortified wines. The exceptions are port-style wines which are destined for laying down, and these are treated as for wines above.

Determining stock levels

All the individual outlets within an establishment such as the lounge, lounge bar, cocktail bar, saloon bar, brasserie, dispense bars and floor service should draw their stock on a daily or weekly basis from the cellar. Each outlet will hold a set stock (or 'par stock') of liquor, which is sufficient for a service period, or for a day or week. The level of the par stock will be determined mainly by the amount of storage space available in the service areas and also taking account of the expected sales demand. At the end of this service period each individual outlet will requisition for the amount of drink consumed in that one service period, day or week, thus bringing their total stock back up to the par stock level.

For the establishment as a whole, the central stock levels that are required in order to meet expected sales demand may be determined by using past sales data. Using this approach can enable foodservice operations to determine the stockholding that will meet the needs of the expected demand, while at the same time minimising the amount of capital tied up in the stock being held. Good stock control can also be supported by the application of a 'just in time' (JIT) approach to purchasing. JIT involves only ordering stock as required in order to meet forecasted demand, rather than holding unnecessarily high stock levels, just in case.

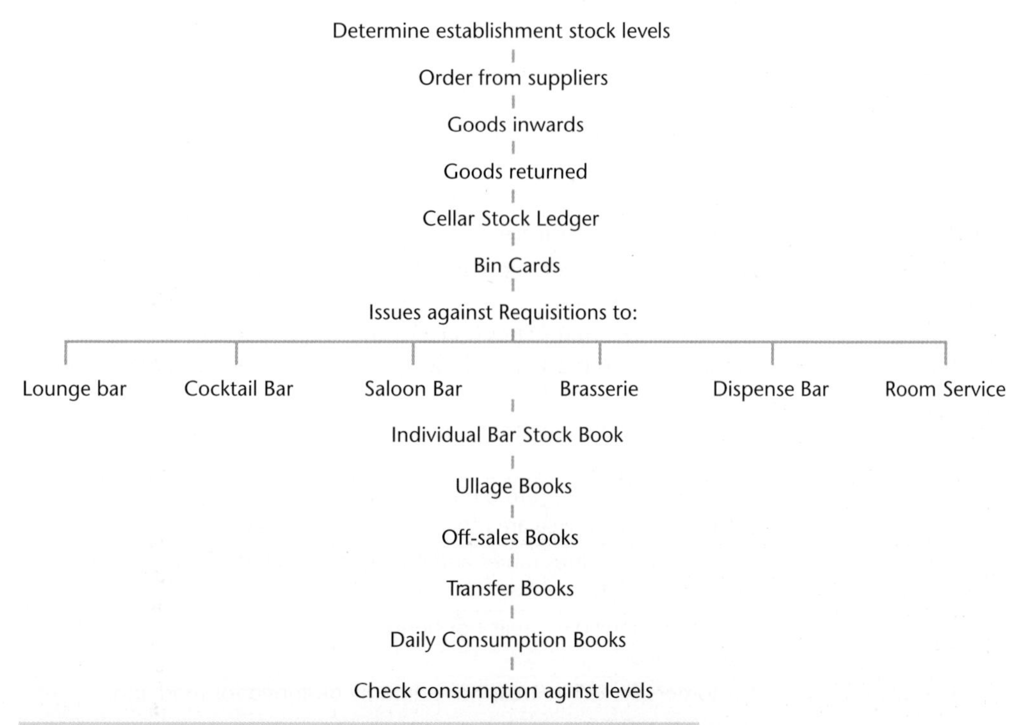

Figure 3.5 Summary of basic steps in bar and cellar control

Beverage control procedures

In any foodservice establishment where income is received from the sale of wine and drink, a system of control and costing must be put into operation. The system used will depend entirely on the policy of the establishment. Some or all of the books listed in Table 3.2 may be necessary, depending upon the requirements of the particular foodservice operation.

Table 3.2 **Books used in beverage control**

Book	Used to record
Order book	Orders made to suppliers
Goods inwards/goods received book	Goods received from suppliers
Goods returned book	Goods that are sent back to suppliers
Returnable containers book	Returnable containers sent back to suppliers
Cellar ledger	Stock movement in and out of the cellar
Bin cards	Stock of individual lines in the cellar
Requisition book	Re-stocking orders for individual service areas
Daily consumption sheets	Usage of stock in individual service areas
Ullage book	Breakage, spillage and wastage
Off-sales book	Items sold at the off-sale prices
Transfers book	Movement of stock between different service areas

Although referred to as books here, most modern-day systems are computer-based. However, the basic processes are the same whatever the method being used to record the data. A summary of the basic steps in bar and cellar control is given in Figure 3.5.

3.6 Furniture

Furniture must be chosen according to the needs of the establishment. Examples of various dining arrangements are shown in Table 3.3.

Table 3.3 **Dining arrangements (based on a chart from Croner's Catering)**

Type	Description of furniture
Loose random	Freestanding furniture positioned in no discernable pattern within a given service area
Loose module	Freestanding furniture positioned within a given service area to a pre-determined pattern, with or without the use of dividers to create smaller areas within the main area
Booth	Fixed seating (banquette), usually high-backed, used to create secluded seating
High density	Furniture with minimum dimensions and usually fixed, positioned within a given service area to create maximum seating capacity
Module	Seating incorporates tables and chairs constructed as one and may be fixed to the floor
In situ	Customers served in areas not designed for service, e.g. aircraft and hospital beds
Bar and lounge areas	Customers served in areas not primarily designed for food and beverage service

By using different materials, designs and finishes of furniture and by their careful arrangement, often the atmosphere and appearance of the service area can be changed to suit different occasions.

Tables

Tables come in three main shapes: round, square and rectangular. An establishment may have a mixture of shapes to give variety, or tables of all one shape depending on

Figure 3.6 **Restaurant area with traditional seating and with banquette seating shown on right of picture (image courtesy of Dunk Ink UK)**

the shape of the room and the style of service being offered. As a guide, tables are usually found in the following sizes:

Square

- 76 cm (2 ft 6 in) square to seat two people.
- 1 m (3 ft) square to seat four people.

Round

- 1 m (3 ft) in diameter to seat four people.
- 1.52 m (5 ft) in diameter to seat eight people.

Rectangular

- 137 cm × 76 cm (4 ft 6 in × 2 ft 6 in) to seat four people, extensions being added for larger parties.

Sideboards

The sideboard or workstation is used to store spare cutlery and linen, close to the service point, that might be needed during service. It is also an area to place trays for service and clearing of equipment used during service.

The style and design of a sideboard varies from establishment to establishment and is dependent upon:

- the style of service and the food and beverages on offer
- the number of service staff working from one sideboard
- the number of tables to be served from one sideboard
- the amount of equipment it is expected to hold.

Figure 3.7 **Example of a tray jack**

It is essential that the sideboard is of minimum size and portable so that it may be easily moved if necessary. Some establishments use smaller fixed sideboards and also use tray jacks (movable folding tray stands, as shown in Figure 3.7) when serving and clearing.

After service the sideboard is either completely emptied out or restocked for the next service. In some establishments the waiters are responsible for their own equipment on their station.
If sideboards are restocked after service, the sideboard will also carry its own stock of linen. Examples of sideboards are shown in Figure 3.8.

Figure 3.8 **Examples of sideboards (images courtesy of Euroservice UK)**

3.7 Linen

The type of linen used will depend on the class of establishment, type of clientele, the cost involved, the style of menu and service to be offered. The main items of linen normally to be found are shown below.

Tablecloths

- 137 cm × 137 cm (54 in × 54 in) to fit a table 76 cm (2 ft 6 in) square or a round table 1 m (3 ft) in diameter
- 183 cm × 183 cm (72 in × 72 in) to fit a table 1 m (3 ft) square
- 183 cm × 244 cm (72 in × 96 in) to fit rectangular-shaped tables
- 183 cm × 137 cm (72 in × 54 in) to fit rectangular-shaped tables.

Slip cloths

- 1 m × 1 m (3 ft × 3 ft) used to cover a slightly soiled tablecloth.

Napkins (serviettes)

- 46–50 cm (18–20 in) square if linen.
- 36–42 cm (14–17 in) square if paper.

Buffet cloths

- 2 m × 4 m (6 ft × 12 ft) – this is the minimum size; longer cloths will be used for longer tables.

Waiter's cloths or service cloths

- Servers use these as protection against heat and to help keep uniforms clean.

Tea and glass cloths

- These are used for drying items after washing; tea cloths should be used for crockery and glass cloths for glassware.

Use and control of linen

Linen should be used only for its intended purpose in the restaurant and not for cleaning purposes, as this often results in permanent soiling which will render the item unusable in the future.

The stock of clean linen is usually issued upon receipt of a requisition signed by a responsible person from the service department. A surplus linen stock is usually held in the food service area in case of emergency.

At the end of each service the dirty linen should be counted, recorded and sent to the issuing department to be exchanged for clean.

A range of disposable linen, including napkins, placemats and tablecloths, are available in varying colours and qualities. There are also now reversible tablecloths with a thin polythene sheet running through the centre that prevents any spillages from penetrating from one side to the other. For more information on disposables, see Section 3.11 (page 65).

3.8 Crockery

The crockery must blend in with the general decor of the establishment and also with the rest of the items on the table. An establishment generally uses one design and pattern of crockery, but when an establishment has a number of different service areas it is easier, from the control point of view, to have a different design in each service area.

Foodservice crockery

There are various classifications of foodservice crockery. Although referred to as crockery here (and throughout the book), all glazed tableware was traditionally referred to as china. Items include:

- flatware, for example, plates and saucers and serving flats
- cups and bowls, for example, tea and coffee cups, soup and sweet bowls and serving dishes
- hollow-ware, for example, pots and vases.

Types of crockery

There are four main types of crockery used in food service operations and these are described in Table 3.4 below.

Table 3.4 Types of crockery

Type	Description of crockery
Bone china	This very fine, hard china is expensive. Decorations are only found under the glaze. It can be made to thicker specifications, if requested, for hotel use
Hotel earthenware	Vitrified (or vitreous) earthenware is produced in the United Kingdom in vast quantities. It is the cheapest but least durable hotelware although it is much stronger than regular domestic earthenware
Stoneware	This is a natural ceramic material traditionally made in the United Kingdom and fired at a very high temperature, about 1,200°C–1,315°C (2,200°F). It is shaped by traditional handcrafting techniques so there are a wide variety of shapes and finishes available, from matt to a high-gloss glaze. It is non-porous and extremely durable with high thermal and shock resistance. The price is slightly higher than earthenware due to its long-life guarantee
Porcelain	This is of a different composition with a semi-translucent body, normally cream/grey, and has a high resistance to chipping

As well as crockery items modern contemporary styles now include other materials such as glass, slate, plastic or wood.

Crockery sizes

A wide range of crockery items is available (see Figures 3.9(a) and (b)) and their exact sizes will vary according to the manufacturer and the design produced. As a guide, the sizes are as follows:

- side plate: 15 cm (6 in) diameter
- sweet plate: 18 cm (7 in) diameter
- fish plate: 20 cm (8 in) diameter
- soup plate: 20 cm (8 in) diameter
- joint plate: 25 cm (10 in) diameter
- cereal/sweet bowl: 13 cm (5 in) diameter
- breakfast cup and saucer: 23–28 cl (8–10 fl oz)
- teacup and saucer: 18.93 cl (6⅔ fl oz)
- coffee cup and saucer (demi-tasse): 9.47 cl (3½ fl oz)
- teapot: 28.4 cl (½ pint), 56.8 cl (1 pint), 85.2 cl (1½ pint), 113.6 cl (2 pint)

Other items of crockery required include:

- consommé cup and saucer
- soup bowl/cup
- platter (oval plate)
- salad crescent
- egg cup
- butter dish
- ashtray
- teapot
- hot water jug
- coffee pot
- milk jug
- cream jug
- hot milk jug
- sugar basin
- salt and pepper pots.

Figure 3.9(a) **Selection of tableware – traditional style**

Figure 3.9(b) **Selection of tableware – contemporary style**

Storage

Crockery should be stored on shelves in piles of approximately two dozen. Any higher may result in their toppling down or damage to plates at the bottom of the stack because of the weight bearing down on them.

Crockery should be stored at a convenient height for placing on and removing from the shelves without fear of accidents occurring. If possible, crockery should be kept covered to prevent dust and germs settling on it.

3.9 Tableware (flatware, cutlery and hollow-ware)

Tableware includes all items of flatware, cutlery and hollow-ware and may be classified as follows:

- flatware in the catering trade denotes all forms of spoon and fork, as well as serving flats
- cutlery refers to knives and other cutting implements
- hollow-ware consists of any other item, apart from flatware and cutlery, e.g. teapots, milk jugs, sugar basins and serving dishes.

Although traditionally flatware included spoons and forks, and cutlery referred to knives, the modern usage of these terms has changed. All spoons, forks and knives used as eating implements are now referred to as cutlery. The term 'cutlery' is therefore used throughout the rest of this book.

Manufacturers produce varied patterns of flatware, hollow-ware and cutlery in a range of prices to suit all demands. There are also patterns of flatware and cutlery that are scaled down to three-quarters the normal size specifically for tray service.

Figure 3.10 **Examples of cutlery: (left to right) fish fork, sweet fork, joint fork, fish knife, small (side) knife, joint knife, coffee spoon, tea spoon, soup spoon, sweet spoon, table (service) spoon)**

Silver

Silver-plated tableware comes in two grades:

- standard for general use
- restaurant thicker grade for restaurant use and marked with an 'R'.

The minimum thickness of silver plating quoted should give a life of at least 20 years, depending on usage.

Plain cutlery and flatware is more popular than patterned for the simple reason that it is cheaper and easier to keep clean.

Silver-cleaning methods

All the service silver should be cleaned on a rota basis to ensure all silver is cleaned regularly. Items that are in constant use will require more attention.

There are various methods of silver-cleaning and the method used generally depends on the size and class of establishment. The main methods used are summarised in Table 3.5.

Table 3.5 **Summary of silver-cleaning methods**

Method	Description
Silver dip	Items to be cleaned are completely immersed in dip in a plastic bowl for a very short time, rinsed in clean water and polished with a tea cloth
Burnishing machine	Items to be cleaned are placed in a drum containing ball bearings, soap powder and water. The drum rotates and the tarnish is rubbed off
Polvit	An enamel or galvanised iron bowl within which is the Polvit aluminium metal sheet containing holes, together with some soda. At least one piece of silver needs contact with the Polvit. Boiling water is poured onto the silver and a chemical reaction causes the tarnish to be lifted
Plate powder	Pink powder is mixed with a little methylated spirit to a smooth paste and rubbed well onto the tarnished silver with a clean piece of cloth. (Information based on that obtained from the Cutlery and Allied Trades Research Association (CATRA).)

Stainless steel

Stainless steel tableware is available in a variety of grades. The higher-priced designs usually incorporate alloys of chromium (which makes the metal stainless) and nickel (which gives a fine grain and lustre). Good British flatware and cutlery is made of 18/8 or 18/10 stainless steel.

Stainless steel is finished by different degrees of polishing:

- high polish finish
- dull polish finish
- light grey matt, non-reflective finish.

Stainless steel resists scratching far more than other metals and may therefore be said to be more hygienic. Although it does not tarnish it can stain. There are special cleaning products for stainless steel such as a commercial powder that is applied with a wet sponge or cloth and rubbed on the surface before being rinsed off. Such products can be used to keep stainless steel looking clean and polished.

Storage

In larger establishments the silver room, or plate room as it is sometimes known, is a separate service area within which a complete stock of tableware required for the service of meals, together with a slight surplus stock in case of emergency, is stored. Tableware for banqueting service may be of a different design and kept specifically for that purpose within the banqueting department. In smaller establishments it is often combined with the wash-up area.

- *Large tableware*: Flats, salvers, soup tureens and cloches – store on shelves, with all the flats of one size together. All shelves should be labelled showing where each different item goes. Heavier items should go on lower shelves and the smaller and lighter items on higher shelves.
- *Small tableware*: Smaller items such as cruets, butter dishes, special equipment, table numbers and menu holders, can be stored in drawers lined with green baize to protect items and reduce noise.

Ideally all tableware should be stored in a room or cupboard that can be locked, as it is a large part of the capital investment of the foodservice operation. Cutlery may be stored in cutlery trolleys or trays ready for use, which can also be locked in a store.

3.10 Glassware

Glassware contributes to the appearance of the table and the overall attraction of the service area. All glassware should be clean and well polished.

Most manufacturers now supply hotel glassware in standard sizes for convenience of ordering, availability and quick delivery. An example of drinking glasses and their use is shown in Figure 16.1, page 281.

A good wine glass should be plain and clear so that the colour and brilliance of a wine can be clearly seen. It should have a stem for holding the wine glass so that the heat of a customer's hand does not affect the wine on tasting. There should be a slight incurving lip to help hold the aroma and it should be large enough to hold the particular wine being tasted.

Type and sizes of glassware

Glassware is made by various processes. The main ones are shown in Table 3.6 below.

Table 3.6 **Types of glassware**

Type of glass	Method of production
Soda lime glass	This glass contains sand, soda ash and limestone as the principal ingredients. It is used for day-to-day, relatively inexpensive glassware
Lead crystal	This form of glass includes sand, red lead and potash, which produces a slightly softer glass of high brilliance. The surface can be left plain or can be cut to produce prismatic effects and sparkle.
Borosilicate glass	This is glass made with the addition of borax, which increases its hardness and heat resistance. This type of glass is used for flame ware
Tempered and toughened glass	This glass has additional treatments to make it more resistant to the effects of heat. It is mostly used as ovenware glass, but the treatment is also used to produce glassware that needs to withstand heavy usage

Glassware decoration

The surface of glassware may be decorated by:

- cutting to produce patterns or badging
- sand-blasting to texture the surface
- acid-etching to make patterns or to add badging
- engraving using grinding wheels to add patterns
- surface printing with patterns from transfers.

Sizes for glassware

Examples of sizes for drinking glasses are shown in Table 3.7.

Table 3.7 **Examples of sizes for glassware**

Glass	Size
Wine goblet	14.20, 18.93, 22.72, 28 cl (5, 6⅔, 8, 10 fl oz)
Flute/tulip	18–23 cl (6–8 fl oz)
Saucer champagne	18–23 cl (6–8 fl oz)
Cocktail glass	4–7 cl (2–3 fl oz)
Sherry, port	5 cl (1.75 fl oz)
Highball	23–28 cl (9–10 fl oz)
Lowball	18–23 cl (6–8 fl oz)
Worthington	28–34 cl (10–12 fl oz)
Lager glass	28–34 cl (10–12 fl oz)
Brandy balloon	23–28 cl (8–10 fl oz)
Liqueur glass	2.5 cl (0.88 fl oz)
Tumbler/Slim Jim	28.40 cl (½ pint)
Beer	25–50 cl (½–1 pint)

Storage and cleaning

Drinking glasses are normally stored in a glass pantry and should be placed in single rows on thin plastic grid matting, upside down to prevent dust settling in them. Plastic racks made specifically for the purpose of stacking and storing glasses are another alternative. These racks are also a convenient method of transporting glassware from one point to another, which cuts down on breakages. Tumblers and other straight-sided glassware should not be stacked inside one another as this may result in breakages and can cause accidents to staff.

Most day-to-day glassware used in the industry can be washed using dishwashers. However, for certain glassware this is not recommended. This includes lead crystal and other forms of fine glassware, which should be hand washed. Over time most glassware will become milky in appearance and will then need to be replaced. Finer glassware will become like this very quickly, unless hand washed.

3.11 Disposables

There has been considerable growth in the use of disposables or 'throw-aways' as they are sometimes called.

Although many establishments use disposables to cut costs, the disposables must be attractive, presentable and acceptable to the client and also help to attract customers. The choice of which disposables to use may be determined by:

- necessity because of operational needs for:
  - outdoor catering
  - automatic vending
  - fast food
  - takeaways
- cost considerations such as:
  - traditional forms of service equipment
  - cost of laundry
  - wash-up costs.

Types of disposables

The main varieties of disposables generally used are as follows:

- storage and cooking purposes
- service of food and beverages, e.g. plates, knives, forks, cups
- decor – napkins, tablecloths, slip cloths, banquet roll, placemats
- hygiene – wipes
- clothing, e.g. aprons, chef hats, gloves
- packaging – for marketing and presentation purposes.

The types of disposables that may be used to replace the regular restaurant linen would be napkins, placemats, tray cloths, tablecloths and coasters, etc. Today, most forms of disposables can be of various colours, patterned or have the house-style motto or crest reproduced on them. The vast range of colours available also allows for changes in a service area with different colours being used for each meal.

Throwaway packs of knives, forks and spoons are more convenient and hygienic where the turnover of custom is very high over very short periods of time. This might apply in industrial canteens and transport catering. Throwaway packs eliminate delays at service points where the speed of washing-up is inadequate.

A considerable advance in the range of disposables available has been the introduction of disposables whose approximation to crockery tableware is very close. For instance, they may have a high-quality overall finish and a smooth, hard, white surface. The plates themselves are strong and rigid with no tendency to bend or buckle, and a plasticising ingredient ensures that they are greaseproof and moisture-proof, even against hot fat and gravy. Oval meal plates, snack trays and compartmentalised plates are all available to the caterer.

Figure 3.11 Examples of disposable products used in food service

Environmental issues

When purchasing disposable items it is important to consider products that are environmentally friendly. With the development of new materials many disposable products are now totally compostable and biodegradable, as they are made from renewable resources such as:

- sugar cane fibre off-cuts – very similar to conventional paper products and used for bowls, plates and cups
- clear polylactic acid (PLA) from carbon stored in plants such as corn and used for cups, containers and straws. Not suitable for hot liquids but can be frozen
- cornstarch cutlery, made from a starch-based polymer and chalk
- bamboo ware, used to make plates, bowls, cups and cutlery from reconstituted bamboo.

Advantages of disposables

- **Equipment and labour:** disposables reduce the need for washing-up equipment, staff and materials.
- **Hygiene:** usage improves the standard of hygiene in an establishment.
- **Time:** disposables may speed up service, e.g. for fast food.

- **Properties:** disposables have good heat retention and insulation properties.
- **Marketing:** disposables can be used as a promotional aid.
- **Capital:** usage reduces the amount of capital investment.
- **Carriage:** disposables are easily transported.
- **Cost:** disposables may be cheaper than hiring conventional equipment.

Disadvantages of disposables

- **Acceptability:** customer acceptability may be poor.
- **Cost:** disposables can be more expensive than some conventional equipment.
- **Storage:** back-up quantities are required.
- **Supply:** there is heavy reliance on supply and delivery time.
- **Environment:** unless they are made from renewable resources and are completely biodegradable they have a negative impact on the environment.

3.12 Automatic vending

Automatic vending is a form of automatic retailing and uses one of the following methods of payment:

- coin
- banknote
- money card
- token
- free vend.

Types of foodservice vending machine

Within foodservice operations, automatic vending is used for the supply of a wide variety of food and beverages, both hot and cold. Vending machines used for foodservice operations include:

- **Merchandiser:** Customers can view the products for sale, e.g. confectionery machines. Can also be used for refrigerated drinks (bottles and cans) and pre-packaged meals and snacks as well as for hot meals and snacks through internal heating.
- **Hot beverage vendor:** This mixes the powdered ingredients with hot water to produce the product.
- **In-cup system:** Ingredients are already in individual cups to which hot water is added.

Figure 3.12 Examples of foodservice vending machines (image courtesy of Sodexo UK and Ireland)

- **Cold beverage vendor:** Post-mix syrup mixed with water (carbonated or non-carbonated).
- **Micro-vend system:** Provides a range of hot or cold foods from which the customer may make a selection and heat in an accompanying microwave oven.

Cleaning of vending machines

Automatic vending machines are neither self-cleaning nor self-maintaining or filling. Therefore, regular service maintenance is required and should be guaranteed if the vending service is to run smoothly and without the problems of mechanical breakdown. The type of vending machine and the service demand upon it will help to determine the regularity of the service requirements. All vending machines come with instruction about cleaning, maintenance and stocking.

CHAPTER 4

Personal workplace skills

This chapter will help you to learn about:

1 Key factors for success in food and beverage service
2 Essential attributes of service personnel
3 Contributing to the team
4 Applying for a job
5 Developing a personal development plan

4.1 Key factors for success in food and beverage service

Today more than ever people are eating outside the home, and to meet this demand there is a wide diversity in the nature and type of food and beverage on offer.

Food and beverage service is the essential link between the customers and the menu on offer in an establishment. The server is the main point of contact between the customers and the establishment and therefore plays an important role. The skills and knowledge of food and beverage service are transferable between establishments, sectors and throughout the world.

To be successful in food and beverage service members of staff should have:

- sound product knowledge
- well-developed interpersonal skills
- a range of technical skills
- an ability to work as part of a team.

4.2 Essential attributes of service personnel

Professional and hygienic appearance

How staff look and the first impressions they create are a reflection of the hygiene standards of the establishment and the quality of service to come.

All staff should be aware of the factors listed below and it is their individual responsibility to ensure that they are put into practice.

- Staff should be clean and use subtle-smelling deodorants.
- Staff should ensure they have sufficient sleep, an adequate and healthy intake of food and regular exercise to maintain good health and the ability to cope with the pressures and stress of work.

- Particular attention must be paid to the hands. They must always be clean, free of nicotine stains and with clean, well-trimmed nails.
- Teeth should be brushed immediately before coming on duty and the breath should be fresh smelling.
- Men should normally be clean-shaven or with moustache or beard neatly trimmed.
- Women should only wear light make-up. If nail varnish is worn then it should be clear.
- Earrings should not be worn with the possible exception of studs/sleepers.
- Uniforms must be clean, starched as appropriate, neatly pressed and in good repair. All buttons must be present. Being smart and wearing the correct clothing is an important part of working in the hospitality industry.
- Hair must be clean and well groomed. Long hair should be tied up or back to avoid hairs falling into food and drinks, and to avoid repeated handling of the hair.
- Shoes must be comfortable and clean, and of a plain, neat design. Fashion is not as important here as safety and foot comfort.
- Cuts and burns must be covered with waterproof dressings.
- Any colds or other possible infections must be reported immediately.
- Hands must be washed immediately after using the toilet, smoking or dealing with refuse. Hot water and soap must be used.
- Staff should try to avoid any mannerisms they may have, such as running their fingers through their hair, chewing gum or scratching their face.
- Excessive jewellery should not be worn. The establishment policy should be followed.

Figure 4.1 **An example of a waiter in correct uniform**

Knowledge of food and beverages and technical ability

Staff must have sufficient knowledge of all the items on the menu and wine and drink lists in order to advise and offer suggestions to customers. Staff must also know how to serve correctly each dish on the menu, what its accompaniments are, the correct cover, the make-up of the dish and its garnish. For beverage service, the staff should know how to serve various types of wine and drink, in the correct containers (e.g. glasses, cups) and at the right temperature.

Punctuality

Punctuality is all-important. When staff are continually late on duty, it shows a lack of interest in their work and a lack of respect for the management and customers.

Local knowledge

The staff should have a reasonable knowledge of the area in which they work so they may be able to advise guests on the various forms of entertainment offered, the best means of transport to places of interest, local transport, parking, and so on.

Personality

Staff must be tactful, courteous, good-humoured and of an even temper. They must converse with the customer in a pleasing and well-spoken manner, and having the ability to smile at the right time pays dividends.

Attitude to customers

The correct approach to the customer is of the utmost importance. Staff should be able to anticipate the customer's needs and wishes without being servile. A careful watch must be kept on customers during the service to check the progress of the meal.

Memory

A good memory is an asset to food and beverage service staff. It may help them in various ways in their work if they know the likes and dislikes of customers, where they like to sit in the food service area, what are their favourite drinks, and so on.

Honesty

Trust and respect in the triangle of staff, customer and management relationships lead to an atmosphere at work that encourages efficiency and a good team spirit.

Loyalty

The obligations and loyalty of staff are first to the establishment in which they are employed and its management.

Conduct

Staff conduct should be impeccable at all times, especially in front of customers. The rules and regulations of an establishment must be followed and respect shown to all senior members of staff.

Sales ability

All members of staff reflect the image of the establishment. They are sales people and must therefore have a complete knowledge of all forms of food and drink and their correct service, and so be able to contribute to personal selling and merchandising.

Sense of urgency

In order for an establishment to generate the maximum amount of business over the service period, with as high net profit as possible, staff must develop a sense of urgency in their work.

Complaints

While staff should have a pleasant manner, show courtesy and tact, demonstrate an even temper and good humour, they should never show their displeasure even during a difficult situation. Staff should never argue with a customer and if they are unable to resolve a situation, they should refer immediately to a senior member of the team. They should be able to reassure the customer and put right any fault, as loss of time in dealing with complaints only makes the situation worse.

4.3 Contributing to the team

Staff must be able to work as part of a team, both within and between departments. The people in a team depend on each other to be successful and as a member of the food and beverage department, you will need to be able to work as part of a team. Each team will have targets and deadlines and in order to meet these there must be good communication and planning within the team. All members of the team need to understand what deadlines and targets have been set and what is expected of them.

It is also important that you:

- do your job in a professional way
- are punctual for work
- inform your employer, ideally your line manager, if you are ill
- are reliable and courteous because other people depend on you; if one person is away, it puts pressure on the other members of staff and, in some cases, temporary staff may have to be employed as cover
- manage your time and deadlines well and are able to prioritise – food has to be served on time; breakfast, lunch and dinner must be ready when the customer is ready.

Figure 4.2 **Staff working as a team**

Understanding yourself

In order to be a good employee it is important that you try to understand yourself. To do this, ask yourself the following questions:

- What are you capable of doing?
- What development do you need to help the team and yourself?
- What are your strengths?
- What are your weaknesses?
- Do you know when to ask for help?
- What training do you need? For example, would you like to improve your:
  - culinary skills
  - writing skills
  - IT skills
  - equipment skills?

Communication

Everyone in the team should be working towards the same goals and targets. Listening is also an important part of effective communication. You should learn to listen carefully and to understand facial expressions, gestures and body language. Good listeners:

- avoid any distractions
- concentrate on what is being said
- think about what is being said
- show interest in the person speaking and do not look bored
- maintain eye contact with the person talking and acknowledge what is being said
- if necessary, ask sensible questions
- paraphrase, in other words, clarify what has been said in their own words.

Be an active listener. Show the person you are listening to that you are interested in what they are saying by maintaining eye contact and responding to what they say. Listen before you form your own opinion.

Communication can also be non-verbal, in other words, unspoken. It is important to understand other people's body language. Body language refers to such things as:

- how you dress
- your posture
- how far you are from the other person
- your stance – how you sit or stand
- your facial expressions
- your movements and gestures
- your eye movements.

Body language is often unconscious and can tell us what people really think and feel. If someone is telling a lie, for instance, their body language will usually give them away because they may be unable to maintain eye contact. By focusing on other people's body language, you can discover their true feelings about you and what you are saying. Think about how you approach people and what body language you use. Everyone uses body language, but it can mean different things in different cultures and to different people.

Signs and meanings

Some gestures are open and positive. For example, leaning forwards with the palms of your hands open and facing upwards shows interest, acceptance and a welcoming attitude. On the other hand, leaning backwards, with your arms folded and head down might show that you are feeling closed, uninterested, defensive and negative or rejected.

If someone uses plenty of gestures this may indicate that they are warm, enthusiastic and emotional. If someone does not use many gestures this may indicate that they are cold, reserved and logical.

However, a gesture does not necessarily reveal exactly what a person is thinking. For example, if someone has their arms folded this may mean that:

- they are being defensive about something
- they are cold
- they are comfortable.

Barriers to effective communication

In order to communicate effectively:

- speak clearly
- speak slowly
- remember that not speaking the same language can cause difficulties
- avoid using too much unfamiliar terminology and jargon
- speak clearly and slowly to those who have a hearing impairment, as they may be able to lip read
- read through any letters or emails you write to check for grammar and spelling mistakes; if possible use a word-processing program and use the grammar and spellchecker.

Try to be confident, not shy, when you are communicating with other people.

Working with colleagues

It is important to develop good working relationships with your colleagues, work as a team and be supportive of each other. Seek guidance from other team members and your line manager in order to identify suitable role models.

Usually there will be a work plan developed for the day and for the week. Your manager will have discussed duty rotas and work schedules with team members in order to determine who will be covering what duties. The manager will also discuss targets and required outcomes with team members, and will be responsible for evaluating your performance and the team's performance. This may be done informally perhaps through a social occasion by meeting for a drink after work, or formally through a team meeting. Within your own establishment you should be able to identify how both your performance and that of your team is being monitored and measured.

4.4 Applying for a job

When applying for a job you will usually be asked to supply various documents and letters and then, if the first stage of your application is successful, you will be asked to go for an interview.

Writing a CV

When you apply for a job, you will probably be asked to send in a current CV (curriculum vitae). This requires you to list all your educational qualifications and work history, your interests and any other activities you participate in. Employers will generally want to know where you have demonstrated certain skills, how you have dealt with certain situations in the workplace and whether you carry out any voluntary work.

When preparing a CV, you should also bear in mind the following points:

- Your work experience and work placements should be included in the CV.
- Always keep your CV up to date and keep track of all your experience, jobs, dates of employment, employers and any awards you have won (that are relevant to the employment you are seeking).
- Always check spelling, layout and punctuation.
- Always update your personal records.
- As you develop your career, personal qualities and skills, write a short sketch about yourself.
- Write down what inspires you and how you use existing skills.
- Specify what your long-term goals are, as well as your immediate goals and targets.
- Broaden your life experience – identify ways of broadening your outlook, your range of skills and your ability to deal with a range of different people, personalities and cultural diversity.

An example layout of a curriculum vitae is shown in Figure 4.3(a) overleaf.

Writing a covering letter

A covering letter introduces you to the company; it explains why you are suitable for the job on offer, and the skills and qualities you can bring to it (see the example in Figure 4.3(b)). A covering letter may also give you an opportunity to say how you would be able to contribute positively to the establishment and organisation as a whole. The letter will usually accompany a copy of your CV.

Interview techniques

First impressions are important so always make sure you prepare thoroughly for an interview. Good preparation will help to ensure that you are in control of the interview. When preparing for an interview, you should also bear in mind the following points:

- Prepare any questions in advance.
- Consider how you are going to introduce yourself at the start of the interview.
- Make sure you are well groomed, smart and look professional.
- It is sometimes useful to practise interviews beforehand – this is known as role play.
- Before the interview, plan your journey and work out the travelling time – allow yourself plenty of time to get there so you do not feel rushed.

Personal presentation for interview

Before interviews make sure you research the job you are applying for and find out about the company. Make sure you:

- create a good first impression
- use the correct vocabulary
- know the questions you are going to ask

- demonstrate good communication skills
- show that you understand the importance of time management.

CURRICULUM VITAE

Name

Current position:
Home address:
Telephone:
Home email:
Date of birth:

General career overview:
[Include bullet point list of key features and achievements of career, including key experience and skills]

- X years' industry experience in food and beverage operations, including X years at craft and supervisory level.
- Experienced in *[give details]*.
- Proven record of achievement recognised through promotion and career advancement.
- Commitment to continuing professional development through undertaking various in-company training programmes *[give details]*.

Professional experience:

- Dates *[write as month and year in full]* – include job title and name of place, name of specific place and indication of level of operation e.g. 5*.
- Reporting to *[give details]*.
- Give some descriptive information, such as services provided, for how many people and how many staff responsible for. *[For example, à la carte and table d'hôte all day dining for up to 000 people, function catering for up to 000 people, with a staffing of 000 people.]*
- List key responsibilities.
- List other job features and unique experience.

[Then repeat this format for all employment going back in time. Write in the third person as it is easier to write in that format and much easier for other people to read.]

Professional activities:

- *[Bullet point list of any professional memberships and any contributions to industry activities.]*

Competitions and awards:

Education, training and qualifications:

Hobbies and interests:

Marital status:

Nationality: *[Include visa status if appropriate.]*

Figure 4.3(a) **Example of a CV**

4 Maynard Avenue
Compton
Sturbridge
X00 0XX
Telephone: 0000 000 000
Email: william.johns@xxxxxx.xxx

Mr James Bryant
Human Resources Manager
Hambury Hotels Ltd
Hertford Road
Birmingham
X00 0XX

23 May 2010

Dear Mr Bryant

Re: 55/001: Commis Chef Trainee program

I am writing to you to apply for the Commis Chef trainee program, currently advertised on the Hambury Hotels' website. My current CV is enclosed for your consideration.

Having always been interested in cooking, I applied after my GCSEs to study a GNVQ Chef and Restaurant Diploma course. Interest in becoming a chef started when my school attended an open day at Birmingham College of Food, my local catering college.

Hambury Hotels has an excellent reputation, focusing on high standards, and I would relish the opportunity to study for higher qualifications while training and contributing to the work of the hotel. At the college's February open day, I met with current graduate trainees and was impressed by the friendliness of your employees and very positive descriptions of working life at the hotel.

As well as completing my current course in May, my practical experience has included working on a three-month placement at The Weigh Bridge Hotel, Sturbridge. I am hard-working and a good team member.

I am available for an interview from 1st June onwards. In the meantime, I look forward to taking the opportunity to talk with you further about my application.

Yours sincerely,

William Johns

Figure 4.3(b) **Example of a covering letter**

During the interview maintain eye contact with the interviewer and smile occasionally. Be confident and polite. Think about the questions you are asked before you answer them and do not waffle! Be clear and concise in your answers. If you do not understand a question, ask for it to be clarified.

When the interview is over, reflect on your performance. If you are unsuccessful, ask for feedback and learn from the experience. Assess what you did well and what you did less well. Think about how you might improve in the future.

4.5 Developing a personal development plan

Whatever your job role, it is often useful to evaluate and check your progress. Feedback from your peers and managers is a useful way of evaluating your performance. Keeping records (e.g. personal development plans) provides a further way to check your progress, refer back to your targets and think about the outcome. Monitoring performance to check whether targets have been met therefore involves three key stages:

- work plans (e.g. personal development plans) – seeking guidance
- targets – evaluating them and taking corrective action when necessary
- outcomes – must be measurable in order to know whether they have been achieved.

Gathering information to improve your workplace skills is useful because once you have achieved a successful outcome, you can use that information to inform and help others.

Having a personal development plan will help you identify targets and timescales to improve your skills and advance your career for personal and professional success.

The next step is to identify which skills you need to develop further. Table 4.1 provides an opportunity for you to assess the skills you currently possess and those you would like to develop and then rank them in order of priority.

Table 4.1 Skills development progress chart

Knowledge, skills, qualities and experience	Already experienced	Want to know more	Want to develop further	Order of importance
Preparation skills				
Bar skills				
Wine skills				
Service skills				
Order-taking skills				
Billing skills				

Knowledge, skills, qualities and experience	Already experienced	Want to know more	Want to develop further	Order of importance
Managing your time				
Identifying barriers to personal success				
Being able to reflect positively				
Knowing what kind of career you want				
Preparing a job application				
Writing a job application covering letter				
Writing an attractive CV				
Understanding what is required to be successful				
Team-building skills				
Developing professional relationships				
Being assertive				
Dealing with difficult people				
Developing confidence				
Dealing with basic problem-solving				
Being self-motivated				
Evaluating personal competitiveness				
Understanding effective interview techniques				
Preparing for an interview				
Developing personal records				
Recording evidence				

Table 4.2 shows a personal target chart which you can use to identify a skill you wish to develop. The chart enables you to explain why the skill is important, describe how you will achieve it and provide evidence that the skill has been achieved.

Table 4.2 **Personal target chart**

	Target 1	Target 2	Target 3
What is the target?			
Importance of the skill and why you need it			
How you will achieve the skill and what support and guidance you will need			
Evidence that you have achieved your aim			

Your personal development plan will help you to evaluate your performance feedback from your mentor, manager or tutor, and will help you to improve your own performance. The plan will help you to achieve your aims and become successful – to be where you want to be and who you want to be. An example of an action plan for personal development is shown in Table 4.3.

Table 4.3 **Action plan for personal development**

Target	Steps to take in milestones	Indicators of successful completion	Start date	Target completion date	Done
1	a				
	b				
	c				
2	a				
	b				
	c				

CHAPTER 5

Legislation in food and beverage service

This chapter will help you to learn about:

1 The importance of legal compliance
2 Health, safety and security
3 Liquor and other licensing
4 Legal aspects of the sale of goods
5 Avoiding discrimination
6 Data protection

5.1 The importance of legal compliance

There are a wide variety of legal requirements for foodservice operations. These include company law, liquor licensing regulations and employment law. Summaries of the key responsibilities for the foodservice operation are described throughout this chapter.

Enforcement bodies include representatives of:

- Trading standards
- Local councils
- Police
- Weights and measures enforcement
- Information Commissioner's Office
- Equality and Human Rights Commission.

Penalties for non-compliance with the legislation can be severe, both for the business and for the management and staff. It is important that all members of staff contribute to ensuring compliance with the legal requirements.

Note: All food and beverage service personnel must at least hold a current Basic Food Hygiene Certificate.

5.2 Health, safety and security

An establishment has a common law duty to care for all staff and lawful visitors. In addition, establishments must not:

- sell (or keep for sale) food and beverages that are unfit for people to eat
- cause food or beverages to be dangerous to health

- sell food or beverages that are not what the customer is entitled to expect, in terms of content or quality
- describe or present food in a way that is false or misleading.

A foodservice operator must be able to demonstrate that steps have been taken to ensure good food hygiene (this is called due diligence).

The Health and Safety at Work Act, 1974, the Fire Safety Order 2006 and Fire (Scotland) Act 2005 cover areas of safety within the workplace. Key responsibilities under the legislation include ensuring that:

- there is a written health and safety policy
- service standards comply with health, safety, environmental and food hygiene regulations
- there are adequate arrangements in place to ensure the safety, security and well-being of staff and customers
- periodic risk assessments are carried out and recorded
- emergency exits are clearly marked and regular fire drills are carried out
- staff are trained in fire procedures and know how to use fire-fighting equipment
- staff are aware of evacuation procedures in the event of a fire or security risk such as a bomb threat
- health and safety notices are displayed in working areas
- staff and customers are trained, as appropriate, on correct usage of equipment and facilities
- all food handlers are trained in safe and hygienic working practices.

In addition the Employers' Liability Act (1969) and Employers' Liability (Northern Ireland) Order (1972) require employers to ensure that they have valid employer liability insurance cover at all times and a notice is displayed to that effect.

Note: More detailed information on health, safety and security is presented in Chapter 6, Health, safety and security (page 86).

5.3 Liquor and other licensing

The sale of alcoholic liquor is subject to the Licensing Act (2003) requirements, which have four key objectives:

1. The prevention of crime and disorder
2. Public safety
3. The prevention of public nuisance
4. The protection of children from harm.

The usual requirements of the Act are:

- the display of a summary of the premises licence, including the days and times of opening, the name of the registered licence holder, the licence number and a valid date
- drinks price lists to be displayed
- restrictions on under-aged persons being served alcohol and employed to serve alcohol
- the need for an authorised person (or the personal licence holder) to be on site at all times.

Other types of licences may include, for example, licences for music (live or pre-recorded), dancing, gambling, theatrical performance and television display. In all cases the supervisor and the staff should be aware of the provisions and limitations of the licences to ensure compliance.

5.4 Legal aspects of the sale of goods

There are three Acts of Parliament that cover the sale of goods:

- Sale and Supply of Goods Act (1994)
- Trade Descriptions Act (1968)
- Consumer Protection Act (1987).

In addition to the above Acts is the Consumer Protection from Unfair Trading Regulations 2008 and the Consumer Protection (Northern Ireland) Order.

Broadly, the legislation requires the foodservice operator and members of staff to follow good practice to ensure:

- all food, beverages and other services provided are fit for purpose and of satisfactory quality in relation to price and description
- food, beverages and other services are accurately described in terms of size, quality, composition, production, quantity and standard
- all statements of price, whether in an advertisement, brochure, leaflet, on the web, or those given by letter or orally in person or over the telephone are clear and accurate
- pricing and the display of priced items complies with the Price Marking Order 2004
- food, beverages and other services correspond to their description in brochures/promotional material
- times, dates, locations and nature of service promised are adhered to
- customer billing is fair, transparent and reflects the prices quoted either orally or in writing.

To ensure compliance with the legislation, care must be taken when:

- wording menus and wine lists
- describing menu and beverage items to customers
- stating if prices include local and/or government taxes
- describing conditions such as cover charges, service charges or extras
- describing the service provision.

Selling goods by weights and measures

All sales of goods by weight or measure should be in accordance with the legislative requirements of the Weights and Measures Act (1985) and the Weights and Measures (Packaged Goods) Regulations 1986. This usually requires:

- a display of the prices and the measures used for all spirits, wines, beers, ciders and any other alcohol served
- the food and beverage items for sale to be of the quantity and quality demanded by the customer
- the use of officially stamped measures.

Providing services

Generally a food and beverage operator is under no specific requirement to serve anyone. However, it is important that the supervisor and staff are aware of:

- circumstances where there may be a mandatory requirement to provide services
- valid reasons for refusal.

Contracts

A contract is made when one party agrees to the terms of an offer made by another party; this can be written or verbal. In food and beverage service there are essentially two types of customer: those who pre-book and those who do not (often called chance or casual customers).

All foodservice establishments should be clear on how they will deal with these different types of customers, including:

- circumstances where the restaurant may seek compensation from the customer if they do not turn up or pay for their meals or services
- taking care when making contracts with minors (i.e. persons under 18).

Customer property and customer debt

Good practice usually means that supervisors need to ensure:

- care is taken of customers' property in order to minimise potential loss or damage. Notices warning customers of 'no responsibility' may help in defence but do not guarantee exemption from liability for the food and beverage operator
- clear guidance is given on the procedures to follow if the customer is unable or unwilling to pay.

5.5 Avoiding discrimination

There are a number of Acts that the foodservice operator and staff should be aware of relating to discrimination on grounds of ethnic origin, race, creed, sex or disability:

- Race Relations Act (1976)
- Race Relations (Northern Ireland) Order (1997)
- Sex Discrimination Act (1970)
- Sex Discrimination (Northern Ireland) Order (1975)
- Disability Discrimination Act (1995)
- Age Discrimination Act (2006)

Both the foodservice operator and staff must ensure that steps are taken to ensure that discrimination under the terms of the Acts does not occur. There are potentially three ways in which discrimination can take place.

1. **Direct discrimination**: e.g. refusing service to customers of particular ethnic origin, race, creed, sex or disability.
2. **Indirect discrimination**: e.g. denying consumer services by imposing unjustifiable conditions or requirements that have ethnic origin, sex or disability implications.
3. **Discrimination through victimisation**: e.g. by (a) refusal of provision, i.e. refusal of admission on the basis of ethnic origins, sex or disability; or (b) omission of provision, i.e. providing services to ethnic customers that are markedly inferior to those available to the public in general or which may only be available at a price premium.

It is the responsibility of the business and the members of staff to ensure that no such discrimination occurs.

Under the legislation there are requirements to ensure:

- a commitment to providing consistently high levels of service to all internal and external customers to ensure they are not discriminated against on the grounds of race, sex, age, disability, sexual orientation, religion or belief
- the publishing of an equal opportunities policy
- job adverts use wording that indicates equal opportunities
- a diversity of staff are employed or considered for employment including mixed sexes, ages and races and people with disabilities
- reasonable adjustments are made to the way services are delivered to make it easier for disabled guests to use them, including easy wheelchair access for disabled customers and staff, disabled toilet facilities, elevator facilities as an alternative to stairs for disabled customers and staff, and assistance being given to any disabled customer on request.

5.6 Data protection

Customers generally have a right under the Data Protection Act (1998) to expect that data about them is kept secure and is only used for the published business purposes. The general requirements for businesses are to ensure that:

- the company is registered with the Data Protection Registrar
- information on customers is kept up to date, fairly, lawfully and securely
- customer information is not passed on to third parties without prior consent from the customer
- staff are aware of the importance of the protection of customer information and the procedures to follow to ensure it is held securely.

CHAPTER 6

Health, safety and security

This chapter will help you to learn about:

1 Maintaining a safe environment
2 Ensuring fire safety
3 Ensuring food safety
4 Maintaining a secure environment

6.1 Maintaining a safe environment

Every day, people are injured at work. Some may be permanently disabled and some may even die. Be safe and do not let this happen to you or your work colleagues. Foodservice operations can be dangerous places so it is important to work in a safe and systematic way in order to avoid accidents or injury to yourself or anyone else.

Stress and accidents are currently the two biggest causes of absence from work.

Absence due to sickness costs the UK economy approximately £400–£500 per employee each year. Over 200 people die in accidents at work each year; accidents can happen in any workplace. The average number of days taken as sick leave each year in the UK is approximately 30 million.

Potential benefits of good health and safety practices:

- reduction in accidents and ill health
- motivated workers
- enhanced reputation
- increased productivity
- improved profitability.

Potential costs of accidents in the workplace:

- employees off work due to illness and stress
- compensation claims
- prosecution
- fines
- legal costs
- damage to the business's reputation
- high staff turnover.

Who is responsible for health and safety?

The simple answer is that everyone is responsible for health and safety. More specifically, the following can be said to have a responsibility:

- employers/employees
- people in control of work premises
- self-employed
- designers

- manufacturers
- suppliers
- local authorities
- Health & Safety Executive (HSE)
- enforcement officers
- environmental health officers
- health and safety inspectors

Under the terms of the Health and Safety at Work Act, an employer must make sure all staff are safe while at work. This means that the employer must:

- provide safe equipment and utensils
- train staff in safe working practices
- provide first aid equipment
- keep an accident book
- produce a policy document telling everyone how to work safely
- provide good welfare facilities for staff including rest facilities, drinking water, toilets, washing facilities, changing rooms and lockers.

Essentially safety is a civil duty and negligence is a criminal offence. The implications for staff under the above legislation are that they should:

- understand the food hygiene regulations and that it is their responsibility to act within the bounds of these regulations
- notify management of any major illnesses
- perform duties in any area concerned with the handling of food in a hygienic manner, paying attention to food and hygiene regulations
- make themselves familiar with all escape routes and fire exits in the building
- ensure that fire exits remain clear at all times
- participate in fire evacuation drills and practices
- take reasonable care for the health and safety of themselves and of others, and ensure that health and safety regulations are followed
- report to heads of department or duty managers any hazards which may cause injury or ill health to customers and/or staff.

Managing health and safety

Employers must have appropriate arrangements in place (which must be recorded if there are five or more employees) for maintaining a safe workplace. These should cover the usual management functions of:

- planning
- organisation
- control.

Avoiding risks

Risk is the chance of somebody being harmed by a hazard. There may be a high risk or a low risk of harm.

Here are five steps to assessing risk:

1. Look for hazards, i.e. the things that can cause harm.
2. Identify who could be harmed and how.
3. Work out the risks and decide if the existing precautions are good enough or whether more should be done to prevent harm being caused.
4. Write down what the hazard is and what the risk is and keep this as a record.
5. Re-check the hazard and the risk at regular intervals and go back and change the risk assessment (the written record) if necessary.

Table 6.1 **Common risks and hazards and ways to minimise them**

Common risks and hazards	Ways to minimise risks
• Poor design and structure of building • Poor signage • Poor housekeeping standards • Poor lighting and ventilation • Dangerous working practices • Distraction and lack of attention • Working too quickly • Ignoring the rules • Not wearing protective clothing	• Improved and safe design of the building • Correct and clear/visible signage • Good housekeeping • Well-lit and ventilated areas • Well-trained staff • Strict enforcement of rules • Wearing correct protective clothing • Concentrating on the work and avoiding distractions

Avoiding hazards

The Health and Safety at Work Act covers all full-time and part-time workers and unpaid workers. The Health & Safety Executive (HSE) is responsible for enforcing health and safety in the workplace.

- The HSE has the power to investigate premises, check, dismantle and remove equipment, inspect records, ask questions, seize and destroy articles.
- It can give verbal or written advice, order improvement and prohibition notices and will, if necessary, prosecute, which can result in unlimited fines or even imprisonment.

A hazard is anything that can cause harm, such as:

- extremes of cold and heat
- uneven floors
- excessive noise
- chemicals
- electricity
- working using ladders
- moving parts and machinery
- dust and fumes.

The following aspects of the foodservice environment have the potential to give rise to hazards:

- equipment – liquidisers, food processors, mixers, mincers, etc.
- substances – cleaning chemicals, detergents, sanitisers
- work methods – carrying knives and equipment incorrectly and not following a logical sequence
- work areas – spillages not cleaned up, overcrowded work areas, insufficient work space, uncomfortable work conditions due to extreme heat or cold.

Employees have a responsibility to themselves, work colleagues and customers to be aware of hazards that may arise when working. Many accidents occur through carelessness or through lack of thought, for example:

- not having the correct protective clothing such as an apron
- not wearing sensible (stable and properly fitted) shoes
- delay in clearing spillages or picking up items of equipment that have fallen on the floor
- not being aware of customers' bags placed on the floor
- items of equipment not stored correctly
- broken glass or crockery not wrapped up sufficiently before being placed in the bin
- forgetting to unplug electrical appliances prior to cleaning
- putting ashtray debris into rubbish bins containing paper (a fire hazard)
- forgetting to switch off and unplug an appliance after use, or at the end of the service

- not being observant with table lamps or lit candles on a buffet
- overfilling coffee pots, soup tureens, glasses, etc.
- using cups, glasses, soup bowls, etc. for storing cleaning agents
- stacking trays incorrectly
- carrying a mix of equipment on a tray, such as cutlery, crockery and glassware
- carpet edges turned up
- faulty wheels on trolleys or castors on sideboards
- being unaware of customers' walking sticks and crutches
- lack of adequate space for the safe service of food and drink due to bad planning
- lack of knowledge in carrying out certain tasks, e.g. opening a bottle of sparkling wine.

Control of substances hazardous to health

The Control of Substances Hazardous to Health (COSHH) Regulations state that an employer must not carry out any work that might expose employees to any substances that are hazardous to health, unless the employer has assessed the risks of this work to employees. In foodservice establishments there are many chemicals and substances used for cleaning that can be harmful if not used correctly (see Table 6.2).

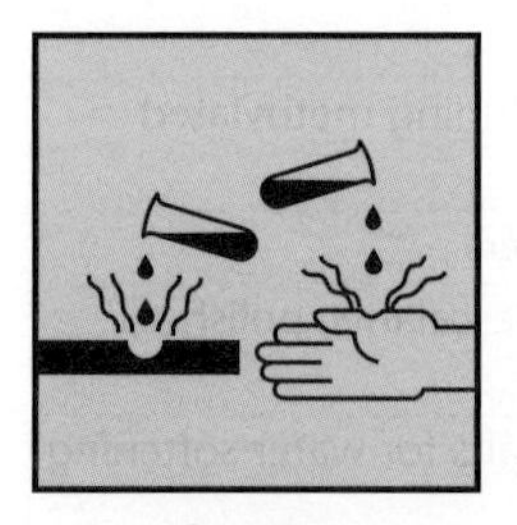
Corrosive

Flammable

Harmful

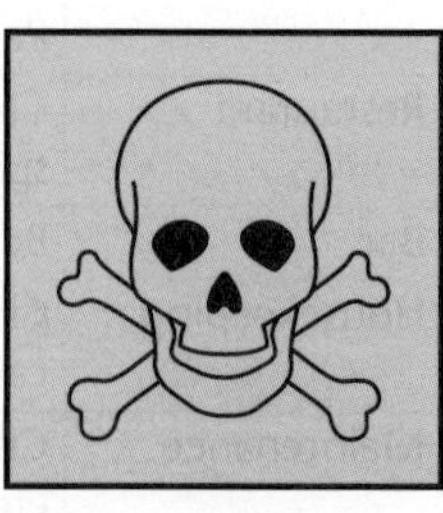
Toxic

Figure 6.1 **Hazardous substances' symbols**

Substances that are dangerous to health are labelled as very toxic, toxic, harmful, irritant or corrosive. Figure 6.1 shows some hazardous substances' symbols. People using these chemical substances must be trained to use them correctly. They must also wear protective clothing such as goggles, gloves and facemasks. Hazardous substances can enter the body through the skin, eyes, nose (by inhaling) and mouth (by swallowing).

Preventing accidents

The COSHH Regulations state that the employer must assess the risk from chemicals and decide what precautions are needed. The employer should make sure that measures are in place to control the use of chemical substances and monitor their use. Some guidelines for using chemical substances include the following:

- Inform, instruct and train all staff in their use and safety.
- Ensure the manufacturer's instructions are followed.
- Make sure the chemicals are always stored in their original containers, away from heat.
- Keep lids tightly closed.
- Do not expose chemicals to heat or naked flames.
- Read all the labels carefully.

- Never mix chemicals.
- Know the first aid procedure.
- Get rid of empty containers immediately.
- Get rid of waste chemical solutions safely.
- Wear safety equipment and clothing.

Hazardous substance monitoring

In order to comply with legal obligations under the COSHH Regulations, all areas should be surveyed to ascertain which chemicals and substances are used. Table 6.2 lists the different work areas and the chemicals and substances likely to be found in them.

Table 6.2 **Work areas and the chemicals and substances likely to be found in them**

Area	Chemicals and substances
Kitchen	Cleaning chemicals including alkalis and acids, detergents, sanitisers and descalers Chemicals associated with burnishing; possibly some oils associated with machines Pest control chemicals, insecticides and rodenticides
Restaurant	Cleaning chemicals, polishes, fuel for flame lamps including methylated spirits, LPG
Bar	Beer-line cleaner, glass-washing detergent and sanitisers
Housekeeping	Cleaning chemicals including detergents, sanitisers, descalants, polishes, carpet-cleaning products, floor-care products
Maintenance	Cleaning chemicals, adhesives, solvents, paint, LPG, salts for water softening etc., paint stripper, varnishes, etc.
Offices	Correction fluid, thinners, solvents, methylated spirits, toner for photocopier, duplicating fluids and chemicals, polishes

A COSHH register should be kept by the manager of all substances used in the establishment. Technical data sheets should be attached to the completed COSHH assessment sheet.

Personal protective equipment

According to the Personal Protective Equipment (PPE) at Work Regulations (1992), employees must wear personal protective clothing and equipment (e.g. safety shoes, eye protection such as goggles) for tasks that may pose a risk or hazard.

Manual handling

Picking up and carrying heavy or difficult loads can lead to accidents if not done properly. Poor handling of loads is the main cause of back problems in the workplace. The safest way to lift objects is to bend your knees rather than your back (see Figure 6.2). It is also better if two people lift the object together, rather than one person trying to do it on their own. This will help to prevent straining and damage to your back.

Handling checklist

- When you move goods on trolleys, trucks or other wheeled vehicles:
  - load them carefully
  - do not overload them
  - load them in a way that allows you to see where you are going.

- In stores, stack heavy items at the bottom.
- If steps are needed to reach higher items, use them with care.
- Take particular care when moving large pots of liquid, especially if the liquid is hot. Do not fill pots to the brim.
- Use a warning sign to let people know if equipment handles, lids, and so on might be hot. This is traditionally done by sprinkling a small amount of flour, or something similar, onto the part of the equipment that might be hot.
- Take extra care when removing a tray from the oven or salamander to avoid burning someone else.

Figure 6.2 **How to lift correctly**

Safety signs

Safety signs are used to control a hazard and they should not replace other methods of controlling risks.

Figure 6.3 **Yellow warning sign**

Yellow warning signs

These are warning signs to alert people to various dangers, such as slippery floors, hot oil or hot water. They also warn people about hazards such as corrosive material.

Blue mandatory signs

These signs inform people about precautions they must take. They tell people how to progress safely through a certain area. They must be used whenever special precautions need to be taken, such as wearing protective clothing.

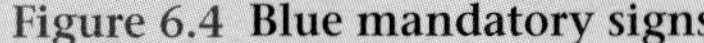

Figure 6.4 **Blue mandatory signs**

Red prohibition signs – firefighting signs

Red signs tell people that they should not enter. They are used to stop people from doing certain tasks in a hazardous area. Red signs are also used for firefighting equipment.

Figure 6.5 **Red prohibition signs**

Green safe signs

These are route signs designed to show people where fire exits and emergency exits are. Green is also used for first aid equipment.

Electricity and gas

Great care must be taken when dealing with electricity. If a person comes into direct contact with electricity, the consequences can be very serious and sometimes fatal. If a person has an electric shock, switch off the current. If this is not possible, free the person using something that is dry and will insulate you from the electricity, such as a cloth, or something made of wood or rubber. You must take care not to use your bare hands otherwise the electric shock may be transmitted to you. If the person has stopped breathing, call an ambulance and summon a first aider.

In an emergency you should always:

- switch off the electrical current
- raise the alarm
- summon an ambulance/first aid help.

Figure 6.6 **Green safe signs**

RIDDOR (Reporting Injuries, Diseases and Dangerous Occurrences) Act (1996)

The law says that all work-related accidents, diseases and dangerous occurrences must be recorded and reported. Employers must report the following injuries to the Incident Contact Centre (ICC) at the HSE:

- fractures (apart from fractures to fingers, thumbs or toes)
- amputation (cutting off) of limbs – legs, arms, etc.
- dislocation of a hip, knee or spine
- temporary or permanent loss of sight (blindness)
- eye injuries from chemicals getting into the eye, a hot metal burn to the eye or any penetration of the eye
- any injury from electric shock or burning that leads to unconsciousness or the need to resuscitate the person or send them to hospital for more than 24 hours
- any injury resulting in hypothermia (when someone gets too cold), or illness due to heat, that leads to unconsciousness or the need to resuscitate the person or send them to hospital for more than 24 hours (e.g. an electric shock or a gas flame blown back and causing burns)

- unconsciousness caused by exposure to a harmful substance or biological agents (e.g. cleaning products and solvents)
- unconsciousness or illness requiring medical treatment caused by inhaling a harmful substance or absorbing it through the skin (e.g. breathing in poisonous carbon monoxide leaking from a gas appliance)
- illness requiring medical treatment caused by a biological agent or its toxins or infected material (e.g. harmful bacteria used in laboratories).

Some diseases are also reportable under RIDDOR and these include:

- dermatitis
- skin cancer
- asthma
- hepatitis
- tuberculosis
- tetanus
- anthrax.

Incident/accident reporting

Health and safety has to be monitored regularly in the workplace by the designated Health & Safety Officer. Any incidents or near misses must be recorded, even if no one is injured.

Full name of injured person:			
Occupation:		Supervisor:	
Time of accident:	Date of accident:	Time of report:	Date of report:
Name of injury or condition:			
Details of hospitalisation:			
Extent of injury (after medical attention):			
Place of accident or dangerous occurrence:			
Injured person's evidence of what happened (include equipment/items and/or other persons):			
Witness evidence (1):		Witness evidence (2):	
Supervisor's recommendations:			
Date:		Supervisor's signature:	

Figure 6.7 An incident report form

All accidents should be reported to your line manager, chef or a supervisor. Each accident is recorded in an accident book, which must be provided in every business. Below is an example of an incident report form showing all the details required.

First aid

When people at work suffer injuries or fall ill, it is important that they receive immediate attention and that, in serious cases, an ambulance is called. The arrangements for providing first aid in the workplace are set out in the Health and Safety (First Aid) Regulations (1981). First aiders and first aid facilities should be available to give immediate assistance to casualties with common injuries or illness.

As the term implies, first aid is the immediate treatment given on the spot to a person who has been injured or is ill. Since 1982 it has been a legal requirement that adequate first aid equipment, facilities and personnel are provided at work. If the injury is serious, the injured person should be treated by a doctor or nurse as soon as possible.

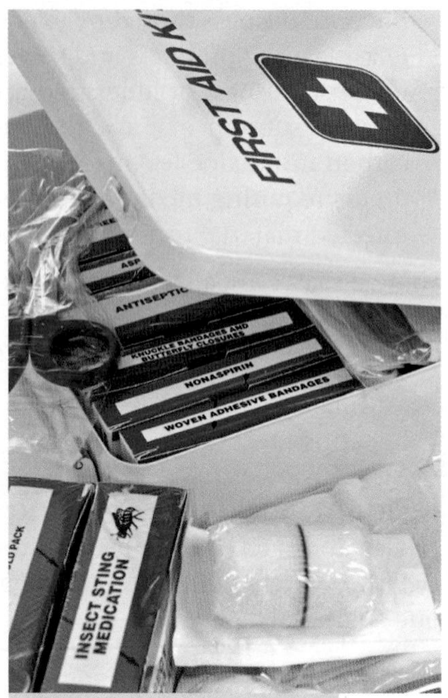

Figure 6.8 **A first aid box**

If you are involved in or witness an accident you will be required to give information and/or to complete an accident form. For this reason it is wise to make notes on the event at the earliest opportunity. The information should include:

- the location of the accident
- the time of the accident
- a statement of the event
- details of witnesses
- the treatment administered.

Cleaning programmes

Clean areas play an essential part in the production of safe food, and the team must plan, record and check all cleaning as part of a cleaning schedule. Clean premises, work areas and equipment are important to:

- control the bacteria that cause food poisoning
- reduce the possibility of physical and chemical contamination
- reduce the possibility of accidents (e.g. slips on a greasy floor)
- create a positive image for customers, visitors and employees
- comply with the law
- avoid attracting pests to the kitchen.

The cleaning schedule needs to include the following information:

- *What* is to be cleaned.
- *Who* should do it (name if possible).
- *How* it is to be done and how long it should take.
- *When it is to be done*, i.e. time of day.
- *Materials* to be used, including chemicals and their dilution, cleaning equipment and protective clothing to be worn.
- *Safety* precautions that must be taken.
- *Signatures* of the cleaner and the supervisor checking the work, along with the date and time.

Cleaning products

There are different cleaning products designed for different tasks.

- **Detergent** is designed to remove grease and dirt. It may be in the form of liquid, powder, gel or foam and usually needs to be added to water before use. Detergent will not kill pathogens (bacteria), although the hot water it is mixed with may help to do this. Detergent will clean and degrease surfaces so that disinfectant can work properly. Detergents usually work best with hot water.
- **Disinfectant** is designed to destroy bacteria when used properly. Make sure you only use a disinfectant intended for kitchen use. Disinfectants must be left on a cleaned grease-free surface for the required amount of time (contact time) to be effective.
- **Heat** may also be used to disinfect, for example, using steam cleaners or the hot rinse cycle of a dishwasher. Items that should be both cleaned and disinfected include all items in direct contact with food, all hand contact surfaces, hand wash basins and cleaning equipment.
- **Sanitiser** cleans and disinfects. It usually comes in spray form. Sanitiser is very useful for work surfaces and equipment, especially when cleaning them between tasks.

All food and beverage service staff should be made aware of the importance of cleaning programmes to reduce and minimise the build up of dust, bacteria and other forms of debris. For this reason, together with the considerations needed for safety and hygiene, full attention needs to be paid by all concerned to cleaning tasks and when they should be carried out. Regular maintenance will make the service area look attractive and will project a positive image for the establishment.

A cleaning programme should be set up for any cleaning tasks that must be done in a particular area. Some tasks are done daily, even twice daily, for instance, the washing and polishing of crockery before each service period. Other tasks might be done weekly, monthly or every six months. Certain items of equipment will need cleaning immediately after each service period is finished.

Points to note:

- always use the correct cleaning materials for the task in hand
- clean frequently
- rinse all surfaces well
- dusters should only be used for dusting and not other cleaning tasks
- use cleaning procedures that are adequate and efficient
- cloths used for cleaning toilets must not be used for any other purpose
- clean and store equipment safely and in its correct place
- do not use cleaning cloths for wiping down food preparation surfaces
- consider safety at all times and do not stretch or stand on chairs to reach high points – use a stepladder.

6.2 Ensuring fire safety

Every employer has an explicit duty for the safety of his or her employees in the event of a fire. The Regulatory Fire Safety Order (2005) emphasises that fires should be prevented. It says that fire safety is the responsibility of the occupant of the premises and the people who might be affected by fire, so in catering this will usually be the employer (the occupant) and the employees (who will be affected by fire).

The responsible person must:

- make sure that the fire precautions, where reasonably practicable, ensure the safety of all employees and others in the building
- make an assessment of the risk of and from fire in the establishment; special consideration must be given to dangerous chemicals or substances and the risks that these pose if a fire occurs
- review the preventative and protective measures.

Fire precautions

A fire requires heat, fuel and oxygen – known as 'the fire triangle' (see Figure 6.9). Without any one of these elements there is no fire, so taking precautions to avoid the three coming together will reduce the chances of a fire starting.

Some fire precaution guidelines are shown below:

- Remove all hazards or reduce them as much as possible.
- Make sure that everyone is protected from the risk of fire and the likelihood of a fire spreading.
- Make sure that all escape routes are safe and used effectively, in other words, ensure they are signposted, easy to access and people know where they are.
- Some way of fighting fires (e.g. a fire extinguisher or fire blanket) must be available on the premises.
- There must be some way of detecting a fire on the premises (e.g. smoke alarms) and instructions on what to do in case of fire.
- There must be arrangements in place for what to do if a fire breaks out on the premises. Employees must be trained in what to do in the event of a fire.
- All fire precaution devices must be installed and maintained by a competent person.

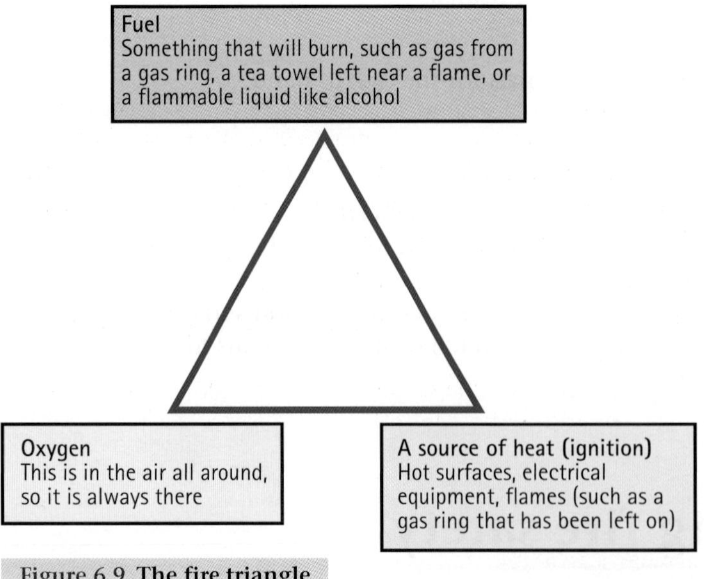

Figure 6.9 **The fire triangle**

Fire risk assessments

A fire risk assessment will:

- determine how likely it is that a fire might happen
- highlight the dangers from fire in the workplace.

You should always report:

- dangerous electrical equipment
- gas leaks
- faulty equipment.

Always use qualified professionals for problems with gas, electricity and water.

There are five steps to complete for a fire risk assessment:

1. Identify the potential fire hazards in the workplace.
2. Decide who will be in danger in the event of a fire, e.g. employees, visitors.
3. Identify the risks caused by the hazards. Decide whether the existing fire precautions are adequate or whether more needs to be done, e.g. to remove a hazard to control the risk.
4. Anything arising from points 1–3 above should be written down and a record kept, and all staff should be informed of them.
5. The risk assessment should be reviewed regularly to check that it is up to date. If things change it should be revised as necessary.

Fire detection and fire warning

It is important that there is an effective way of detecting a fire and warning people about it quickly enough to allow them to escape before the fire spreads too far.

In small workplaces, such as small restaurants, a fire will be detected easily and quickly and is unlikely to cut off the escape routes. In this case, if people can see the exits clearly, shouting 'FIRE!' may be all that is necessary.

In larger establishments fire warning systems are needed. Manually operated call points are likely to be the minimum that is needed. These are the type of fire alarm where you break glass to set off the alarm (as seen on the wall in schools, etc.).

Firefighting equipment

Methods of extinguishing fires concentrate on cooling (as in a water extinguisher or fire hose) or depriving the fire of oxygen (as in an extinguisher that uses foam or powder to smother it). Portable fire extinguishers enable people to tackle a fire in its early stages. People should be trained to use the extinguishers and should only use them if they can do so without putting themselves in danger.

Fires are classified in accordance with British Standard EN2 as follows:

- Class A – fires involving solid materials where combustion (burning) normally forms glowing embers (e.g. wood).
- Class B – fires involving liquids (e.g. methylated spirits) or liquefiable solids (e.g. any kind of flammable gel used under a burner).
- Class C – fires involving gases.
- Class D – fires involving metals.
- Electrical fires.
- Class F – fires involving cooking oils or fats.

Table 6.3 **Fire extinguishers and their uses**

Contents	Water	Foam	CO_2	Dry powder	Halon
Label colour*:	White on red	Cream on red	Black on red	Blue on red	Green on red
Electrical suitability:	Dangerous – electrically conductive		Safe – non-electrically conductive		
Suitable for:	Solids	Some liquids	Electrical	Liquid	Liquid
Unsuitable for:	Oil	Electrical	Solids	Very little	Solids

* Under European Union standards the body of every extinguisher must be coloured red. However, a colour zone is used to indicate what the extinguishing medium is – the colours used for these mediums are the ones given here, and they are the same as the previous whole-body colour-coding system.

There are different types of fire extinguishers that are suitable for different types of fire. Portable extinguishers all contain a substance that will put out a fire. The substance will vary, but whatever it is it will be forced out of the extinguisher under pressure. Generally, portable fire extinguishers contain one of the following five substances (known as extinguishing mediums):

- water
- foam
- powder
- carbon dioxide
- vaporising liquids.

Procedure in case of fire

All employees should be given fire drill training within their induction programme. This initial training should then be followed up by regular training sessions on the procedures to be followed in the event of fire. This training should include:

- fire procedures in employee's own specific area of work
- fire drill instructions for both customers and staff
- the location of fire points (safe places where staff and customers should assemble after an evacuation) nearest to own particular area of work
- the location of the fire exits
- the correct type of fire extinguisher to be used in relation to the type of fire (see Table 6.3)
- an identification of employee's own specific responsibilities in the event of fire.

In the event of the fire alarm ringing, employees must be aware of the following rules:

1. Follow the fire instructions as laid down for the establishment.
2. Usher all customers and staff out of the work area promptly and calmly.
3. Pay special attention to customers with special needs such as those with mobility problems.
4. Walk quickly but do not run. Display a sense of urgency.
5. Do not panic; remain calm as composure will be imitated by others.
6. Proceed as promptly as possible to the nearest assembly point.
7. Ensure that someone watches to see that there are no stragglers.
8. Follow the exit route as laid down in the establishment fire instructions.
9. Never use a lift.
10. Never re-enter the building until told it is safe to do so by the Fire Service.
11. Do not waste time to collect personal items.

Employees have a responsibility to assist in fire prevention, control and safety. They must therefore ensure that:

- fire exits are not obstructed
- firefighting equipment is not damaged or misused
- no smoking rules are observed at all times
- as far as is possible all electrical and gas equipment is switched off when not in use
- all doors and windows are closed when not being used for evacuation purposes
- fire doors are not locked or wedged open
- sufficient ashtrays/stands are available outside for the disposal of cigarette ends and used matches
- the procedure for making an emergency fire call is known.

6.3 Ensuring food safety

Everyone consuming food prepared for them by others when they are away from home (for example, in canteens and restaurants) has the right and expectation to be served safe food that will not cause illness or harm them in any way.

Food safety means putting in place all of the measures needed to make sure that food and drinks are suitable, safe and wholesome through all of the processes of food provision, from selecting suppliers and delivery of food right through to serving the food to the customer.

Note: All food and beverage service personnel must at least hold a current Basic Food Hygiene Certificate.

Why is food safety important?

Eating 'contaminated' food can cause illness (food poisoning) and, in some cases, even death. The number of reported cases of food poisoning each year in England and Wales remains very high, between 70,000 and 94,000 reported cases each year. However, as a large number of food poisoning cases are not reported, no one really knows the actual number.

Food poisoning is an illness of the digestive system that is the result of eating foods contaminated with pathogenic bacteria and/or their toxins. It can be an unpleasant illness for anyone, but it can be very serious or even fatal for some people. High-risk groups include:

- babies and very young children
- elderly people
- pregnant women
- those who are already unwell
- people with a repressed immune system.

It is therefore essential to take great care to prevent food poisoning, and The Food Standards Agency has committed to reduce significantly the numbers of reported food poisoning cases in the UK.

Food poisoning may also be caused by eating poisonous fish or plants, allergens or foods contaminated with chemicals, metal deposits or physical contaminants.

Symptoms of food poisoning may include:

- nausea
- vomiting
- diarrhoea
- fever
- dehydration.

How is food contaminated?

There are three main ways that food is contaminated:

1. **Bacteria** are all around us in the environment – on raw food, on humans, animals, birds and insects. When bacteria multiply in food which is then eaten they can make people ill.
2. **Chemicals** can sometimes get into food accidentally and can make the consumer ill. The kinds of chemical that may get into food include cleaning fluids, disinfectants, machine oil, insecticides and pesticides, etc.
3. **Physical contamination** is caused when something gets into food that should not be there. This could be anything that a person should not eat, such as glass, pen tops, paperclips, blue plasters, hair, fingernails, etc.

Two further reasons why people can become ill after eating food are allergens and food intolerance:

- **Allergens** cause allergic reactions. An allergy is when someone's immune system reacts to certain foods (allergens). Symptoms of an allergic reactions can include swelling, itching, rashes and breathlessness. In the case of a severe reaction anaphylactic shock can occur, which often causes swelling of the throat and mouth, preventing breathing. Medical help should be sought immediately in such an event.
- **Food intolerance** is different and does not affect the immune system, but there may still be a reaction to some foods. Foods usually associated with allergies and food intolerances are nuts, dairy products, wheat-based products, eggs and shellfish.

All of these are potentially dangerous and in the case of the three contaminants, great care must be taken to avoid them, especially bacteria. In the case of allergens and food intolerance it is important for customers to be aware of what is in their food and drink so they can make an informed choice.

High-risk food

Some foods pose a greater risk to food safety than others and are called high-risk foods. They are usually ready to eat, so do not need to be cooked to the high temperatures that would kill bacteria. Such foods are usually moist, contain protein and need to be stored in the fridge. Examples of high-risk foods include:

- soups, stocks, sauces, gravies
- eggs and egg products
- milk and milk products
- cooked meat and fish, and meat and fish products
- any foods that need to be handled or reheated.

Bacteria and contamination

Not all bacteria are harmful. In fact, some are very useful and are used in foods and medicines. For example, the processes of making milk into yogurt and making cheese both use bacteria.

The bacteria that are harmful are called pathogenic bacteria (pathogens) and can cause food poisoning. Bacteria are so small that you need to use a microscope to see them – you cannot taste them or smell them on food. This is why pathogenic bacteria are so dangerous – you cannot tell when they are in food. Under the right conditions (food, warmth, moisture and time) they can multiply approximately every 10–20 minutes by dividing in half. This is called binary fission.

Pathogenic bacteria can act in different ways to cause food poisoning. Bacteria may multiply in food until it is heated to very high temperatures, and will then cause infection when the food is eaten. Other pathogens use food to get into the body, where they then multiply. Some can produce toxins, while other can produce spores.

- Some pathogens produce **toxins** (poisons) that can survive boiling temperatures for half an hour or more. Because they are so heat resistant, the toxins are not killed by the normal cooking processes that kill bacteria, so remain in the food and can cause illness. Some bacteria produce toxins as they die, usually in the intestines of the person who has eaten the food.
- Others can produce **spores** to protect themselves. The bacteria form spores when the conditions surrounding them become hostile, for example, as temperatures rise, or in the presence of chemicals such as disinfectant. A spore forms a protective 'shell' inside the bacteria, protecting the essential parts from the high temperatures of normal cooking, disinfection, dehydration, etc. Once spores are formed, the cells cannot divide and multiply as before but simply survive until conditions improve, for example, the high temperatures drop to a level where multiplication can start again. Normal cooking temperatures will not kill spores. Time *is* very important in preventing the formation of spores. If food is brought to cooking temperature slowly it allows time for spores to form. To avoid this, bring food up to cooking temperature quickly and cool food quickly.

Common food-poisoning bacteria include:

- *Salmonella*
- *Staphylococcus aureus*
- *Clostridium perfringens*
- *Bacillus cereus*
- *Clostridium botulinum.*

Some bacteria cause food-borne illnesses but do not multiply in food. Instead, they use food to get into the human gut, where they then multiply and cause a range of illnesses, some of them serious, including severe abdominal pain, diarrhoea, vomiting, headaches, blurred vision, flu symptoms, septicaemia and miscarriage. These organisms may be transmitted from person to person, in water or through the air, as well as through food.

Food-borne pathogens include:

- *Campylobacter*
- *E coli* 0157
- *Listeria*
- Norovirus.

Personal hygiene

Because humans are a source of food-poisoning bacteria it is very important for all food handlers to take care with personal hygiene and to adopt good practices when working with food.

- Arrive at work clean (bathe or shower daily) and ensure hair is clean.
- Wear approved, clean kitchen clothing and only wear it in the kitchen. This must completely cover any personal clothing.

- Keep your hair neatly contained in a suitable hat/hairnet.
- Keep your nails short and clean and do not wear nail varnish or false nails.
- Do not wear jewellery or watches when handling food (a plain wedding band is permissible but could still trap bacteria).
- Avoid wearing cosmetics and strong perfumes.
- Smoking should not be allowed in food preparation areas (ash, smoke and bacteria from touching the mouth area could get into food).
- Do not eat food or sweets or chew gum when handling food as this may also transfer bacteria to food.
- Cover any cuts, burns or grazes with a blue waterproof dressing, then wash your hands.
- Report any illness to the supervisor as soon as possible. You should report diarrhoea and/or vomiting, infected cuts, burns or spots, bad cold or flu symptoms or if you were ill while on holiday.

Hand washing

Hands are constantly in use in the kitchen and will be touching numerous materials, foods, surfaces and equipment. Contamination from hands can happen very easily and you must take care with hand washing to avoid this.

- A basin should be provided that is used only for hand washing. Make sure that you use this.
- Wet your hands under warm running water.
- Apply liquid soap.
- Rub your hands together, and rub one hand with the fingers and thumb of the other.
- Remember to include your fingertips, nails and wrists.
- Rinse off the soap under the warm running water.
- Dry your hands on a paper towel and use the paper towel to turn off the tap before throwing it away.

You should always wash your hands:

- when you enter the kitchen, before starting work and handling any food
- after a break (particularly if you have used the toilet)
- between different tasks, but especially between handling raw and cooked food
- if you touch hair, nose, mouth or use a tissue for a sneeze or cough
- after you apply or change a dressing on a cut or burn
- after cleaning preparation areas, equipment or contaminated surfaces
- after handling kitchen waste, external food packaging, money or flowers.

Cross-contamination

Cross-contamination is when bacteria are transferred from contaminated food (usually raw food), equipment or surfaces to ready-to-eat food. It is the cause of significant amounts of food poisoning and care must be taken to avoid it. Cross-contamination could be caused by:

- foods touching each other, such as raw and cooked meat
- raw meat or poultry dripping onto high-risk foods
- soil from dirty vegetables coming into contact with high-risk foods
- dirty cloths or dirty equipment
- equipment (such as chopping boards or knives) used with raw food and then used with cooked food

- hands touching raw food and then cooked food, without being washed between tasks
- pests spreading bacteria from their own bodies around the kitchen.

Controlling cross-contamination

Sources of bacteria (where they come from) include raw meat and poultry, pests, dirty vegetables and unwashed hands. Cross-contamination can be avoided by following hygienic working practices and storing, preparing and cooking food safely.

- Separate working areas and storage areas for raw and high-risk foods are strongly recommended. If this is not possible, keep them well away from each other and make sure that working areas are thoroughly cleaned and disinfected between tasks.
- Vegetables should be washed before preparation/peeling and again afterwards. Leafy vegetables may need to be washed in several changes of cold water to remove all of the soil clinging to them.
- Good personal hygiene practices by staff, especially frequent and effective hand washing, are very important in controlling cross-contamination and will avoid the significant amounts of contamination caused by faecal/oral routes (when pathogens normally found in faeces are transferred to ready-to-eat foods, resulting in cross-contamination and illness). An obvious way that this may happen is when food handlers visit the toilet, do not wash their hands and then handle food.

Colour-coding equipment

Colour-coded chopping boards are a good way to keep different types of food separate. Worktops and chopping boards will come into contact with the food being prepared, so need special attention. Make sure that chopping boards are in good condition – cracks and splits could trap bacteria that could be transferred to food.

As well as colour-coded chopping boards, some kitchens also provide colour-coded knives, cloths, cleaning equipment, storage trays, bowls and even staff uniforms to help prevent cross-contamination.

Figure 6.10 Colour code chart for chopping boards (image courtesy of Russums)

Cleaning and sanitising

As a food handler it is your responsibility, along with those working with you, to keep food areas clean and hygienic at all times. Clean and tidy as you go and do not allow waste to build up. It is very difficult to keep untidy areas clean. Clean up any spills straight away.

The importance of temperature

An important way of controlling bacteria is to ensure that it is kept in controlled temperatures as much as possible.

- Temperatures between 5°C and 63°C are called the **danger zone** because it is possible for bacteria to multiply between these temperatures, with most rapid multiplication at around body temperature (37°C). Keep food held for service above 63°C, or cool it rapidly and keep it below 5°C.
- Thorough cooking is one of the best methods available to control bacteria. Cooking to 75°C and holding that temperature for at least two minutes will kill most pathogens (but not spores and toxins).
- Never put hot or warm food into a fridge or freezer as this will raise the temperature in the fridge or freezer and put food into the danger zone.

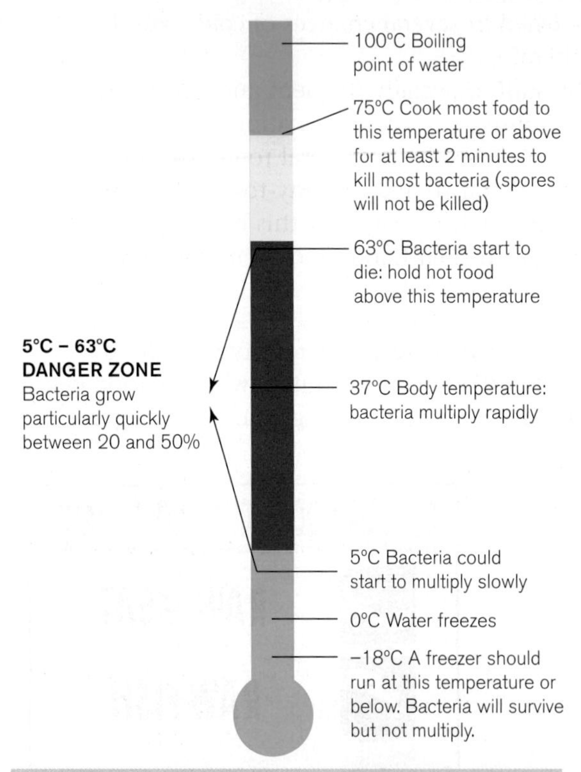

Figure 6.11 **Important food safety temperatures**

Food deliveries and storage

For food to remain in the best condition and be safe to eat, it is essential that it is stored correctly. This should be planned and the procedures fully understood by staff. Only approved suppliers who can assure that food is delivered in the best condition should be used. Food must be delivered in suitable packaging, properly date-coded and at the correct temperature.

Storing food in multiuse fridges:

- Ensure the fridge operates at a temperature of 1°C to 4°C.
- All food must be covered and labelled with the name of the item and the date.
- Always store raw food at the bottom of the fridge, with other items above.
- Keep high-risk foods well away from raw foods.

- Never overload the fridge – to operate properly cold air must be allowed to circulate between items.
- Wrap strong-smelling foods very well as the smell (and taste) can transfer to other foods such as milk.
- Record the temperature at which the fridge is operating. Do this at least once a day (this is an example of monitoring) and keep the fridge temperatures with other kitchen records.
- Clean fridges regularly.

'First in – first out'

This term is used to describe stock rotation, and is applied to all categories of food. It simply means that foods already in storage are used before new deliveries (providing stock is still within recommended dates and in sound condition). Food deliveries should be labelled with the delivery date and preferably the date by which they should be used. Use this information along with food-labelling codes (see below). Written stock records should form part of a 'food safety management system'.

Food-labelling codes

- **Use by dates** appear on perishable foods with a short life. Legally, the food must be used by this date and not stored or used after it.
- **Best before dates** apply to foods that are expected to have a longer life, for example, dry products or canned food. A 'best before' date advises that food is at its best before this date; using it after this date is legal but not advised.

Pests

When there are reports of food premises being forcibly closed down, an infestation of pests is often the reason. As pests can be a serious source of contamination and disease, having them near food cannot be allowed and is against the law. Pests can carry food poisoning bacteria into food premises in their fur/feathers, feet/paws, saliva, urine and droppings. Other problems caused by pests include damage to food stocks and packaging, damage to buildings, equipment and wiring, blockages in equipment and piping.

Beware! Pest control measures can also introduce food safety hazards. The bodies of dead insects or even rodents may remain in the kitchen (causing physical and bacterial contamination). Pesticides, insecticides and baits could cause chemical contamination if not managed properly. Pest control is best managed by professionals.

Premises

Suitable buildings with well-planned fittings, layout and equipment allow for good food safety practices. Certain basics need to be available if a building is to be used for food production. There must be:

- electricity supplies and preferably gas supplies
- drinking water and good drainage
- suitable road access for deliveries and refuse collection
- no risk of contamination from surrounding areas and buildings, e.g. chemicals, smoke, odours or dust.

Table 6.4 Signs of pest presence and how to keep them out

<table>
<tr><th>Pest</th><th>Signs that they are present</th><th>Ways to keep them out/eliminate them</th></tr>
<tr><td>Rats and mice</td><td>Sightings of rodents or droppings; gnawed wires; greasy marks on lower walls; damaged food stock; paw prints; unpleasant smell</td><td rowspan="7">Block entry by making sure there are no holes around pipework
Fill all gaps and cavities where they could get in
Use sealed drain covers
Damage to the building or fixtures and fittings should be repaired quickly
Use window/door screening/netting
Check deliveries/packaging for pests
Use baits and traps
Use electronic fly killer
Use sealed containers and ensure no open food is left out
Do not allow build-up of waste in kitchen
Do not keep outside waste too close to the kitchen
Arrange professional and organised pest management control, surveys and reports</td></tr>
<tr><td>Flies and wasps</td><td>Sighting of flies and wasps; hearing them; sightings of dead insects; sightings of maggots</td></tr>
<tr><td>Cockroaches</td><td>Sightings (dead or alive), usually at night; unpleasant smell</td></tr>
<tr><td>Ants</td><td>Sightings, including in food. The tiny, pale-coloured Pharaohs ants are difficult to spot but can still be the source of a variety of pathogens</td></tr>
<tr><td>Weevils</td><td>Sightings of weevils in stored products, e.g. flour/cornflour. They are tiny black insects that are very difficult to see but can be spotted by their movement in flour, etc.</td></tr>
<tr><td>Birds</td><td>Sighting; droppings in outside storage areas and around refuse</td></tr>
<tr><td>Domestic pets</td><td>These must be kept out of food areas as they carry pathogens in fur, whiskers, saliva, urine, etc.</td></tr>
</table>

Layout

- When planning food premises, a linear workflow should be in place, e.g. delivery → storage → preparation → cooking → hot holding → serving. This type of workflow means there will be no crossover of activities that could result in cross-contamination.
- There must be adequate storage areas – proper refrigerated storage is especially important.
- Staff hand washing/drying facilities suitable for the work being carried out must be provided.
- Clean and dirty (raw and cooked) processes should be kept apart.
- Cleaning and disinfection should be planned with separate storage for cleaning materials and chemicals.
- All areas should allow for good cleaning, disinfection and pest control.
- Personal hygiene facilities must be provided for staff, as well as changing facilities and storage for personal clothing and belongings.

Food safety management systems

It is good practice for all food businesses to have a food safety management system in place. In line with the Food Standards Agency's commitment to reduce food poisoning cases, it became a legal requirement from January 2006 for all food businesses to operate such a system. When environmental health officers/practitioners inspect the premises of these businesses they will also check that food safety management systems are in place and are working well.

Hazard Analysis Critical Control Point (HACCP)

- All food safety management systems must be based on the Hazard Analysis Critical Control Point (HACCP). This is an internationally recognised food safety management system that aims to identify the critical points or stages in any process. The system must provide a documented record of the stages *all* food will go through right up to the time it is eaten. Once the hazards have been identified, measures are put in place to control the hazards and keep the food safe.

The HACCP system involves seven stages:

1. Identify hazards – what could go wrong.
2. Identify CCP (critical control points), i.e. the important points where things could go wrong.
3. Set critical limits for each CCP, e.g. the temperature that fresh chicken should be at when it is delivered.
4. Monitor CCPs and put checks in place to stop problems from occurring.
5. Identify corrective action – what will be done if something goes wrong.
6. Verification – check that the HACCP plan is working.
7. Documentation – record all of the above.

The system must be updated regularly, especially when the menu or systems change (for instance, when a new piece of equipment is brought into the kitchen). Specific new controls must be put in place to include any changes.

'Safer food, better business' and 'CookSafe'

The HACCP system described above may seem complicated and difficult to set up for a small business. With this in mind, the Food Standards Agency launched its 'Safer food, better business' system for England and Wales. This is based on the principles of HACCP but is in a format that is easy to understand, with pre-printed pages and charts in which to enter the relevant information, such as temperatures for individual dishes. It is divided into two parts.

- The first part is about safe methods (e.g. avoiding cross-contamination, personal hygiene, cleaning, chilling and cooking).
- The second part covers opening and closing checks. These are checks that procedures are in place (e.g. safe methods, recording of safe methods, training records, supervision, stock control and the selection of suppliers and contractors) to ensure that the operation is working to the standards required to produce safe food. There is a diary entry page for every day that the business is open. Each day, the preset opening checks and closing checks are completed and the diary page signed. Nothing else needs to be recorded unless something goes wrong, e.g. a piece of equipment not working would be recorded along with the action that was taken.

A copy of 'Safer food, better business' is available from www.food.gov.uk.

A similar system called 'CookSafe' has been developed by the Food Standards Agency (Scotland) and details of this can also be found at www.food.gov.uk.

What the law says

The latest laws of importance to food businesses took effect from 1 January 2006. Almost all of the requirements in these regulations remain the same as the previous 1990/1995 regulations. These set out the basic food safety requirements for all aspects of a food business, from premises to personal hygiene of staff, with specific attention to temperatures relating to food.

The main difference in the 2006 laws is that they provide a framework for EU legislation to be enforced throughout the UK and they require food establishments to have an approved Food Safety Management Procedure in place, with up-to-date records available.

Food safety legislation

Food safety standards and legislation are enforced by environmental health officers (EHOs), also known as environmental health practitioners (EHPs). They may visit food premises as a matter of routine, after problems have occurred or after a complaint. The frequency of visits depends on the type of business, the food being handled and whether there have been previous problems.

EHOs can enter a food business at any reasonable time, usually when the business is open. The main purpose of inspections is to identify any possible risks from the food business to the consumer, and to assess how well the food safety management systems are working.

Serving of notices

A **Hygiene Improvement Notice** will be served if the EHO/EHP believes that a food business does not comply with regulations. The notice states the details of the business, what is wrong, why it is wrong, what needs to be put right and the time in which this must be completed (usually not less than 14 days). It is an offence if the work is not carried out in the specified time.

A **Hygiene Emergency Prohibition Notice** is served if the EHO believes that the business poses an imminent risk to people's health. This would include serious issues such as sewage contamination, lack of water supply, rodent infestation, etc. Serving this notice would mean immediate closure of the business for three days, during which time the EHO must apply to magistrates for a **Hygiene Emergency Prohibition Order** to keep the premises closed. A Hygiene Prohibition Order prohibits a person (i.e. the owner/manager) from working in a food business.

Fines and penalties for non-compliance

Magistrate's courts can impose fines of up to £5,000, a six-month prison sentence or both. For serious offences, magistrates could impose fines of up to £20,000. In a Crown court, unlimited fines can be imposed and/or two years' imprisonment.

Due diligence

'Due diligence' can be an important defence under food safety legislation. This means that if there is proof that a business took all reasonable care and did everything it could to prevent food safety problems, legal action may be avoided. Proof would need to be provided in the form of accurate written documents such as pest control reports, staff training records, fridge temperature records, etc.

Food businesses must ensure that all staff who handle food are supervised and instructed and/or trained in food hygiene appropriate to the work they do. Training can take place in house or with a training provider. All records of staff training must be kept for possible inspection.

Food Standards Agency

The Food Standards Agency was set up in 2000 'to protect public health and to protect the interest of customers in relation to food'. The agency is committed to putting customers first, being open and accessible and being an independent voice on food-related matters.

'Scores on the Doors' is a strategy that has been introduced by the Food Standards Agency to raise food safety standards and reduce the incidence of food poisoning. Various schemes were piloted and tested, and in 2008 a star-rating scheme was selected for England and Wales. On inspection, food premises can be awarded up to 5 stars (0 stars = very poor food safety; 5 stars = excellent food safety). The intention is that the given star-rating certificate will be placed in a prominent position on the door or window of a premises, but as yet it is not mandatory to do so.

It is expected that the Scores on the Doors scheme will have a positive impact on food safety standards. No matter how good the food in a particular establishment, few people will want to eat there if the food safety score is low!

6.4 Maintaining a secure environment

Security is a major concern these days. The main security risks in the hotel and catering industry are:

- theft: where customers' property, employers' property (particularly food, drink and equipment) or employees' property is stolen
- burglary: where the burglar comes onto the premises (trespasses) and steals customers' property, employers' property or employees' property
- robbery: theft with assault, e.g. when staff are banking or collecting cash
- fraud: false insurance claims, counterfeit money, stolen credit cards
- assault: fights between customers; assaults on staff by customers (e.g. if a customer is not happy with the service, and may also be drunk, they may become violent towards staff); attacks on staff while they are taking cash to or collecting cash from the bank
- vandalism: damage to property caused by customers, intruders or employees
- arson: setting fire to the property
- undesirables: having people such as drug traffickers and prostitutes on the premises
- terrorism: bombs, telephone bomb threats.

The Health and Safety at Work Regulations now require employers to conduct a risk assessment regarding the safety of staff in the catering business. Preventing crime is better than having to deal with it once it has happened. Here are some ideas for helping to prevent crime.

- The best way to prevent theft is to stop the thief entering the premises in the first place. Reception staff should be trained to spot suspicious individuals. Everyone who comes in should be asked to sign in at reception and, if they are a legitimate visitor, be given a security badge. It is also essential to make sure that any suspicious person does not re-enter the building.
- All contract workers should be registered and given security badges, and they may be restricted to working in certain areas.
- There should be a good security system at the back door, where everyone delivering goods has to report to the security officer.
- Many establishments restrict access to their premises by using a security keypad (see Figure 6.12) which

Figure 6.12 A security keypad

requires staff to enter a numerical code to gain access. The code is changed on a regular basis to maintain security.
- All establishments should try to reduce temptation for criminals, e.g. by reducing the amount of cash that is handled. The use of credit and debit cards does cost the establishment a small amount of money (a fee must be paid to the credit card companies), but it reduces the amount of cash that is used and therefore reduces the risk of cash being stolen. However, there is also an increase in crime due to fraud (e.g. using stolen credit cards).
- Staff who handle money should be trained in simple anti-fraud measures such as checking bank notes, checking signatures on plastic cards, etc.
- It is impossible to remove all temptation, so equipment such as computers, fax machines and photocopiers should be marked with some type of security identification or tag.
- There are many simple and obvious security measures that can also be taken, such as locking doors and windows.
- Good lighting is also important for security reasons – criminals are less likely to come onto the premises at night if people can see them easily. Supervisors and managers should regularly check the lighting in all areas. Leaving lights on in some areas that can be seen by passers-by can also help.
- Closed-circuit television (CCTV) cameras are also used as a deterrent against crime.
- With regard to staff, the first step is to appoint honest staff by checking their references from previous employers.
- Some companies write into employee contracts the 'right to search'. This means that from time to time the employer can carry out searches of the employees' lockers, bags, and so on. This discourages employees from stealing. It is not legal to force a person to be searched even if they have signed a contract about it, but if they refuse they may be breaking their employment contract.

Personal safety

Below is a personal safety checklist to help you stay safe:

- Wear protective clothing.
- Do not work under the influence of alcohol or drugs.
- Keep hair short, or tied back if long.
- Do not wear jewellery as this, like long hair, can be caught in machinery.
- Walk – do not run.
- Use the gangways provided and never take shortcuts.
- Look out for and obey all warning notices and safety signs.
- Back problems can cause a lot of pain and may last a lifetime. Always use trolleys, wheelbarrows or other appropriate lifting equipment if available.
- You must be shown how to lift and carry items correctly. Take care that you:
  - lift or carry only what you can manage
  - can see clearly where you are going
  - get help with anything that you think might be too heavy or awkward to manage on your own.

If in doubt, ask for help!

General procedures

Depending upon the nature of the establishment, the security measures that are laid down may vary considerably. As employees, staff should be aware of all such measures as they relate to their own work environment. Consideration needs to be given to the aspects of security outlined below:

- The importance of wearing some form of recognised identity badge.
- Being observant and reporting 'suspicious' persons and/or packages.
- Not discussing work duties with customers or outside of the workplace.
- Allowing bags, packages and one's person to be searched upon request when either entering or leaving the workplace.
- Being aware of the security procedures for the establishment, should sudden and urgent action need to be taken.
- Ensuring external fire doors are kept shut but not locked, nor left ajar in error.
- Ensuring that all areas have been vacated when responsible for 'locking up' duties. All toilets/cloakrooms must be carefully checked and at the same time all windows and doors should be checked to ensure they are locked.
- Keys should only be handled by someone in authority. A signing-out book should be available when staff request keys.
- Keys are never to be left unattended.
- When handling cash, all large denomination notes should be checked carefully as well as all cheque and credit card payments to prevent fraud, the passing of illegal notes and the acceptance of altered credit cards.
- Being alert and observant at all times and not hesitating in reporting anything suspicious to the immediate superior.

Dealing with a suspicious item or package

All employees should be constantly alert for suspicious items or packages.

- If an object is found then it must immediately be reported to the security officer, manager or supervisor.
- Do not touch or attempt to move the object.
- If there are customers in the immediate vicinity, discreetly attempt to establish ownership of the object.
- If the ownership is established then ask the customer to keep the object with them, or to hand it in for safe keeping.
- If no immediate ownership is established, then the area should be cleared and the authorities notified without delay.

Dealing with a bomb threat

Immediate action needs to be taken as a bomb could go off at any moment. As a result staff should:

- be aware of and follow establishment policy with regard to bomb threats and evacuation procedures
- evacuate the immediate work area
- search the work area to ensure it is cleared, if this is part of their own responsibility
- evacuate the premises and usher all customers/staff through the nearest usable exits to specified assembly areas
- count all persons present to determine their safety and minimise the risk of fatal accidents.

CHAPTER 7

Customer service and customer relations

This chapter will help you to learn about:

1. Factors that contribute to the meal experience
2. Providing good customer service
3. Ensuring good customer relations
4. Dealing with incidents during service

7.1 Factors that contribute to the meal experience

There are many different kinds of foodservice operation, designed to meet a wide range of demand. These different types of operation are designed for the needs people have at a particular time, rather than for the type of people they are. For example, a person may be a business customer during the week, but a member of a family at the weekend; they may want a quick lunch on one occasion, a snack while travelling on another and a meal with the family on another occasion. Additionally, the same person may wish to book a wedding or organise some other special occasion.

The main aim of food and beverage operations is to achieve customer satisfaction, in other words, to meet the customers' *needs*. The needs that customers might be seeking to satisfy include:

- **Physiological:** e.g. the need to sate one's appetite or quench one's thirst, or the need for special foods such as diabetic or vegetarian.
- **Economic:** e.g. the need for good value, rapid service or a convenient location.
- **Social:** e.g. going out with friends or business colleagues; attending a function in order to meet others.
- **Psychological:** e.g. the need for enhancement of self-esteem; fulfilling life-style needs; the need for variety; as a result of advertising and promotion.
- **Convenience:** e.g. as a result of being unable to get home (shoppers, workers) or attending some other event (cinema, theatre); the desire for someone else to do the work; the physical impossibility of catering at home (weddings and other special functions).

Customers may want to satisfy some or all of these needs.

As the reasons for eating out vary, then so do the types of operation that may be appropriate at the time. Differing establishments offer different service, in both the extent of the menu and the price, as well as varying service levels. The choice offered may be restricted or wide.

It is important to recognise that the specific reasons behind a customer's choice will often determine the customer's satisfaction (or dissatisfaction), rather than the food and beverage service by itself. One example is the social need to go out with friends: if one person fails to turn up or behaves in a disagreeable way, then the customer may be dissatisfied with the meal.

The customer who is not able to satisfy his or her needs will be a dissatisfied customer. The customer may, for instance, be dissatisfied with unhelpful staff, cramped conditions or the lack of choice available. These aspects are the responsibility of the food and beverage operation. However, sometimes the reasons for the customer being dissatisfied are beyond the operation's control, for example, location, the weather, other customers or transport problems.

In **non-captive markets** the customer has a choice of opportunities for eating out, both in terms of the food and drink to be consumed and the type of operation they may wish to patronise. While it is true that certain types of catering operations might attract certain types of customer, this is by no means true all the time. The same customers may patronise a variety of different operations depending on the needs they have at a given time, for example, a romantic night out, a quick office lunch or a wedding function.

In **semi-captive markets** the availability of choice is also important. Customers may choose, for example, a certain airline, ship or hotel based upon the identification of certain needs they wish to satisfy.

In **captive markets** where the customer does not have a choice of operation, there is still a need for satisfaction. For instance, it is generally recognised that better-fed workers work better and that better-fed patients recover quicker. 'Better-fed' here, though, does not just refer to the food and drink provided but the whole experience of the meal.

It is important to recognise that the customer's needs may vary, and food and beverage operators should therefore be aware of factors that might affect the customer's meal experience. Much research has been carried out in recent years identifying these factors. They range from location to the acceptance of credit cards, and from attitudes of staff to the behaviour of other customers. These factors are summarised in Table 7.1.

Table 7.1 **Meal experience factors**

Factor	Description
Food and beverages on offer	Includes the range of foods and beverages, choice, availability, flexibility for special orders and the quality of the food and beverages
Level of service	The level of service sought will depend on the needs people have at a particular time. For example, a romantic night out may require a quiet table in a top-class restaurant, whereas a group of young friends might seek a more informal service. This factor also takes into account the importance to the customer of other services such as booking and account facilities, acceptance of credit cards and the reliability of the operation's product
Level of cleanliness and hygiene	This factor relates to the premises, equipment and staff. Over the last few years this factor has increased in importance in customers' minds. The recent media focus on food production and the risks involved in buying food have heightened awareness of health and hygiene aspects

Perceived value for money and price	Customers have perceptions of the amount they are prepared to spend and relate this to differing types of establishments and operations. Value is the personal estimate of a product's capacity to satisfy a set of goals and also a perception of the balance between worth and cost. Good value for a food and beverage operation is where the worth is perceived as greater than the total cost. Poor value is where the costs involved are perceived as greater than the worth
Atmosphere of the establishment	This factor takes account of issues such as design, decor, lighting, heating, furnishings, acoustics and noise levels, other customers, the smartness of the staff and the attitude of the staff

7.2 Providing good customer service

In order the meet the customers' expectations and to enhance their meal experience, a foodservice operation will determine the level of customer service that the customer should expect within that operation. The main job of people working in the hospitality industry is to look after customers' needs, wants and expectations. Every organisation must have good customer service if it is to be successful. The most successful businesses are those that are customer focused.

Customer service in foodservice operations can be defined as being a combination of five characteristics. These are:

1 **Service level:** the intensity of or limitations in, the individual personal attention given to customers.
2 **Service availability:** e.g. the opening times and variations in the menu and beverage list on offer.
3 **Level of standards:** e.g. the food and beverage quality, decor, standard of equipment used and professionalism of staff.
4 **Service reliability:** the extent to which the product is intended to be consistent and its consistency in practice.
5 **Service flexibility:** the extent to which alternatives are available, and to which there can be variations in the standard products that are offered.

A foodservice operation will determine the **customer service specification** of the operation by taking account of these five customer service factors.

Use of resources

Although a foodservice operation is designed to provide customer service, it must also be efficient in its use of resources. The three resources used in foodservice operations are:

1 **Materials:** food, beverages and short-use equipment (such as paper napkins)
2 **Labour:** staffing costs
3 **Facilities:** premises, plant and equipment.

Figure 7.1 A formal restaurant (Strathern Restaurant, image courtesy of Gleneagles Hotel, Scotland)

The management team must take into account the effect that the level of business has on the ability of the operation to maintain customer service requirements, while at the same time ensuring productivity in all of the resources being used.

Level of customer service

Within foodservice operations the level of service in a specific operation may be defined as follows:

1 **Technical specification:** refers to the food and beverage items on offer, the portion size or measure, the cooking method, the degree of cooking, the method of presentation, the cover, accompaniments and the cleanliness of items, etc.
2 **Service specification:** refers to two aspects: first, the procedures for service and second, the method in which the procedures are carried out.
   - Procedures include meeting and greeting, order-taking, seeking customer comments, dealing with complaints, receiving payment and the special needs of customers.
   - The method in which the service is carried out includes paying attention to the level of staff attentiveness, their tone of voice and body language, etc.

All foodservice operations will have written statements of both technical and service specification (often called a customer service specification). These may also be detailed in staff manuals that outline expected standards of performance.

Level of service and standards of service

There can be confusion when referring to the level of service and the standards of service.

- The **level of service** in foodservice operations can range from being very limited to complex, with high levels of personal attention.
- The **standards of service** are a measure of the ability of the operation to deliver the service level it is offering.

An operation might be offering low levels of service, such as a fast-food operation, but may be doing this at a very high standard. Equally, an operation may be offering a high level of service, such as a full service restaurant, but may be doing so with low standards.

Figure 7.2 **Informal restaurant (Dormy House, image courtesy of Gleneagles Hotel, Scotland)**

The starting point for all customer service is good manners: saying 'please', 'thank you' and 'I beg your pardon'; being pleasant to people; showing that you care about what they want and apologising for anything that has been unsatisfactory, such as having to wait.

7.3 Ensuring good customer relations

Customer relations are also referred to as interpersonal skills, and in food and beverage service it refers to the relationship between the customer and the food and beverage service staff. Conversations between customers and staff are of the highest importance and override conversations between staff. Customers should always be made to feel that they are being cared for rather than an intrusion into the operation.

When in conversation with customers, staff should not:

- talk to other members of staff without first excusing themselves from the customer
- interrupt interactions between customers and staff, but should wait until there is a suitable moment to catch the attention of the other member of staff so that they may excuse themselves from the customer first
- serve customers while carrying on a conversation between themselves
- talk across a room, either to each other or to customers.

In food and beverage service operations interaction also takes place with people outside the service areas, such as kitchen staff, bill office staff, dispense bar staff and still room staff. It is important that the customer can see that the provision of food and beverages and service within an establishment is a joint effort between all departments, with each department understanding the needs of the others in order to meet the customers' demands.

Dealing with customers

When addressing customers, 'Sir' or 'Madam' should be used when the customer's name is not known. If the name is known, then the members of staff should also address the customer as 'Mr Smith' or 'Miss Jones', etc. First names should only be used in less formal operations and where the customer has explicitly indicated that this is acceptable.

Greetings such as 'Good morning' and 'Good evening' should be used upon receiving customers, or when the member of staff first comes into contact with the customer, for example, when lounge service staff attend people already seated in the lounge.

The list below identifies examples of interpersonal skills needed at particular points during the service.

- **Showing customers to their table:** always lead and walk with them at their pace.
- **Seating customers:** ladies first, descending in age unless the host is a lady.
- **Handling coats/wraps:** handle with obvious care.
- **Handing menus/wine lists to customers:** offer the list the right way round and open for the customer and wait for the customer to take it.
- **Opening and placing a napkin:** open carefully, do not shake it like a duster, place it on the customer's lap after saying 'Excuse me' to the customer.
- **Offering water or rolls:** say, e.g. 'Excuse me sir/madam, may I offer you a bread roll?'
- **Offering accompaniments:** only offer them if you have them at the table. Offering them when they are not at the table usually means 'I will get them if you really want them!'
- **Serving and clearing:** always say 'Excuse me' before serving or clearing and 'Thank you' after you have finished with each customer.

- **Explaining food and beverage items:** use terms the customer understands, not technical terms, such as turned vegetable or pane. Use terms that make the item sound attractive, such as casserole not stew, creamed or purée potatoes not mashed. Do not use abbreviations, such as 'veg'.
- **Talking to customers:** only talk when standing next to them and looking at them.

Dealing with children

If children are among the customers arriving in the foodservice area then take the lead in how to care for them from the parents, guardian or accompanying adults. Where applicable, the following factors should be determined:

- Are highchairs/seat cushions required?
- Restrictions on the service of alcohol to minors.
- Are children's meal menus required?
- The portion size required if items are ordered from the standard menu.
- The provision of children's 'give aways', such as crayons, colouring books, etc.
- For the safety of both children and others, the staff should be aware of children's movements.
- Should the children be older, then they should be addressed as either 'Sir' or 'Miss'.
- Younger children should be served as promptly as possible as this will lessen the stress on the parents.

Customers with additional needs

Customer mobility

Extra awareness is needed to meet the requirements of customers who may have additional needs, such as mobility difficulties. The following considerations should be made:

- Offer wheelchair users places at tables where there is adequate space for manoeuvrability.
- Offer wheelchair users a place out of the main thoroughfare of customer/ staff movement.
- Offer wheelchair users a place with easy access to cloakrooms, exits and fire exits.
- Always ensure that menus, wine lists and the like are immediately available to any wheelchair user.
- Never move the wheelchair without asking the customer first.
- Crutches/walking sticks should be placed in a safe but accessible and readily available position.
- Customers with dexterity difficulties may be assisted by first asking the customer how best they can be helped. Assistance may include, e.g. ensuring that all items served or placed on to the table are near to the customer, offering to fillet/bone fish and meat items and offering to cut up potato and vegetable items.

Blind and partially sighted customers

Awareness is also required to meet the needs of those customers who may be blind or partially sighted. The following considerations should be taken into account:

- Talk to and treat the customer with special needs as you would any other customer.
- Remember it is by touch that blind people 'see' and are made aware that they are involved in what is happening around them.

- If in doubt, ask the person directly how they may best be helped.
- Do not talk to their companions as if the person was not there.
- Offer to read menus or wine and drink lists.
- Immediately prior to taking the customer's order, a gentle touch on the hand or arm will attract his or her attention to you.
- Offer to fillet/bone fish and meat items.
- Offer to cut up potato and vegetable items should it be necessary.
- Never overfill cups, glasses or soup bowls.
- Should you feel it appropriate, use bowls instead of plates for specific food items, but always ask the customer first.
- Ask if you should describe where the food items are on the plate. Use the clock method to explain the location of food on a plate, e.g. 6 o'clock for meat, 10 to 10 for vegetables and 10 past 2 for potatoes, as shown in Figure 7.3.

Figure 7.3 **Standard placement of food items**

Customers with communication difficulties

Be aware of communication difficulties that may arise when dealing with, for example, customers who are hearing impaired or who have little understanding of the English language. In such cases the steps shown below may be helpful:

- Speak directly to the customer.
- Stand in such a position that the customer is able to see your face clearly.
- Speak normally but more distinctly.
- Describe food/drink items in simple, precise and plain language.
- Seat customers away from possible excessive noise, as this is most uncomfortable for customers wearing hearing aids.
- Always read back the food or beverage order received to confirm all requests.
- Listen attentively to what is being said to you to ensure you understand the customer's requirements.

7.4 Dealing with incidents during service

Always deal with incidents promptly and efficiently without causing more disturbance than is necessary to any of the other customers. Quick action will usually soothe the irate customer and enable a good impression of the waiting staff and the establishment to be maintained. Complaints, of whatever nature, should be referred immediately to the supervisor; any delay will only cause confusion and very often the situation may be wrongly interpreted if it is not dealt with straight away. In the case of accidents, a report of the incident must be kept and signed by those involved.

Spillages

If during the service of a course a few drops of sauce or gravy have fallen onto the tablecloth, the following steps might be taken:

1. Check immediately that none has fallen on the customer being served. Apologise to the customer.
2. If some has fallen on the customer's clothing, allow the customer to rub over the dirtied area with a clean damp cloth. This will remove the worst of the spillage.
3. If it is necessary for the customer to retire to the cloakroom to remove the spillage then the meal should be placed on the hotplate until he or she returns.
4. Depending on the nature of the spillage the establishment may offer to have the garment concerned cleaned.
5. If the spillage has gone on the tablecloth, the waiter should first of all remove any items of equipment that may be dirtied or in the way.
6. The waiter should then mop or scrape up the spillage with either a clean damp cloth or a knife.
7. An old menu card should then be placed on top of the table but under the tablecloth beneath the damaged area.
8. A second menu should be placed on the tablecloth over the damaged area.
9. A clean rolled napkin should then be brought to the table and rolled completely over the damaged area. The menu will prevent any damp from soaking into the clean napkin.
10. Any items of equipment removed should be returned to their correct position on the tabletop.
11. Any meals taken to the hotplate should be returned and fresh covers put down where necessary.
12. Again, apologies should be made to the customer for any inconvenience caused.

If a customer accidentally knocks over a glass of water, then the following steps might be taken:

1. Ensure none has gone on the customer.
2. If some of the water has fallen on the customer's clothing then follow steps 2 and 3 for spillages as described above.
3. Where possible, as this form of accident usually involves changing the tablecloth, the party of customers should be seated at another table and allowed to continue their meal without delay.
4. If the customers cannot be moved to another table then they should be seated slightly back from the table so that the waiter can carry out the necessary procedures to rectify the fault speedily and efficiently.

Figure 7.4 **(a)–(d) Example process for covering spillages**

5 The customers' meals should be placed on the hotplate to keep warm.
6 All dirty items should be removed on a tray to the waiter's sideboard ready to go to the wash-up area.
7 All clean items should be removed and kept on the waiter's sideboard for relaying.
8 The tablecloth should be mopped with a clean absorbent cloth to remove as much of the liquid as possible.
9 A number of old menus should be placed on the tabletop but underneath the spillage area of the soiled tablecloth.
10 A clean tablecloth of the correct size should be brought to the table. It should be opened out and held in the correct manner as if one were laying a tablecloth during the pre-service preparation period. The table should then be clothed up in the usual manner except that when the clean tablecloth is being drawn across the table towards the waiter, the soiled tablecloth should be removed at the same time so that the customers cannot see the bare tabletop at any time. The old menus will prevent any dampness penetrating to the clean tablecloth.
11 When the table has its clean tablecloth on it should be re-laid as quickly as possible.
12 The customers should then be re-seated at the table and the meals returned to them from the hotplate.

Returned food

If, for example, a customer suggests that their chicken dish is not cooked, then the following steps might be taken.

1. Apologise to the customer.
2. The dish should be removed and returned to the kitchen.
3. The customer should be asked if he or she would like another portion of the same dish or would prefer to choose an alternative.
4. The new dish should be collected as soon as possible and served to the customer.
5. Apologies should be made for any inconvenience caused.
6. The policy of the establishment will dictate whether or not the customer is to be charged for the alternative dish.

Lost property

If a waiter finds lost property in a service area that has recently been vacated by a customer, the steps listed below might be taken.

1. A check should be made immediately as to whether or not the customer has left the service area. If they are still in the area, the property may be returned to them.
2. If the customer has left the service area, the waiter should hand the property to the headwaiter or supervisor in charge.
3. The supervisor should check with reception and the hall porter to see if the customer has left the building.
4. If the customer concerned is a resident, then reception may ring their room, stating the property has been found and can be collected at a convenient time.
5. If the customer is a regular customer, it is possible that the head waiter or receptionist may know where to contact them to arrange for them to collect the property.
6. If the customer is a regular customer but cannot be contacted, the property should be kept in the lost property office until the customer's next visit.
7. If the owner has not been found or contacted immediately, the headwaiter or supervisor should list the items found including the contents if appropriate with the waiter who found the property. The list should be signed by both the headwaiter or supervisor and the finder. The list must be dated and also indicate where the property was found and at what time.

Lost property record sheet	
Date:	Establishment:
Item description:	
Found by:	
Checked by:	
Where stored:	
Claimed by:	Date:
Contact details:	
Proof of identity seen:	
Customer signature:	

Figure 7.5 Example of a lost property record sheet

8 A copy of this list should go with the property to the lost property office where the contents of the property must be checked against the list before it is accepted. The details of the find are then entered in a lost property register.
9 Another copy of the list should go to the hall porter in case any enquiries are received concerning the property. Anyone claiming lost property should be passed on to the lost property office.
10 Before the lost property office hands over any lost property, a description of the article concerned and its contents should be asked for to ensure as far as possible that it is being returned to the genuine owner. The office should also see proof of identity of the person claiming ownership.
11 In the case of all lost property, the steps mentioned above should be carried out as quickly as possible as this is in the best interests of the establishment and causes the customer minimum inconvenience. On receipt of lost property, the customer should be asked to sign for the article concerned and to give his address and telephone number.
12 Any lost property unclaimed after three months may become the property of the finder who should claim it through the headwaiter or supervisor.

Illness of a customer

If a customer falls ill in your establishment then the steps below might be taken.

1 As soon as it is noticed that a customer is feeling unwell while in the dining room or restaurant, a person in authority should be called immediately.
2 If the customer falling ill is a woman then a female member of staff should attend to her.
3 The person in authority must enquire if the customer needs assistance. At the same time they must try to judge whether the illness is of a serious nature or not. If in any doubt it is always better to call for medical assistance.
4 It is often advisable to offer to take the customer to another room to see if they are able to recover in a few minutes. If this happens, their meal should be placed on the hotplate until their return.
5 If the illness appears to be of a serious nature, a doctor, nurse or someone qualified in first aid should be called for immediately.
6 The customer should not be moved until a doctor has examined him/her.
7 If necessary the area should be screened off.
8 Although this is a difficult situation to deal with in front of the general public, minimum fuss should be made and service to the rest of the customers should carry on as normal.
9 The medical person will advise whether an ambulance should be called.
10 The customer may have had a sudden stomach upset and wish to leave without finishing the meal. Assistance should be offered in helping the customer leave the restaurant.
11 Payment for the part of the meal consumed and any ensuing travel costs would be according to the policy of the establishment.
12 It is most important that for all accidents (minor or serious) all details are recorded in an accident book. This is in case of a claim against the establishment at a later date.
13 If after a short period of time the customer returns and continues with the meal, a fresh cover should be laid and the meal returned from the hotplate or a new meal served.

Over-consumption of alcohol

If a customer is suspected of having too much to drink, the following steps might be taken.

1. If a prospective customer asks for a table and the staff believe the client is under the influence of drink, they may refuse the customer a table, even though there may be one available. It is not always possible, however, to recognise a customer who may prove objectionable later on.
2. If difficulty is found in handling this type of person, then assistance in removing the person from the eating area may come from other members of staff (depending on establishment policy; physical contact should be avoided).
3. If a customer is suspected of being drunk this must first of all be ascertained by the supervisor.
4. The customer should then be asked to leave rather than be allowed to become objectionable to other customers.
5. If the customer has already consumed part of the meal but is not being objectionable then the remainder of the meal should be served in the normal fashion, but the supervisor must ensure no more alcoholic beverage is offered.
6. On finishing, the customer should be watched until he or she has left the premises.
7. It is always advisable to make out a report of all such incidents. They should also be brought to the immediate attention of the manager in case of any claim at a later date concerning a particular incident.

Note: It is an offence to serve alcohol to a customer who appears to be drunk, or to serve their companions if you think the drunken person may receive the alcohol.

Unsatisfactory appearance

If a customer's appearance is not satisfactory according to the policy of the establishment, the following steps might be taken.

1. If a customer's appearance does not meet the dress code policy of the establishment or is likely to give offence to others, then the customer should be asked to correct their dress to the approved fashion required by the establishment.
2. Staff should be made aware of the need for sensitivity towards cultural dress.
3. If the customer will not comply with the request, he or she should be asked to leave.
4. If they have partly consumed a meal then whether they will be charged or not depends on the policy of the house and the discretion of the head waiter or supervisor.
5. A report of this incident must be made and signed by the staff concerned.

Lost children

Should a child be reported lost, the steps listed below must be taken.

1. A complete description of the lost child should be obtained:
   - male/female
   - name
   - age
   - where last seen
   - clothing worn
   - any predominant features
   - colour of hair
   - whether any accessories were being carried, e.g. a doll.
2. Immediately inform the supervisor/security.
3. Put a constant watch on all entrances/exits.
4. Check all cloakroom/rest areas, play areas and the immediate vicinity where the child has been reported missing.
5. Should nothing result from taking the above actions, immediately inform the police.

Handling complaints

Should a problem arise and the customer makes a complaint, the following steps should be taken.

1. Do not interrupt the customer – let them have their say and make their point.
2. Apologise – but only for the specific problem or complaint.
3. Restate the details of the complaint briefly back to the customer to show you have listened and understood.
4. Agree by thanking the customer for bringing the matter to your attention. This shows you are looking at the problem from the customer's perspective.
5. Act quickly, quietly and professionally and follow the establishment's procedures for handling complaints.

Never:

- lose your temper
- take it personally
- argue
- lie
- blame another member of staff or another department.

Valid complaints provide important feedback for a foodservice operation and can be used as valuable learning opportunities to improve service.

Recording incidents

It is advisable that when any incident occurs a report is made out immediately. The basic information that should be found in the report is as follows:

- place
- date
- time
- nature of incident
- individual, signed reports from those concerned
- action taken
- name, address and phone number of the customer involved
- names of the staff involved.

All reports should be kept in case similar incidents occur at a later date. Such reports also provide a record in case there is a subsequent complaint from a customer and the record can also be used when revising procedures for dealing with various incidents.

PART C

Product Knowledge

CHAPTER 8

Menus and wine and drinks lists

This chapter will help you to learn about:

1 The purpose of the menu
2 Classes of menu
3 Influences on menus
4 The classic menu sequence
5 Other types of menus
6 Types of wine and drinks lists
7 Contents of wine and drinks lists
8 General information given on wine and drinks lists

8.1 The purpose of the menu

The menu is primarily a selling aid. The design of the menu should be such that it is appealing to the customer and encourages him or her to accept it and want to open it to view its contents. Design considerations include:

- size and shape
- artwork
- colour
- ease of handling
- layout
- information it contains
- logical flow of information
- headings
- prices clearly indicated
- service charge
- description of dishes
- speciality of the house
- details of the dish of the day.

Adequate information, easily found and followed, will make the customer feel more at home and will assist in selling your menu.

8.2 Classes of menu

Menus may be divided into two classes, traditionally called *à la carte* ('from the card') and *table d'hôte* ('table of the host'). The key difference between these two is that the à la carte menu has dishes separately priced, whereas the table d'hôte menu has an inclusive price either for the whole meal or for a specified number of courses, for example, any two or any four courses. There are, however, usually choices within each course.

Sometimes the term 'menu du jour' is used instead of the term 'table d'hôte menu'. Another menu term used is 'carte du jour' (literally 'card of the day'), or 'menu of the day', which can also be a fixed meal with one or more courses for a set price. A 'prix fixe' (fixed price) menu is similar. A 'tasting menu' ('menu degustation') is a set meal with a range of courses (often between 6 and 10). These tasting menus are offered in restaurants where the chef provides a sample of the range of dishes available on the main menu. These tasting menus can also be offered with a flight (selection) of wines (sometimes this can be a different wine for each course). For all classes of menu the price of the meal might also include wine or other drinks.

Table d'hôte menu

The key characteristics of the table d'hôte menu are:

- the menu has a fixed number of courses
- there is a limited choice within each course
- the selling price is fixed
- the food is usually available at a set time.

À la carte menu

The key characteristics of the à la carte menu are:

- the choice is generally more extensive
- each dish is priced separately
- there may be longer waiting times as some dishes are cooked or finished to order.

> All menus, no matter how simple or complex, are based on the two basic menu classes of table d'hôte or à la carte. Some menus also offer combinations of these two classes, with a number of menu items being offered together at a set price and other menu items being priced separately.

8.3 Influences on menus

Modern-day menus are the result of a combination of a number of factors. Menu content, traditionally based on classic cuisine, is continually being influenced by food trends, fads and fashions. In the main, customer demand is being affected by a greater understanding of:

- the relationship between health and eating
- dietary requirements
- cultural and religious influences
- vegetarianism
- ethical influences.

Because of these influences there is now a greater emphasis on offering alternatives such as low-fat milks (for example, skimmed or semi-skimmed), non-dairy creamers for beverages, alternatives to sugar such as sweeteners, sorbets alongside ice creams and polyunsaturated fat and non-animal fats as alternatives to butter. These influences have also affected cooking ingredients and methods, with the development of lower fat dishes, lighter cuisine and attractive and decent alternatives for non-meat eaters, with greater use of animal protein substitutes such as Quorn and tofu.

Health and eating

The key issue in the relationship between health and eating is a healthy diet. This means eating a balanced diet rather than viewing individual foods as somehow healthier or less healthy. Customers are increasingly looking for the availability of

All Day Dining

STARTERS

Pomodoro tomato, red pepper and pesto soup	£8.50
Spicy corn fed chicken and coriander velouté with ginger wonton	£8.25
Smoked organic Scottish salmon Old England	£16.00
Parma Ham, white balsamic and mango	£12.00

SALADS & SANDWICHES

Classic Blue Fin Tuna Nicoise	£13.00
℗ Salad with avocado, tomato and asparagus	£14.00
Classic Caesar Salad	10.00
with corn fed chicken	£13.50
with Tiger prawns and avocado	£15.00
Confit duck salad with saladaise potatoes	£14.50
Crotin goats cheese, poached pear, chicory and walnut salad	£14.00
100% pure Angus beef burger with hand cut chips	£16.00
Croque Madame - baked chicken, Gruyère cheese with fried free range egg	£15.50
Croque Monsieur ham and Gruyère cheese	£15.50
℗ Club with corn fed chicken, and hand cut chips	
Baked Ruben on rye pastrami, sauerkraut, Savora mustard and Montgomery cheddar	
Angus beef steak sandwich with Pomodoro tomatoes, onion rings and iceberg lettuce	

All sandwiches served on either bloomer, rye bread or sliced white a

MAIN

Pink Paris mushroom risotto	£16.75
Deep fried plaice fillets and chips with mushy peas	£17.00
Seared Scottish Salmon, spring onion mashed potatoes and grain mustard sauce	£18.50
Tiger prawn penne pasta, garlic and crispy shallots	£18.00
Tomato tart, goats cheese, roquette and confit onions	£17.50
Rump of English lamb with thyme and seasonal vegetables	£20.50

FROM THE GRIDDLE

Corn fed chicken Supreme 160g	£17.00
Angus rib eye steak 175g / 225g	£20.00 / £24.00
Castle of Mey sirloin steak 175g / 225g	£21.50 / £25.50

All griddle mains are served with a baked Pomodoro tomato with confit onions, field mushroom and gaufrette potatoes with either béarnaise, red wine or green peppercorn sauce

SIDE ORDERS

Petit pois, spring onion and mint	£3.75
Green beans and shallots	£3.75
Potatoes chipped, mashed or buttered	£3.75
Market vegetables	£3.75
Green salad with tomato and cucumber	£3.75

All prices are inclusive VAT. A discretionary 12.5% service charge will be added to your bill.

Figure 8.1 **Palm Court all day dining menu (courtesy of The Langham Hotel, London)**

choices that will enable them to achieve a balanced diet. Customers also require more specific information on methods of cooking used, for example, low-fat or low-salt methods. General consensus suggests that the regular diet should be made up of at least one third based on a range of bread, cereals, rice and potatoes; one third based on a variety of fruit and vegetables; and the remainder based on dairy foods, including low-fat milk, low-fat meats and fish, and small amounts of fatty and sugary food.

Dietary requirements

There are a variety of medical conditions, including allergies, which are more common than was previously understood. Customers may therefore require a certain diet for medical reasons (including the prevention of allergic reactions). Such customers will need to know about the ingredients used in a dish, since eating certain things may make them very ill and may even be fatal. Although such customers will usually know what they can and cannot eat, it is important that when asked, a server is able to accurately describe the dishes so that the customer can make the appropriate choice. The server should *never* guess and if in doubt, should seek further information. Some examples of dietary requirements are given in Table 8.1.

Cultural and religious dietary influences

Different religious faiths have differing requirements with regard to the dishes/ ingredients that may be consumed, and these requirements often also cover preparation methods, cooking procedures and the equipment used. Examples are given in Table 8.2 below.

Table 8.1 **Examples of dietary requirements**

Allergies	Food items that are known to cause allergies include the gluten in wheat, rye and barley (known as coeliac), peanuts and their derivatives, sesame seeds and other nuts such as cashew, pecan, brazil and walnuts, as well as milk, fish, shellfish, eggs and tropical fruits. Sometimes these foods can cause anaphylactic shock resulting in the lips, tongue or throat swelling dramatically over a very short period of time. Prompt medical treatment is needed in such cases
Diabetic	This refers to the inability of the body to control the level of insulin within the blood. An appropriate diet may include foods listed in the low cholesterol section below and the avoidance of dishes with high sugar content
Low cholesterol	Diets will include polyunsaturated fats and may include limited quantities of animal fats. Other items eaten may include lean poached or grilled meats and fish, fruit and vegetables and low-fat milk, cheese and yogurt
Low sodium/salt	This requires a reduction in the amount of sodium or salt consumed. Diets will include low sodium/salt foods and cooking with very limited or no salt

Table 8.2 **Dietary requirements according to the various faiths**

Hindus	Do not eat beef and rarely pork. Some Hindus will not eat any meats, fish or eggs. Diets may include cheese, milk and vegetarian dishes
Jews	Only 'clean' (kosher) animals may be consumed. Jews do not eat pork or pork products, shellfish or animal fats and gelatine from beasts considered to be unclean or not slaughtered according to the prescribed manner. There are restrictions placed on methods of preparation and cookery. The preparation and eating of meat and dairy products at the same meal is not allowed

Muslims	Will not eat meat, offal or animal fat unless it is halal (i.e. lawful, as required under Islamic Dietary Law) meat. Will not consume alcohol, even when used in cooking
Sikhs	Do not eat beef or pork. Some will keep to a vegetarian diet. Others may eat fish, mutton, cheese and eggs. Sikhs will not eat halal meat
Rastafarians	Will not eat any processed foods, pork or fish without fins (e.g. eels). Will not consume tea, coffee or alcohol
Roman Catholics	Few restrictions on diet. Usually will not eat meat on Ash Wednesday or Good Friday. Some keep with the past requirement for no meat to be eaten on Fridays. Fish and dairy products may be eaten instead

Vegetarianism

Vegetarianism may derive from cultural, religious, moral, ethical or physiological considerations. It is therefore important that food descriptions are accurate.

The various forms of vegetarianism are summarised in Table 8.3 below.

Table 8.3 **Forms of vegetarianism**

Vegetarians: semi	Do not eat red meats, or all meats other than poultry, or all meats. Diet will include fish and may include dairy produce and other animal products
Vegetarians: lacto-ovo	Do not eat meat, fish or poultry but may eat milk, milk products and eggs
Vegetarians: lacto	Do not eat meat, fish, poultry and eggs but may eat milk and milk products
Vegans	Do not eat any foods of animal origin. Diet will mainly consist of vegetables, vegetable oils, cereals, nuts, fruits and seeds
Fruitarians	More restricted form of vegetarianism. Excluded are all foods of animal origin together with pulses and cereals. Diet may include mainly raw and dried fruit, nuts, honey and olive oil

Ethical influences

Customers have become increasingly aware of ethical issues, such as:

- ensuring sustainability of foods consumed
- fair trade
- the acceptability or otherwise of genetically modified foods or irradiated foods
- reducing food packaging and food waste
- reducing the effects that food production and food transportation have on the environment generally.

There is also a greater trend towards using more seasonal and locally sourced food and beverage items, when the quality, taste, freshness and nutritional value are all at their peak, and when supplies are more plentiful and cheaper. For foodservice businesses, the benefits can also include:

- improved menu planning, as suppliers can give information in advance on what they are able to provide
- more reliable products and service, with greater flexibility to respond to customer needs

- increased marketing opportunities through making a feature of using locally sourced food and beverage items, and through special promotions related to local and seasonal food and beverage specialities
- support for training of staff from local suppliers.

Legal considerations are summarised in Chapter 5, Section 5.4 (page 83) and additional information about how to meet customer needs is given in Chapter 18, Section 18.3 (page 306).

8.4 The classic menu sequence

Over the last 100 or so years the sequence of the European menu has taken on a classical format or order of dishes. This format is used to lay out menus as well as to indicate the order of the various courses. Although the actual number of courses on a menu, and dishes within each course, will depend on the size and class of the establishment, most follow the classic sequence. This sequence is as follows:

1. **Hors-d'oeuvres**
   Traditionally this course consisted of a variety of compound salads. These would contain a selection of vegetables, fish or smoked meats with suitable dressings, e.g. Russian salad or Italian salad. Hors-d'oeuvre today now include such items as pâtés, mousses, fruit, charcuterie and smoked fish.
2. **Soups *(potages)***
   Includes all soups, both hot and cold, e.g. consommé, crèmes, veloutés, purées, potages, bisques (shellfish base), and national soups such as minestrone (Italian).
3. **Egg dishes *(œufs)***
   There are a great number of egg dishes beyond the usual omelettes, but these have not retained their popularity on modern menus.
4. **Pasta and rice *(farineux)***
   Includes all pasta and rice dishes. Can be referred to as farinaceous dishes.
5. **Fish *(poisson)***
   This course consists of fish dishes, both hot and cold and their accompanying sauces. Fish dishes such as smoked salmon, smoked eel or seafood cocktails are mainly considered to be hors-d'oeuvre dishes and therefore would be served earlier in a meal.
6. **Entrée**
   Entrées are generally small, well-garnished dishes which come from the kitchen ready for service. They are usually accompanied by a rich sauce or gravy. Potatoes and vegetables are not usually served with this course if it is to be followed by a main course. If this is the main meat course then it is usual for potatoes and vegetables to also be offered. Examples of this type of dish are tournedos, noisettes, sweetbreads, garnished cutlets or filled vol-au-vent cases.
7. **Sorbet**
   Traditionally sorbets (sometimes now called granites) were served to give a pause within a meal, allowing the palate to be refreshed. They are lightly frozen water ices, often based on unsweetened fruit juice, and may be served with a spirit, liqueur or even champagne poured over. Russian cigarettes also used to be offered at this stage of a meal.

8 **Relevé**
This refers to the main roasts or other larger joints of meat which would be served together with potatoes and vegetables, such as roast ribs of beef or sirloin of beef.

9 **Roast *(rôti)***
This term traditionally refers to roasted game or poultry dishes, such as roast pheasant, partridge and chicken.

10 **Vegetables *(légumes)***
Apart from vegetables served with the relevé or roast courses, certain vegetables (e.g. asparagus and artichokes) may be served as a separate course, although these types of dishes are now more commonly served as starters.

11 **Salad *(salade)***
Often refers to a small plate of salad that is taken after a main course (or courses) and is quite often simply a green salad and dressing (plain salad).

12 **Cold buffet *(buffet froid)***
This course includes a variety of cold meats and fish, cheese and egg items together with a range of salads and dressings.

13 **Cheese *(fromage)***
Includes the range of cheeses – fresh, soft, semi-hard, hard and blue cheese – and their various accompaniments, including cruet set, biscuits (water, Ryvita, digestive, cream crackers, savoury), breads, celery, radishes (when available), grapes and apples. This course can also refer to cheese-based dishes such as soufflés (hot).

14 **Sweets *(entremets)***
Refers to both hot and cold puddings. A wide variety is available.

15 **Savoury *(savoureux)***
Sometimes simple savouries, such as Welsh rarebit or other items on toast or in pastry, or savoury soufflés, may be served at this stage.

16 **Fruit *(dessert)***
Fresh fruit, nuts and sometimes candied fruits.

17 **Beverages**
Traditionally this referred to coffee but nowadays includes a much wider range of beverages, including tea, coffee (in both standard and decaffeinated versions) and a range of other beverages such as tisanes, milk drinks (hot or cold) and proprietary drinks such as Bovril or Horlicks. These are commonly available throughout the day, with a choice of milks, creams (including non-dairy creamers) and sugars (including non-sugar sweeteners).

Note: Although listed here to indicate the sequence for meals, beverages are not counted as a course as such and therefore should not be included when the number of courses for a meal is stated. Thus if a meal is stated as having four courses, this means that there are four food courses and that the beverages at the end are in addition to these.

The classic menu sequence outlined above is based on a logical process of taste sensations. This classic sequence also provides the guide for the compilation of both à la carte and table d'hôte menus, as is evident in many examples of modern menus. However, a number of courses are often now grouped together. At its most simple this might comprise:

- starters – courses 1 to 4
- main courses – courses 5, 6 and 8 to 12
- afters – courses 13 to 16
- beverages.

The classic menu sequence is also used as a guide for the compilation and determination of the order of courses for event and special party menus. This sequence shows the cheese course after the main course and before the sweet course. However, the sweet course is still sometimes offered before the cheese course.

Note: The modern European classic menu sequence outlined here is derived from traditional European (mainly Franco-Russian, Swiss and English) cuisine and service influences. The menu structure and menu sequence can change considerably within the various world cuisines. Menu terms also vary, for instance, in the USA a main course is commonly called an entrée and sweets are commonly called dessert. The term 'dessert' is also now becoming more commonly used to denote sweets generally.

8.5 Other types of menus

The breakfast menu

The current trend is for breakfasts to be offered in a variety of establishments. Many hotels now offer room-only rates or only serve a continental breakfast inclusive in the room rate, with a full breakfast available at an extra charge.

Types of breakfast

There are a variety of terms indicating the various forms in which a breakfast may be offered. These terms encompass in themselves what the customers might expect to receive for their breakfast meal. For example:

Café complet

The term 'café complet' is widely used in continental Europe and means a continental breakfast with coffee as the beverage. The term 'thé complet' is also used, with tea provided as the beverage.

Café simple or thé simple

Café simple or thé simple is just a beverage (coffee or tea) with nothing to eat.

Continental breakfast

The traditional continental breakfast consisted of hot croissant, brioche or toast, butter and preserves and coffee as the beverage. The current trend in the continental breakfast menu is to offer a wider choice, including cereals, fruits, juices, yogurts, ham, cheese, assorted bread items and a wider selection of beverages.

Full breakfast

A full breakfast menu may consist of from two to eight courses and usually includes a cooked main course. Traditionally this was a very substantial meal and included such items as chops, liver, game, steak, kippers and porridge as the main part of the meal. This type of breakfast was traditionally known as an English Breakfast, but is now also known as Scottish, Irish, Welsh or more simply British Breakfast. The term 'full breakfast' is also becoming more common.

Modern full breakfast menus have changed to include a much more varied choice of items. Today customers expect to see such items as fresh fruit juices, fresh fruit, yogurt, muesli, continental pastries, homemade preserves, decaffeinated coffee and mineral waters on the full breakfast menu. Examples of breakfast menu items are given in Table 8.4.

Table 8.4 **Examples of breakfast menu items**

Menu	Examples of food items
Juices	Orange, pineapple, grapefruit, tomato, prune, carrot, apple
Fresh and stewed fruit	Melon, strawberries, grapefruit (half or segments), pineapple, apricots, peaches, mango, paw paw, lychees, figs, prunes (fresh and stewed)
Cereals	Cornflakes, Weetabix, Special K, muesli, bran flakes, Rice Krispies, porridge
Yogurt	Natural and fruit, regular and low-fat
Fish	Fried or grilled kippers, poached smoked haddock (sometimes with poached eggs), grilled herring, fried or grilled plaice, fried or grilled sole, kedgeree, smoked fish (sometimes including dishes like smoked salmon with scrambled eggs), marinated fish such as gravadlax
Eggs	Fried, poached, scrambled, boiled, plain or savoury filled omelette, eggs Benedict
Meats	Bacon in various styles, various sausages, kidney, steak, gammon
Potatoes and vegetables	Hash browns, sauté potatoes, home fries, mushrooms, baked beans, fresh or grilled tomato
Pancakes and waffles	Regular pancakes or waffles, with maple syrup or other toppings, blueberry pancakes, wholemeal pancakes, griddle cakes
Cold buffet	Hams, tongue, chicken, smoked cold meats, salamis, cheeses (often accompanied by fresh salad items)
Bread items	Toast, rolls, croissants, brioches, crispbreads, plain sliced white or brown bread, rye and gluten-free bread, Danish pastries, American muffins, English muffins, spiced scones, tea cakes, doughnuts
Preserves	Jams (strawberry, blackcurrant), marmalade, honey
Beverages	Tea, coffee (including decaffeinated), chocolate, tisanes, proprietary beverages, milk, soy/rice milk, mineral waters

Buffet breakfast menus are often priced and offered at three levels:

- **Continental:** Including juices, bread items and beverages.
- **Cold buffet:** Including those items of continental breakfast plus a selection of cold items from the buffet.
- **Full breakfast:** Full selection from the buffet including hot cooked items.

Afternoon tea menus

Afternoon tea is served in many establishments and in a variety of forms. Afternoon tea may be classified into two main types:

1 Full afternoon tea as served in a first-class hotel or restaurant.
2 High tea as served in a popular price restaurant, department store or café.

Full afternoon tea

The menu for a full afternoon tea usually consists of some or all of the items listed in Figure 8.2. These are generally served in the order in which they are listed. Note that beverages are served first. An afternoon tea stand is often used as part of the service of afternoon tea (see Figure 8.3).

Full afternoon tea menu

Variety of teas, tisanes and coffees

~

Assorted afternoon tea sandwiches:
smoked salmon, cucumber, tomato, sardine,
egg, Gentleman's Relish

~

Brown and white bread and butter
Fruit bread and butter

~

Hot buttered toast or toasted teacake or crumpets
Warmed scones (with butter or whipped or clotted cream)
Raspberry or strawberry jams

~

Gâteaux and pastries

Figure 8.2 **Full afternoon tea menu**

Figure 8.3 **Example of an afternoon tea stand**

High tea menu

A high tea may be available in addition to the full afternoon tea. It is usually in a modified à la carte form and the menu will offer, in addition to the normal full afternoon tea menu, such items as grills, toasted snacks, fish and meat dishes, salads, cold sweets and ice creams. The meat dishes normally consist of pies and pastries, whereas the fish dishes are usually fried or grilled.

The following accompaniments (proprietary sauces) may be offered with high tea:

- tomato ketchup
- brown sauce (e.g. 'HP')
- Worcestershire sauce
- vinegar
- mustards.

Reception or buffet tea menus

A reception or buffet tea is offered for special functions and private parties only, and, as the name implies, the food and beverage are served from a buffet table and not at individual tables. The foods that will be available might be a selection from either the full afternoon tea or the high tea menu.

Event menus

The term 'event' covers a wide variety of occasions that may be requested by customers, such as a golden wedding anniversary, formal dinners, cocktail parties, promotion of a special event and conferences.

Following an enquiry about a special event or function to be held, the potential host will receive an 'event sales pack'. Included in this will be:

- examples of meal packages such as a range of set menus, snack menus and conference lunches
- details of the service methods available, such as formal table service, buffets and in-room service.

To assist the customer there should be:

- a varied choice of menu within a wide price range
- special menus available for occasions such as weddings, 21st birthday parties and New Year's Eve.

The number of courses at a banquet is normally four plus beverages, but can be many more and often includes:

- hors-d'oeuvre or other appetisers
- soup or fish
- meat/vegetarian – with a selection of seasonal vegetables
- sweet
- coffee or tea – with a selection of petits fours.

This approach is generally popular, but extra or alternative courses such as entrées, cheese or savouries may be added.

Floor/room service menus

Floor or room service varies from basic tea- and coffee-making facilities in the room and possibly a mini-bar, to vending machines on floors, or the service of a variety of meals in rooms. The extent of service in hotel guest rooms will depend on the nature of the establishment. In five-star hotels, 24-hour room service is expected, whereas in two- and three-star hotels, service may be limited to tea- and coffee-making facilities in the room and only continental breakfast available to be served in the room.

An example of a room service menu is shown in Figure 8.5. In this establishment full room service is offered and the room service staff are employed to provide 24-hour service.

Figure 8.4 Room service (image courtesy of Six Continents Hotels)

Breakfast service

An example of a breakfast menu is shown in Figure 8.6. This menu also acts as an order which, when completed, is hung on the outside of the hotel guest's bedroom door.

Lounge service menus

Lounge service may include the service of continental breakfast, morning coffee, luncheon snacks, afternoon tea, dinner or late evening snacks as well as alcoholic beverages. Although mainly associated with hotels, it is also found in public houses, wine bars and on ships. Examples of lounge and bar service menus are given in Figure 8.7.

8.6 Types of wine and drinks lists

The purpose of a wine and drinks list is similar to that of the menu and is a selling aid. Careful thought is needed in its planning, design, layout, colour and overall appearance to ensure it complements the style of the establishment.

Bar and cocktail lists

These lists may range from a basic standard list offering the common everyday aperitifs such as sherries, vermouths, bitters, a selection of spirits with mixers, beers and soft drinks, together with a limited range of cocktails, through to a very comprehensive list offering a good choice in all areas. The actual format and content of the list will be determined by the style of operation and clientele that the establishment wishes to attract. Depending on this, the emphasis may be on:

- cocktails: traditional or fashionable
- malt whiskies
- beers
- New World wines
- non-alcoholic drinks.

Restaurant lists

These lists may take various formats such as:

- a full and very comprehensive list of wines from all countries, with emphasis on the classic areas such as Bordeaux/Burgundy plus a fine wine/prestige selection
- a middle-of-the-road, traditional selection, e.g. some French, German and Italian wines, together with some New World wines
- a small selection of well-known or branded wines – a prestige list
- predominantly wines of one particular country.

Wake Up And Smell The Bacon

If you would like breakfast served in your room please fill in the breakfast menu door hanger and place on the outside doorknob of your room before 3am. Alternatively call room service direct on extension 4.

Served from 11am till 10.45pm

Hilton Classics

Caesar salad with parmesan shavings	£6.95 / £10.95
With chicken breast or Atlantic prawns	£9.95 / £14.95
Club sandwich with back bacon, chicken breast, vine tomato and egg	£12.95
100% beef Hilton burger with back bacon or mature Scottish cheddar or both	£13.95

Club sandwich and Hilton burger are both served with fries

Sandwiches and Paninis

Sandwiches come on your choice of traditional white or wholemeal bread. All sandwiches and paninis are served with vegetable crisps, dill pickle and marinated olives.

Oak smoked salmon, lemon mayonnaise (Served 24 hours)	£8.95
Honey roast ham, apple relish (Served 24 hours)	£8.95
Tuna mayonnaise, spring onion and rocket (Served 24 hours)	£8.95
Spinach, ricotta and vine tomato wrap wit balsamic reduction (Healthy Option) (Vegetarian Option) (Served 24 hours)	£8.95
Hot Turkish flat breadwith smoked turkey breast, Howgate brie and cranberry	£8.95
Warm sun blushed vine tomato, mozzarella and basil panini (Vegetarian Option)	£8.95
Warm chicken breast, caramelised onion and grain mustard panini (Healthy Option)	£8.95
Your choice of today's soup with any of the above sandwich or panini	£10.95
Mature Mull cheddar and ham toastie	£8.95
Mild cheddar and pickle toastie (Vegetarian Option)	£8.95
Fillet steak sandwich with fried onions, cos lettuce and fries	£11.95

From Our Pizza Oven

Margherita (Vegetarian Option) (Served 24 hours)	£12.00
Smoked chicken, rocket, fresh pineapple (Served 24 hours)	£12.00
Pepperoni (Served 24 hours)	£12.00
Woodland mushrooms, char grilled vegetables, pesto and mozzarella (Vegetarian Option) (Served 24 hours)	£12.00

Healthy Option · Vegetarian Option · Served 24 hours

All weights are uncooked. Please note an order charge of £3.50 will be added to your bill, all prices include VAT at the current rate. For those with special dietary requirements or allergies who may wish to know about ingredients used, please ask the Manager.

From Our Pasta Range

Linguini, penne or gnocchi £13.95

Add your own sauce

Pesto, pine nut and mushroom (Vegetarian Option)	Arabiatta (Vegetarian Option)
Bolognese	Carbonara

Light Bites

Soups of the day (Healthy Option) (Vegetarian Option) (Served 24 hours) *Freshly prepared, always 2 choices available, served with crusty bread rolls*	£5.95
Bards Bree – Full bodied soup of haggis, neeps and tatties *(vegetarian alternative available)*	£5.95
Stornoway black pudding, Ayrshire bacon and crushed hash	£7.95
Shetland mussels, marinière or with lemon grass and coconut milk	£7.95
Greek salad; feta cheese with vine tomato, basil and marinated olives (Healthy Option) (Vegetarian Option) (Served 24 hours)	£6.95
Nachos with mozzarella, jalapenos, salsa and sour cream (Vegetarian Option) (Served 24 hours)	£7.95
Gravadlax with new potato salad, young spinach, keta caviar and dill (Healthy Option)	£7.95
Prawn and Uig smoked salmon cocktail (Served 24 hours)	£7.95
Antipasti plate – Prosciutto ham, chorizo, galia melon, mozzarella, sun blushed tomatoes, marinated olives, roasted vegetables, anchovies feta cheese and wild leaves (Healthy Option)	£8.95

Main Meals

Add all dishes from the "Old Favourites" section in the new bar menu.

Baked field mushrooms, goats cheese, herb crust (Vegetarian Option)	£11.95
Highland game venison sausage, creamed potato, caramelised onion jus	£11.95
Tempura haddock, hand cut chips, tartare sauce and lemon	£15.95
Lime and ginger stir fried chicken strips, egg noodles, pak choi and prawn crackers (Served 24 hours)	£15.95
Crumbed scampi tails, hand cut chips, tossed salad	£15.95
Dry aged Scottish ribeye (280g), Cherry vine tomatoes, field mushrooms and hand cut chips	£20.00
Roasted North Sea halibut, tender greens, white wine sauce	£19.00
Beef madras with basmati rice, naan bread and poppadoms	£16.95
From Minsky's Buffet –	
Selection of cold appetisers	£6.95
Roast joint, entrée or fish of the day with vegetables and potatoes	£16.95

Side Orders

£3.50 each

Panache of seasonal vegetables (Vegetarian Option)	Parsley new potatoes (Vegetarian Option)
Hand cut chips (Vegetarian Option)	Onion rings (Vegetarian Option)
Fries (Vegetarian Option)	Rocket, endive and watercress salad (Vegetarian Option)
Garlic bread (Vegetarian Option)	

Desserts And Cheese

White and dark chocolate indulgence	£6.95
Warm apple tart tartin, calvados anglâise	£6.95
Warm Eccles cake, vanilla pod ice cream	£6.95
Movenpick ice cream (please ask for our daily selection)	£5.95
Sticky toffee pudding	£6.95
Exotic fruit salad h	£5.95

Figure 8.5 Example of part of a room service menu (image courtesy of The Glasgow Hilton Hotel, Scotland)

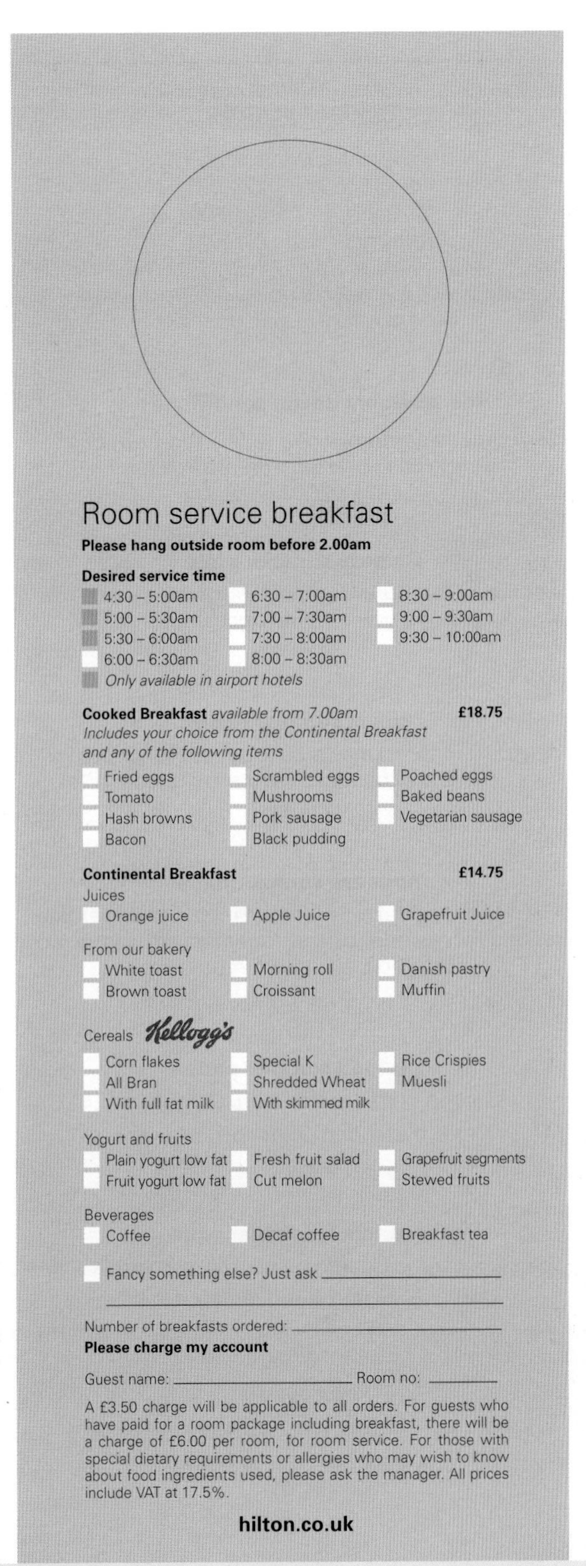

Room service breakfast

Please hang outside room before 2.00am

Desired service time

- 4:30 – 5:00am
- 5:00 – 5:30am
- 5:30 – 6:00am
- 6:00 – 6:30am
- 6:30 – 7:00am
- 7:00 – 7:30am
- 7:30 – 8:00am
- 8:00 – 8:30am
- 8:30 – 9:00am
- 9:00 – 9:30am
- 9:30 – 10:00am

Only available in airport hotels

Cooked Breakfast *available from 7.00am* **£18.75**

Includes your choice from the Continental Breakfast and any of the following items

- Fried eggs
- Tomato
- Hash browns
- Bacon
- Scrambled eggs
- Mushrooms
- Pork sausage
- Black pudding
- Poached eggs
- Baked beans
- Vegetarian sausage

Continental Breakfast **£14.75**

Juices

- Orange juice
- Apple Juice
- Grapefruit Juice

From our bakery

- White toast
- Brown toast
- Morning roll
- Croissant
- Danish pastry
- Muffin

Cereals Kellogg's

- Corn flakes
- All Bran
- With full fat milk
- Special K
- Shredded Wheat
- With skimmed milk
- Rice Crispies
- Muesli

Yogurt and fruits

- Plain yogurt low fat
- Fruit yogurt low fat
- Fresh fruit salad
- Cut melon
- Grapefruit segments
- Stewed fruits

Beverages

- Coffee
- Decaf coffee
- Breakfast tea

- Fancy something else? Just ask ______________________

____

Number of breakfasts ordered: ______________________

Please charge my account

Guest name: ______________________ Room no: __________

A £3.50 charge will be applicable to all orders. For guests who have paid for a room package including breakfast, there will be a charge of £6.00 per room, for room service. For those with special dietary requirements or allergies who may wish to know about food ingredients used, please ask the manager. All prices include VAT at 17.5%.

hilton.co.uk

Figure 8.6 **Room service breakfast menu and order card (image courtesy of the Belfast Hilton Hotel, Northern Ireland)**

SAMPLER PLATES

CASPIAN CAVIAR (30g)

Royal Beluga	£240.00
Oscietra	£210.00
Sevruga	£175.00

Unpasteurised, specially selected for The Westbury, served with a classic garnish

The Westbury caviar sandwiches

Sevruga caviar sandwiched with buckwheat and lemon blinis and fresh crème fraîche
£95.00

Chinese sampler plate

Selection of aromatic duck with pancakes, spring rolls, sweet and sour chicken and prawn toast
£28.00

Italian sampler plate

Selection of sliced meats antipasti, bruschetta, mini olive and buffalo mozzarella calzone
£28.00

Japanese sampler plate

Selection of hand made tuna, salmon and vegetable rolls and thinly sliced sashimi, together with carpaccio of marinated beef, and tempura prawns
£30.00

Seafood sampler plate

Selection of smoked salmon, Cornish crab, rock oyster and Dublin bay prawns
£40.00

Vegetarian sampler plate

Selection of crudités with humus dip, spring rolls with sweet chilli, bruschetta and antipasti
£26.50

Rock oysters

Half a dozen rock oysters, garnished with shallot vinegar, lemon and bread
£22.50

1

Figure 8.7(a) **Example of a lounge and bar menu (image courtesy of The Westbury Hotel, London)**

CANAPES

Mini foie gras burgers
Six mini sauté foie gras burgers served canapé style with a selection of chutneys
£22.50

Duck Spring Rolls
With a plum sauce
£14.95

Panko crusted prawns
Nine prawns in panko breadcrumbs served with chilli
£19.00

Bar sushi and sashimi
Selection of hand made tuna, salmon and vegetable rolls and thinly sliced sashimi
£19.50

SANDWICH SELECTION

The Bookmaker
Grilled fillet of Caledonian Crown with melted Stilton, plum tomatoes and shallot mayonnaise on ciabatta
£19.00

The Bond Street
Slices of roasted sirloin of Aberdeen Angus beef served with Swiss cheese, horseradish, lettuce on Viennoise bread
£16.00

Peppered Pastrami
New York style peppered pastrami with shaved fennel and Swiss cheese on toasted bagel
£16.00

Thai spiced chicken
Breast of chicken with lime leaf, lemon grass, and ginger on ciabatta
£16.50

The Savile Row
Croque Monsieur with hand sliced smoked salmon, cream cheese, horseradish, capers and beetroot
£18.50

Mediterranean vegetable club
Wood roasted peppers, hummus, mozzarella, artichoke, with grilled asparagus on toasted granary
£14.00

2

Figure 8.7(b) **Example of a lounge and bar menu (image courtesy of The Westbury Hotel, London)**

After meal drinks lists (digestifs)
These lists are often combined with the wine list, although occasionally they are presented as a separate liqueur list. The list should offer a full range of liqueurs, and may also include a specialist range of brandies and/or malt whiskies. Vintage and Late Bottled Vintage (LBV) port may also be offered here. A range of speciality liqueur/spirit coffees might also be included.

Banqueting and events lists
The length of the list will generally depend on the size and style of operation. In most instances there is a selection of popular wine names/styles on offer. There would be a range of prices from house wines to some fine wines to suit all customer preferences. In some operations the banqueting wine list is the same as the restaurant wine list.

Room service lists
There may be a mini-bar in the room, or the room service menu may offer a choice from a standard bar list. The range of wines offered is usually limited and prices will vary according to the type of establishment.

Lounge service lists
These are often reduced forms of the restaurant lists and may also offer a choice from a standard bar list. The range of wines offered is usually limited and prices will vary according to the type of establishment.

8.7 Contents of wine and drinks lists

The contents of wine and drinks lists are commonly listed in the order in which they might be consumed:

1. aperitifs – which alongside sparkling and still wines can include a range of aromatised wines, fortified wines and natural spring and mineral waters
2. cocktails
3. spirits and associated mixers such as aerated waters
4. wines – sparkling and still
5. beers, cider, aerated waters and squashes
6. digestifs – which as well as liqueurs may also include various spirits, such as brandy, malt whiskies and also ports, other fortified wines, sweet table wines and vins doux naturels
7. speciality coffees

Listing of wines
Wines are usually listed in three main ways:

- by place of origin (geographical)
- by type
- by grape.

Geographical listing for wines
The traditional approach is to list wines by geographical area. Within this approach the wines are presented country by country or region, for instance, France or

Australasia (which includes Australia and New Zealand), and then area by area. It is also usual to have the wines presented under each country, region or area with the white wines first, followed by rosé wines and then red wines. Using this approach the listing of wines within a wine list might be:

1 Champagne and sparkling
2 France
3 Germany
4 Italy
5 Spain
6 Portugal
7 England
8 Other European wines
9 Australia
10 Australasia
11 The Americas (USA and South America)
12 South Africa
13 Other world wines
14 House wines.

Listing wines by type

A modern approach is to have wines listed by type:

- sparkling wines
- white wines
- rosé wines
- red wines
- dessert (sweet) wines.

The wines can then be listed under each type of wine in three main ways:

- country by country
- region by region (similar to the geographical listing described above)
- by the style of the wine.

If the wines are to be listed by type and by style, then the wines may be presented under the following headings:

- sparkling wines
- rosé wines
- white wines
  - grapey whites
  - grassy-fruity whites
  - richer whites
- red wines
  - fruity reds
  - claret style reds
  - herby-spicy reds.

To help the customer choose a wine and to enable staff to make recommendations, it is also useful for each of the groups of wines to be listed in order from the lighter wines to the more full wines.

Listing wines by grape

If the wines are to be listed by grape, then one approach is to list the grapes in alphabetical order as follows:

White grapes

- Chardonnay
- Chenin blanc
- Gewürztraminer
- Pinot Blanc
- Pinot Gris/Pinot Grigio
- Riesling
- Sauvignon Blanc
- Sémillon
- Other white grapes

Red grapes

- Cabernet Sauvignon
- Gamay
- Merlot
- Pinot Noir
- Sangiovese
- Shiraz/Syrah
- Tempranillo
- Zinfandel
- Other red grapes

Under each heading the wines made with that grape are listed, as well as the principal blends that are made with that grape as the predominant grape. When the wines are listed under the headings 'Other white grapes' or 'Other red grapes', then the grape(s) of the wine should also be listed next to the name of the wine.

Again, to help the customer choose a wine and to aid staff in making recommendations, it is useful for each of the groups of wines to be listed in order from the lighter wines to the more full wines.

8.8 General information given on wine and drinks lists

It is usual to give information on wine and drinks lists that help the customer to make a decision and the staff in making recommendations. This information is shown below.

Wines

- Bin number
- Name of wine
- Country and area of origin
- Quality indication (e.g. AOC, Qmp etc.)
- Shipper
- Château/Estate bottled
- Varietal (grape type(s))
- Vintage
- Alcoholic strength
- ½ bottle, bottle, magnum
- Price
- Supplier
- Descriptive notes as appropriate

Other drinks

- Type of drink, e.g. juices, whisky, gin, sherry
- Brand name if appropriate, e.g. Martini
- Style (sweet, dry, etc.)
- Description, e.g. for cocktails
- Alcoholic strength in percentage by volume as appropriate
- Descriptive notes as appropriate

CHAPTER 9

Menu knowledge

This chapter will help you to learn about:

1 Basic sauces and food items used in service
2 Hors-d'oeuvre and other appetisers
3 Soups
4 Egg dishes
5 Pasta and rice dishes
6 Fish dishes
7 Meats, poultry and game
8 Potatoes, vegetables and salads
9 Cheese
10 Sweets
11 Savouries
12 Dessert *(fresh fruit and nuts)*

9.1 Basic sauces and food items used in service

Knowledge about the product is at the core of successful food and beverage service. This knowledge enables the server to advise the customer of:

- the content of dishes
- the methods used in making the dishes
- the correct accompaniments to be offered with a selected dish.

The rest of this chapter provides information on the accompaniments for a selection of menu items by course.

A note on sauces

Although there appears to be a wide variety of sauces, they are almost always variations on the same base sauces. These base sauces are summarised in Table 9.1

Table 9.1 **Base sauces**

Fond brun	Basic brown meat sauce
Velouté	White sauce using fish, meat, poultry or vegetable stock
Allemande	A velouté thickened with cream and egg yolks
Béchamel	Savoury white sauce made with milk
Tomato sauce	Made with fresh, tinned or puréed tomatoes
Mayonnaise	Cold sauce made from egg yolks, oil, vinegar, salt, pepper and mustard

Hollandaise	Hot sauce made from melted butter, egg yolks, shallots, vinegar and seasonings
Vinaigrette	Cold sauce made from mixing oil, vinegar and a selection of seasonings

These sauces provide the base for other sauces by adding a variety of different ingredients. For example:

- cheese to a béchamel sauce to create a Mornay sauce
- whipped cream to a Hollandaise sauce to create sauce Mousseline
- tarragon and other herbs added to Hollandaise to make Béarnaise
- gherkins, capers and fines herbes to mayonnaise to form tartare sauce.

Thus a wide range of sauces can be created.

Accompaniments

There are a number of dishes where traditional accompaniments are normally served. Accompaniments offered with certain dishes are mainly to assist in:

- improving the flavour
- counteracting richness.

The sections that follow contain guides to these accompaniments. However, these guides are not intended to be prescriptive, as changes are constantly taking place and new accompaniments being tried. In addition, the desire for healthier eating has led to a number of changes, for example:

- alternatives to butter such as Flora are often provided
- frequently bread is not buttered in advance, thereby allowing the customer to choose his or her requirements
- the availability of lower fat milks, non-dairy creamers and non-sugar sweeteners is also now standard.

There are a variety of food items available which support the service of a range of dishes. Some of these items have specific uses for particular dishes and others are used generally across a number of dishes. Table 9.2 gives a list of examples of accompaniments used in food and beverage service.

Table 9.2 **Examples of food items used in food service**

Item	Description	Use
Aioli/Ailloli	Garlic mayonnaise	Cold fish dishes and as a salad dip, e.g. for crudités
Apple sauce	Purée of cooking apples, slightly sweetened, served hot but more usually cold	Roast pork, roast duck and roast goose
Balsamic vinegar	Aromatic vinegar, acid product made from sweet grape wine, aged in oak	Dressings
Cayenne	Hot, red pepper (actually a species of powdered capsicum)	Oysters, smoked salmon
Chilli sauce	Hot sauce, mostly Chinese made	With Chinese-style foods
Chilli vinegar	Vinegar flavoured with chillies	Oysters
Chives	Herb (fresh chopped)	Salad garnish and for the surface of chilled soups, e.g. Vichyssoise

Item	Description	Use
Chutney	Generic name for Indian sauces. Common varieties are sweet mango or hot mango, also Piccalilli and others such as the proprietary Branston Pickle	Indian chutneys for Tandoori and other Indian dishes. Other chutneys for cold meats, with cheeses and Ploughman's lunch
Cider vinegar	Acid product made from cider	Can be used in salad dressings. Viewed by some as a product for the health conscious
Cocktail gherkins	Small gherkins	Appetisers or garnish for charcuterie
Cocktail onions	Small, pearl onions	Appetisers or garnish for charcuterie
Cocktail sauces	Manufactured sauces of mayonnaise with added flavourings, e.g. tomato	Seafood cocktails
Corn oil	Light-flavoured oil made from corn	Dressings
Cranberry sauce	Sauce made from cranberries, usually available as a proprietary sauce. Can be served hot or cold	Roast turkey
Croutons	Small cubes of fried or toasted bread	Garnish for soups and also used in some salad dishes, e.g. Caesar salad
Cucumbers, pickled	Pickled cucumbers	For meats, salad dishes, charcuterie and cheese
Cumberland sauce	Sweet-and-sour sauce including orange and lemon juice and zest, redcurrant jelly and port. Can be kitchen made or proprietary bottled	Game dishes and for charcuterie
Dill pickle	Pickled gherkins or cucumbers flavoured with dill	Meats, salad dishes, charcuterie and cheese
French dressing	Dressing made from oil and usually wine vinegar or lemon juice, with seasoning. Mustards and herbs may be added	Salads
Gherkins	Small pickled cucumbers	Charcuterie
Ginger	Spicy root used in many forms. Ground ginger is most common in restaurants	Melon
Gros sel	Literally 'fat salt', not finely ground. Also called rock salt	Boiled beef but also widely used in table grinders
Groundnut oil	Bland oil made from groundnuts	Dressings
Horseradish sauce	Hot-tasting sauce made from horseradish root, usually available as proprietary sauce, often needs creaming down	Roast beef and Chicken Maryland and also for cold smoked fish dishes when creamed down
HP Sauce	Brown proprietary, spicy, vinegar-based sauce	Cold meats and other dishes
Indian pickles	Unsweetened hot pickles, featuring limes, mango, brinjals, etc.	Accompaniment for Indian (and other) savoury dishes
Kasundi	Hot Indian pickle featuring chopped mango	Accompaniment for Indian (and other) savoury dishes

Item	Description	Use
Ketchup, mushroom	Old-style English proprietary sauce now seldom seen. Chinese mushroom sauce is substituted	Flavouring in lamb cookery and for other dishes
Ketchup, tomato	Sauce of tomato pulp, vinegar and sweetening. Usually available as a proprietary sauce	Grills, fish, burgers
Lemon	Citrus fruit (slices, segments or halves)	Infinite variety of uses, especially smoked fish, fried fish and a range of drinks including tea
Lime	Citrus fruit (slices, segments or halves)	Similar to lemon above
Malt vinegar	Acid product of brewed malted barley	Dressings and traditionally (in UK) for chips
Mayonnaise	Made from combination of oil and egg yolks, flavoured with vinegar, herbs and seasoning	Dressing for poached fish and sauce for salads
Mint jelly	Sweetish jelly made with mint. Proprietary versions often used	Roast lamb, as an alternative to mint sauce. Also offered with roast mutton
Mint sauce	Vinegar-based sauce with chopped mint and sweetening. Proprietary versions usually used	Roast lamb
Mixed pickles	Assortment of vegetables pickled in vinegar	Cold meats, charcuterie
Mustard, English	Generally the hottest. Available as powder for making up or as proprietary bottled, sometimes with other ingredients such as whole seeds	Roast beef, boiled beef, grills, cold meats, pâtés and as ingredient in dressings, e.g. vinaigrette
Mustard, other	Wide variety including French, au poivre, vert, Bordeaux, Meaux, Dijon, Douce, German (*Senf*)	Cold meats, grills, dressings
Mustard sauce	Warm sauce, generally kitchen made, but also available as proprietary sauce	Traditionally grilled herring but is used for other meat and fish dishes
Oil (general)	Many varieties, usually low in unsaturated fats	Dressings and increasingly for cooking
Olive oil	Oil made from olive pressings (cholesterol free)	Dressings
Olives	Black or green fruit lightly pickled in brine	Appetisers but also garnish for food and drinks, or chopped as flavouring
Onions – pickled	Small onions pickled in malt vinegar (brown) or white vinegar (silverskin)	Cold meats, Ploughman's lunch
Oriental vinegars	Several varieties	Give character to dressings and food dishes
Paprika	Powdered, mild, red capsicum	Garnish on and in seafood cocktails
Parmesan	Italian hard cheese (grated or shredded)	Used in soups, e.g. minestrone and for pasta dishes

Item	Description	Use
Parsley	Chopped or sprig	Garnish on wide variety of dishes. Sometimes deep fried with fried fish
Pepper	Ground white pepper	Traditional form of pepper in table shaker
Peppercorns	Green are usually pickled in brine and soft. White and black	In food dishes. Black used for the table in pepper mills but sometimes mixed
Piccalilli	Mixed pickle in thickened, spiced sauce (predominantly turmeric and sugar)	Cold meats, Ploughman's lunch, buffet, snacks
Piri-piri	Hot chilli sauce of Portuguese/African origin	Prawns, crayfish, chicken
Redcurrant jelly	Proprietary sauce	Traditionally offered with hare. Also traditionally offered with roast mutton but now often offered with roast lamb
Rouille	Provençale sauce made from pounded chillies, garlic and breadcrumbs (or cooked potatoes) blended with olive oil and fish stock	Used as accompaniment to boiled fish and fish soups such as bouillabaisse. If served with chicken bouillabaisse then chicken stock is used
Salt, refined	Ground table salt	Traditionally used as salt in table cellar or shakers
Sea salt	Salt derived from evaporated sea water	Seasoning, especially with boiled beef and used in table grinders
Soy sauce	Clear, dark brown sauce, usually Chinese, made from soy beans	Chinese and sometimes other dishes
Soya oil	Oil made from crushed soya beans	Dressings
Sunflower oil	Light textured and flavoured oil from sunflower seeds	Dressings
Tabasco sauce	Hot, spicy, pepper proprietary sauce	Oysters, clams, other seafood and in other dishes
Tartare sauce	Mayonnaise-based sauce with addition of chopped gherkins, capers and lemon juice	All deep fried fish
Vinaigrette	Combination of oil and vinegar or lemon juice with seasoning. May also include mustards and herbs	Dressings
Walnuts, pickled	Whole pickled walnuts	Cold meats and some savouries
Wine vinegar	Acid product of wine, red or white	Dressings
Worcestershire sauce	Maceration of blend of spices and fruit in vinegar. Often known by the maker's brand name 'Lea and Perrins'	Tomato juice, Irish stew, Scotch broth, seafood cocktails and in dressings. Also used as a flavouring in a variety of other dishes

9.2 Hors-d'oeuvre and other appetisers

Traditionally, hors-d'oeuvre was a selection of salads, fish and meats. Oil and vinegar were also traditionally offered but this has become less common because such foods are usually already well dressed. Buttered brown bread is also offered less often, thereby allowing the customer a choice of breads and butter or alternatives. A selection of common hors d'oeuvre items are shown in Table 9.3. A list of other appetisers is given in Table 9.4.

Table 9.3 **Common hors d'oeuvre items**

Canapés	These are slices of bread with the crusts removed, cut into a variety of shapes, then toasted or fried in oil or butter and garnished. Garnishes can include smoked salmon, foie gras, prawns, cheese, asparagus tips, tomato, egg, capers, gherkins, salami and other meats.
Eggs	These can be poached, presented in aspic or mayonnaise, or hard-boiled, cut in two and garnished or stuffed with various fillings, which include the yolk.
Fish	May include items such as anchovies, herring (fresh or marinated), lobster, mackerel (marinated, smoked or fresh), smoked eel (filleted or sliced) and prawns (plain, in cocktail sauce or in a mousse).
Meats	Includes items such as pâtés, ham (raw, boiled or smoked) and salamis of all varieties.
Salads	Plain or compound. Examples of plain salads include fish and meat salads, cucumber salad, tomato salad, potato salad, beetroot salad, red cabbage and cauliflower. Compound salads include, e.g. Russian (mixed vegetables in mayonnaise); Andalouse (celery, onions, peppers, tomatoes, rice and vinaigrette); Italienne (vegetable salad, cubes of salami, anchovy fillets and mayonnaise).

Generally the cover is a small knife and fork. Some establishments use the traditional fish knife and fork.

Table 9.4 **Other appetisers**

Asparagus (Asperges)	Fresh asparagus may be eaten hot with, e.g. melted butter or Hollandaise sauce or cold with vinaigrette or mayonnaise. Generally now eaten with a knife and fork. Sometimes asparagus holders are used.
Avocado (Poire d'avocat)	Generally served in halves with a salad garnish on a fish plate. Can be served with vinaigrette (now more likely to be made with a wine vinegar), which is served separately, or with prawns in a cocktail sauce. Brown bread and butter is less common now.
Caesar salad	Salad of cos (or Romaine) lettuce, dressed with vinaigrette or other similar dressing (originally containing near-raw egg), garlic, croutons and grated (or shaved) parmesan cheese. There are a number of variations to these ingredients.
Caviar (Caviare)	Served with a caviar knife (broad blade knife) or side knife, on the right hand side of the cover. Accompaniments include blinis (buck wheat pancakes) or hot breakfast toast, butter, segments of lemon, chopped shallots and chopped egg yolk and egg white. Portion size is usually up to about 30 g (1 oz).

Charcuterie	This can include a range of meat (mainly pork) items including Bayonne ham, salamis, smoked ham, Parma ham and also pâtés and terrines. Accompaniments are peppermill and cayenne pepper, gherkins and sometimes onions. Occasionally a small portion of potato salad is offered. Bread is usually offered but brown bread and butter is now less common.
Corn on the cob (Maïs naturel)	These are usually served with special corn-on-the-cob holders that are similar to small swords or forks. Hollandaise sauce or melted butter would accompany this appetiser. A peppermill is offered.
Fresh fruit	Caster sugar may be offered upon request. Both caster sugar and ground ginger are offered with melon if served alone.
Fruit juices	Caster sugar may be offered should grapefruit juice be ordered. For tomato juice, salt and Worcestershire sauce (shaken) are offered.
Gravlax (Gravadlax)	Salmon pickled with salt, sugar and dill. Traditional accompaniments are a slightly sweetened sauce of mustard and dill and often half a lemon (which may be wrapped in muslin to prevent the juice squirting onto the customer when the lemon is squeezed). A variety of unbuttered breads may be offered, with butter and alternatives served separately.
Mousses and pâtés	Hot, unbuttered breakfast toast or bread is offered. Butter or alternatives may be offered and other accompaniments appropriate to the dish itself, e.g. lemon segments with fish mousses, although lemon is often offered with meat-based pâtés.
Niçoise salad	There are a number of versions of this salad. Generally it includes boiled potatoes, whole French beans, tomatoes, hard-boiled eggs (quartered or sliced), stoned black olives, flakes of tuna fish and anchovy fillets. This salad is usually made up and plated. Vinaigrette is often offered.
Oysters (huîtres)	Cold oysters are usually served in one half of the shell on a bed of crushed ice in a soup plate on an underplate. An oyster fork is usually offered but a small sweet fork can also be used. These would be placed on the right hand side of the cover. Oysters are usually eaten by holding the shell in one hand and the fork in the other. Thus a finger bowl on an underplate and containing luke warm water and a slice of lemon together with an extra napkin could be offered. Accompaniments include half a lemon and the oyster cruet (cayenne pepper, pepper mill, chilli vinegar and Tabasco sauce). Traditionally brown bread and butter is also offered.
Potted shrimps	Accompaniments include hot, unbuttered, breakfast toast (there is plenty of butter already in this dish), cayenne pepper, a peppermill and segments of lemon.
Seafood cocktails (Cocktail de crevettes)	The traditional accompaniments are a lemon segment, peppermill, sometimes cayenne pepper and traditionally brown bread and butter, although this is less common now.
Smoked salmon (saumon fumé)	Traditional accompaniments are half a lemon (which may be wrapped in muslin to prevent the juice squirting onto the customer when the lemon is squeezed), cayenne pepper, peppermill and brown bread and butter. Nowadays a variety of unbuttered bread may be offered with butter and alternatives served separately. Oil is sometimes offered and also chopped onions and capers.
Other smoked fish	As well as the accompaniments offered with smoked salmon, creamed horseradish has become a standard offering with all other smoked fish including trout, mackerel, cod, halibut and tuna.

9.3 Soups

Soups are divided into a number of categories. These include consommés, veloutés, crèmes, purées, potages, bisques (shellfish soups) and broths. Examples of these are shown in Table 9.5. There are also various national soups and examples of these are shown in Table 9.6.

Table 9.5 Types of soup

Consommé	Clarified soup made from poultry, beef, game or vegetable bouillon. There are no traditional accompaniments to consommé although warmed sherry or sometimes Madeira might be added to the consommé in the restaurant just before serving.
Veloutés, crèmes and purées	Traditionally croutons were only offered with purées and Cream of Tomato soup, but they are now commonly offered with a range of soups.
Potages, broths and bisques	There are no traditional accompaniments offered here. Bisques are shellfish soups.

Consommé is usually served in consommé cups on a consommé saucer and set on a fish plate. Traditionally it is eaten with a sweet spoon but a soup spoon is acceptable. There are now a number of modern designs of soup bowls and saucers acceptable for the service of consommé.

Other soups are usually eaten from a soup plate/bowl, placed on its underplate, and eaten with a soup spoon. However, it is common today to see soup bowls of varying modern designs together with their underplate.

Table 9.6 National soups

Bortsch (Polish)	Duck-flavoured consommé garnished with duck, diced beef and turned root vegetables. The accompaniments are sour cream, beetroot juice and bouchées filled with duck pâté.
Bouillabaisse (French)	This is really a form of fish stew. Although a soup plate on its underplate and soup spoon is used, it is common for a side knife and sweet fork to also be laid as part of the cover. Thin slices of French bread, dipped in oil and grilled (sippets), are offered as well as rouille.
Chowder (USA)	Chowders are thick soups usually containing seafood, potatoes and cream or milk. The most well known is New England clam chowder made with potatoes, onion, bacon or salt pork, flour and clams. Served with clam cakes, which are deep fried balls of buttery dough with chopped clam inside.
Cock-a-leekie (Scottish)	Veal and chicken consommé garnished with shredded leeks and chicken. Served with prunes which may have been put into the soup plate at the service point.
Gazpacho (Spanish)	A cold, tomato-based soup. It contains tomatoes, onions, breadcrumbs, peppers, cucumber, garlic, ice water, sugar and spices. Croutons, diced cucumber, peppers, tomato and onion may all be offered as accompaniments.
Minestrone (Italian)	Vegetable paysanne soup with pasta. Traditional accompaniments are grated (shaved) Parmesan cheese and grilled flûtes.
Miso (Japanese)	Miso is a paste made from fermented soya beans. The soup is made by adding this paste to dashi soup stock. The stock itself is made from bonito flakes and konbu seaweed. Ingredients that provide contrasts such as spring onion and the delicate tofu, and those that float and sink such as potatoes and seaweed, may be paired together and offered as a garnish at the last moment.

Petit marmite (French)	Beef and chicken-flavoured soup garnished with turned root vegetables and dice of beef and chicken. Usually served in a special marmite pot, which resembles a small casserole. This marmite pot would sit on a doily on an underplate. A sweet spoon is used to eat this soup, as it is easier to get this spoon into the small pot. Accompaniments are grilled flûtes, poached bone marrow and grated (shaved) Parmesan cheese. Sometimes the bread and cheese are added as a croute on top of the soup before serving at the table.
Soupe à l'oignon (French)	French onion soup. May be served with grilled flûtes and grated (shaved) Parmesan cheese but is often topped with a slice of French bread gratinated with cheese.

9.4 Egg dishes

Egg dishes as separate courses have become less common in recent years. Omelettes have retained their popularity while dishes such as eggs en cocotte occasionally feature on menus. Table 9.7 gives some examples of egg dishes.

Table 9.7 **Egg dishes**

Œuf sur le plat	The egg is cooked in the oven in the œuf sur le plat dish (small, round, white earthenware or metal dish with two ears). A sweet spoon and fork are used but a side knife may be given, depending on the garnish.
Œuf en cocotte	The egg is cooked in the cocotte dish, in a bain-marie in the oven, and served in this dish with various garnishes. A cocotte dish is a small round earthenware dish with straight sides about the size of a small teacup. The dish is placed on an underplate and will be eaten with a teaspoon.
Omelettes	Two or three egg omelettes with various fillings. Omelettes can also be made just with egg whites. As a first course the omelette is eaten usually with a large fork. As a main course it would be eaten with a knife and fork.

9.5 Pasta and rice dishes

These dishes, which are also referred to as farinaceous dishes, include all pastas such as:

- spaghetti
- macaroni
- nouilles
- ravioli
- rice dishes such as pilaff or risotto
- other pasta dishes, such as gnocchi.

Grated Parmesan cheese is normally offered with all these dishes. Sometimes the Parmesan cheese is shaved from a large piece rather than grated.

Most pasta and rice dishes are now served plated. For spaghetti, a joint fork should be laid on the right hand side of the cover and a sweet spoon on the left. For all other farinaceous dishes a sweet spoon and fork are used, with the sweet spoon on the right and the fork on the left.

9.6 Fish dishes

Traditionally, fish dishes were eaten with a fish knife and fork but this practice is declining. For a fish course the lay-up is a hot fish plate and side knife and sweet fork. If fish is to be served as a main course, a hot joint plate with fish knife and fork or a joint knife and fork should be used. The general accompaniments for fish dishes are shown in Table 9.8.

Table 9.8 **Accompaniments for fish dishes**

Hot fish dishes with a sauce	Usually no accompaniments.
Hot fish dishes without a sauce	These often have Hollandaise or another hot butter-based sauce offered. Lemon segments may also be offered.
Fried fish which has been breadcrumbed (à l'Anglaise)	These dishes often have tartare sauce or another mayonnaise-based sauce offered, together with segments of lemon.
Fried or grilled fish dishes, not breadcrumbed	These dishes are usually offered with lemon. Sometimes sauces such as Hollandaise or tartare are offered.
Deep fried fish which has been dipped in batter (à l'Orly)	A (kitchen-made) tomato sauce is sometimes offered together with segments of lemon. Proprietary sauces can also be offered, as can vinegar if chips are being served.
Cold poached fish dishes	Usually mayonnaise or another mayonnaise-based sauce such as Sauce Verte is offered, together with segments of lemon.
Grilled Herring (hareng grillé)	Usually served with a mustard sauce.
Whitebait (blanchailles)	Accompaniments are cayenne pepper, peppermill, segments of lemon and brown bread offered with butter or alternatives.
Mussels (moules marinières)	Served with brown bread and butter, or more commonly now a variety of breads offered with butter or alternatives. Cayenne pepper may be offered.
Cold lobster (homard froid)	Lemon and sauce mayonnaise are the usual accompaniments.

9.7 Meats, poultry and game

Roast meats

In all cases roast gravy is offered. For dishes where the roast is plain (not roasted with herbs, for instance) the accompaniments are shown in Table 9.9.

Table 9.9 **Accompaniments for plain roast meats**

Roast beef (bœuf rôti)	Horseradish sauce, French and English mustards and Yorkshire pudding.
Roast lamb (agneau rôti)	Traditionally mint sauce, although redcurrant jelly is sometimes also offered.
Roast mutton (mouton rôti)	Traditionally redcurrant jelly, although mint sauce is sometimes also offered. An alternative traditional accompaniment is a white onion sauce.
Roast pork (porc rôti)	Apple sauce and sage and onion stuffing.
Veau rôti	Thickened roast gravy, lemon, parsley and thyme stuffing.

Boiled meats

Accompaniments for boiled meats are listed in Table 9.10.

Table 9.10 **Accompaniments for boiled meats**

Boiled mutton (mouton bouilli)	Caper sauce is traditionally served.
Salt beef (silverside)	Turned root vegetables, dumplings and the natural cooking liquor.
Boiled fresh beef (bœuf bouilli)	Turned root vegetables, natural cooking liquor, rock salt and gherkins.
Boiled ham (jambon bouilli)	Parsley sauce or white onion sauce.

Other meat dishes

Table 9.11 **Accompaniments for other meat dishes**

Irish stew	Accompaniments are Worcestershire sauce and pickled red cabbage.
Curry (kari)	Accompaniments are poppadums (crisp, highly seasoned pancakes), Bombay Duck (dried fillet of fish from the Indian Ocean) and mango chutney. Also offered is a Curry Tray, which will have items such as diced apple, sultanas, sliced bananas, yogurt and desiccated coconut.
Mixed grill and other grills	These dishes may be garnished with cress, tomato, straw potatoes and parsley butter. Various mustards (French and English) and sometimes proprietary sauces (tomato ketchup and brown sauce) are offered as accompaniments.
Steaks	As for mixed grill. Sauce Béarnaise is offered with Chateaubriand (double fillet) and sometimes with other grilled steaks.

Poultry, furred and feathered game

Table 9.12 **Accompaniments for poultry, furred and feathered game**

Poultry	
Roast chicken (poulet rôti farci)	The accompaniments are bread sauce, roast gravy, parsley and thyme stuffing, game chips, grilled bacon and watercress. Sage and onion stuffing is also used.
Roast duck (caneton rôti)	Sage and onion stuffing, apple sauce and roast gravy are served.
Wild duck (caneton sauvage rôti)	Roast gravy and traditionally an orange salad with an acidulated cream dressing is offered as a side dish.
Roast goose (oie rôti)	Sage and onion stuffing, apple sauce and roast gravy.
Roast turkey (dinde rôti)	Cranberry sauce, chestnut stuffing, chipolata sausages, game chips, watercress and roast gravy are the usual accompaniments.
Furred game	
Jugged hare	Heart-shaped croutons, forcemeat balls, redcurrant jelly and roast gravy.
Venison (venaison)	Cumberland sauce, redcurrant jelly and roast gravy. Sauce poivrade might also be offered.

Feathered game	
When roasted	The accompaniments for all feathered game such as partridge (perdreau), grouse (lagopède), woodcock (bécasse), quail (caille) and pheasant (faisan) are fried breadcrumbs, hot liver pâté spread on a croute on which the meat sits, bread sauce, game chips, watercress and roast gravy.

9.8 Potatoes, vegetables and salads

A wide variety of potatoes and vegetables, including salads, may be served with various main dishes and courses. These can be either:

- silver served onto the main plate alongside the main dish
- pre-plated onto the main plate alongside the main dish
- silver served onto a crescent-shaped dish or side plate, separate from the main plate, and which has been positioned at the top left hand corner of the cover. A separate sweet fork for the salad, and service spoon and fork for the potatoes and vegetables may be offered
- pre-plated onto a crescent-shaped dish or side plate, separate from the main plate, and then placed at the top left hand corner of the cover. A separate sweet fork for the salad, and service spoon and fork for the potatoes and vegetables may be offered
- placed on the table in multi-portion serving dishes from which customers can serve themselves, using service spoons and forks (family service).

Baked potato

A baked potato (pomme au four) accompanied by cayenne pepper, peppermill and butter (or substitutes). Butter is not now automatically put on the top of the potato, but is offered separately, together with alternatives.

Salads

Salads can be offered with a course and may also be eaten separately as a course. There are two main types of salad:

1. **Plain salads**, which consist of two main types. These may be either green salads made up of green leaf ingredients or vegetable salads made up of one main vegetable ingredient which will dominate the overall flavour of the dish. Plain salads may often be served with a main course or as a separate course after a main course. Various types of dressings are either included in the salad or offered separately.
2. **Compound salads**, which may be a plain salad plus other ingredients, such as meat, fish and mushrooms, or a combination of a number of ingredients, mixed together using specific dressings or sauces.

Table 9.13 **Examples of salads**

Française	Lettuce hearts, sections of skinned tomato, hard-boiled egg, with vinaigrette offered separately
Verte	Lettuce hearts, vinaigrette offered separately
Saison	Lettuce hearts plus other salad vegetables in season, vinaigrette offered separately
d'orange	Lettuce hearts, in sections, filleted orange, freshly made acidulated cream dressing

Mimosa	Lettuce hearts, filleted orange, grapes skinned and stoned, sliced banana, sprinkled with egg yolk, acidulated cream dressing offered separately
Russian	Macédoine of mixed cooked vegetables including potato, often decorated with other ingredients such as tomatoes, eggs, anchovies, lobster, ham and tongue and bound in mayonnaise sauce
Niçoise	French beans, tomato quarters, sliced potatoes, anchovies, capers, olives, vinaigrette
Endive	Hearts of lettuce, endive, sauce vinaigrette

All salads should be served chilled, crisp and attractive. Remember that a salad is not complete without a well-made salad dressing or sauce, such as vinaigrette or mayonnaise.

9.9 Cheese

Cheeses are distinguished by flavour and categorised according to their texture. They differ from each other for a number of reasons, mainly arising through variations in the making process. Differences occur in the rind and how it is formed and in the paste and the cooking process (relating here to both time and temperature). Cheeses also vary because the milk used comes from different animals such as cows, sheep and goats. The texture of a cheese depends largely on the period of maturation.

Storage

Dependent upon use, cheeses may be purchased either whole or pre-portioned. Cheese should be stored:

- in a cool, dark place, with good air circulation
- in a refrigerator
- with its original wrapping, otherwise it should be wrapped in either greaseproof paper, cling film or aluminium foil to prevent it drying out
- away from food items that absorb flavours/odours, such as dairy produce.

Categories

The recognised categories of cheese are:

- fresh
- soft
- semi-hard
- hard
- blue.

Table 9.14 Examples of cheeses within the five categories

Fresh cheese	
Cottage	Unripened low-fat, skimmed milk cheese with a granular curd. Originated in the USA and now has many variations.
Cream	Similar to cottage cheese but is made with full-fat milk. There are a number of different varieties available, some made from non-cow's milk.
Mozzarella	Italian cheese made from buffalo milk but may now also be made from cow's milk.
Ricotta	Italian cheese made from the whey of cow's milk. A number of other Italian varieties are available, made from sheep's milk.

Soft cheese	
Bel Paese	This light and creamy Italian cheese has a name that means 'beautiful country' and was first produced in 1929.
Brie	Famous French cheese made since the eighth century. Other countries now make this style of cheese, distinguishing it from the original French brie by the addition of the name of the country or county of origin, e.g. German brie, Somerset brie.
Camembert	Famous French cheese which is stronger and often more pungent than Brie.
Carré de l'est	A soft cheese produced in France that is made from pasteurised cow's milk, and packed in square boxes. Like Camembert, it softens on ripening and is darker in colour than Brie. When ripe it has a mild flavour.
Mont d'Or, Vacherin du Haut-doubs	Soft, slightly acidic, full-flavoured, herby, washed-rind cheese made from cow's milk. Vacherin Mont d'Or (Swiss) and Vacherin du Haut-doubs/Le Mont d'or (French) come from the Swiss/French border region. Only produced between 15 August and 31 March and therefore exclusive to the autumn and winter months. Sold in characteristic round pine or spruce wood boxes and traditionally served from the box, but may also be enjoyed directly from the box with a spoon.
Semi-hard cheese	
Caerphilly	Buttermilk-flavoured cheese with a soft paste. Some people will find it almost soapy. Originally a Welsh cheese but now manufactured all over Britain.
Cheddar	Classic British cheese now made all over the world and referred to as, e.g. Scottish cheddar, Canadian cheddar.
Cheshire	Crumbly, slightly salty cheese, available as either white or red. It was originally made during the 12th century in Cheshire but is now made all over Britain.
Edam	A Dutch cheese that is similar to, but harder than, Gouda. It has a fairly bland, buttery taste and a yellow or red wax coated rind. It is sometimes flavoured with cumin.
Emmenthal	The name of this Swiss cheese refers to the Emme Valley. It is similar to Gruyère, although it is softer and slightly less tasty.
Gloucester/Double Gloucester	Full-cream, classic English cheeses originally made only from the milk of Gloucestershire cows.
Gouda	Buttery textured, soft and mild-flavoured, well-known Dutch cheese with a yellow or red rind.
Gruyère	Mainly known as a Swiss cheese, but both the French and Swiss varieties can legally be called by this name. It has small pea-size holes and a smooth, relatively hard texture. The French varieties may have larger holes.
Jarlsberg	Similar to Emmenthal, this Norwegian cheese was first produced in the late 1950s. It has a yellow wax coating.
Lancashire	Another classic English cheese similar to Cheshire (white Cheshire is sometimes sold as Lancashire).
Leicester	Mild-flavoured and orange-coloured English cheese.
Monterey	Creamy, soft American cheese with many holes. A harder version known as Monterey Jack is suitable for grating.
Pont l'Evêque	Similar to Camembert, but square in shape, this French cheese originates from Normandy.

Port Salut	Mild-flavoured cheese with a name meaning 'Port of Salvation', referring to the abbey where exiled Trappist monks returned after the French Revolution.
Wensleydale	Yorkshire cheese originally made from sheep or goat's milk but now made from cow's milk. This cheese is the traditional accompaniment to apple pie.
Hard cheese	
Parmesan	Classic Italian hard cheese, more correctly called Parmigiano Reggiano. It is also known as the grated cheese used in and for sprinkling over Italian dishes, especially pasta, and also minestrone.
Provolone	Smoked cheese made in America, Australia and Italy. Now made from cow's milk but originally from buffalo milk. Younger versions are softer and milder than the longer-kept and more mature varieties.
Blue cheese	
Blue Cheshire	One of the finest of the blue cheeses which only becomes blue accidentally, although the makers endeavour to assist this process by pricking the cheese and maturing it in a favourable atmosphere.
Blue de Bresse	Fairly soft and mild-flavoured French cheese from the area between Soane-et-Loire and the Jura.
Danish Blue	One of the most well known of the blue cheeses. Softish and mild flavoured, it was one of the first European blue cheeses to gain popularity in Britain.
Dolcelatte	Factory-made version of Gorgonzola. The name is Italian for 'sweet milk' and the cheese is fairly soft with a creamy texture and greenish veining.
Dorset Blue	A strong, hard-pressed cheese, being close textured and made from skimmed milk. It is straw-coloured with deep blue veins, rather crumbly and has a rough rind.
Gorgonzola	Softish, sharp-flavoured, classic Italian cheese with greenish veining, which is developed with the addition of mould culture.
Roquefort	Classic, sheep's milk cheese from the southern Massif Central in France. The maturing takes place in caves, which provide a unique humid environment that contributes to the development of the veining.
Stilton	Famous and classic English cheese made from cow's milk. So called because it was noted as being sold in the Bell Inn at Stilton by travellers stopping there. According to legend it was first made by a Mrs Paulet of Melton Mowbray. The White Stilton has also become popular and is slightly less flavoursome than the blue variety.

Accompaniments

Accompaniments set on the table may include:

- cruet (salt, pepper, and mustard)
- butter or alternative
- celery served in a celery glass part filled with crushed ice, on an underplate
- radishes (when in season) placed in a glass bowl on an underplate with teaspoon
- caster sugar for cream cheeses
- assorted cheese biscuits (cream crackers, Ryvita, sweet digestive, water biscuits, etc.) or various breads.

Cheese is often served plated. The cover is a small/sweet knife and fork. Cheese may also be served from a selection presented on a cheese board or a cheese trolley. For service of cheese from a selection then the procedure would be as follows:

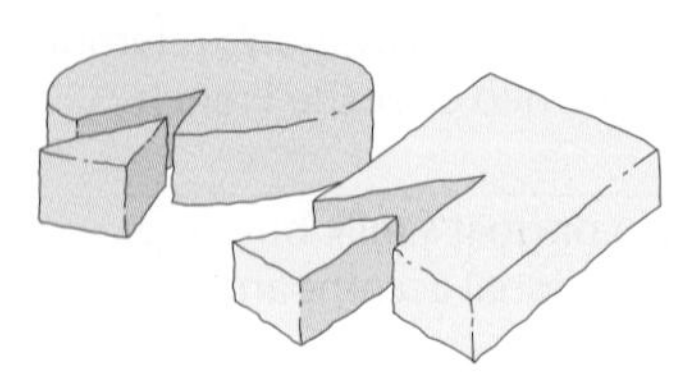

Round and square cheeses can be presented whole and then portioned by being cut into triangular pieces. Note that with square or oblong cheeses one of the cuts is at an angle.

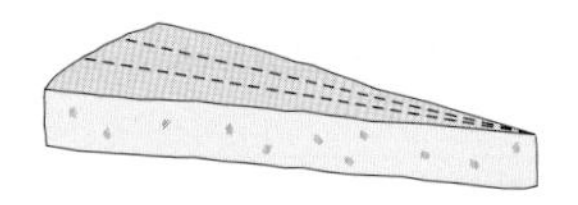

Brie or similar type cheeses may be either presented whole or cut into triangular slices and then portioned by being sliced (much like a cake) as required.

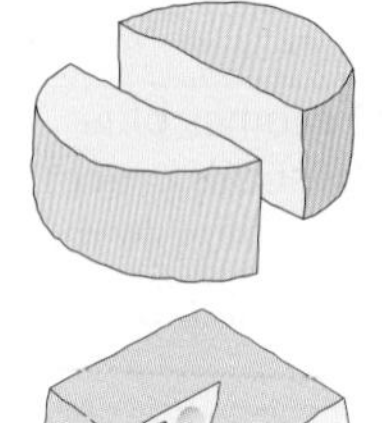

Small soft cheeses such as goat's cheeses may be presented whole and then portioned by being cut in half or quarter as the customer requests.

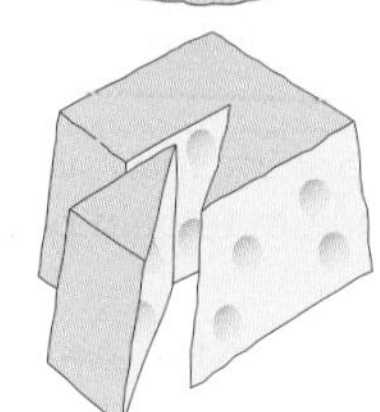

Flattened or pyramid shaped cheeses may be presented whole and then portioned by being cut into small triangles by keeping one side of each cut at an angle.

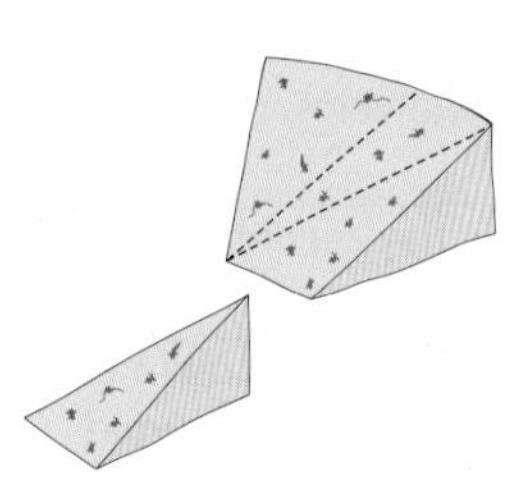

Largish wedges of blue cheeses can be cut from a cylinder or half cylinder of cheese for presentation, and these wedges are then cut into smaller wedges for service. Other cheeses bought in cylinders or half cylinders can be cut and presented for service and then portioned in the same way.

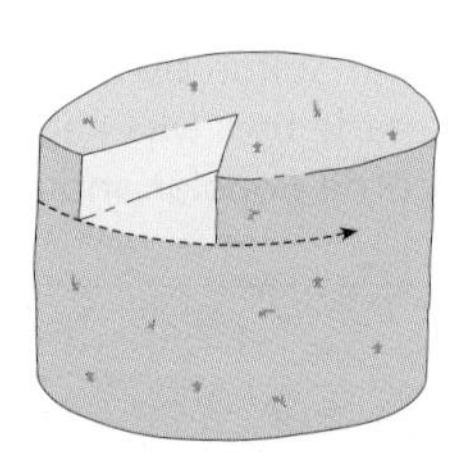

A cylinder (truckle) or half cylinder of cheese may also be presented whole and then portioned by individual wedges being cut from it. In order to do this the cheese is first cut around at about 25 to 30 cm. This is also an alternative to the tradition of Stilton being portioned by scooping the cheese out from the top of the cylinder after removing the top rind.

Figure 9.1 **Examples of methods for cutting, portioning and presenting cheeses**

Equipment

- Cheese board or cheese trolley
- Sufficient cheese knives for cutting and portioning the different cheeses
- Plates for the service of cheese – often a fish or sweet plate

Cover

- Fish or sweet-size plate
- Side knife and sometimes a small/sweet fork

Method

1 Ensure all the 'mise en place' (term meaning literally 'put in place' but also meaning preparation for service) is complete before commencing.
2 Check that all the cheeses on the trolley are known so as to be able to explain them to the customer.
3 Check cheeses are properly presented (if cheese is wrapped in foil this must be removed by the waiter before serving. The waiter should remove the cheese rind if it is not palatable (edible). This is not necessary in the case of Camembert and Brie as the rind of these two French cheeses is palatable.
4 Present the cheese board or trolley at the table.
5 Explain the cheeses available to the customer.
6 Cut or portion the cheeses and present on plates as required. Figure 9.1 gives examples of the methods for cutting, portioning and presenting.
7 Present in front of the customer and offer accompaniments at the table.

9.10 Sweets

The range of possible sweets is very extensive and varied. Examples of the range of sweet dishes are listed in Table 9.15.

Table 9.15 **Sweet dishes**

Bavarois, mousses, syllabubs	Either served in individual dishes or glassware or portioned and served
Charlottes	Moulds lined with sponge and filled with bavarois in various flavours and sometimes with fruits
Coupes and sundaes	Usually ice cream and various fruit combinations, served in coupe dishes or sundae dishes
Creams	Examples include Chantilly (sweetened whipped cream flavoured with vanilla), custard (Sauce Anglaise) and dishes such as Egg Custard or Crème Brûlée
Fritters (beignets)	For example, Beignets de pomme (apple)
Fruit dishes	Examples are fruit salads, poached fruits (compôte) and baked apples
Gâteaux	Examples include au chocolat (chocolate) and forêt noir (black forest)
Ices and sorbets	Ices refer to ice cream and frozen yogurt. Sorbets refer to water ices. Presented in various forms, including bombs (ice cream preparations made into bomb shapes using moulds)
Omelettes	With a variety of fillings and flavourings, e.g. rum, jam, or apple
Pancakes	With a variety of fillings, e.g. cherries or other fruits
Pies, flans and other pastries	Examples include flan aux poires (pear), Bakewell tart, Dutch apple pie
Puddings	Includes Bread and Butter, Cabinet, Diplomate and various fruit puddings
Soufflés	Can be served hot or cold and include soufflé au citron and soufflé au café

Sweets are often served plated or presented in a sweet dish such as a sundae glass. If served from a trolley then they are plated at the trolley. Cut portions of cakes or pies are normally put on the table so that the point is towards the customer.

There are no particular accompaniments to sweets. Often the customer may require a sugar sifter or, depending on the nature of the sweet selected, sauces such as custard or sauce à l'Anglaise may be offered. Alternatives to this might be single cream or double whipped cream.

9.11 Savouries

On the lunch and dinner menu a savoury may generally be served as an alternative to a sweet. In a banquet it may be a separate course served in addition to either a sweet or cheese course. Examples of savouries are given in Table 9.16.

Table 9.16 **Examples of savouries**

On toast	Usually shaped pieces of toast with various toppings such as anchovies, sardines, mushrooms, smoked haddock and the classic Welsh rarebit (toasted seasoned cheese, egg and Béchamel sauce mixture) or Buck rarebit (Welsh rarebit with a poached egg on the top).
Canapés or croûtes	Shaped pieces of bread about 6 mm (¼" inch) thick, brushed with melted butter and grilled, or may be shaped shallow fried bread. Examples include Scotch woodcock (scrambled egg, topped with a trellis of anchovies and studded with capers), Devils on horseback (prunes wrapped in bacon) and Angels on horseback (poached oysters wrapped in bacon).
Tartlettes	Round pastry cases with various fillings such as mushrooms, or cheese soufflé mixtures with various garnishes, or prawns or other fish in various sauces.
Barquettes	Filled boat-shaped pastry cases, similar to tartlettes.
Bouchées	Filled small, round puff pastry cases. A small edition of a vol-au-vent.
Omelettes	Two- and three-egg omelettes with various flavours/fillings such as parsley, anchovy, cheese or fines herbes (mixed herbs).
Soufflés	Made in a soufflé dish with various flavours such as mushroom, spinach, sardine, anchovy, smoked haddock or cheese.
Flans	Either single or portioned savoury flans such as Quiche Lorraine.

Savouries are usually pre-portioned by the kitchen and are served to the customer plated, after the cover has been laid and the accompaniments placed on the table. The cover for a savoury is usually a side knife and a sweet fork.

Accompaniments

The accompaniments are:

- salt and pepper
- cayenne pepper
- pepper mill
- Worcestershire sauce (usually only with meat savouries).

9.12 Dessert (fresh fruit and nuts)

Dessert may include all types of fresh fruits and nuts according to season, although the majority of the more popular items are now available all the year round. Some of the more popular items are dessert apples, pears, bananas, oranges, mandarins, tangerines, black and white grapes, pineapple and assorted nuts such as Brazils. Sometimes a box of dates may appear on the fruit basket.

Accompaniments

The following accompaniments should be set on the table:

- caster sugar holder on a sideplate
- salt for nuts.

CHAPTER
10
Non-alcoholic beverages

This chapter will help you to learn about:

1. Tea
2. Coffee
3. Chocolate
4. Other non-alcoholic beverages
5. Non-alcoholic bar beverages

10.1 Tea

Tea is prepared from the leaf bud and top leaves of a tropical evergreen bush called *Camellia sinensis*. It produces what is regarded as a healthy beverage, containing approximately only half the caffeine of coffee, and at the same time it aids muscle relaxation and stimulates the central nervous system.

The leaf particle size is referred to as grades. The main ones are:

- Pekoe (pecko) – the delicate top leaves
- Orange Pekoe – a rolled leaf with a slim appearance
- Pekoe Dust – the smallest particle of leaf size.

In between these grades there is a set of grades known as 'fannings'. In tea terminology, 'flush' refers to a picking, which can take place at different times of the year.

Tea-producing countries

Tea is grown in more than 25 countries around the world. The crop benefits from acidic soil, a warm climate and where there is at least 130 cm of rain a year. It is an annual crop and its flavour, quality and character is affected by the location, altitude, type of soil and climate. The main tea-producing countries are shown in Table 10.1.

Note: Teas are fermented (oxidised) during the process of manufacture, which gives them their black colour. The one exception is the China green tea.

Table 10.1 **Tea-producing countries**

China	Oldest tea-growing country and is known for speciality blends such as Keemun, Lapsang Souchong, Oolongs and green tea.
East Africa (Kenya, Malawi, Tanzania and Zimbabwe)	Produces good-quality teas, which are bright and colourful and used extensively for blending purposes. Kenya produces teas that are easily discernible and have a reddish or coppery tint and a brisk flavour.

India	Largest producer of tea, producing about 30 per cent of the world's tea. Best known are the teas from Assam (strong and full bodied), Darjeeling tea (delicate and mellow) and also Nilgiri, which is second only to Assam, and produces teas similar to those of Sri Lanka.
Indonesia	Produces light and fragrant teas with bright colouring when made and are used mainly for blending purposes.
Sri Lanka (formerly Ceylon)	Teas here are inclined to have a delicate, light lemon flavour. They are generally regarded as excellent afternoon teas and also lend themselves to being iced.

Purchasing tea

Most teas are blended teas sold under proprietary brands or names. Other teas, sometimes called speciality or premium teas, are sold by the name of the specific tea (see Table 10.2, Characteristics and service of teas, below). The word 'blend' indicates that a named tea may be composed of a variety of different teas to produce one marketable tea, which is acceptable to the average consumer taste. For instance, what is sometimes termed a standard tea may contain somewhere in the region of 15 different teas, and which would almost certainly include Indian tea for strength, African tea for colour and China tea for flavour and delicacy.

Tea may be purchased in a variety of forms depending on requirements such as:

- volume of production
- type of establishment
- clientele
- the occasion
- method of service
- storage facilities available
- cost.

The different means of purchasing are:

- **Bulk:** this is leaf tea (also called loose tea), which allows the traditional method of serving.
- **Tea bags:** these are heat-sealed and contain either standard or speciality teas. They come in one-cup, two-cup, and pot-for-one or bulk brew sizes up to several litres.
- **String and tag:** this comes as a one-cup teabag with string attached and a tag that remains outside the cup or teapot for easy and quick identification of the type of tea by the customer.
- **Envelopes:** this is again a string and tag teabag but in an envelope for hygienic handling. It is used for trays for in-room tea- and coffee-making facilities.
- **Instant:** instant tea granules, soluble in hot water.
- **Pods:** these are specially designed individual portions of tea that are used in proprietary tea and coffee makers. Each pod makes one portion of tea and the pod is then disposed of.

Storage

Tea should be kept:

- in a dry, clean and covered container
- in a well-ventilated area
- away from excess moisture
- away from any strong-smelling foods as it very quickly absorbs strong odours.

Making of tea

The type of tea used will of course depend on the customer's choice, but most establishments carry a varied stock of Indian, Ceylon, China and speciality teas, together with a variety of tisanes (fruit-flavoured teas and herbal infusions) available upon request.

The quantities of dry tea used per pot or per gallon may vary slightly with the type of tea used, but the following may be used as an approximate guide:

- 42.5–56.7 g (1½–2 oz) dry tea per 4.546 litres (1 gallon)
- ½ litre (1 pint) of milk will be sufficient for 20–24 cups
- ½ kilogram (1 lb) sugar for approximately 80 cups.

When brewing smaller amounts in the stillroom, such as a pot for one or two, it is often advisable to install a measure for the loose tea. This ensures standardisation of the brew and control on the amount of loose tea being used. Alternative methods of pre-portioning tea may also be used, such as tea bags.

When making tea in bulk and calculating quantities of tea required for a party, allow approximately ⅙ litre (⅓ pint) per cup or 24 cups per 4.546 litres (1 gallon). If breakfast cups are used, capacity approximately ¼ litre (½ pint), then allow only 16 cups to 4.546 litres (1 gallon).

Because tea is an infusion, the flavour is obtained by allowing the tea to brew. The following checklist will enable good results.

1. Heat the pot before putting in the dry tea so that the maximum heat can be obtained from the boiling water.
2. Measure the dry tea exactly.
3. Use freshly boiled water.
4. Make sure the water is boiling on entering the pot.
5. Allow the tea to brew for 3–6 minutes (depending on the type of tea) to obtain maximum strength from the brew.
6. Remove the tea leaves at the end of the brewing period if required, but especially if making the tea in multi-pot insulated urns.
7. Ensure all the equipment used is scrupulously clean.

Table 10.2 **Characteristics and service of teas**

Afternoon tea	Usually a blend of delicate Darjeeling tea and high-grown Ceylon tea to produce a refreshing and light tea. As the name of the blend suggests, this tea is suitable for afternoon tea but may be taken at any time. Served with milk or lemon and sugar offered separately.
Assam	Rich, full and malty flavoured tea, suitable for service at breakfast, usually with milk. Sugar would be offered separately.
China	Tea made from a special blend of tea that is more delicate in flavour and perfumed than any other tea. Less dry tea is required than for making Indian or Ceylon tea. Traditionally China tea is rarely served with milk. It is made in the normal way and is best made in a china pot. China tea is normally drunk on its own, but may be improved, according to taste, by the addition of a slice of lemon. Slices of lemon would be offered on a side plate with a sweet fork. Sugar may be offered separately.
Darjeeling	Delicate tea with a light grape flavour and known as the 'Champagne of teas'. Usually served as an afternoon or evening tea with either lemon or a little milk if preferred. Sugar may be offered separately.

Earl Grey	Blend of Darjeeling and China tea, flavoured with oil of Bergamot. Usually served with lemon or milk. Sugar would be offered separately.
English Breakfast	Often a blend of Assam and Kenya teas to make a bright, flavoursome and refreshing tea. Usually served as a breakfast tea but may be offered at any time. Usually served with milk but can also be taken with lemon. Sugar is offered separately.
Iced tea	This is strong tea that is made, strained and well chilled. The tea is then stored chilled until required. It is traditionally served in a glass, such as a tumbler. A slice of lemon may be placed in the glass and some additional lemon slices served separately as for Russian tea. Sugar may be offered.
Indian or Ceylon Blend	Indian or Ceylon Blend tea may be made in either china or metal teapots. These teas are usually offered with milk. Sugar is offered separately.
Jasmine	Green (unoxidised) tea that is dried with Jasmine Blossom and produces a tea with a fragrant and scented flavour.
Kenya	Consistent and refreshing tea usually served with milk. Sugar would be offered separately.
Lapsang Souchong	Smoky, pungent and perfumed tea, delicate to the palate and may be said to be an acquired taste. Usually served with lemon. Sugar would be offered separately.
Multi-pot	There are many occasions when tea has to be produced in bulk. Such occasions might be a reception tea, tea breaks in an industrial catering concern, or for functions catering for large numbers. In these instances tea may be made in multi-pots/urns, which may be described as teapots or urns, varying in capacity up to 25 litres (1 to 5 gallons). These containers have infusers which hold the required quantity of tea leaves for the size of pot/urn being used. The infuser would be placed in the pot/urn and freshly boiled water added. The mix would then be allowed to brew for a number of minutes – a maximum of 10 minutes for a 25-litre urn – and the infuser is then removed to ensure a good-quality product is served. The quantity of tea made should always relate to the number to be served – this will ensure minimum delay in the service and minimum wastage.
Russian or lemon tea	Tea that is brewed from a special blend similar to China tea, but is also often made from either Indian or Ceylon tea. It is made in the normal way and is usually served with a slice of lemon. The tea is served in quarter litre (half pint) glasses, which stand in a silver holder with a handle and on a side plate with a teaspoon. A slice of lemon may be placed in the glass and a few slices of lemon served separately. Sugar would be served separately.
Sri Lanka	Makes a pale golden tea with a good flavour. Ceylon blend is still used as a trade name. Served with lemon or milk. Sugar would be offered separately.
Tisanes	These are fruit-flavoured teas and herbal infusions which are often used for medicinal purposes and are gaining in popularity with trends towards healthier eating and drinking. Often these do not contain caffeine. Examples are: *Herbal teas*: • camomile • peppermint • rosehip • mint *Fruit teas*: • cherry • lemon • blackcurrant • mandarin orange These teas are usually made in china pots or can be made by the cup or glass. Sometimes served with sugar.

10.2 Coffee

The trees that produce coffee are of the genus *Coffea*, which belongs to the *Rubiaceae* family. There are somewhere in the region of 50 different species, although only two of these are commercially significant. These are known as *Coffea arabica* and *Coffea canephora*, which is usually referred to as *Robusta*. Arabica accounts for some 75 per cent of world production.

The coffee tree is an evergreen shrub, which reaches a height of two to three metres when cultivated. The fruit of the coffee tree are known as the 'cherries' and these are about 1.5 cm in length and have an oblong shape. A cherry usually contains two coffee seeds. The coffee tree will not begin to produce fruit until it is 3–5 years old and it will then usually yield good crops for up to 15 years.

Coffee-producing countries

Coffee is a natural product grown in many countries of the tropical and sub-tropical belt in South and Central America, Africa and Asia. It is grown at different altitudes in different climates and in different soils and is looked upon as an international drink consumed throughout the world. Brazil is the world's largest grower of coffee, Columbia is second, the Ivory Coast third and Indonesia fourth.

Purchasing coffee

The different means of purchasing coffee are:

- **Bulk:** (either as beans or in vacuum packs of pre-ground beans) allowing for the traditional methods of making and serving.
- **Coffee bags:** these are heat-sealed and come in one-cup, two-cup, pot-for-one or bulk brew sizes up to several litres.
- **Instant:** coffee granules, soluble in hot water and available in sizes from one cup to pot size.
- **Individual filters:** vacuum packed and containing one portion.
- **Pods:** these are specially designed individual portions of pre-ground coffee that are used in proprietary coffee and tea makers. Each pod makes one portion of coffee and the pod is then disposed of.

The blend

Companies who sell coffee have their own blending experts whose task it is to ensure that the quality and taste of their particular coffee brand is consistent, despite the fact that the imported beans will vary from shipment to shipment.

Samples of green coffee beans are taken from bags in the producing countries and the port of arrival. The samples are sent to prospective buyers whose experts roast, brew and taste samples to test their quality before deciding on the type of blend for which the particular coffee is suitable.

The roasting

Most brands of coffee sold in shops are, in fact, a blend of two or more batches of beans. Because they have no smell or taste, green beans have to be roasted in order to release the coffee aroma and flavour. The roasting process should give a uniform colour. The outputs from different 'roastings' are used to form different blends.

The common degrees of roasting are:

- **Light or pale roastings:** suitable for mild beans to preserve their delicate aroma.

- **Medium roastings:** give a stronger flavour and are often favoured for coffees with well-defined character.
- **Full roastings:** popular in many Latin countries, they have a bitter flavour.
- **High roasted coffee:** accentuates the strong bitter aspects of coffee, although much of the original flavour is lost.

Commercial coffee roasters can either convert the beans into instant (soluble) coffee or prepare them for sale as roasted or ground beans. The higher the roast, the less acidity and the more bitterness there is in the coffee.

Certain coffees also have flavourings added, either in the blend or during the process of making. Examples of these include:

- Turkish coffee – vanilla
- French coffee – chicory
- Viennese coffee – fig.

The grind

Roasted coffee must be ground before it can be used to make the brew. Coffee is ground to different grades of fineness to suit the many different methods of brewing. The most suitable grinds for some common methods of brewing coffee are shown below.

Method	**Grinding grade**
Cafetière	Medium
Espresso	Very fine
Filter/Drip	Fine to medium
Jug	Coarse
Percolator	Medium
Turkish	Pulverised
Vacuum infusion	Medium-fine to fine

Storage

Some tips for storing coffee:

- Store in a well-ventilated storeroom.
- Use an airtight container for ground coffee to ensure that the oils do not evaporate, causing loss of flavour and strength.
- Keep coffee away from excess moisture.
- Do not store near any strong-smelling foods or other substances, as coffee will absorb their odours.

Making coffee

Methods of brewing can vary, ranging from instant coffee brewed by the cup, through to 1½–3 litre (3–6 pints) units and up to machines that may produce large quantities for functions. Coffee beans may be purchased and then ground according to requirements. The beans should not be ground until immediately before they are required as this will ensure the maximum flavour and strength from the oils within the coffee bean. If ground coffee is purchased it normally comes in vacuum-packed packets in order to maintain its qualities until use. These packets contain set quantities to make 4.5 litres (1 gallon) and 9 litres (2 gallons), and so on.

When making coffee in bulk, 283.5–340 g (10–12 oz) of ground coffee is sufficient to make 4.5 litres (1 gallon) of black coffee.

- Assuming that cups with a capacity of ⅓ pint will be used then 283.5–340 g (10–12 oz) of ground coffee is sufficient to provide 24 cups of black coffee or 48 cups if serving half coffee and half milk.
- When breakfast cups are used then 16 cups of black coffee or 32 cups of half coffee and half milk will be available.
- Capacity, at a dinner where demi-tasse 10 cl (⅙ pint) cups are used, is 48 cups of black coffee or 96 cups half black coffee and half milk.

The rules to be observed when making coffee in bulk are as follows:

- Use freshly roasted and ground coffee.
- Buy the correct grind for the type of machine in use.
- Ensure all equipment is clean before use.
- Use a set measure of coffee to water: 283.5–340 g per 4.5 litres (10–12 oz per gallon).
- Add boiling water to the coffee and allow to infuse.
- The infusion time must be controlled according to the type of coffee being used and the method of making.
- Control the temperature since to boil coffee is to spoil coffee (it will develop a bitter taste).
- Strain and serve.
- Offer milk (hot or cold) or cream separately and sugar and alternatives.
- The best serving temperatures are 82°C (180°F) for coffee and 68°C (155°F) for milk.

Characteristics of good coffee

Coffee should have:

- good flavour
- good aroma
- good colour when milk or cream are added – not grey
- good body.

Reasons for bad coffee

Weak coffee

- Water has not reached boiling point
- Insufficient coffee used
- Infusion time too short
- Stale or old coffee used
- Incorrect grind of coffee used for equipment in operation

Stale or lifeless coffee

- All points for weak coffee listed above
- Coffee kept too long before use or kept at wrong temperature
- Dirty equipment
- Water not fresh
- Coffee reheated

Bitter coffee

- Too much coffee used
- Infusion time too long
- Coffee not roasted correctly
- Sediment remaining in storage or serving compartment
- Infusion at too high a temperature
- Coffee may have been made and kept hot too long before being used

Coffee-making methods

Coffee may be made in many ways and the service depends on the method used. A description of the main methods is given below.

Instant

This may be made in individual coffee or teacups, or in large quantities. It involves the mixing of soluble coffee solids with boiling water. When making instant coffee in bulk, approximately 71 g (2½ oz) to each 4.5 litres (one gallon) of water should be allowed. This form of coffee may be made very quickly, immediately before it is required, by pouring freshly boiled water onto a measured quantity of coffee powder. Stir well.

Figure 10.1 **Coffee-brewing methods (clockwise from top): pour through filter machine, single filter, Turkish/Greek/Arabic coffee, jug and plunger/cafetière**

La cafetière (coffee maker)

La cafetière, or jug and plunger method, makes coffee simply and quickly by the infusion method and to order. This ensures that the flavour and aroma of the coffee are preserved. La cafetière comes in the form of a glass container with a lip held in a black, gold or chrome-finished holder and sealed with a lid which also holds the plunger unit in position.

The method of making is completed simply by adding boiling water to the ground coffee, stirring and then placing the plunger unit and lid in position. A guideline to the quantity of coffee to be used might be:

- 2 level sweet spoonfuls for the 3-cup size
- 6 level sweet spoonfuls for the 8-cup size
- 9 level sweet spoonfuls for the 12-cup size.

Infusion time is from 3 to 5 minutes. During this time the coffee grains will rise to the top of the liquid. After this if the plunger is moved slightly the coffee grains will fall to the bottom of the glass container. When the grains have fallen it is easier to push the plunger down.

Filter (café filtre)

This is a method originating from and traditionally used in France and may be made individually in the cup or in bulk. The filter method produces excellent coffee. Fresh boiled water is poured into a container with a very finely meshed bottom, which stands on a cup or pot. Within the container is the required amount of ground coffee. The infusion takes place and the coffee liquid falls into the cup/pot below. Filter papers may be used to avoid the grounds passing into the lower cup, but this will depend on how fine or coarse the ground coffee being used is. There are now many electronic units available of differing capacities. Cold water is poured into a reservoir and is brought to boiling point and then dripped onto the ground coffee.

Pour-through filter method

This is an excellent method of making filter coffee, which has increased in popularity over the past few years. Many of these pour-through filter machines are available for purchase, or on loan from a number of the main coffee suppliers.

The principle behind this method is that when the measured quantity of freshly drawn water is poured into the top of the pour-through filter machine this water displaces the hot water already in the machine. This hot water infuses with the ground coffee and runs into the serving container as a coffee liquid ready for immediate use. It takes approximately 3–4 minutes to make one brew.

When coffee is made by this method, ensure that:

- the machine is plugged in and switched on at the mains
- the brew indicator light is on. This tells the operator that the water already held in the machine is at the correct temperature for use
- the correct quantity of fresh ground coffee, which will usually come in the form of a vacuum-sealed pack, is used. A fresh pack should be used for each new brew of filter coffee being made
- a new clean filter paper is used for each fresh brew.

Individual filter

This is an alternative way of making bulk filter coffee. It is a disposable plastic individual filter, bought with the required amount of coffee already sealed in the base of the filter. Each individual filter is sufficient for one cup and after use the whole filter is thrown away. The advantage of this method is that every cup may be made to order. It appeals to customers, as they are able to see that they are receiving entirely fresh coffee and it also has a certain novelty value.

When making a cup of coffee by this method, the individual filter is placed onto a cup. Freshly boiled water is then poured into the individual filter to the required level. The liquid then infuses with the ground coffee within the individual filter and drips into the cup. A lid should be placed over the water in the filter to help retain the temperature. Time of making is approximately 3–4 minutes.

Espresso

This method is Italian in origin. The machines used in making this form of coffee can provide cups of coffee individually in a matter of seconds, some machines being capable of making 300–400 cups of coffee per hour.

Figure 10.2 **Espresso machine**

The method involves passing steam through the finely ground coffee and infusing under pressure. The advantage is that each cup is made freshly for the customer. Served black, the coffee is known as espresso and is served in a small cup. If milk is required, it is heated for each cup by a high-pressure steam injector and transforms a cup of black coffee into cappuccino. As an approximate guide, from 12 kg (1 lb) of coffee used, 80 cups of good-strength coffee may be produced. The general rules for making coffee apply here, but with this special and delicate type of equipment extra care should be taken in following any instructions.

Still-set

This method normally consists of a small central container into which the correct sized filter paper is placed. A second, fine-meshed metal filter with a handle is then placed on the filter paper and the ground coffee placed on top of this. There is an urn on either side of varying capacities according to requirements. The urns may be 4½, 9, 13 or 18 litres (1, 2, 3 or 4 gallons) in size.

Figure 10.3 **Modern still-set**

These still-sets are easy to operate, but must be kept very clean at all times and regularly serviced. The urns should be rinsed before and after each brew until the water runs clear. This removes the thin layer of cold coffee that clings to the side of the urn that, if left, will spoil the flavour and aroma of the next brew.

Boiling water is passed through the grounds and the coffee passes into the urn at the side. Infusion should be complete in 6–8 minutes for 4½ litres (1 gallon) of coffee, using medium-ground coffee. The milk is heated in a steam jacket container. It should be held at a constant temperature of 68°C because if held at too high a temperature or boiled or heated too soon, on coming into contact with the coffee it will destroy its flavour and taste. At the same time, the milk itself becomes discoloured. The coffee and milk should be held separately, at their correct temperatures, ready for serving.

Decaffeinated

Coffee contains caffeine, which is a stimulant. Decaffeinated coffee is made from beans after the caffeine has been extracted. The coffee is made in the normal way.

Figure 10.4 **Examples of insulated jugs and dispensers for coffee and tea service (images courtesy of Elia®)**

Iced coffee

Strong black coffee should be made in the normal way. It is then strained, chilled well and stored in the refrigerator until required. It may be served mixed with an equal quantity of cold milk for a smooth beverage, or with cream, and is often served in a glass.

Turkish or Egyptian coffees

These are made from darkly roasted mocha beans, which are ground to a fine powder. The coffee is made in special copper pots, which are placed on top of a stove or lamp, and the water is then allowed to boil. The sugar should be put in at this stage to sweeten the coffee, as it is never stirred once poured out. The finely ground coffee may be stirred in or the boiling water poured onto the grounds. The amount of coffee used is approximately one heaped teaspoonful per person.

Once the coffee has been stirred in, the copper pot is taken off the direct heat and the cooling causes the grounds to settle. It is brought to the boil and allowed to settle twice more and is then sprinkled with a little cold water to settle any remaining grains. The coffee is served in small cups. While making the coffee it may be further flavoured with vanilla pods but this is optional.

Irish and other speciality coffees

Speciality coffees are often completed and served at the table using the following equipment:

- service salver
- tray cloth or napkin
- 20 cl (7 fl oz) stemmed glass on a side plate
- teaspoon
- jug of double cream
- 25 ml measure
- coffee pot
- sugar basin of coffee sugar with a teaspoon
- bottle of the spirit or liqueur being used.

The procedure for making Irish coffee is:

1. A Paris goblet or other suitable stemmed glass of about 20 cl (7 fl oz) capacity is used.
2. Brown sugar is added first (a certain amount of sugar is always required when serving this form of coffee, as it is an aid to floating the double cream on the surface of the hot coffee).
3. One measure of Irish whiskey is added.
4. The teaspoon is then placed in the goblet before the coffee is poured into the glass. This is so the spoon will help to conduct the heat and avoid cracking the bowl of the glass as the hot, strong black coffee is poured in.
5. The coffee should then be stirred well to dissolve the sugar and to ensure the ingredients are blended. The liquid should now be within 2½ cm (1 in) of the top of the glass. The liquid may still be swirling but not too much, as this will tend to draw the cream down into the coffee as it is poured.
6. The double cream should be poured slowly over the back of a teaspoon onto the surface of the coffee until it is approximately 1.9 cm (¾ in) thick. The coffee must not be stirred: the best flavour is obtained by drinking the whiskey-flavoured coffee through the cream.
7. When the Irish coffee has been prepared, the glass should be put on a doily on a side plate and placed in front of the customer.

Figure 10.5 **Tray laid for the service of Irish coffee**

Other forms of speciality, or liqueur, coffees include:

Café Royale or *Café Parisienne*:	Brandy	*Jamaican coffee or Caribbean coffee*:	Rum
Monk's coffee:	Bénédictine	*Calypso coffee*:	Tia Maria
Russian coffee:	Vodka	*Highland coffee*:	Scotch whisky
Seville coffee:	Cointreau	*Swiss coffee*:	Kirsch

Table 10.3 **Various modern coffee styles**

Filter (filtre)	Traditional method of making coffee. Often served with hot or cold milk or cream
Cafetière	Popular method of making and serving fresh coffee in individual or multi-portion jugs. Often served with hot or cold milk or cream
Espresso	Traditional short, strong black coffee
Espresso doppio	Double espresso served in larger cup
Café crème	Regular coffee prepared from fresh beans, ground fresh for each cup, resulting in a thick cream-coloured, moussy head
Espresso ristretto	Intense form of espresso, often served with a glass of cold water in continental Europe
Americano	Espresso with added hot water to create regular black coffee. May also be regular black coffee made using filter method
Espresso macchiato	Espresso spotted with a spoonful of hot or cold milk or hot milk foam
Espresso con panna	Espresso with a spoonful of whipped cream on top
Cappuccino	Espresso coffee topped with steamed frothed milk, often finished with a sprinkling of chocolate (powdered or grated)
Caffè (or café) latte	Shot of espresso plus hot milk, with or without foam
Flat white	Double shot of espresso topped with frothed milk which has been stirred together with the flat milk from the bottom of the jug, to create a creamy rather than frothy texture
Latte macchiato	Steamed milk spotted with a drop of espresso
Caffè mocha (or mochaccino)	Chocolate compound (syrup or powder) followed by a shot of espresso. The cup or glass is then filled with freshly steamed milk topped with whipped cream and cocoa powder

Iced coffee	Chilled regular coffee, sometimes served with milk or simply single espresso topped up with ice cold milk
Turkish/Egyptian	Intense form of coffee made in special jugs with finely ground coffee
Decaffeinated	Coffee with caffeine removed. Can be used as alternative to prepare the service styles listed above
Instant coffee	Coffee made from processed powder (often freeze dried). Regular and decaffeinated styles are available

10.3 Chocolate

Chocolate and cocoa come from the fruit of the plant *Theobroma cacao*, in the form of beans containing up to 25–30 white seeds. This cocoa plant is grown in countries as far afield as Mexico, Central and South America, West Africa and Asia.

Production process

The seeds are fermented, dried, shipped abroad, and then roasted, blended, and pressed or ground for use as powdered or solid products. They then become cocoa powder, drinking chocolate, eating chocolate and couverture chocolate used for decorating purposes.

Beverage preparation

This beverage is very popular and may come sweetened or non-sweetened, and as a powder or soluble granules. It may be mixed with hot water or hot milk. Whipped cream, from a whipped cream dispenser, marshmallows or a sprinkling of powdered chocolate may be added upon request.

Product characteristics

The characteristics of these beverages may vary according to the exact ingredients used and in what proportions. This has an impact on:

- flavour
- consistency
- sweetness/bitterness
- milkiness/smoothness
- overall presentation.

Some products on the market only have to be mixed with hot water as dried skimmed milk and milk proteins are among the ingredients making up the product.

Purchasing and storage

These drinking chocolate products may come in individual vacuum-sealed packs, or pods for use with electronic beverage-making machines or in containers of varying sizes to suit demand and turnover. When not in use, these containers should be kept airtight, in cool, dry and well-ventilated conditions and away from excess moisture and sunlight.

Hygiene

All equipment used should be thoroughly cleaned and sterilised on a daily basis. The manufacturer's cleaning instructions should always be adhered to. Checklists are a great help here to ensure continuity of the cleaning process because staff may change due to shift work and the opening hours of an establishment.

Potential problems

Any problems arising concerning the beverage produced may be due to:

- incorrect amount of drinking chocolate (powder or granules) to liquid (water or milk), thus consistency and strength will be affected
- the temperature of the liquid used is not sufficient to dissolve the powder or granules
- poor storage has affected the commodity being used
- lack of the correct cleaning processes may result in lack of steam, no power, leaks, or excess limescale build-up in the equipment being used.

10.4 Other non-alcoholic beverages

Other beverages may be offered for service and are often made in the still room. These include proprietary drinks such as Horlicks, Ovaltine and Bovril. They should all be prepared and served according to the maker's instructions.

If milkshakes are requested, then the following basic ingredients are required:

- chilled milk
- syrups (flavourings) (see Section 10.5, page 179)
- ice cream.

These may be served from either the still room or the bar after making in a mixer or blender.

10.5 Non-alcoholic bar beverages

Non-alcoholic dispense bar beverages may be classified into five main groups:

1. aerated waters
2. natural spring/mineral waters
3. squashes
4. juices
5. syrups.

Aerated waters

These beverages are charged (or aerated) with carbon dioxide gas. Artificial aerated waters are by far the most common. The flavourings found in different aerated waters are obtained from various essences.

Examples of aerated waters are:

- **soda water:** colourless and tasteless
- **tonic water:** colourless and quinine flavoured
- **dry ginger:** golden straw-coloured with a ginger flavour
- **bitter lemon:** pale, cloudy yellow-coloured with a sharp lemon flavour.

Other flavoured waters which come under this heading are:

- 'fizzy' lemonades
- orange
- ginger beer
- cola, etc.

Aerated waters are available in bottles and cans and many are also available as post-mix. The term post-mix indicates that the drink mix of syrup and the carbonated (filtered) water is mixed after (post) leaving the syrup container, rather than being pre-mixed (or ready-mixed) as in canned or bottled soft drinks. The post-mix drinks are served from hand-held dispensing guns at the bar. These have buttons on the dispensing gun to select the specific drink.

The key advantage of the post-mix system is the saving on storage space, especially for a high-turnover operation. Dispensing systems need regular cleaning and maintenance to ensure that they are hygienic and working properly.

The proportions of the mix need to be checked regularly: too little syrup and the drinks will lack taste; too much syrup and the flavours become too strong.

Natural spring waters/mineral waters

The European Union has divided bottled water into two main types: mineral water and spring water.

- Mineral water has a mineral content (which is strictly controlled).
- Spring water has fewer regulations, apart from those concerning hygiene.

Waters can be still, naturally sparkling or carbonated during bottling.

Bottle sizes for mineral and spring waters vary considerably from, for example, 1.5 l to 200 ml. Some brand names sell in both plastic and glass bottles, while other brands prefer either plastic or glass bottles depending on the market and the size of container preferred by that market.

Table 10.4 **Examples of mineral waters**

Name	Type	Country
Appollinaris	Naturally sparkling	Germany
Badoit	Slightly sparkling	France
Buxton	Still or carbonated	England
Contrex	Still	France
Evian	Still	France
Perrier	Sparkling and also fruit-flavoured	France
San Pellegrino	Carbonated	Italy
Spa	Still, naturally sparkling and also fruit-flavoured	Belgium
Vichy	Naturally sparkling	France
Vittel	Naturally sparkling	France
Volvic	Still	France

Table 10.5 **Examples of spring waters**

Name	Type	Country
Ashbourne	Still or carbonated	England
Ballygowen	Still or sparkling	Ireland
Highland Spring	Still or carbonated	Scotland
Llanllry	Still or sparkling	Wales
Malvern	Still or carbonated	England
Strathmore	Still or sparkling	Scotland

Natural spring waters are obtained from natural springs in the ground, the waters themselves being impregnated with the natural minerals found in the soil and sometimes naturally charged with an aerating gas.

The value of these mineral waters, as they are sometimes termed, has long been recognised by the medical profession. Where natural spring waters are found, there is usually what is termed a spa, where the waters may be drunk or bathed in according to the cures they are supposed to effect. Many of the best-known mineral waters are bottled at the spring (bottled at source).

Recently there has been a shift in consumer demand for bottled waters. The reasons for this include:

- environmental and sustainability concerns. In some cases demand has reduced considerably. Regular utility tap water, from safe commercial supplies, has become more popular in food service operations and customers increasingly expect this to be available, chilled or served with ice
- the emergence of commercial filter systems being used by foodservice operations. Utility supplied tap water is filtered at the establishment and then offered either as chilled still or sparking water in branded carafes or bottles, for which the establishment makes a charge.

Squashes

A squash may be served on its own diluted by water, soda water or lemonade. Squashes are also used as mixers for spirits and in cocktails, or used as the base for such drinks as fruit cups. Examples are:

- orange squash
- lemon squash
- grapefruit squash
- lime juice.

Juices

The main types of juices held in stock in the dispense bar are:

Bottled or canned

- Orange juice
- Pineapple juice
- Grapefruit juice
- Tomato juice

Fresh

- Orange juice
- Grapefruit juice
- Lemon juice

Apart from being served chilled on their own, these fresh juices may also be used in cocktails and for mixing with spirits.

Syrups

The main uses of these concentrated, sweet, fruit flavourings are as a base for cocktails, fruit cups or mixed with soda water as a long drink. The main ones used are:

- *Cassis* (blackcurrant)
- *Cerise* (cherry)
- *Citronelle* (lemon)
- *Framboise* (raspberry)
- *Gomme* (white sugar syrup)
- *Grenadine* (pomegranate)
- *Orgeat* (almond).

Syrups are also available as 'flavouring agents' for cold milk drinks such as milkshakes.

Information on the service of non-alcoholic bar beverages may be found in Chapter 16, Section 16.6, page 289.

CHAPTER 11

Alcoholic beverages

This chapter will help you to learn about:

1. Alcoholic strength
2. Safe, sensible drinking
3. Cocktails and mixed drinks
4. Bitters
5. Wine
6. Spirits
7. Liqueurs
8. Beer
9. Cider and perry
10. Tasting techniques
11. Matching food with wine and other drinks

11.1 Alcoholic strength

Although there are various types of alcohol, the two main ones are methyl alcohol (methanol) and ethyl alcohol (ethanol). Methanol is used for various industrial purposes but is a dangerous poison when drunk; alcoholic beverages are drinks that contain ethanol. Alcoholic beverages are divided into three general classes: beers, wines and spirits.

The two main scales of measurement of alcoholic strength may be summarised as:

- OIML Scale (European): range 0% to 100% alcohol by volume.
- American Scale (USA): range 0° to 200°.

The Organisation Internationale Métrologie Légale (OIML) Scale (previously called Gay Lussac Scale) is directly equal to the percentage of alcohol by volume in the drink at 20°C. It is the universally accepted scale for the measurement of alcohol. The by volume measurement indicates the amount of pure alcohol in a liquid. Thus, a liquid measured as 40% alcohol by volume will have 40 per cent of the contents as pure alcohol (under the American Scale, alcoholic strength of 80° equals 40 per cent by volume). The alcoholic content of drinks, by volume, is now almost always shown on the label. Table 11.1 gives the approximate alcoholic strength of a variety of drinks.

Table 11.1 **Approximate alcoholic strength of drinks (OIML scale)**

0%	non-alcoholic
not more that 0.05%	alcohol free
0.05–0.5%	de-alcoholised
0.5–1.2%	low alcohol
1.2–5.5%	reduced alcohol
3–6%	beer, cider, FABs* and 'alcopops'** with any of these being up to 10%
8–15%	wines, usually around 10–13%
14–22%	fortified wines (liqueur wines) such as sherry and port, aromatised wines such as vermouth, vin doux naturels (such as Muscat de Beaumes-de-Venise) and Sake***
37.5–45%	spirits, usually at 40%
17–55%	liqueurs, very wide range
* FABs is a term used to describe flavoured alcoholic beverages, e.g. Bacardi Breezer (5.4%).	
** 'Alcopops' is a term used to describe manufactured flavoured drinks (generally sweet and fruity) which have had alcohol, such as gin, added to them. They are also known as alcoholic soft drinks or alcoholic lemonade. Usually 3.5 to 5% but can be up to 10%.	
*** Sake is a strong (18%), slightly sweet form of beer made from rice.	

11.2 Safe, sensible drinking

Most people who drink alcohol do so for many reasons: to quench a thirst, as a relaxant or simply because it is enjoyable. A small amount of alcohol does no harm and can even be beneficial. However, the more you drink and the more frequently you drink, the greater the health risks.

Alcohol depresses the brain and nerve function, affecting a person's judgement, self-control and skills. The four general stages of becoming drunk are:

Stage 1: Happy (relaxed, talkative and sociable).
Stage 2: Excited (erratic and emotional; movement and thinking affected).
Stage 3: Confused (disorientated, loud, out of control).
Stage 4: Lethargic (unable to stand, talk or walk).

Most of the alcohol consumed passes into the bloodstream from where it is rapidly absorbed. This absorption may be slowed down if drink is accompanied by food but the amount of alcohol consumed will be the same. The liver must then burn up almost all the alcohol consumed, with the remainder being disposed of in urine or perspiration. It takes approximately one hour for the liver to burn up one unit of alcohol; if it has to deal with too much alcohol over a number of years, it will inevitably suffer damage.

Sensible limits

So what are the sensible limits to avoid damage to health? Of course, not drinking alcohol cuts out any risk. However, medical opinion in the UK has set the limit at 21 units spread throughout the week for men and 14 units spread throughout the week for women (excluding pregnant women). Drinking in excess of these limits is likely to be damaging to health.

One unit of alcohol is equal to 10 millilitres (liquid) or 8 grams (weight) of alcohol. This is roughly equivalent to:

- ½ pint of ordinary beer or lager
- one glass of wine (125 ml)
- one glass of sherry (50 ml)
- one measure of vermouth or other aperitif (50 ml)
- one measure of spirits (25 ml).

It is important to note the following, however:

- Some extra-strength lagers and beer have two or three times the strength of ordinary beers. Remember too that some low-calorie beers can contain more alcohol than their ordinary equivalents.
- The number of units required to reach the maximum permitted levels for driving varies between individuals but it can be as little as three units.
- Some alcohol remains in the bloodstream for up to 18 hours after consumption. This should be considered in relation to the legal limits for alcohol in the blood when driving.
- There are about 100 calories in a single unit of alcohol. The amount of calories quickly adds up and can lead to weight gain. Replacing food with alcohol as a source of calories denies the body essential nutrients and vitamins.

Calculating alcohol intake

The amount of alcohol being consumed is a measure of both the strength of the alcoholic drink and the amount or volume of the drink being consumed.

To calculate the alcohol unit intake for wines:

Wine at a specific percentage of alcohol by volume multiplied by the amount in litres equals the units of alcohol per bottle. For example:

- Wine at 12% alcohol by volume × 0.75 cl bottle = 9 units per 0.75 cl bottle. Therefore this 0.75 cl bottle of wine will give 6 × 125 ml individual glasses of wine and each glass will contain 1.5 units of alcohol (9 units in the whole bottle divided by the 6 glasses).

Further examples for calculating the alcohol unit intake for other drinks are:

- Lager at 5% alcohol by volume × 50 cl measure = 2.5 units per half litre measure.
- Spirit at 40% alcohol by volume × 25 ml measure = 1 unit per 25 ml measure.
- Sherry at 18% alcohol by volume × 50 ml measure = 0.9 unit per 50 ml measure.

11.3 Cocktails and mixed drinks

A modern cocktail is normally a short drink of up to about 10 cl (3½–4 oz) – anything larger often being called a 'mixed drink' or 'long drink'. However, the term cocktail is now generally recognised to mean all types of mixed drinks. Table 11.2 gives the range of drinks that can be included under the heading cocktails.

Table 11.2 **Types of cocktails**

Blended drinks	Made using a liquidiser
Champagne cocktails	For example, Bucks Fizz, which has the addition of orange juice

Cobblers	Wine and spirit based, served with straws and decorated with fruit
Collins	Hot-weather drinks, spirit-based, served with plenty of ice
Coolers	Almost identical to the Collins but usually containing the peel of the fruit cut into a spiral; spirit or wine-based
Crustas	May be made with any spirit, the most popular being brandy; edge of glass decorated with powdered sugar and crushed ice placed in glass
Cups	Hot-weather, wine-based drinks
Daisies	Made with any spirit; usually served in tankards or wine glasses filled with crushed ice
Egg noggs	Traditional Christmas drink; rum or brandy and milk-based; served in tumblers
Fixes	Short drink made by pouring any spirit over crushed ice; decorated with fruit and served with short straws
Fizzes	Similar to a Collins; always shaken and then topped with soda; must be drunk immediately
Flips	Similar to Egg Noggs, containing egg yolk but never milk; spirit, wine or sherry-based
Frappés	Served on crushed ice
Highball	American; a simple drink that is quickly prepared with spirit and a mixer
Juleps	American; containing mint with claret, Madeira or Bourbon whiskey base
Pick-me-ups	To aid digestion
Pousse-Café	Layered mix of liqueurs and/or spirits using differences in the specific densities of drinks to create layers – heaviest at the bottom, lightest at the top
Smashes	Smaller version of a julep
Sours	Always made with fresh juices to sharpen the flavour of the drink
Smoothies	Blended, chilled and sometimes sweetened beverage usually made from fresh fruit or vegetables
Swizzles	Take their name from the stick used to stir the drink; 'swizzling' creates a frost on the outside of glass
Toddies	Refreshers that may be served hot or cold; contain lemon, cinnamon and nutmeg

Figure 11.1 **Cocktails (illustration courtesy of Six Continents Hotels)**

Making of cocktails

A true cocktail is made by one of two methods: shaking or stirring. The art of making a good cocktail is to blend all the ingredients together by shaking or stirring so that upon tasting no one ingredient is predominant.

A rule of thumb to determine whether a cocktail should be shaken or stirred is that if it contains a fruit juice as one of the ingredients, then it should be shaken, and if the ingredients are wine based and clear, then it should be stirred.

The key equipment required when making a cocktail depends on the method being used.

Shaken

- Cocktail shaker or Boston shaker with Hawthorn strainer.
- Blender (for mixes).

Stirred

- Bar mixing glass.
- Bar spoon with muddler.
- Hawthorn strainer.

More recently **smoothies** have become popular and are often seen as health drinks. These are made in a blender. In addition to fresh fruit or vegetables these are sometimes sweetened. The recipe may also include crushed ice, frozen fruit, honey or frozen yogurt. Pre-made bottled or carton versions are also available.

Note: For examples of bar equipment see Chapter 3, Section 3.5, page 51.

11.4 Bitters

Bitters are used either as aperitifs or for flavouring mixed drinks and cocktails. The most popular varieties are shown in Table 11.3.

Table 11.3 **Popular varieties of bitters**

Amer Picon	A very black and bitter French aperitif. Grenadine or Cassis is often added to make the flavour more acceptable. Traditionalists add water in a proportion of 2:1.
Angostura bitters	Takes its name from a town in Bolivia. However, it is no longer produced there but in Trinidad. Brownish-red in colour, it is used in the preparation of pink gin and the occasional cocktail and may be regarded as mainly a flavouring agent.
Byrrh	(Pronounced beer.) This is a style of bitters made in France near the Spanish border. It has a base of red wine and is flavoured with quinine and herbs and fortified with brandy.
Campari	A pink, bittersweet Italian aperitif that has a slight flavour of orange peel and quinine. Serve in an 18.93 cl (6⅔ fl oz) Paris goblet or Highball glass. Use one measure on ice and garnish with a slice of lemon. Top up according to the customer's requirements with soda or water (iced).
Fernet Branca	The Italian version of Amer Picon. Best served diluted with water or soda. Good for hangovers!
Underberg	A German bitter that looks like, and almost tastes like, iodine. It may be taken as a pick-me-up with soda.
Other bitters	Orange and peach bitters are used principally as cocktail ingredients. Other well-known bitters are Amaro Montenegro, Radis, Unicum, Abbots, Peychaud and Boonekamp. Many are used as hangover cures. Cassis or Grenadine is sometimes added to make the drink more palatable.

11.5 Wine

Wine is the alcoholic beverage obtained from the fermentation of the juice of freshly gathered grapes. The fermentation takes place in the district of origin, according to local tradition and practice.

Table 11.4 Principal white and red grapes used for wine-making

White grapes	Where grown	General characteristics of the wine
Chardonnay	Worldwide	The white grape of Burgundy, Champagne and the New World. Aromas associated with Chardonnay include ripe melon and fresh pineapple. The fruity, oaky New World wines tend to be buttery and syrupy, with tropical fruits and richness. In Burgundy the wines are succulent but bone-dry, with a nutty intensity. Chablis, from the cooler northern Burgundy, produces wines that have a sharp, steely acidity that may also be countered by the richness of oak. Also one of the three grapes for champagne.
Chenin blanc	Loire, California and South Africa (known as Steen)	Variety of styles: bone-dry, medium-sweet, intensely sweet or sparkling wines, all with fairly high acidity making the wines very refreshing. Aroma association tends to be apples.
Gewürztraminer	Alsace, Australia, Chile, Eastern Europe, Germany, New Zealand, USA	One of the most pungent grapes, making wines that are distinctively spicy, with aromas like rose petals, grapefruit and tropical fruits such as lychees. Wines are aromatic and perfumed and are occasionally off-dry.
Muscat	Worldwide	Mainly sweet, perfumed wines, smelling and tasting of grapes and raisins and made in styles from pale, light and floral to golden, sweet and orangey, or brown, rich and treacly. Often fortified (as in the French *vins doux naturels*, e.g. Muscat des Beaumes-de-Venise). Also principal grape for sparkling Asti.
Pinot Blanc/ Weissburgunder	Alsace, Eastern Europe, northern Italy, Germany, USA	Dry, neutral, fresh and fruity wines with the best having appley and soft spicy and honeyed aromas.
Pinot Gris/Pinot Grigio/Ruländer/ Tokay-Pinot Gris	Alsace, Canada, Germany, Hungary, Italy, New Zealand, Slovenia, USA	Generally full bodied, spicy white wines, often high in alcohol and low in acidity. Wines are crisp and neutral in Italy and aromatic and spicy in Alsace and elsewhere, with a hint of honey. Also used to make golden sweet wines, especially from Alsace.
Riesling	Alsace, Australia, Canada, Germany, New Zealand, South Africa, USA	Range of wines from the steely to the voluptuous, always well perfumed, with good ageing potential. Aromas tend towards apricots and peaches. Germany makes the greatest Riesling in all styles. Piercing acidity and flavours ranging from green apple and lime to honeyed peaches, to stony and slate-like. Styles can range from bright and tangy to intensely sweet.
Sauvignon Blanc	Worldwide	Common aroma association with gooseberries, the wines are green, tangy, fresh and pungent. When made with oak, it can be a different wine: tropical fruits in the Californian examples, while the Bordeaux classic wines are often blended with Sémillon and begin with nectarine hints and then become more nutty and creamy with age. May be called Blanc Fumé.
Sémillon	Mainly Bordeaux but also Australia and New Zealand	Lemony, waxy dry whites; when oaked they can gain flavours of custard, nuts and honey. Luscious golden sweet wines when grapes are affected by *Botrytis Cinerea* (Noble Rot), e.g. Sauternes.
Viognier	Rhône Valley and southern France, Australia, USA	Rhône wines, e.g. Condrieu, are aromatic, with hints of apricots and spring flowers; wines from other areas tend to be less perfumed.

Red grapes	Where grown	General characteristics of the wine
Cabernet Sauvignon	Worldwide	Principal grape of Bordeaux, especially in the Médoc. New World wines deliver big wines with upfront blackcurrant fruit; Bordeaux wines need time to mature. Generally benefits from being blended, e.g. with Merlot, Cabernet Franc, Syrah, Tempranillo, Sangiovese. Also used to make aromatic rosé wines.
Gamay	Beaujolais, Loire, Savoie, Switzerland and USA	The grape of Beaujolais, making light and juicy wines. Characteristic pear drop aroma association indicating wine made using *macération carbonique* method. Makes lighter wine in the Loire Valley in central France and in Switzerland and Savoie. Known as 'Napa Gamay' in California.
Grenache/ Garnacha	Southern France and Rhône, Australia, Spain, USA	Makes strong, fruity but pale wines, and fruity rosé wines. Important grape as part of blends, e.g. for Châteauneuf-du-pape in the Rhône and for Rioja in Spain. Characteristics of ripe strawberries, raspberries and hints of spice.
Malbec	South-west France, Argentina	French wines tend to be plummy and tannic. In Bordeaux it is used for blending. The Argentinean wines tend to be rich and perfumed.
Merlot	Worldwide	Principal grape of Saint-Emilion and Pomerol in France. Aromas tend towards plums and damsons. The wines are low in harsh tannins and can be light and juicy, smooth and plummy or intensely blackcurrant.
Nebbiolo	Italy	One of Italy's best red grapes, used in Barolo and Barbaresco. Fruity and perfumed wines with a mixture of tastes and flavours of black cherry and sloes, tar and roses. Aroma association tends towards prunes. Traditionally tough and tannic when young, with good plummy flavours as they develop.
Pinot Noir/ Spätburgunder/ Pinot Nero	Worldwide	Principal grape of Burgundy's Côte d'Or. Aromas can be of strawberries, cherries and plums (depending on where grown). Silky and strawberry-like; simple wines have juicy fruit; the best mature wines, such as the great red wines of Burgundy, are well perfumed. Loire and German wines are lighter. Also one of the three grapes of champagne and used elsewhere (e.g. California and Australia) for making white, sparkling or red and very pale pink wines.
Sangiovese	Italy, Argentina, Australia, USA	Principal grape of Chianti. Also known as Brunello and Morellino. Mouth-watering, sweet-sour red fruit in young wines, reminiscent of juicy cherries, which intensifies in older wines.
Shiraz/Syrah	Worldwide	Warm, spicy, peppery wines with aromas of raspberries; French Syrah tends to be smoky, herby and packed with red fruits (raspberries, blackberries or blackcurrants); Australian Shiraz has sweeter black cherry fruit and often black chocolate or liquorice aromas. Very fruity rosé wines are also made.
Tempranillo	Spain, Portugal, Argentina	Early ripening, aromatic Rioja grape (Ull de Llebre in Catalonia, Cencibel in La Mancha, Tinto Fino in Ribera del Duero, Tinta Roriz in Douro and Aragonez in southern Portugal). Wines are light and juicy with hints of strawberries and plums, silky and spicy with hints of prunes, tobacco and cocoa. Wines in cooler climates are more elegant and those in warmer climates are more beefy.
Zinfandel (Pimitivo in Italy)	California, Italy	Aromas of blackberries, bramble and spice. In California wines have blackberry flavours, which are sometimes slightly metallic. Can be structured and lush and also used to make the pale pink 'blush' white wine. Genetically linked and known as Primitivo in Southern Italy, where it makes big, rustic wines.

Only a relatively small area of the world is wine producing. This is because the grape will only provide juice of the quality necessary for conversion into a drinkable wine where two climatic conditions prevail:

- sufficient sun to ripen the grape

- winters that are moderate yet sufficiently cool to give the vine a chance to rest and restore its strength for the growing and fruiting season.

These climatic conditions are found in two main wine-producing zones, which lie between the latitudes 30° and 50° north of the equator and 30° and 50° south of the equator.

Three-quarters of the world's wine is produced in Europe and just under half in the EU. France and Italy produce the most wine, with Italy being the largest producer. Next in order come Spain, USA, Australia, Argentina, Germany, Portugal, Chile and South Africa.

Vinification

The process central to vinification (wine-making) is fermentation – the conversion of sugar by yeast to alcohol and carbon dioxide. This process is also necessary to the making of all alcoholic beverages – not only for still, sparkling and fortified wines, but also as the start point for the making of spirits, liqueurs and beers (although some variations and further processes will be applied for the different types of beverages).

Vine species

The vine species that produces grapes suitable for wine production, and which stocks most of the vineyards of the world, is named *Vitis vinifera*. Most varieties now planted in Europe and elsewhere have evolved from this species through cross-breeding, to suit local soils and climates. The same grape in different regions may be given a different name, for example, Grenache in the Rhône region is also known as Garnacha, which produces fine Spanish wines. There are a number of grapes that have become known as having distinctive characteristics. Examples of these principal grapes of the world, and their general characteristics, are given in Table 11.4.

The grape

The grape consists of:

- skin – which provide tannins and colour
- stalk – which provides tannins
- pips – provide bitter oils
- pulp – contains sugar, fruit acids, water and pectins.

The yeast required for the fermentation process is found on the outside of the grape skin in the form of a whitish bloom. The colour in wine comes mainly from the skin of the grape, being extracted during the fermentation process. Red wine can only be made from red grapes. However, white wine can be made from white or red grapes, provided that, in the case of red grapes, the grape skins are removed before fermentation begins.

Factors that influence the quality and final taste of wine

The same vine variety, grown in different regions and processed in different ways, will produce wines of differing characteristics. The factors that affect the quality and final taste of wines include:

- climate and microclimate
- nature of the soil and subsoil
- vine family and grape species
- method of cultivation – viticulture
- composition of the grape(s)
- yeast and fermentation
- method of wine-making – vinification
- luck of the year – vintage
- ageing and maturing process
- method of shipping or transportation
- storage temperature.

Pests and diseases

The vine is subject to pests and diseases in the form of birds, insects, fungi, viruses and weeds. The main ones are shown in Table 11.5.

Table 11.5 **Pests and diseases affecting the vine**

Phylloxera vastatrix	A louse-like, almost invisible aphid, which attacks the roots of the vine. *Phylloxera* arrived in Europe in the mid 1800s almost by accident, transported on American vines imported into various European countries from the eastern states of North America. It ravaged many of the vineyards of Europe at this time. The cure was to graft the European vine onto resistant American rootstocks. This practice has since become standard throughout the world wherever *Vitis vinifera* is grown.
Grey rot or Pourriture grise	This fungus attacks the leaves and fruit of the vine during warm damp weather. It is recognised by a grey mould. The fungus imparts an unpleasant flavour to the wine.
Noble rot or pourriture noble (Botrytis cinerea)	This is the same fungus in its beneficent form, which may occur when humid conditions are followed by hot weather. The fungus punctures the grape skin, the water content evaporates and the grape shrivels, thus concentrating the sugar inside. This process gives the luscious flavours characteristic of Sauternes, German Trockenbeerenauslese and Hungarian Tokay Aszu.

Faults in wine

Faults occasionally develop in wine as it matures in bottles. Nowadays, through improved techniques and attention to detail regarding bottling and storage, faulty wine is a rarity. Some of the more common causes of faulty wine are shown in Table 11.6.

Table 11.6 **Faults in wine**

Corked wines	These are wines affected by a diseased cork caused through bacterial action or excessive bottle age. TCA (trichloroanisole) causes the wine to taste and smell foul. This is not to be confused with cork residue in wine, which is harmless.
Maderisation or oxidation	This is caused by bad storage leading to too much exposure to air, often because the cork has dried out. The colour of the wine browns or darkens and the taste slightly resembles that of Madeira, hence the name. The wine tastes 'spoilt'.
Acetification	This is caused when the wine is overexposed to air. The vinegar microbe develops a film on the surface of the wine and acetic acid is produced, making the wine taste sour, resembling wine vinegar (vin vinaigre).
Tartare flake	This is the crystallisation of potassium bitartrate. These crystal-like flakes, sometimes seen in white wine, may cause anxiety to some customers as they spoil the appearance of the wine, which is otherwise perfect to drink. If the wine is stabilised before bottling, this condition should not occur.
Excess sulphur dioxide (SO_2)	Sulphur dioxide is added to wine to preserve it and keep it healthy. Once the bottle is opened, the smell will disappear and, after a few minutes, the wine is perfectly drinkable.
Secondary fermentation	This happens when traces of sugar and yeast are left in the wine in the bottle. It leaves the wine with an unpleasant, prickly taste that should not be confused with the pétillant or spritzig characteristics associated with other styles of healthy and refreshing wines.

Foreign contamination	Examples include splintered or powdered glass caused by faulty bottling machinery or re-used bottles which previously held some kind of disinfectant.
Hydrogen sulphide (H_2S)	The wine smells and tastes of rotten eggs and should not be drunk.
Sediment, lees, crust or dregs	This is organic matter discarded by the wine as it matures in the cask or bottle. It can be removed by racking, fining or, in the case of bottled wine, by decanting.
Cloudiness	This is caused by suspended matter in the wine that disguises its true colour. It may also be caused by extremes in storage temperatures.

Classification of wine types

Still (or light) wine

This is the largest category. The alcoholic strength may be between 9% and 15% by volume. The wines may be:

- **Red:** produced by being fermented in contact with grape skins (from which the wine gets its colour). Normally dry wines.
- **White:** usually produced from white grapes, but the grape juice (must) is usually fermented away from the skins. Normally dry to very sweet.
- **Rosé:** can be made in three ways – from black grapes fermented on the skins for up to 48 hours; by mixing red and white wines together; or by pressing grapes so that some colour is extracted. Rosé wine may be dry or semi-sweet. Rosé wines are called 'blush' wines in the USA when made wholly from red grapes.

Sparkling wines

Sparkling wines are available from France, Spain (Cava), Italy (Prosecco), Germany (Sekt) and many other countries.

The most famous sparkling wine is champagne. This is made by the *méthode champenoise* (secondary fermentation in the bottle) in an area of north-eastern France.

Effervescent wines made outside this area are called *vins mousseux* or sparkling wines. A summary of the four methods for making sparkling wines is given in Table 11.7.

Table 11.7 **Key differences in methods of production of sparkling wines**

Method	Fermentation and maturation	Removal of sediment
Méthode traditionnelle	In bottle	By the processes of *remuage* and *dégorgement* (moving the sediment to the neck of the bottle and then opening the bottle to remove it, topping up the bottle with more wine and then resealing).
Méthode transvasement or transfer method	In bottle	By transfer under pressure to a vat and then filtering before rebottling.
Charmat or méthode cuve close	In tank	By filtration process.
Méthode gazifié or carbonation method	Sometimes termed 'impregnation', where carbon dioxide is injected into a vat of still wine that has been chilled and which is then bottled under pressure. Least expensive method.	

Other sparkling wine terms

French

- *Vin mousseux*: sparkling wine other than champagne.
- *Méthode traditionnelle*: sparkling, made by the traditional method.
- *Pétillant/perlant*: slightly sparkling.
- *Crémant*: less sparkling than mousseux.

German

- *Spritzig*: slightly sparkling.
- *Flaschengarung nach dem traditionellen Verfahren*: sparkling wine made by the traditional method.
- *Sekt*: sparkling (also used to mean the wine itself).
- *Schaumwein*: sparkling of lesser quality than Sekt.
- *Perlwein*: slightly sparkling.

Italian

- *Prosecco*: name of the northern Italian village, where the grape is believed to have originated; the term is now often used as the generic name for Italian sparkling wines.
- *Frizzante*: semi-sparkling.
- *Spumante*: sparkling.
- *Metodo classico/tradizionale*: sparkling wine made by the traditional method.

Portuguese

- *Espumante*: sparkling.
- *Vinho verde*: meaning 'green wine', slightly sparkling.

Spanish

- *Espumoso*: sparkling.
- *Método tradicional*: sparkling, made by the traditional method.
- *Cava*: sparkling, made by the traditional method, also used as generic name for Spanish sparkling wines.

Organic wines

These wines, also known as 'green' or 'environmentally friendly' wines, are made from grapes grown without the aid of artificial insecticides, pesticides or fertilisers. The wine itself will not be adulterated in any way, save for minimal amounts of the traditional preservative, sulphur dioxide, which is controlled at source.

Alcohol-free, de-alcoholised and low-alcohol wines

These wines are made in the normal way and the alcohol is removed either by hot treatment – distillation – which unfortunately removes most of the flavour as well, or, more satisfactorily, by a cold filtration process, also known as reverse osmosis. This removes the alcohol by mechanically separating or filtering out the molecules of alcohol through membranes made of cellulose or acetate. At a later stage, water and a little must are added, thus attempting to preserve much of the flavour of the original wine. The definitions for these wines are:

- alcohol free: maximum 0.05% alcohol
- de-alcoholised: maximum 0.50% alcohol
- low alcohol: maximum 1.2% alcohol.

Vins doux naturels

These are sweet wines that have had their fermentation muted by the addition of alcohol in order to retain their natural sweetness. Muting takes place when the alcohol level reaches between 5% and 8% by volume. They have a final alcoholic strength of about 17% by volume. One of the best known is Muscat de Beaumes-de-Venise, named after a village in the Côtes du Rhône where it is made. The wine is fortified with spirit before fermentation is complete so that some of the natural sugar remains in the wine. It is usually drunk young.

Fortified (liqueur) wines

Fortified wines such as sherry, port and Madeira have been strengthened by the addition of alcohol, usually a grape spirit. These are now known within the EU as liqueur wines or *vins de liqueur*. Their alcoholic strength may be between 15% and 22% by volume. Examples are:

- **Sherry** (from Spain) 15–18% – Fino (dry), Amontillado (medium), Oloroso (sweet).
- **Port** (from Portugal) 18–22% – ruby, tawny, vintage character, late bottled vintage, vintage.
- **Madeira** (made on the Portuguese island of Madeira) 18% – Sercial (dry), Verdelho (medium), Bual (sweet), Malmsey (very sweet).
- **Marsala** (dark sweet wine from Marsala in Sicily) 18%.
- **Málaga** (from Málaga, Andalusia, Spain) 18–20%.

Aromatised wines

These are flavoured and fortified wines, often referred to as vermouths.

The four main types of vermouth are:

- *Dry vermouth*: often called French vermouth or simply French (as in Gin and French). It is made from dry white wine that is flavoured and fortified.
- *Sweet vermouth/bianco*: made from dry white wine, flavoured, fortified and sweetened with sugar or mistelle.
- *Rosé vermouth*: made in a similar way to Bianco, but it is less sweet and is coloured with caramel.
- *Red vermouth*: often called Italian vermouth, Italian or more often 'It' (as in Gin and It). It is made from white wine and is flavoured, sweetened and coloured with a generous addition of caramel.

Other aromatised wines include:

- *Chamberyzette*: Made in the Savoy Alps of France. It is flavoured with the juice of wild strawberries.
- *Punt-e-mes*: From Carpano of Turin. This is heavily flavoured with quinine and has wild contrasts of bitterness and sweetness.
- *Dubonnet*: Made in France and is available in two varieties: *blonde* (white) and *rouge* (red) and is flavoured with quinine and herbs.
- *St Raphael*: Red or white, bittersweet drink from France flavoured with herbs and quinine.
- *Lillet*: Popular French aperitif made from white Bordeaux wine and flavoured with herbs, fruit peel and fortified with Armagnac brandy. It is aged in oak casks.
- *Pineau des Charentes*: Although not strictly an aromatised or fortified wine, Pineau des Charentes has gained popularity as an alternative aperitif or digestif. It is available in white, rosé or red and is made with grape must from the Cognac region and fortified with young Cognac to about 17% alcohol by volume.

Quality control for wines

The majority of the world's winemakers must ensure that their products conform to strict quality regulations covering such aspects as the location of the vineyards, the variety of grape used, how the wine is made and how long it is matured.

Many countries now give the name of grape varieties on the wine label. Within the EU, if a grape variety is named on the label then the wine must contain at least 85 per cent of that variety. For EU wines, any number of grapes may be listed as part of descriptive text, but only a maximum of two may appear on the main label. For most countries outside of the EU, the wine must contain 100 per cent of the named variety, although there are exceptions. These include Australia and New Zealand who are permitted 85 per cent and the USA who are permitted 75 per cent. Australia allows up to five varieties, provided each is at least five per cent of the blend.

European Union

European Union directives lay down general rules for quality wines produced in specified regions (QWPSR) or, in French, *vin de qualité produit dans des régions déterminées* (VQPRD).

Countries other than the EU

Developments in the international wine business, especially in the New World, have led to a more marketing-led approach to wines. Simpler information is given on the labels and also on detailed back labels, including the identification of grape varieties (or the use of the Californian term 'varietals') and straightforward advice on storage, drinking and matching the wine with food.

Although most countries have a category for wines that is similar to EU Table Wine, this is mainly sold locally. On the international markets the wines are classified as Wine with Geographical Description. Each country has its own system for dividing its vineyard areas into regions, zones, districts, and so on, and controlling the use of regional names. Where regions, vintages and varieties are named on the label, these wines may also have a small proportion of wine from other regions, vintages and varieties blended with them. All countries have their own legislation covering production techniques and use of label terms to prevent consumers from being misinformed.

Reading a wine label

The EU has strict regulations that govern what is printed on a wine bottle label. These regulations also apply to wine entering the EU. In addition, standard-sized bottles of light (or still) wines bottled after 1988, when EU regulations on content came into force, must contain 75 cl.

Examples of taste and colour terms that appear on wine labels are given in Table 11.8.

Table 11.8 **Examples of wine label terms indicating colour and taste**

Term	France	Germany	Italy	Spain	Portugal
Wine	vin	Wein	vino	vino	vinho
Dry	sec	trocken	secco	seco	seco
Medium	demi-sec	halbtrocken	abboccato	abocado	semi-seco
Sweet	doux/moelleux	süß	dolce	dulce	doce
White	blanc	Weißwein	bianco	blanco	branco
Red	rouge	Rotwein	rosso	tinto	tinto
Rosé	rosé	Rosé	rosato	rosado	rosado

The label on a bottle of wine can give a lot of useful information about that wine. The language used will normally be that of the country of origin. The information always includes:

- the name of the wine
- the country where the wine was made
- alcoholic strength in percentage by volume (% vol)
- contents in litres, cl or ml
- the name and address or trademark of the supplier.

It may also include:

- the varietal(s) (name of the grape(s) used to make the wine)
- the year the grapes were harvested, called the vintage, if the wine is sold as a vintage wine
- the region where the wine was made
- the property where the wine was made
- the quality category of the wine
- details of the bottler and distributor.

An example of the kind of information that is given on a wine label is shown in Figure 11.2. This example shows a guide to a German wine label.

1. Specified growing region: one of the 13 designated regions in Germany
2. Year in which the grapes were harvested (vintage)
3. Town and vineyard from which the grapes come
4. Grape variety – here it is Riesling
5. Indication of taste or style of the wine – in this case it is halbtrocken (medium dry). If it were trocken, it would be dry
6. Quality level of the wine
7. The official testing number: proof that the wine has passed chemical and sensory testing which is required for all German quality wines
8. Alcohol content
9. Bottle size
10. Wines bottled and produced by the grower or a cooperative of growers may be labelled Erzeugerabfüllung. Estates and growers can use Gutsabfüllung as an alternative. Other wineries and bottlers are identified as Abfüller

Figure 11.2 **Guide to the German wine label (source: The German Wine Information Service)**

Closures for wine bottles

There are now four main types of closures for wine bottles:

Natural corks

These closures are made from whole pieces of cork. Each is individual and unique, and so there can be variations in quality. However, natural cork has a high degree of elasticity and compressibility and it can mould itself around tiny imperfections in the neck of the bottle. It is well proven for the long-term storage of wines. Natural cork is, however, susceptible to trichloroanisole (TCA) (see corked wine, page 188). If the cork dries out or is loose fitting the bottle can leak and the wine can become oxidised through being exposed to the air.

Technical (or composite) corks

These are agglomerate corks made from small pieces of natural cork moulded into a cork shape and held with food-grade glue. The better-quality closures are agglomerate with solid cork discs at either end. The solid end is the only part that comes into contact with the wine. However, as with natural cork, it is susceptible to TCA. The opening process is similar to natural corks.

Synthetics (plastics)

These are synthetic closures that may be used for wines that are to be drunk within about 18 months of bottling. After this time synthetic closures may lose their elasticity, resulting in the risk of the seal being broken and the wine becoming oxidised through exposure to the air. Although not susceptible to TCA, there are some risks of the closure taking up fruit flavours from the wine or adding plastic flavours to the wine. The opening process is similar to traditional corks, although this type of closure can be more difficult to extract than cork and re-inserting the closure into the neck of the bottle is also difficult.

Screw caps

Various makes of screw cap and linings are used which are easy to open and reseal. The closure provides a tight seal for the bottle and TCA is unlikely. However, these closures are still relatively new and the longer-term effects on wines for laying down (ageing) are yet to be determined.

11.6 Spirits

Production

All spirits are produced by the distillation of alcoholic beverages. The history of distillation goes back over 2,000 years when it is said that stills were used in China to make perfumes and by the Arabs to make spirit-based drinks.

The principle of distillation is that ethyl alcohol vaporises (boils) at a lower temperature (78°C) than water (100°C). Thus, where a liquid containing alcohol (alcoholic wash) is heated in an enclosed environment the alcohol will form steam first and can be taken off, leaving water and other ingredients behind. This process raises the alcoholic strength of the resulting liquid.

There are two main methods of producing spirits: the pot still method, which is used for full, heavy flavoured spirits such as brandy, and the patent still (Coffey) method, which produces the lighter spirits such as vodka.

Types of spirit

The main types of spirits are shown in Table 11.9.

Table 11.9 **Types of spirit**

Aquavit	Made in Scandinavia from potatoes or grain and flavoured with herbs, mainly caraway seeds. To be appreciated fully, Aquavit must be served chilled.
Arrack	Made from the sap of palm trees. The main countries of production are Java, India, Ceylon and Jamaica.
Brandy	Brandy may be defined as a spirit distilled from wine. The word brandy is more usually linked with the names Cognac and Armagnac, but brandy is also made in almost all wine-producing areas.
Calvados	Apple brandy made from the distillation of cider from the French *région* of Basse-Normandie or Lower Normandy – also see *eau de vie*.
Eau de vie	*Eau de vie* ('water of life') is the fermented and distilled juice of fruit and is usually water-clear in appearance. The best *eau de vie* comes from the Alsace area of France, Germany, Switzerland and Eastern Europe. Examples are: • *Calvados*: from apples and often known as apple brandy (France) • *Himbeergeist*: from wild raspberries (Germany) • *Kirschwasser*: (Kirsch) from cherries (Alsace and Germany) • *Mirabelle*: from plums (France) • *Quetsch*: from plums (Alsace and Germany) • *Poire William*: from pears (Switzerland and Alsace) – sometimes known by the brand name Williamine • *Slivovitz*: from plums (Eastern Europe) • *Fraise*: from strawberries (France, especially Alsace) • *Framboise*: from raspberries (France, especially Alsace).
Gin	The term 'gin' is taken from the first part of the word *genièvre*, which is the French term for juniper. Juniper is the principal botanical (flavouring agent) used in the production of gin. The word 'Geneva' is the Dutch translation of the botanical, juniper. Maize is the cereal used in gin production in the UK. However, rye is the main cereal generally used in the production of Geneva gin and other Dutch gins. Malted barley is an accepted alternative to the cereals mentioned above. The two key ingredients (botanicals) recognised for flavouring purposes are juniper berries and coriander seeds. Types of gin: • *Fruit gins*: as the term implies, these are fruit-flavoured gins that may be produced from any fruit. The most popular are sloe, orange and lemon. • *Geneva gin*: this is made in Holland by the pot still method alone and is generally known as 'Hollands' gin. • *London Dry Gin*: this is the most well-known and popular of all the gins. It is unsweetened. • *Old Tom*: this is a sweet gin made in Scotland. The sweetening agent is sugar syrup. As the name implies, it was traditionally used in a Tom Collins cocktail. • *Plymouth Gin*: this has a stronger flavour than London Dry and is manufactured by Coates in Devon. It is most well known for its use in the cocktail Pink Gin, together with the addition of Angostura bitters.
Grappa	An Italian-style brandy produced from the pressings of grapes after the required must – unfermented grape juice – has been removed for wine production. It is similar in style to the French Marc brandy.
Marc	Local French brandy made where wine is made. Usually takes the name of the region, e.g. Marc de Bourgogne.
Mirabelle	A colourless spirit made from plums. The main country of origin is France.
Pastis	Pastis is the name given to spirits flavoured with anis and/or liquorice, such as Pernod. The spirit is made in many Mediterranean countries and is popular almost everywhere. It has taken over from absinthe, once known as the 'Green Goddess'.

Quetsch	A colourless spirit with plums being the main ingredient. The key countries of production are the Balkans, France and Germany. It has a brandy base. Also see *eau de vie*.
Rum	This is a spirit made from the fermented by-products of sugar cane. It is available in dark and light varieties and is produced in countries where sugar cane grows naturally, e.g. Jamaica, Cuba, Trinidad, Barbados, Guyana and the Bahamas.
Schnapps	A spirit distilled from a fermented potato base and flavoured with caraway seed. The main countries of production are Germany and Holland.
Tequila	A Mexican spirit distilled from the fermented juice (pulque) of the agave plant. It is traditionally drunk after a lick of salt and a squeeze of lime or lemon.
Vodka	A highly rectified (very pure), patent still spirit. It is purified by being passed through activated charcoal, which removes virtually all aroma and flavour. It is described as a colourless and flavourless spirit.
Whisk(e)y	Whisky or whiskey is a spirit made from cereals: Scotch whisky from malted barley; Irish whiskey usually from barley; North American whiskey and Bourbon from maize and rye. The spelling *whisky* usually refers to the Scotch or Canadian drink and *whiskey* to the Irish or American. • Scotch whisky is primarily made from barley, malted (hence the term malt whisky) then heated over a peat fire. Grain whiskies are made from other grains and are usually blended with malt whisky. • Irish whiskey differs from Scotch in that hot air rather than a peat fire is used during malting, thus Irish whiskey does not gain the smoky quality of Scotch. It is also distilled three times (rather than two as in the making of Scotch) and is matured longer. • Canadian whisky is usually a blend of flavoured and neutral whiskies made from grains such as rye, wheat and barley. • American whiskey is made from various mixtures of barley, maize and rye. Bourbon is made from maize. • Japanese whisky is made by the Scotch process and is blended.

11.7 Liqueurs

Liqueurs are defined as sweetened and flavoured spirits. They should not be confused with liqueur spirits, which may be whiskies or brandies of great age and quality. For instance, a brandy liqueur is a liqueur with brandy as a basic ingredient, while a liqueur brandy may be defined as a brandy of great age and excellence.

Table 11.10 **Popular liqueurs**

Liquer	Colour	Flavour/spirit base	Country of origin
Abricotine	Red	Apricot/brandy	France
Advocaat	Yellow	Egg, sugar/brandy	Holland
Amaretto	Golden	Almonds	Italy
Anisette	Clear	Aniseed/neutral spirit	France, Spain, Italy, Holland
Archers	Clear	Peaches/Schnapps	UK
Arrack	Clear	Herbs, sap of palm trees	Java, India, Sri Lanka, Jamaica
Baileys Irish Cream	Coffee	Honey, chocolate, cream, whiskey	Ireland
Bénédictine D.O.M.	Yellow/green	Herbs/brandy	France

Liquer	Colour	Flavour/spirit base	Country of origin
Chartreuse	Green (45% abv) Yellow (55% abv)	Herbs, plants/brandy	France
Cherry Brandy	Deep red	Cherry/brandy	Denmark
Cointreau	Clear	Orange/brandy	France
Crème de cacao	Dark brown	Chocolate, vanilla/rum	France
Disaronno	Amber	Almonds with herbs and fruits soaked in apricot kernel oil	Italy
Drambuie	Golden	Heather, honey, herbs/whisky	Scotland
Frangelico	Golden	Hazelnut	Italy
Galliano	Golden	Herbs/berries/flowers/roots	Italy
Glayva	Golden	Herbs, spice/whisky	Scotland
Grand Marnier	Amber	Orange/brandy	France
Kahlúa	Pale chocolate	Coffee/rum	Mexico
Kümmel	Clear	Caraway seed/neutral spirit	East European countries
Malibu	Clear	Coconut/white rum	Caribbean
Maraschino	Clear	Maraschino cherry	Italy
Parfait amour	Violet	Violets, lemon peel, spices	France/Holland
Sambuca	Clear	Liquorice/neutral spirit	Italy
Southern Comfort	Golden	Peaches/oranges/whiskey	United States
Strega (The Witch)	Yellow	Herbs/bark/fruit	Italy
Tia Maria	Brown	Coffee/rum	Jamaica
Van der hum	Amber	Tangerine/brandy	South Africa

Production

Liqueurs are made by two basic methods:

1. Heat or infusion method: best when herbs, peels, roots, etc., are being used, as heat can extract their oils, flavours and aromas.
2. Cold or maceration method: best when soft fruits are used to provide the flavours and aromas.

The heat method uses a pot still for distillation purposes. The cold method allows the soft fruit to soak in brandy in oak casks over a long period of time.

For all liqueurs a spirit base is necessary and this may be brandy, rum or a neutral spirit. Many flavouring ingredients are used to make liqueurs.

Types of liqueurs

Table 11.10 lists some of the more popular liqueurs. The service of liqueurs is discussed in Chapter 16, Section 16.5, page 288.

11.8 Beer

Beer in one form or another is an alcoholic beverage found in all bars and areas dispensing alcoholic beverages. Beers are fermented drinks, deriving their alcoholic content from the conversion of malt sugars into alcohol by brewers yeast. The alcoholic content of beer varies according to type and is usually between 3.5% and 10% alcohol by volume.

Types of beer

There are a number of different types of beer, as shown in Table 11.11.

Table 11.11 **Types of beer**

Abbey-style	Ale brewed in the monastic tradition of the Low Countries but by secular brewers, often under license from a religious establishment.
Barley wine	Traditionally an all-malt ale. This beer is sweet and strong and sold in small bottles or nips (originally ⅓ of a pint, now 190 ml).
Bitter	Pale, amber-coloured beer served on draft. May be sold as light bitter, ordinary bitter or best bitter. When bottled it is known as pale ale or light ale depending on alcoholic strength.
Burton	Strong, dark, draft beer. This beer is also popular in winter when it is mulled or spiced and offered as a winter warmer.
Fruit beers and flavoured beers	Variety of beers with additional flavourings such as heather or honeydew, or fruit beers, which have fresh fruits such as raspberry or strawberry introduced during the making process to add flavour.
IPA (India Pale Ale)	Heavily hopped strong pale ale, originally brewed in the UK for shipping to British colonies. The modern style is a light-coloured, hoppy, ale.
Lager	The name comes from the German *lagern* (to store). Fermentation takes place at the bottom of the vessel and the beer is stored at low temperatures for up to six months and sometimes longer. Sold on draft, in a bottle or can.
Mild	Can be light or dark depending on the colour of the malt used in the brewing process. Generally sold on draft and has a sweeter and more complex flavour than bitter.
Old ale	Brown, sweet and strong. Can also be mulled or spiced.
Pilsner	Clear, pale lagers (originally from Pilsen, hence the name). Modern styles are characterised by a zesty, hop taste and bubbly body.
Porter	Brewed from charred malt, highly flavoured and aromatic. Its name comes from its popularity with market porters working in Dublin and London.
Reduced-alcohol beer	There are two categories of beer with reduced alcohol levels: • Non-alcoholic beers (NABs) which, by definition, must contain less than 0.5% alcohol by volume. • Low alcohol beers (LABs) which, by definition, must contain less than 1.2% alcohol by volume. The beer is made in the traditional way and then the alcohol is removed.
Smoked beers	Beers made with grains that have been smoked as part of the malting process. Various woods are used, including alder, cherry, apple, beech or oak. Sometimes the process uses peat smoke.
Stout	Made from scorched, very dark malt and generously flavoured with hops. Has a smooth, malty flavour and creamy consistency. Sold on draft or in bottles and was traditionally not chilled (although today it often is). Guinness is one example.
Strong ale	Colour varies between pale and brown and taste between dry and sweet. Alcoholic content also varies.
Trappist beer	Beer brewed in Trappist monasteries, usually under the supervision of monks. Six Belgian breweries produce this beer, which is strong, complex and unpasteurised, and often includes candy sugar in the recipe.
White beer	Traditional beers made with a high proportion of wheat, sometimes known as wheat beers.

Cask-conditioned beers

Cask-conditioned ale is ale that has its final fermentation in the cask (or barrel) from which it is dispensed.

Bottle-conditioned beers

Also known as sediment beers, bottle-conditioned beers tend to throw a sediment in the bottle while fermenting and conditioning takes place. These beers need careful storage, handling and pouring. Available in bottles only.

Draught beer in cans

These draft-flow beers have an internal patented system that produces a pub-style, smooth creamy head when poured from the can. A range of beers are available in this format.

Faults in beer

Although thunder has been known to cause a secondary fermentation in beer, thereby affecting its clarity, faults can usually be attributed to poor cellar management. The common faults in beer are described below.

- **Cloudy beer:** This may be due to too low a temperature in the cellar or, more often, may result from the beer pipes not having been cleaned properly.
- **Flat beer:** Flat beer may result when a wrong spile has been used – a hard spile builds up pressure, a soft spile releases pressure. When the cellar temperature is too low, beer often becomes dull and lifeless. Dirty glasses, and those that have been refilled for a customer who has been eating food, will also cause beer to go flat.
- **Sour beer:** This may be due to a lack of business resulting in the beer being left on ullage for too long. Sourness may also be caused by adding stale beer to a new cask or by beer coming into contact with old deposits of yeast that have become lodged in the pipeline from the cellar.
- **Foreign bodies:** Foreign bodies or extraneous matter may be the result of production or operational slip-ups.

Beer measures

- Nips 7–8 fl oz (about 22.72 cl)
- Half pint 10 fl oz (about 28.40 cl)
- Pint 20 fl oz (about 56.80 cl)
- Litre
- Half litre

Draft beer containers

- Pin 20.457 litres (4½ gallons)
- Firkin 40.914 litres (9 gallons)
- Kilderkin 81.828 litres (18 gallons)
- Barrel 163.656 litres (36 gallons)
- Hogshead 245.484 litres (54 gallons)
- 2½ barrel tanks 205 litres (45 gallons)
- 5 barrel tanks 410 litres (90 gallons)

Mixed beer drinks

A selection of beverages based on beer is given below:

- mild and bitter
- stout and mild
- brown and mild
- light and mild

- shandy: draught bitter or lager and lemonade or ginger beer
- black velvet: Guinness and champagne
- black and tan: half stout and half bitter
- lager and lime
- lager and blackcurrant.

11.9 Cider and perry

Cider is an alcoholic beverage obtained through the fermentation of apple juice, or a mixture of apple juice and up to 25 per cent pear juice. Perry is similarly obtained from pear juice and up to 25 per cent apple juice.

Cider and perry are produced primarily in England and Normandy, but may also be made in Italy, Spain, Germany, Switzerland, Canada, the USA, Australia and New Zealand. The English areas of production are the counties of Devon, Somerset, Gloucester, Hereford, Kent and Norfolk where the best cider orchards are found.

Cider

The characteristics of the apples that are required for making cider are:

- the sweetness of dessert apples
- the acidity of culinary apples
- the bitterness of tannin to balance the flavour and help preserve the apple.

Main types of cider

- **Draught:** This is unfiltered. Its appearance, while not cloudy, is also not 'star-bright'. It may have sugar and yeast added to give it condition. Draught cider may be completely dry (known as 'scrumpy') or sweetened with sugar. It is marketed in oak casks or plastic containers.
- **Keg/bottled:** This cider is pasteurised or sterile filtered to render it star-bright. During this stage, one or more of the following treatments may be carried out:
  - it may be blended
  - it may undergo a second fermentation, usually in a tank, to make it sparkling
  - it may be sweetened
  - its strength may be adjusted
  - it will usually be carbonated by the injection of carbon dioxide gas.

The characteristics of keg and bottled ciders are:

- Medium sweet (carbonated): 4% vol alcohol.
- Medium dry (carbonated): 6% vol alcohol.
- Special (some carbonated): 8.3% vol alcohol – some special ciders undergo a second fermentation to make them sparkling.

Perry

Perry is usually made sparkling and comes into the special range. It may be carbonated or the sparkle may come from a second fermentation in sealed tanks. In the production of perry the processes of filtering, blending and sweetening are all carried out under pressure.

Perries were traditionally drunk on their own, chilled and in saucer-shaped sparkling wine glasses. Today the tulip-shaped sparkling wine glass is more commonly used.

11.10 Tasting techniques

The tasting, or evaluation, of wine and other drinks is carried out to:

- develop learning from experience
- help in the assessment of the quality of a wine in terms of value (the balance between price and worth) when making purchasing decisions
- monitor the progress of a wine which is being stored, to determine the optimum selling time and as part of protecting the investment
- assist in the description of a wine when explaining its qualities or deficiencies to customers
- provide a personal record of wines tasted, which helps to reinforce the experience and the learning.

To appreciate the tasting of wine to the full it should be carried out in an environment that supports the wine evaluation process. That is with:

- no noise to distract the taster
- good ventilation to eliminate odours
- sufficient light (daylight rather than artificial if possible), preferably north facing in the northern hemisphere (south facing in the southern hemisphere), as the light is more neutral
- a white background for tables so as not to affect the perception of the colour of the wine
- a room temperature of about 20°C (68°F).

The tool of the taster is the glass, which must be the correct shape. A wine glass with a stem and of sufficient capacity should be chosen (see Figure 11.3). The glass should be fairly wide but narrowing at the top. This allows the elements making up the bouquet to become concentrated and thus better assessed. The wine-tasting glass should never be filled to more than one-third capacity. This allows the taster to swirl the wine round the glass more easily. It goes without saying that the tasting glass should be spotlessly clean.

Figure 11.3 **Wine taster's glass (International Standards Organisation)**

Professional approach

The purpose of the wine tasting is to attempt to identify characteristics that describe the wine, which are then used to assess its quality. The professional tasting, or evaluation, of wines includes three key stages:

1. Recording the details of each individual wine.
2. Looking at, smelling and tasting the wine.
3. Recording the findings.

Approaching the process in this way ensures the development of confidence and the ability to make sound judgements.

Recording wine details

To ensure a complete record of the tasting of each wine, it is important to record the following details:

- name of wine
- country and area of origin
- quality indication (e.g. AOC, Qmp etc.)
- shipper

- château/estate bottled
- varietal(s) (grapes)
- vintage
- alcohol level
- ½ bottle, bottle, magnum
- price
- supplier.

Looking at, smelling and tasting the wine

Professional wine tasting is really an analysis and evaluation of qualities of the wine by the senses. This includes:

- looking at the wine to assess its clarity, colour and intensity, and the nature of the colour by identifying the specific shade of white, rosé or red
- smelling, or nosing, the wine to assess the condition of the wine, the intensity of aroma or bouquet, and to identify other aroma characteristics. Taste is 80 per cent smell!
- tasting the wine to assess the sweetness/dryness, acidity, tannin, body, length and other taste characteristics
- touch, to feel the weight of the wine in the mouth, the temperature, etc.
- hearing, to create associations with the occasion
- drawing conclusions about the evaluation (summing up) and making a judgement of the quality of the wine (poor, acceptable, good, outstanding).

Examples of the terms that might be used as part of the evaluation of the wine are given in Table 11.12.

Table 11.12 **Examples of wine evaluation terms**

Sight	*Clarity*: clear, bright, brilliant, gleaming, sumptuous, dull, hazy, cloudy *Colour intensity*: pale, subdued, faded, deep, intense *White wine*: water clear, pale yellow, yellow with green tinges, straw, gold, deep yellow, brown, Maderised *Rosé wine*: pale pink, orange-pink, onion-skin, blue-pink, copper *Red wine*: purple, garnet, ruby, tawny, brick-red, mahogany
Smell (nose, aroma, bouquet)	*Condition*: clean – unclean *Intensity*: weak – pronounced *Other aroma descriptors*: fruity, perfumed, full, deep, spicy, vegetal, fine, rich, pleasant, weak, nondescript, flat, corky
Taste	*Sweetness/dryness*: bone dry, dry, medium dry, sweet, medium sweet, sweet, luscious *Acidity*: low – high *Tannin*: low – high *Body*: thin, light, medium, full-bodied *Length*: short – long *Other taste descriptors*: fruity, bitter, spicy, hard, soft, silky, floral, vegetal, smooth, tart, piquant, spritzig/pétillant (slightly sparkling)
Conclusion	*Summing up*: well-balanced, fine, delicate, rich, robust, vigorous, fat, flabby, thick, velvety, harsh, weak, unbalanced, insipid, for laying down, just right, over the hill *Overall quality/value*: poor – acceptable – good – outstanding

Tasting technique

After assessing the clarity, colour and the smell, take a small amount of the wine in the mouth together with a little air and roll it around so that it reaches the different parts of the tongue. Now lean forward so that the wine is nearest the teeth and suck air in through the teeth. Doing this helps to highlight and intensify the flavour.

(Fortified wines, spirits and liqueurs are often assessed by sight and smell without tasting.)

When tasting, the following should be considered:

- The taste-character of the wine is detected in different parts of the mouth but especially by the tongue: sweetness at the tip and the centre of the tongue, acidity on the upper edges, saltiness on the tip and at the sides, sour at the sides and bitterness at the back.
- Sweetness and dryness will be immediately obvious.
- Acidity will be recognised by its gum-drying sensation, but in correct quantities acidity provides crispness and liveliness to a drink.
- Astringency or tannin content, usually associated with red wines, will give a dry coating or furring effect, especially on the teeth and gums.
- Body, which is the feel of the wine in your mouth, and flavour, the essence of the wine as a drink, will be the final arbiters as to whether or not you like it.
- Aftertaste is the finish the wine leaves on your palate.
- Overall balance is the evaluation of all the above elements taken together.

Note: It is important that you make up your own mind about the wines you taste. Do not be too easily influenced by the observations of others.

General grape and wine characteristics

There are a number of grapes that have distinctive characteristics. Examples of these grapes are listed in Table 11.4 (page 185) and information on their general characteristics is also given.

Recording the findings

Whenever wine is being evaluated a written record should be kept. These notes should be made at each stage of the process, otherwise it is possible to become muddled and confused. The process of writing down the findings helps to reinforce the discipline of the approach and leads, over time, to the development of greater confidence and skill, and also provides a record of wine tastings over time.

11.11 Matching food with wine and other drinks

Food and its accompanying wine/drink should harmonise well together, with each enhancing the other's performance. However, the combinations that prove most successful are those that please the individual.

When considering possible food and wine partnerships there are no guidelines to which there are not exceptions. However, general guidelines on matching wine and food are summarised in Table 11.13.

Some general guidelines when selecting and serving wines are given below.

- Dry wines should be served before sweeter wines.
- White wines should be served before red wines.
- Lighter wines should be served before heavier wines.

- Good wines should be served before great wines.
- Wines should be at their correct temperature before serving.
- Wine should always be served to customers before their food.

Table 11.13 **General guidelines for matching wine and food**

Characteristic	Food considerations
Acidity	Can be used to match, or to contrast, acidity in foods, e.g. crisp wines to match lemon or tomato, or to cut through creamy flavours.
Age/maturity	As wine ages and develops it can become delicate with complex and intricate flavours. More simple foods, such as grills or roasts, work better with older wines than stronger-tasting foods, which can overpower the wines.
Oak	The more oaked the wine then the more robust and flavoursome the foods need to be. Heavily oaked wines can overpower more delicate foods.
Sweetness	Generally the wine should be sweeter than the foods or it will taste flat or thin. Sweet dishes need contrast for them to match well with sweeter wines, for example, acids in sweeter foods can harmonise with the sweetness in the wines. Savoury foods with sweetness (e.g. carrots or onions) can match well with ripe, fruity wines. Blue cheeses can go well with sweet wines. Also sweeter wines can go well with salty foods.
Tannin	Tannic wines match well with red meats and semi-hard cheeses (e.g. Cheddar). Tannic wines are not good with egg dishes and wines with high tannin content do not work well with salty foods.
Weight	Big, rich wines go well with robust (flavoursome) meat dishes, but can overpower lighter-flavoured foods.

Beers and food

Recently there has been an increasing trend to offer beers with food, either alongside or as an alternative to wines. As with wines it is a question of trial and error to achieve harmony between particular beers and foods. Generally the considerations for the pairing of beers and foods are similar to those for matching wines with foods, as shown in Table 11.13, and in particular, taking account of acidity, sweetness/dryness, bitterness, tannin, weight and the complexity of the taste.

Making recommendations to customers

A few general pointers are set out below that may be followed when advising the customer on which beverage to choose to accompany a meal. However, customers should at all times be given complete freedom in their selection of wines or other drinks.

- Aperitifs are usually alcoholic beverages that are drunk before the meal. If wine will be consumed with the meal, then the aperitif selected should be a grape (wine-based) rather than a grain (spirit-based) aperitif, since the latter can potentially spoil or dull the palate.
- The aperitif is usually a wine-based beverage. It is meant to stimulate the appetite and therefore should not be sweet. Dry and medium dry sherries, dry vermouths and Sercial or Verdelho Madeira are all good examples of aperitifs.
- Starter courses are often best accompanied by a dry white or dry rosé wine.
- National e.g. Italian red wine with pasta dishes.
- Fish and shellfish dishes are often most suited to well-chilled, dry white wines.

- Red meats such as beef and lamb blend and harmonise well with red wine.
- White meats such as veal and pork are acceptable with medium white wines.
- Game dishes require the heavier and more robust red wines to complement their full flavour.
- Sweets and desserts are served at the end of the meal and here it is acceptable to offer well-chilled, sweet white wines that may come from the Loire, Sauternes, Barsac or Hungary. These wines harmonise best with dishes containing fruit.
- The majority of cheeses blend well with port and other dry robust red wines. Port is the traditional wine, harmonising best with Stilton cheese.
- The grain- and fruit-based spirits and liqueurs all harmonise well with coffee.

PART D

Service Skills

CHAPTER 12

Basic technical skills and service conventions

This chapter will help you to learn about:

1 The importance of technical skills
2 Holding and using a service spoon and fork
3 Carrying plates
4 Using a service salver (round tray)
5 Using a service plate
6 Carrying glasses
7 Carrying and using large trays
8 The importance of service conventions
9 Traditional service conventions

12.1 The importance of technical skills

Developing good technical skills is essential for three main reasons:

- proficiency in technical service skills leads to greater confidence in undertaking the service tasks
- being technically competent allows servers to concentrate on their social skills and contributes to achieving excellence in the service
- technical competence reduces the risks of accidents.

There are six basic technical food and beverage service skills. These are identified in Table 12.1 below, together with examples of their application. The rest of this chapter provides further information on the application of the skills.

These basic technical skills are used specifically for table service and assisted service. However, these skills are also used when providing other forms of service, for example, when carrying trays for room service or using a service salver for bar service.

Table 12.1 Technical skills and their application

Technical skill	Examples of application
Holding and using a service spoon and fork	For the service of food at a customer's table, especially for silver service, and for serving at a buffet or from a trolley
Carrying plates	When placing and clearing plates from a customer's table

Technical skill	Examples of application
Using a service salver (round tray)	For carrying glasses, carrying tea and coffee services, as an underliner for entrée dishes and for potato and vegetable dishes
Using a service plate	For carrying items to and from a table, including clean cutlery, clearing side plates and knives, crumbing down and clearing accompaniments
Carrying glasses	Carrying clean glasses by hand or on a salver and for clearing dirty glasses from a service area
Carrying and using large trays	For bringing equipment or food and beverage items to the service area and for clearing used equipment from the service area

12.2 Holding and using a service spoon and fork

Expertise in this technique can only be achieved with practice. The purpose of the service spoon and fork is to enable the waiter to serve food from a flat or dish on to the customer's plate quickly and to present the food on the plate well.

- The service fork should be positioned above, or on top of, the service spoon.
- The key to developing this skill is the locking of the ends of the service spoon and fork with the small finger and the third finger, as illustrated in Figure 12.1(a).
- The spoon and fork are manoeuvred with the thumb and the index and second fingers (see Figure 12.1(b)). Using this method food items may be picked up from the serving dish in between the service spoon and service fork.
- Alternatively, the service fork may be turned to mould the shape of the items being served, for example, when serving bread rolls (see Figure 12.1(c)).

There are occasions where two service forks may be used, for example, when serving fillets of fish, as this makes the service of this food item easier.

When using a serving spoon and fork for serving at a sweet or cheese trolley, or at a buffet or gueridon, the spoon and fork are held one in each hand.

Other service equipment that may be used includes serving tongs, fish slices, gateaux slices, serving spoons, scoops, small sauce ladles and larger soup ladles, as shown in Figure 12.2.

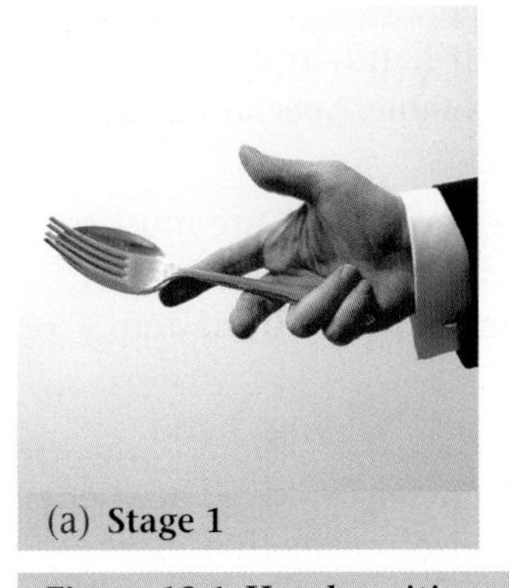

(a) **Stage 1**

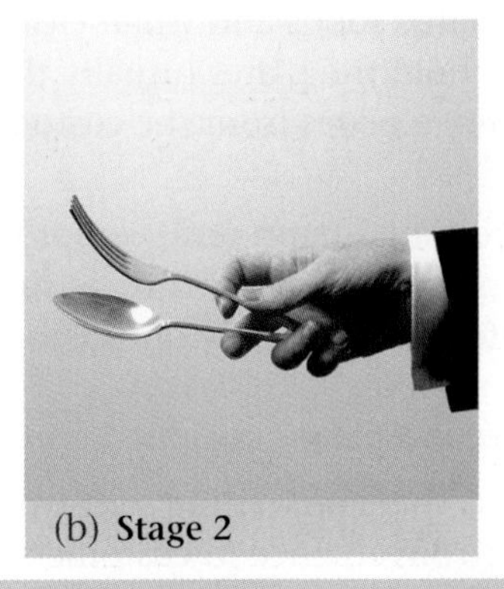

(b) **Stage 2**

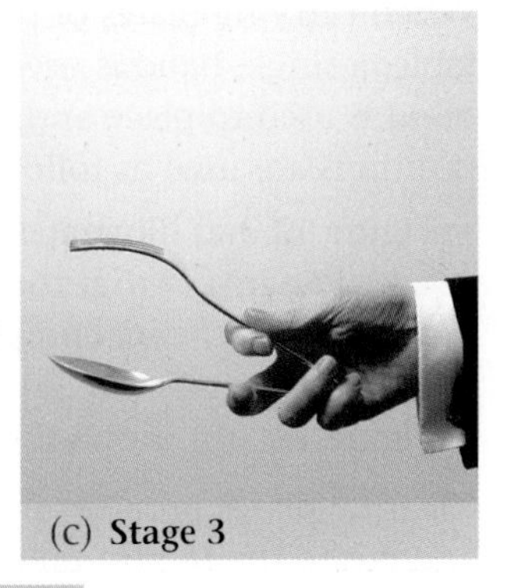

(c) **Stage 3**

Figure 12.1 Hand positions for holding a service spoon and fork

Figure 12.2 Examples of service equipment

12.3 Carrying plates

Clean plates can be carried in a stack, using both hands, or using a tray. When carrying clean plates that are to be placed on the customer's table, a single hand is used to hold the plates (usually the left hand) and the right hand is used to place the plates at each cover on the customer's table. If the plates are hot then the plates are held with a service cloth placed on the palm of the left hand. A separate service cloth is then used in the right hand to hold the hot plates when placing them in front of the customer.

When carrying plates of pre-plated foods and when clearing plates from a customer's table, a single hand is used to hold the plates (usually the left hand) and the right hand is used to place and remove plates from the customer's table. Special hand positions are used as follows:

- Figure 12.3(a) illustrates the initial hand position for the first plate. Care must be taken to ensure that the first plate is held firmly as succeeding plates are built up from here. The second plate will rest firmly on the forearm and the third and fourth fingers.
- Figure 12.3(b) shows the second plate positioned on the left (holding) hand.

Clearing plates properly means that the waiting staff work efficiently, avoid accidents and create the minimum of inconvenience to customers. It also means that more items can be cleared from tables in less time and in fewer journeys between the sideboard or workstation and the customer's table. Clearing properly allows for the stacking of dirties neatly and safely at the sideboard or workstation. (See also Section 17.2, page 294.)

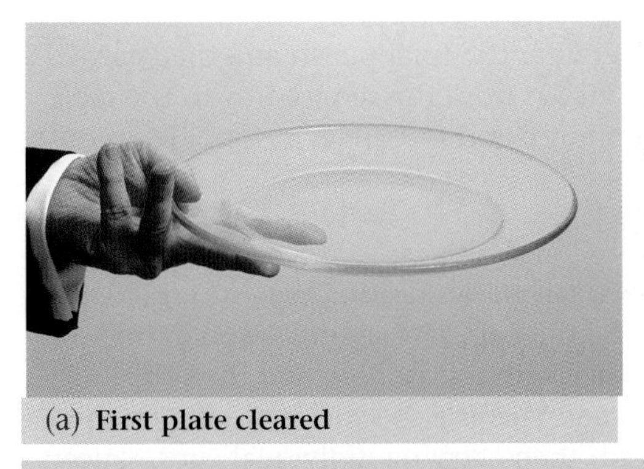

(a) **First plate cleared**

(b) **Second plate cleared**

Figure 12.3 **Hand positions when clearing plates and carrying pre-plated food (cold)**

12.4 Using a service salver (round tray)

A service salver is a round, often silver or stainless steel tray (wood or plastic may also be used). A napkin (folded flat) or non-slip mat is placed on the tray to help prevent items slipping on the tray as they are being carried. Some trays are also made with non-slip surfaces. The service salver may be used to:

- carry clean glasses to, and remove dirty glasses from, a customer's table
- carry clean cutlery to and from a customer's table
- place clean cutlery on the table
- place clean cups and saucers on the table
- provide an underflat when silver-serving vegetables.

Figure 12.4 **Example of cutlery positions when carrying on a service salver**

Carrying clean cutlery

In order to be more efficient, hygienic, safer, and more professional, items to be placed on or removed from a table should be carried on a service salver rather than carrying these items in bunches in the hand.

Clean cutlery is placed onto the service salver after the final polish and then carried to the table on the tray. The cutlery is then placed from the service tray to the table by holding the item of cutlery between the thumb and forefinger at the side, in order to reduce the possibility of finger marks.

Carrying cups and saucers

Tea and coffee cups are carried using a service salver, by stacking the saucers, cups and teaspoons separately. Then before placing the cup, saucer and teaspoon on the table, the cup is put onto a saucer, together with a teaspoon, and then the whole service is placed in front of the customer. This is a speedier and safer method (especially when larger numbers are involved) than carrying individual cups, saucers and teaspoons to the table one by one. (See page 292 and Figure 16.6 on page 293.)

As an underflat

When silver serving food dishes, potatoes or vegetables at the table, an underflat should be used to hold either one large vegetable dish or a number of smaller ones, depending on the customer's order. The purpose of using a service salver as an underflat is to:

- add to the presentation of the food being served
- give the waiter more control when using the service spoon and fork to serve from the food dishes on to the customer's plate
- provide greater protection in case of spillage, therefore not detracting from the presentation of the food on the plate or the overall table presentation
- give the waiter added protection against heat and possible spillage on the uniform.

For more information on silver service see Chapter 15, Section 15.1, page 266.

12.5 Using a service plate

A service plate is a joint plate with a napkin upon it. It has a number of uses during the meal service:

- for placing clean cutlery on and removing it from the table
- for clearing side plates and side knives
- for crumbing down after the main course, or any other stage of the meal if necessary
- for clearing accompaniments from the table as and when necessary.

Carrying clean cutlery

When placing on, or removing, clean cutlery from a table, the items can be carried on a service plate. The reasons for this are the same as given under using a service salver above.

Clearing side plates and knives

When clearing dirty side plates and side knives from the customer's table, the use of a service plate means that the waiter has a larger area on which to stack the side knives and any debris. Using the hand positions shown in Figure 12.3(a) and (b) (page 211), the side plates may be stacked above the service plate and all the debris in a separate pile, together with the side knives laid flat upon the service plate (see Figure 17.4(a)–(b), page 299). This is a much safer and speedier method, especially when larger numbers are involved.

Clearing accompaniments

The service plate is also used to clear such items as the cruet, peppermill or other accompaniments, which may not already be set on an underplate.

Crumbing down

The service plate is used in the crumbing down process. The purpose here is to freshen up the appearance of the tablecloth prior to laying the sweet covers and serving the sweet. For further information see Chapter 17, Section 17.2, page 294.

12.6 Carrying glasses

There are two basic methods of carrying glasses in the food and beverage service areas: by hand or on a service salver.

Carrying by hand

Wine goblets should be positioned between alternate fingers as far as is possible. The wine goblets should only be carried in one hand, allowing the other hand to remain free to steady oneself in case of emergencies.

Figure 12.5 Carrying clean glasses by hand

This method allows wine goblets that are already polished to be handled. They can be carried about the room and set in their correct position on the table without the bowl of the glass being touched. This should only be done if there are no customers present, otherwise a service salver should be used. Clean glassware is always handled by the stem and for non-stemmed glassware by the base.

Carrying glasses on a service salver

The method of carrying clean wine glasses about the restaurant during service using the service salver is illustrated in Figure 12.6.

A service cloth is placed on the palm of the hand, with the service salver placed upon it, to allow the service salver to be rotated more easily in order to remove each wine goblet in turn by the base and to set it on the table.

Figure 12.7 indicates the use of the service salver for clearing dirty wine goblets from the table. The first dirty wine goblet cleared should be placed on the service salver nearest to the server. As the dirty glasses are cleared, they should be placed on the service salver to ensure a better and more even distribution of weight, to lessen the likelihood of accidents occurring. Again, dirty glassware is always handled by the stem and for non-stemmed glassware by the base. This is more hygienic as it avoids touching where the customer has been drinking from the glass.

Figure 12.6 **Carrying clean glasses on a service salver**

Figure 12.7 **Carrying dirty glasses on a service salver**

Carrying glasses using glass racks

Glass racks, usually made of plastic, are often used to carry glasses during the setting up of the restaurant and for functions. These racks enable the transportation of glasses in bulk once they have been washed and polished at a central point. Glass racks are also used for dirty glasses and many can be put through a glass wash machine.

12.7 Carrying and using large trays

Trays are used for:

- carrying food from the kitchen to the restaurant
- service in rooms and lounges
- clearing from sideboards/workstations
- clearing from tables (when the customer is not seated at the table)
- carrying equipment.

The correct method of holding and carrying an oblong tray is to position the tray lengthways onto the forearm and to support it by holding the tray with the other hand.

Figure 12.8 shows how to carry an oblong tray. Note the tray is organised so that the heaviest items are nearest the carrier. This helps to balance the tray. Also note that one hand is placed underneath the tray and the other at the side.

Figure 12.8 Carrying a loaded oblong tray

12.8 The importance of service conventions

There are traditional ways of doing things that have become established over time within food and beverage service. These are known as the 'service conventions' and have proved to be effective and efficient ways in which to carry out the service.

Service conventions also ensure standardisation in the service sequence and the customer process (see Section 2.3, page 35, for the definition of these terms), both for staff and for customers. The service conventions detailed in this chapter are a guide. For food and beverage service to operate efficiently and smoothly it is important that all members of the staff follow the same service conventions. Different establishments may have slight variations on the service conventions listed here but whatever conventions are used, all staff must follow the same ones. Otherwise the service will be inefficient and potentially chaotic and customers will feel that the operation is not well managed and coordinated.

12.9 Traditional service conventions

The various service conventions may be broken down into a number of groups:

- personal service
- service preparation
- order-taking
- general service
- when serving
- conventions for general working and clearing following service.

Examples of these groups of service conventions, and the rationale for them, are given in the tables below:

Table 12.2 Personal service conventions

Convention	Rationale
Always work as part of a team	All members of the team should know and be able to do their own job well, to ensure a smooth, well-organised and disciplined operation.
Work hygienically and safely	For the protection of other staff and customers from harm and to avoid accidents.
Pass other members of staff by moving to the right	Having an establishment rule about each member of staff always moving to the right (or left) avoids confusion and accidents.
Avoid contact between fingers and mouth or hair	If contact between fingers and mouth or hair, etc., is unavoidable, then hands must be washed before continuing with service. Always wash hands after using the toilet.
Cover cuts and sores	Covering cuts and sores with waterproof plasters or dressings is essential health and safety practice.

Table 12.3 Service preparation conventions

Convention	Rationale
Use checklists for preparation tasks	Using checklists ensures that all members of staff complete all preparatory tasks in the same way.
Prepare service areas in sequence	Ensure service areas are laid out and housekeeping duties have been completed before the preparation for service begins. This can save time and unnecessary duplication of effort afterwards.
Consider using white gloves	In some establishments members of staff wear white cotton gloves when carrying out various preparation tasks. The gloves help to prevent the soiling of clean service items and avoid putting finger marks on cleaned and polished service equipment. White gloves are also sometimes used during service, instead of using service cloths, when serving plated foods that are presented on hot plates.
Use a model lay-up	Lay one initial full place setting (cover) to use as a model for all staff to measure against. A place setting is usually about 60 cm wide.
Hold glasses or cups at the base or by the handle	This is hygienic practice. Service staff should not hold glasses or cups, etc., by the rim.
Hold cutlery in the middle at the sides between the thumb and forefinger	This is safer, makes for more accurate placing of items on the table, and also helps to prevent finger marking on the clean cutlery items.
Lay table place settings (covers) from the inside out	This makes table laying easier. Place a centre to the cover (a table mat or side plate for instance) then lay tableware in order from the inside of the cover outwards. When laying a number of covers it is more efficient to lay each piece of tableware for all covers in sequence, i.e., all side plates, then all side knives, etc.
Use of standard lay-ups	Indicates the type of meals being taken, the sequence of the courses and also what stage customers are at within a meal.
Fully or partly lay the table before a meal begins	Most often tables are fully laid before a meal but this may vary, for instance, if the table is likely to become excessively cluttered or where there is not sufficient equipment to fully pre-lay all the tables.
Place items on the table consistently	Make sure that any crested or patterned crockery or glassware is always placed the same way round on the table and that it is evenly spaced.

Table 12.4 Order-taking conventions

Convention	Rationale
Take food, wine and drink orders through hosts	This is common courtesy – agreement needs to be obtained for any items that are to be served. For larger parties, where there may be a choice, orders may be taken individually but it is useful to confirm what has actually been ordered with the host as this may save any disagreements later.
Use order notation techniques	Use of such techniques helps any server to identify which member of a party is having a particular item of food or beverage.
Be aware of customers who may have additional needs	Look out for, and be prepared to deal with, people with sight, hearing, speech, mobility and language difficulties. Also be able to deal with children.

Table 12.5 General service conventions

Convention	Rationale
Use checklists for all aspects of service	These help to ensure that all information is complete and that all managers and staff carry out procedures in the same way.
Avoid leaning over customers	This shows courtesy and respect for physical space. Remember that no matter how clean service staff members are, food and beverage smells do tend to cling to service uniforms.
Place items low to high	Lower items should be placed near to the customer and taller items behind or to the side of these. This makes items easily accessible by the customer and helps to avoid accidents.
Place items according to the customer's position at the table	Items placed on a table should be within reach of the customer. Handles, etc., should be set for the customer's convenience.
Use underplates (liners)	These are used (cold) for four main purposes: to improve presentation on the table; to make carrying of soup plates, bowls and other bowl-shaped dishes easier; to isolate the hand from hot dishes; to allow cutlery to be carried along with the item.
Use service salvers or service plates (with napkins or mats on them to prevent items slipping)	Service salvers or service plates are used for five main purposes: to improve presentation of items to be served; to make carrying of bowl-shaped serving dishes easier and more secure (also avoids the thumb of the server being inside a service dish); to allow for more than one serving dish to be carried at a time; to isolate the hand from hot dishes; to allow service gear to be carried along with the item(s).
Hold flats, food dishes and round trays on the palm of the hand	This is safer and ensures that the food items are best presented for the customer. It also makes for easier carrying and avoids the server's thumb or service cloths being seen on the edge of flats, dishes and round trays. If the flats or dishes are hot then the service cloth can be underneath, folded and laid flat onto the palm to protect the hand.
Use doilies/dish papers on underplates (liners)	Doilies, dish papers (or linen or paper napkins) on underplates are used to improve presentation, to reduce noise and to prevent the dish from slipping on the underplate. Use doilies for sweet food items and dish papers for savoury food items.

Table 12.6 Conventions when serving

Convention	Rationale
Serve cold food before hot food	When the hot food is served the service is complete and customers can enjoy the meal without waiting for additional items to be served. For the same reason, accompaniments should be automatically offered and served at the same time as the food item.
Serve wine before food	Similar to above. Customers will wish to enjoy the wine with their meal. They will not want to wait for the wine service, as their hot food will go cold.
Start service from the right-hand side of the host, with the host last	Honoured guests are usually seated on the right of a host. The convention is to serve a table by moving anti-clockwise to each customer, as this ensures that members of the serving staff are walking forwards to serve the next person.
Serve women first	Often done if it does not slow the service. Particular care needs to be taken so as not to confuse things when the host is a woman. A host of either gender is still the host and should always be served last.
Silver serve food from the left-hand side of a customer	Ensures that the service dish is nearer the plate for ease of service and prevents food being spilt onto the person. Customers can more easily see the food being served and make choices if necessary, and members of the service staff are also able to see and control what they are doing.
Use separate service gear for different food items	This should be standard. It avoids different food items or sauces being transferred from one dish or plate to another and avoids messy presentation of foods on the customers' plates.
Serve foods onto plates consistently	For service of the whole main course onto a joint plate, place the main item at the 6 o'clock position with potatoes served next at the 10 past 2 position and vegetables last at the 10 to 2 position (this also follows the UK Royal National Institute for the Blind (RNIB) recommendations). For main courses with potatoes and vegetables and/or salads served on a separate plate or crescent, the main item is placed in the centre of the main plate with the separate plate or crescent of potatoes and vegetables and/or side salad to the left of this.
Serve plated foods from the right-hand side of a customer	Plates can be placed in front of the customer with the right hand and the stack of other plated food is then behind the customer's chair in the left hand. If there is an accident, the plates held in the left hand will go onto the floor rather than over the customer. Plated foods should be placed so that the food items are consistently in the same position for all customers.
Serve all beverages from the right-hand side of a customer	Glasses are placed on the right-hand side of a cover and the service of beverages follows from this. For individual drinks and other beverages, the tray is held behind a customer's seat in the server's left hand. Other beverages such as coffee and tea are also served from the right. All beverages should also be cleared from the right.
Clear from the right-hand side of a customer	Plates can be removed in front of the customer with the right hand and the stack of plates is then behind the customer's chair, in the server's left hand. If there is an accident, the plates held in the left hand will go onto the floor rather than over the customer. The exception to this is for side plates, which are on the left-hand side of the cover. These are more easily cleared from the left, thus avoiding stretching in front of the customer.

Table 12.7 Conventions for general working and clearing following service

Convention	Rationale
Use trays	Use trays to bring foods and beverage items to the service areas and to clear during and following service. Trays can be brought to, or removed from, sideboards or service tables and also to serve plated foods from (or to clear plates onto) with service staff working as a pair.
Separate the serving at table from food/drink collection and sideboard/workstation clearing	Ensures that there is always someone in the room to attend to customers and to monitor the overall service, while others are bringing in food and beverage orders or clearing items away from the service station. This approach allows for the training of new staff and ensures that customer contact is primarily through experienced staff.
Use checklists for tasks required for clearing after service	In the same way as using checklists for preparatory tasks (see Section 13.6, page 244), using checklists for clearing after service ensures that any member of staff completes all clearing tasks in the same way.

CHAPTER 13

Preparation for service

This chapter will help you to learn about:

1 Preparation for table service
2 Preparation duties
3 Clothing-up and napkin-folding
4 Laying covers for table service and assisted service
5 Preparation for self-service, assisted service and single-point service
6 Checklists for preparatory tasks

13.1 Preparation for table service

The term 'mise-en-place' ('put in place' but also meaning preparation for service) is the traditional term used for all the duties that must be carried out in order to prepare the room for service. The supervisor will draw up a duty rota showing the tasks and duties to be completed before service and the members of staff responsible for them.

Order of working

The duties should proceed in a certain order so that they may be carried out effectively and efficiently. For example, dusting should be done before the tables are laid, and vacuuming should be completed before the tables and chairs are put in place. The duties involved in bar preparation may be included within the duty rota depending upon the type of establishment.

A suggested order of work might be as follows:

1 Dusting
2 Stacking chairs on tables
3 Vacuuming
4 Polishing
5 Arrange tables and chairs according to the table plan
6 Linen
7 Accompaniments
8 Hotplate
9 Still room
10 Sideboards/workstations
11 Silver cleaning
12 Other duties such as preparing trolleys

Some of these duties will be carried out at the same time and the supervisor must ensure they are all completed efficiently. As the necessary preparatory work is completed the staff should report back to the supervisor, who will check that the work has been carried out in a satisfactory manner and then reallocate the member of staff to other work involved in the setting-up of the service areas.

Using white gloves

In some establishments members of staff wear white cotton gloves when carrying out preparation tasks such as:

- handling linen and paper
- clothing up tables
- making napkin folds
- handling clean crockery, cutlery and glassware
- laying tables.

The gloves help to prevent the soiling of clean service items and finger marks on cleaned and polished service equipment. For each separate task carried out, clean gloves should be used. They should not be reused for further tasks as this may present a hygiene risk.

13.2 Preparation duties

The duties to be carried out before the service commences are many and varied according to the particular food and beverage service area concerned. A list of the possible tasks and duties is shown below, but not all of these are applicable to every situation and there may be some jobs not listed which are specific to a particular establishment.

Supervisor

Duties might include:

- checking that a full team of staff is present and that all duties on the duty rota are covered
- checking the booking diary for reservations
- making out the seating plan for the day and allocating customers accordingly
- making out a plan of the various stations and showing where the staff will be working
- going over the menu with staff immediately before service is due to commence.

Housekeeping duties

Housekeeping duties may also include the reception area and might involve the following:

- every day, vacuuming the carpet and brushing surrounds
- cleaning and polishing doors and glass
- emptying waste bins
- performing the daily tasks as indicated on the duty rota – such as:
  - *Monday*: brush and dust tables and chairs
  - *Tuesday*: polish all sideboards, window ledges and cash desk
- each day, on completion of all duties, lining up tables and chairs for laying up.

Linen/paper

This applies not only to table, buffet and slip cloths and glass and waiter cloths, but also to paper slip cloths and napkins plus dish papers and doilies. Duties might include:

- collecting the clean linen from the housekeeping department, checking items against list and distributing them to the various service points. Spare linen should be folded neatly into the linen basket

- ensuring that stocks are sufficient to meet needs
- laying tablecloths
- folding napkins
- ensuring that glass cloths and waiters' cloths are available
- providing dish papers and doilies as required
- the preparation of the linen basket for return to the linen room.

Hotplate

Duties might include:

- switching on the hotplate and checking that all doors are closed
- placing items in the hotplate according to the menu offered, e.g.
  - soup plates
  - consommé cups
  - fish plates
  - joint plates
  - sweet plates
  - coffee cups
- stocking up the hotplate after each service with clean and polished crockery in readiness for the next meal service.

Cutlery

Duties might include:

- collection of cutlery from the storage area (sometimes called a silver room) and polishing and sorting on to trays some or all of the following items, in quantities agreed with the supervisor, and in readiness for laying up the tables and setting up the sideboards:
  - service spoons
  - joint/service forks
  - soup spoons
  - fish knives
  - fish forks
  - joint knives
  - side knives
  - sweet spoons
  - sweet forks
  - tea/coffee spoons
  - specialist service equipment as required for the menu
- identifying broken items or those in need of replacing.

Crockery

Duties might include:

- checking and polishing side plates ready for lay-up
- checking and polishing crockery for the hotplate according to the menu and service requirements
- preparation of service plates for sideboards/workstations
- preparation of stocks of crockery for sideboards/workstations, such as fish plates, side plates and saucers.

Glassware

Duties might include:

- collection of the required glassware from the glass pantry (store)
- checking and polishing glassware needed for the general lay-up
- checking and polishing glassware needed for any special events
- checking and polishing glassware required for the liqueur trolley and any special menu dishes, e.g. goblets for prawn cocktails, tulip glasses for sorbets and liqueur, port and brandy glasses for the liqueur trolley
- stacking the cleaned and polished glassware onto trays or placing into glass racks in readiness for setting up.

Polishing glassware

The following equipment is required to carry out the technique described below:

- a container of near-boiling water
- a clean, dry tea cloth
- the required glassware.

1. Using the base of the glass to be cleaned, hold the wine goblet over the steam from the boiling water so that the steam enters the bowl of the glass (see Figure 13.1(a)).
2. Rotate the wine goblet to allow the steam to circulate fully within the bowl of the glass and then hold the base of the glass over the steam.
3. Now hold the base of the wine goblet in the clean, dry tea cloth.
4. Place the other hand underneath the tea cloth in readiness to polish the bowl of the glass.
5. Place the thumb of the polishing hand inside the bowl of the glass and the fingers on the outside, holding the bowl of the wine goblet gently but firmly. Rotate the wine goblet with the hand holding the base of the glass (see Figure 13.1(b)).
6. When fully polished, hold the wine goblet up to the light to check that it is clean.
7. Ensure that the base of the glass is also clean.

Figure 13.1(a) **Polishing glasses – allowing steam to enter the bowl of the glass**

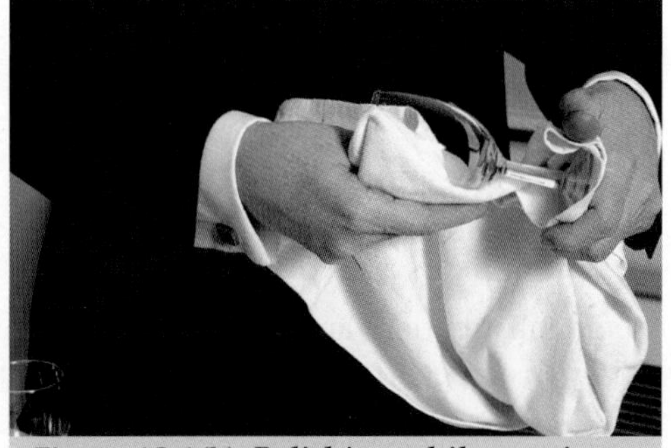

Figure 13.1(b) **Polishing while rotating the glass**

The process described here is for single glasses. Larger quantities of glassware may be polished by first placing a glass rack full of inverted glasses over a sink of very hot water in order to steam the glasses. A number of people would then work together to polish the glassware.

Cruets, table numbers and butter dishes

Duties might include:

- the collection of cruets, table numbers and butter dishes from the silver room
- checking, filling and polishing the cruet sets (salt cellars, pepper and mustard pots)
- the laying on tables of cruet sets, table numbers and butter dishes with butter knives, according to the headwaiter's instructions.

Still room

Duties might include:

- the ordering of stores' requirements (including bar and accompaniment requirements), to hold over the coming service period
- checking with the supervisor/headwaiter the number of accompaniments and sets of cruets to prepare and the number of sideboards/workstations and tables that will be in use during the service period

- the preparation of:
  - beverage service items, e.g. teapots, coffee pots, cold milk jugs
  - butter scrolls/butter pats and alternatives
  - bread items – brioche, croissants, wholemeal rolls, gristicks
- polishing and refilling oil and vinegar stands, sugar basins and caster sugar dredgers, peppermills and cayenne pepper pots
- preparing all accompaniments such as tomato ketchup, French and English mustard, ground ginger, horseradish sauce, mint sauce, Worcestershire sauce and Parmesan cheese
- distributing the accompaniments to the sideboards.

Sideboards/Workstations

After ensuring that the sideboard/workstation is clean and polished it can be stocked up. Figure 13.2 gives an example of a sideboard lay-up including:

Other items might include:

1 water jug
2 butter dish
3 check pad on service plate
4 assorted condiments
5 hotplate
6 side knives
7 joint knives
8 fish knives and forks
9 soup spoons, tea and coffee spoons
10 sweet spoons and forks
11 service spoons and forks
12 bread basket
13 service salver/plate
14 underflats
15 coffee saucers
16 side plates
17 sweet/fish plates
18 joint plates
19 trays

- specialist cutlery according to the menu, e.g. soup and sauce ladles
- various crockery according to the menu, such as saucers for consommé cups.

Note: Gueridons may also have to be laid up in conjunction with the sideboards, according to the type of service offered.

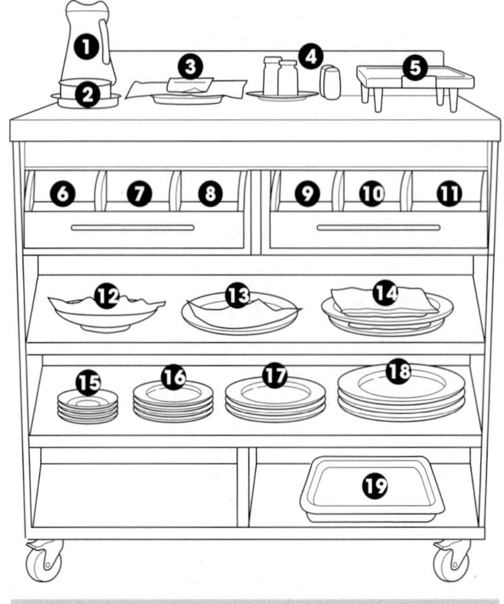

Figure 13.2 Example of a sideboard lay-up

Figure 13.3 Laid sideboard

Bar

Duties may include:

1 Opening the bar.
2 Bar silver requiring cleaning to be taken to the silver person.
3 Clearing any debris left from the previous day.
4 Wiping down bar tops.
5 Cleaning shelves and swabbing the bar floor.
6 Checking optics.
7 Restocking the bar with beverage items as required.
8 Preparing ice buckets, wine coolers, service trays and water jugs.
9 Checking pads and wine lists; lining up, cleaning and polishing aperitif glasses.
10 Preparing and checking the liqueur trolley for glasses, stock and bottle presentation.
11 Preparing the bar service top according to the standards of the establishment which may include:

- cutting board
- fruit knife
- fruit: lemons, oranges, apples
- cucumber
- fresh eggs (for cocktails)
- mixing glass and spoons
- Hawthorn strainer
- wine funnel
- olives, cocktail cherries
- cocktail shaker strainer
- nuts and crisps
- coloured sugar
- Angostura bitters
- peach bitters
- Worcestershire sauce
- cocktail sticks
- cherries in glass
- straws in sherry glass
- tea strainer
- wine coasters
- spirit measures
- soda siphon
- ice bucket and tongs.

Display buffet

Duties may include:

- the preparation of the buffet table to the supervisor's instructions
- the display of:
  - butter dishes and knives
  - accompaniments
  - cold fish plates
  - special cutlery and tableware as required
  - sauce and soup ladles
  - service spoons and forks
  - spare joint plates for used service gear.

Trolleys

Trolleys such as those for cheese or sweets may need to be set up according to the establishment's requirements. For more information about service from trolleys see Chapter 15, Section 15.5, page 272.

Preparing a floral table decoration

A simple centre table display (posy arrangement) can be made in a small shallow bowls with oasis in the bowl to hold the flowers.

Figure 13.4 Centre table posy arrangement

Many establishments, as an alternative to the posy arrangement, purchase blooms, often single stem, on a daily basis or as required. These are presented in a stem vase on the table. This approach is cheaper, less time-consuming and equally effective in providing floral decor for tables.

Note: Oasis is a green-coloured sponge-like material that holds moisture and is soft enough for greenery and flower stems to be pushed into it to hold them secure. The oasis should be kept moist to maximise the life of the flowers. Moisture content can be checked by lightly pressing the oasis – it should feel wet. The flowers can also be kept moist by lightly spraying them from time to time with a water gun.

13.3 Clothing-up and napkin-folding

Nothing is more attractive in the room than tables clothed-up with clean, crisp and well-starched linen tablecloths and napkins. The tablecloth and napkins should be handled as little as possible, which will be ensured by laying the tablecloth quickly and properly first time and folding napkins in the more simpler folds, upon a clean surface, and with clean hands.

Laying the tablecloth

Before laying the tablecloth the table and chairs should be in their correct position. The tabletop should be clean and the table level, with care being taken to ensure that it does not wobble. If the table wobbles slightly, a disc sliced from a cork, a small wedge or an old menu folded neatly can be used to correct the problem. Next, the correct size of tablecloth should be collected. Most tablecloths are folded in what is known as a screen fold.

The waiter should stand between the legs of the table while the tablecloth is being laid, as this ensures that the corners of the cloth cover the legs of the table once the clothing-up has been completed.

The screen fold should be opened out across the table in front of the waiter with the inverted and two single folds facing him, ensuring that the inverted fold is on top.

The tablecloth should then be laid in the following manner:

1. Place the thumb on top of the inverted fold with the index and third fingers either side of the middle fold (see Figure 13.5(a)).
2. Spread out your arms as close to the width of the table as is possible and lift the tablecloth so that the bottom fold falls free.
3. This should be positioned over the edge of the opposite side of the table from where you are standing (see Figure 13.5(b)).
4. Now let go of the middle fold and open the tablecloth out, by drawing it towards you until the table is covered with the tablecloth.
5. Check that the fall of the cloth is even on all sides (see Figure 13.5(c)).
6. Adjustments may be made by pulling from the edge of the cloth (Figure 13.5(d)).

If the tablecloth is laid correctly the following should be apparent:

- the corners of the tablecloth should be over (cover) the legs of the table
- the overlap should be even all round the table: 30–45 cm (12–18 in)
- the creases of all tablecloths laid should run the same way in the room.

If two tablecloths are necessary to cover a table for a larger party, then the overlap of the two tablecloths should face away from the entrance to the room. This is for presentation purposes of both the room and the table.

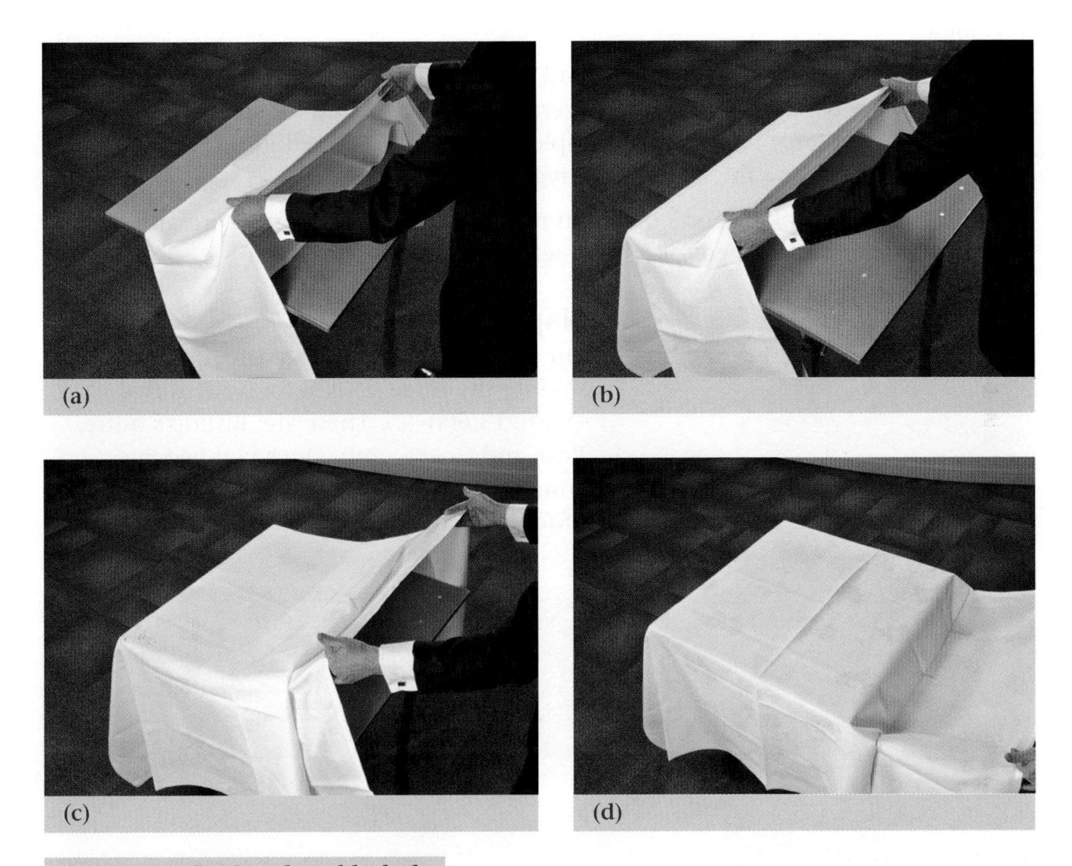

(a) (b) (c) (d)

Figure 13.5 **Laying the tablecloth**

Napkin folds

There are many forms of napkin (or serviette) fold to be found in use in the food and beverage service area. Some are intricate in their detail while others are simpler. The simpler folds are used in everyday service and some of the more complex and difficult folds may only be used on special occasions, such as luncheons, dinners and weddings.

There are three main reasons why the simple folds are better than the more complex ones. The key ones are:

1. The napkin, if folded correctly, can look good and add to the general appearance of the room, whether it is a simple or complex fold.
2. A simpler fold is perhaps more hygienic as the more complex fold involves greater handling to complete. In addition, its appearance, when unfolded to spread over the customer's lap, is poor as it often has many creases.
3. The complex fold takes much more time to complete properly than a very simple fold.

Many of the napkin folds have special names, for example:

- Cone
- Bishop's mitre

- Rose
- Cockscomb
- Triple wave
- Fan
- Candle.

The three napkin folds shown in Figure 13.6(a)–(c) are some of the more common folds used every day in the food and beverage service area and for special occasions. These are simpler folds that may be completed more quickly, requiring less handling by the operator and are therefore more hygienic.

The rose fold of a napkin is one in which rolls or Melba toast may be presented for the table. It is not often used for a place setting.

Figure 13.6(a) Bishop's mitre

Napkin-folding

On the following pages are the methods for folding the three napkin folds identified in Figure 13.6(a)–(c). These are: Bishop's mitre, Rose and Cockscomb. Once you become competent at these, you should learn the art of folding others to extend your repertoire.

Note: The napkins must be clean and well starched. Run the back of your hand over every fold to make the creases firm and sharp.

Figure 13.6(b) Rose

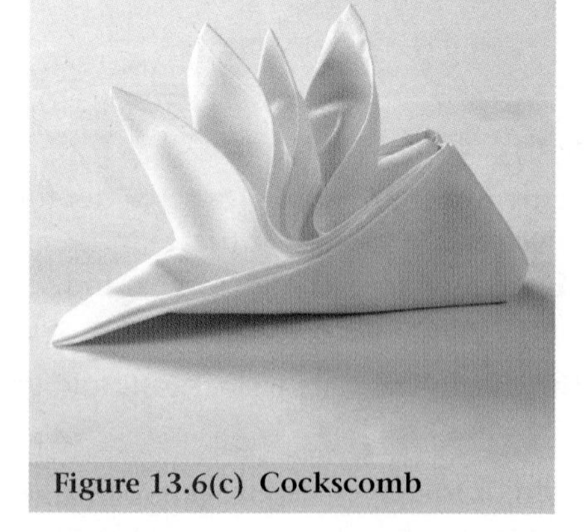

Figure 13.6(c) Cockscomb

Bishop's mitre

1. Lay the napkin out flat in front of you (see Figure 13.7(a)).
2. Fold it in half, straight side to straight side (see Figure 13.7(b)).
3. Take the top right corner and fold it down to the centre of the bottom line (see Figure 13.7(c)).
4. Take the bottom left corner and fold it up to meet the centre of the top line (see Figure 13.7(d)).
5. Turn the napkin over so that the folds are now facing down (see Figure 13.7(e)).
6. Take the top line (edge) and fold it down to meet the base line (bottom edge), leaving the two peaks pointing away from you (see Figure 13.7(f)).
7. Take the bottom right-hand side and fold it under the flap on the left side. Make sure it tucks right under the flap for a snug fit (see Figure 13.7(g)).
8. Turn it completely over (see Figure 13.7(h)).
9. Again take the bottom right-hand side and fold it under the flap on the left side. Now stand the napkin up by pulling the sides of the base out until it is circular in shape (see Figure 13.7(i)).

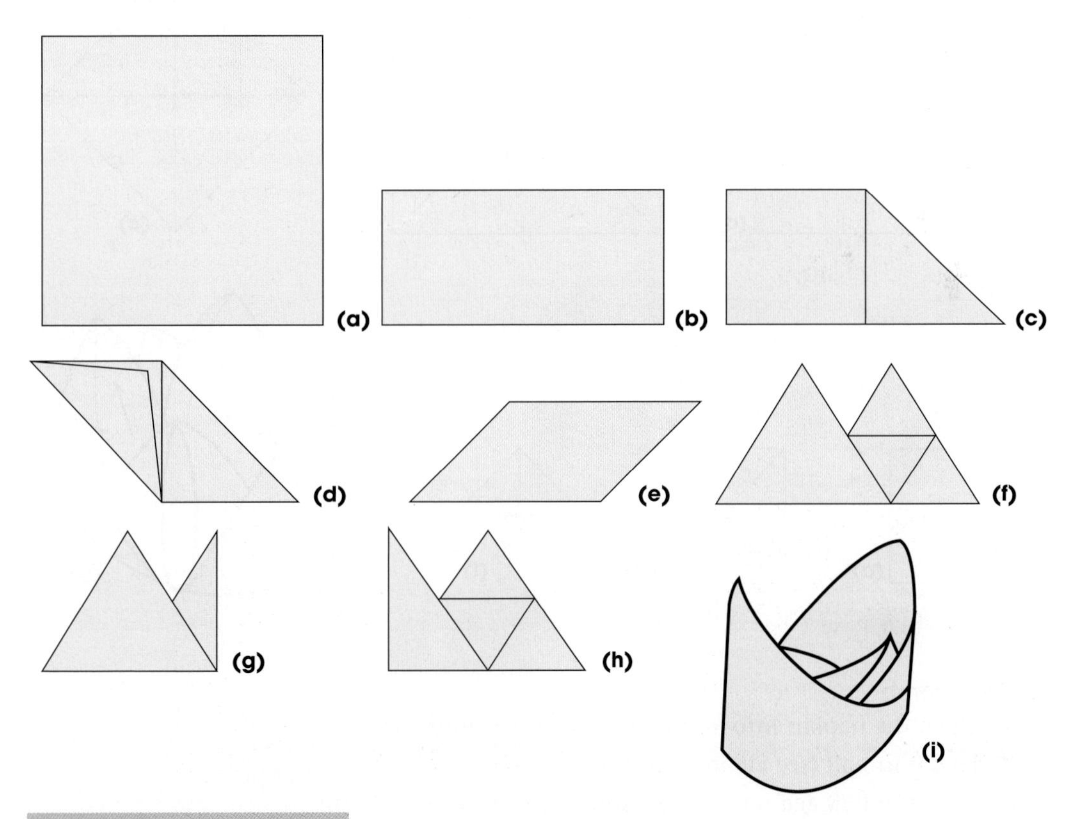

Figure 13.7 Bishop's mitre

Rose

1. Unfold the napkin and lay it out in a square (see Figure 13.8(a)).
2. Fold the corners into the centre of the napkin (see Figure 13.8(b)).
3. Fold the corners into the centre of the napkin for a second time (see Figure 13.8(c)).
4. Turn the whole napkin over so that all the corners folded into the centre are underneath (see Figure 13.8(d)).
5. Fold the corners into the centre once more (see Figure 13.8(e)).
6. Hold the four centre points down by means of an upturned wine goblet (see Figure 13.8(f)).
7. Holding the wine goblet steady, place your hand under each corner and pull up a folded corner of the napkin (petal) on to the bowl of the glass. You now have four petals showing. Now place your hand under the napkin, but between each of the petals, and raise a further four petals. Place on an underplate (see Figure 13.8(g)).

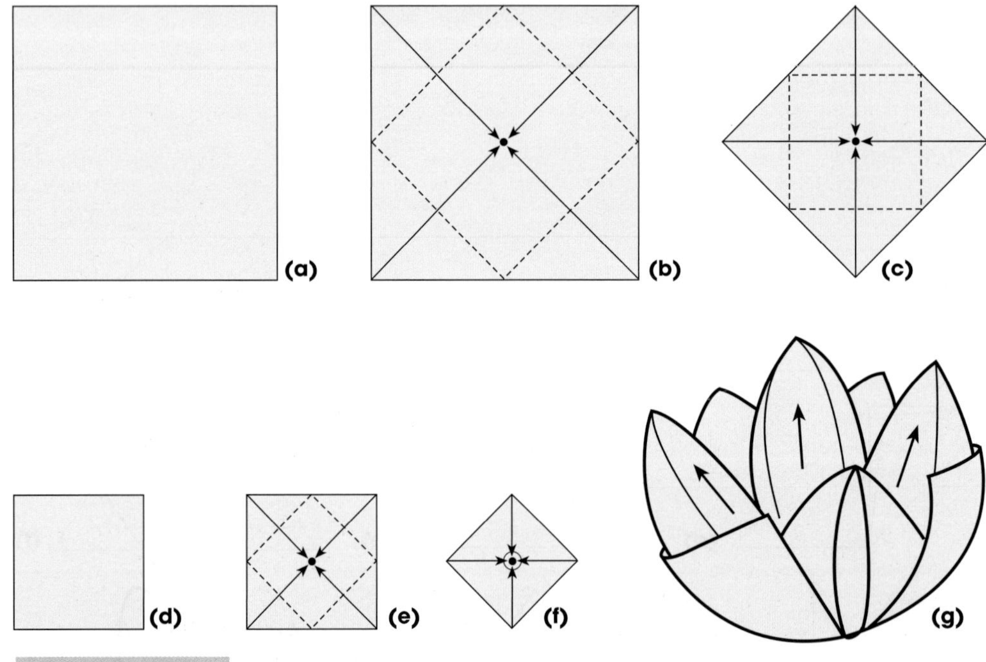

Figure 13.8 Rose

Cockscomb

1. Open the napkin into a square shape (see Figure 13.9(a)).
2. Fold it in half (see Figure 13.9(b)).
3. Fold it in half again to make a square (see Figure 13.9(c)).
4. Rotate the square so that it now forms a diamond shape in front of you. Make sure the four single folds are at the bottom of the diamond (see Figure 13.9(d)).
5. Fold the bottom corner of the diamond to the top corner. You will then have a triangular shape in front of you, with the four single folds on top (see Figure 13.9(e)).
6. Take the right side of the triangle and fold it over on to the centre line (see Figure 13.9(f)).

7 Do the same with the left-hand side (see Figure 13.9(g)).
8 Tuck the two lower triangles (A and B) under the main triangle (see Figure 13.9(h)).
9 Fold the two triangles (C and D) down from the centre line and hold it together. The four single folds should now be on top and at the peak of this fold (see Figure 13.9(i)).
10 Hold this narrow fold firmly, ensuring the four single folds are away from you. In turn, pull each single fold up and towards you (see Figure 13.9(j)).

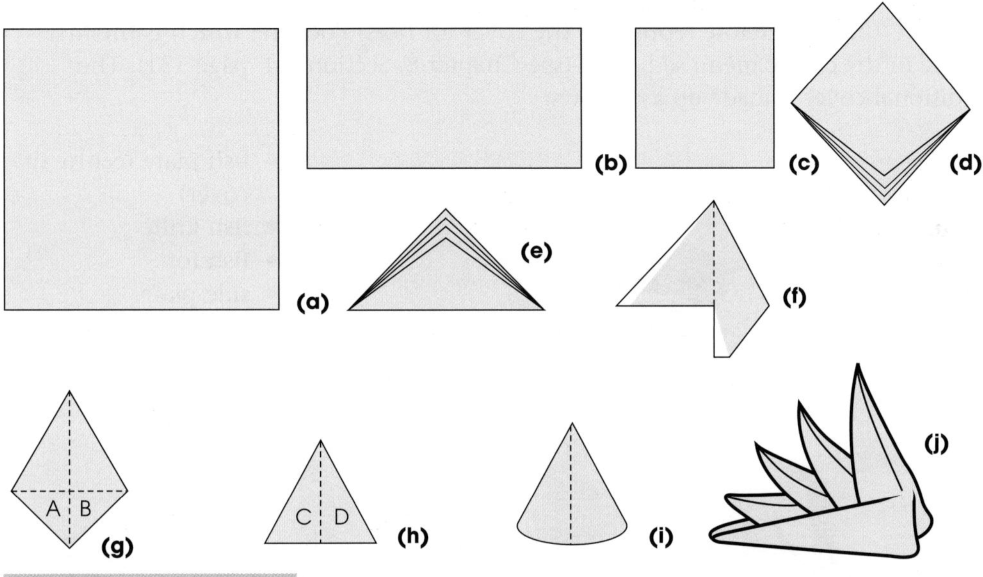

Figure 13.9 Cockscomb

13.4 Laying covers for table service and assisted service

One of the technical terms often used in the foodservice industry is a 'cover' (*couvert*). The term originates from the custom, up to the 15th century, of serving 'under cover' (*couvert*). This meant to cover the courses and dishes with a large white napkin in order to indicate that all precautions had been taken to avoid the poisoning of guests. In modern foodservice operations, the term cover has two definitions, according to the context in which it is being used:

1 When discussing how many customers a restaurant or dining room will seat, or how many customers will be attending a cocktail party, we refer to the total number of customers concerned as so many covers. For example, a restaurant or dining room will seat a maximum of 85 covers (customers); there will be 250 covers (customers) at a cocktail party; this table will seat a party of six covers (customers).
2 When laying a table in readiness for service there are a variety of place settings that may be laid according to the type of meal and service being offered. We refer to this place setting as a certain type of cover being laid. In other words, a cover refers to all the necessary cutlery, crockery, glassware and linen required to lay a certain type of place setting for a specific dish or meal.

When deciding on the laying of covers there are two basic service considerations. The first is when cutlery for the meal is to be laid before each course is served. The second is when the cutlery for the meal is to be laid prior to the start of that meal and for all the courses that are to be served. The first approach is known as the à la carte cover, and the second is known as the table d'hôte cover.

À la carte cover

The à la carte cover follows the principle that the cutlery for each course will be laid just before each course is served. The traditional cover, given below (and shown in Figure 13.10) therefore represents the cover for hors-d'oeuvre, which is the first course in the classic menu sequence (see Chapter 8, Section 8.4, page 131). The traditional cover is made up as follows:

Figure 13.10 À la carte cover

- fish plate (centre of cover)
- fish knife
- fish fork
- side plate
- side knife
- napkin
- water glass
- wine glass.

Where an à la carte cover has been laid, the cutlery required by the customer for the dishes he or she has chosen will be laid course by course. In other words, there should not, at any time during the meal, be more cutlery on the table than is required by the customer at that given moment in time.

Classic or basic lay-up

There is now a variety of approaches to what is laid for the à la carte form of service. This can include using large decorative cover plates and a side plate and side knife only, or replacing the fish knife and fork with a joint knife and fork. This is sometimes known as a classic or basic lay-up. An example of this type of lay-up is shown in Figure 13.11.

Note: If decorative cover plates are used for an à la carte cover it is common for the first course plates to be placed on this plate. The first course and the cover plate are then removed when the first course is cleared.

Figure 13.11 Classic or basic cover

Table d'hôte cover

The table d'hôte cover follows the principle that the cutlery for the whole meal will be laid before the first course is served. The traditional cover is made up as follows.

- joint knife
- fish knife
- soup spoon
- joint fork
- fish fork
- sweet fork
- sweet spoon
- side plate
- side knife
- napkin
- water glass
- wine glass.

Again, there are some possible variations to this approach. The sweet spoon and fork may be omitted, for example, or the fish knife and fork replaced with a side knife and small/sweet fork.

Where a table d'hôte cover has been laid, the waiter should remove, after the order has been taken, any unnecessary cutlery and relay any extra items that may be required. This means that before the customer commences the meal he or she should have the entire cutlery required for the dishes chosen, set out as their place setting or cover.

Figure 13.12 Table d'hôte cover

Breakfast served in the restaurant

The basic mise-en-place (pre-preparation) for the service of breakfast is normally carried out the evening before, after the service of dinners has finished. To ensure protection against dust until the breakfast staff arrives for duty, the corners of the cloths may be lifted up and over the basic mise-en-place on the tables.

The preparation for service is completed the following morning before the actual service of breakfast commences. This will include turning breakfast cups the right way up and laying the breakfast buffet with items usually served for the first course, such as chilled fruit juices, cereals and fruit compôte, together with all the necessary glasses, plates and tableware required for the service.

The breakfast buffet may also contain preserves and butter and alternatives. Jugs of iced water and glasses should be ready on the buffet throughout the meal, especially if the establishment is catering for American visitors. Preserves are usually now served in individual pots.

Breakfast covers

The breakfast cover may be divided into two types:

- continental breakfast cover
- full breakfast cover.

Cover for a continental breakfast

For a continental breakfast consisting of hot croissant/brioches or hot toast, butter, preserves and coffee or tea, the cover would be made up as follows:

- napkin
- side plate and side knife
- sugar basin and tongs or a variety of individual sugar packets in a bowl
- table number
- tea or breakfast cup and saucer with a teaspoon
- stands or underplates for teapot/coffee pot and hot milk/hot water jug.

If the beverage is tea and loose leaves are used then the following additional items will be needed:

- slop basin
- tea strainer.

Figure 13.13 Example of continental breakfast (image courtesy of Six Continents Hotels)

Cover for a full breakfast

The full breakfast consists of a number of courses, usually three or four, with a choice of dishes within each course, as shown on the specimen full breakfast menu in Figure 13.14 below. The cover will therefore include some or all of the following:

- napkin
- side plate and side knife
- fish knife and fork
- joint knife and fork
- sweet spoon and fork
- tea or breakfast cup, saucer and teaspoon
- sugar basin and tongs or individual sugar packets (and alternatives) in a bowl
- slop basin
- tea strainer
- stands or underplates for teapot/coffee pot and hot water jug/hot milk jug
- salt and pepper
- caster sugar in shaker
- table number.

Figure 13.14 **Example of a full breakfast cover**

Many of the items listed above, for the two types of breakfast, are placed on the table as part of the mise-en-place, and before the customer is seated. A number of items are then placed on the table once the customer is seated and has ordered. These include:

- butter dish with butter/alternatives and a butter knife
- preserve dish with preserve and preserve spoon
- jug of cold milk
- other items according to the customer's choice, e.g. mustards
- teapot/coffee pot/hot milk/hot water jug
- toast rack with toast and/or bread basket with hot rolls.

Afternoon tea covers

Two forms of afternoon tea may be available to the customer. These are the full afternoon tea or high tea. The latter comprises the full afternoon tea menu plus a choice from a limited and modified à la carte menu, generally in the form of hot snacks.

Cover for full afternoon tea

The following cover will normally be laid for a full afternoon tea:

- napkin
- side plate with side or tea knife
- pastry fork
- teacup and saucer and a teaspoon
- jug of cold milk and/or side plate with lemon slices (depending on the tea taken)
- teapot and hot water jug stands or underplates
- sugar basin and tongs or individual packets of sugar (and alternatives)
- slop basin and tea strainer
- butter dish with butter and alternatives, together with a butter knife
- preserve dish on an underplate with a preserve spoon, or side plate with small individual preserve pots
- table number.

Note: The beverage, jug of cold milk, preserve dish and butter dish are only brought to the table when the customers are seated and are not part of the mise-en-place.

Figure 13.15 Example of cover for full afternoon tea after the order has been taken

Cover for high tea

The cover for high tea may include:

- napkin
- joint knife and fork
- side plate and side knife
- cruet: salt, pepper, mustard
- teacup, saucer and teaspoon
- jug of cold milk and/or side plate with lemon slices (depending on the tea taken)
- teapot and hot water jug stands or underplates
- slop basin and tea strainer
- sugar basin and tongs or individual packets of sugar (and alternatives)
- butter dish with butter and alternatives, together with a butter knife
- preserve dish on an underplate with a preserve spoon or side plate with small individual preserve pots
- table number.

Note: As for the full afternoon tea cover, the jug of cold milk, butter dish and the preserve dish are not part of the mise-en-place and should only be brought to the table when the customers are seated. Any other items of tableware that may be required are brought to the table as for the à la carte service.

Figure 13.16 Example of cover for high tea

Laying the table

Great care should be taken here to ensure uniformity throughout the food and beverage service area. This is one of the many factors which help to determine the ambiance of the room, thus creating a lasting impression upon the customer on his or her arrival.

Laying up

Once the table is clothed-up it should be laid in readiness for service. Cutlery must be laid consistently:

- This is often at 1.25 cm (½ in) from the edge of the table. An alternative to this is to line up the tops of all cutleries.
- Crockery that has a badge or crest is laid so that the badge is at the head or top of the cover.
- After polishing the glasses should be placed at the top right-hand corner of the cover.
- Napkins would now be folded and placed in the centre of the cover.
- Table accompaniments should now be placed on the table according to the custom of the establishment.

Cutlery should be laid from a service salver or service plate. When handling cutlery it is most often held between the thumb and forefinger in the centre at the sides to reduce the risk of finger marks. An alternative to this is to use a service cloth and to hold the items being laid in the service cloth, giving a final polish before setting the items on the table. In some establishments the service staff wear white gloves when laying cleaned and pre-polished tableware onto the tables in order to avoid finger marks.

When laying a cover:

- The cutlery should be laid from the inside to the outside of the cover. This ensures even spacing of the cover and lessens the need to handle the items laid more than is necessary.
- If an à la carte cover is being laid then the first item set on the table should be the fish plate in the centre of each cover.

- If a table d'hôte cover is being laid then the first item to be set on the table should be the napkin or side plate in the centre of each cover. If the side plate is laid in the centre of each cover it will be moved to the left-hand side of the cover when the entire cutlery has been laid.
- The purpose of initially placing something in the centre of the cover is to ensure that the covers are exactly opposite one another and that the cutlery of each cover is the same distance apart.

Examples of the order of laying covers are as follows:

À la carte

- fish plate at the centre of the cover
- fish knife
- fish fork
- side plate
- side knife
- napkin
- water glass
- wine glass

Table d'hôte

- side plate at centre of cover
- joint knife
- fish knife
- soup spoon
- joint fork
- fish fork
- sweet fork
- sweet spoon
- move side plate to the left of cover
- side knife
- napkin
- water glass
- wine glass

In some operations a trolley is used for storing cutlery. When laying up, without customers in the restaurant, this trolley is pushed around the tables and the cutlery items are laid after a final polish with a clean and dry teacloth or waiter's cloth.

Table accompaniments

The table accompaniments required to complete the table lay-up are the same whether an à la carte or table d'hôte cover has been laid:

- cruet: salt, pepper, mustard and mustard spoon
- table number
- floral table centre.

These are the basic items usually required to complete the table lay-up. In some establishments certain extra items will be placed on the table immediately prior to the service to complete its lay-up. These may include:

- roll basket
- Melba toast
- gristicks
- peppermill
- butter and alternatives.

13.5 Preparation for self-service, assisted service and single-point service

The success of all types of service is determined by the detailed preparation that goes into setting up the service areas prior to the service commencing. It is the success of the preparation duties that helps staff to provide efficient service and to create an ambiance and atmosphere that is attractive and pleasant for the customers.

In order to achieve success in this area, duty rotas and checklists should be drawn up by the supervisor to ensure all tasks are covered and indicating who is responsible for specific tasks. This approach also helps to ensure that staff rotate their duties and are therefore not bored or complacent because they are doing the same job every day.

Cafeteria/counter service

Layout

Within the seating area an allowance of about 0.5–1 m^2 (3–10 sq ft) per person is sufficient to take account of table space, gangways and access to counters.

- A tray stand is placed at the beginning of the service counter or at the entrance to the service area, so that each customer can collect a tray before proceeding along the counter.
- The layout of the dishes on the counter generally follows the order in which they appear on the menu. This could be as follows: starters, cold meats and salads, bread items, soups, hot fish dishes, hot meat dishes, hot vegetables, hot sweets, cold sweets, ice cream, assorted sandwiches, cakes and pastries, beverages and cold drinks.
- The length of the counter will generally be determined by the size of the menu offered, but should not be too long as this will restrict the speed of service.
- Payment points are sited at the end of the service counter or at the exit to the service area so that customers may pay for their meal before they pass to the seating area.
- Cutlery stands should be placed after the cashiers, together with any ancillary items that may be required, such as napkins and accompaniments.

This helps to ensure that the throughput of customers along the service counter remains continuous. Cutlery stands are placed here to allow customers to choose the items they need after making their food and beverage choices. Another advantage of placing the cutlery and ancillary items here is that the customer can return to collect these items, should they initially forget to do so, without interrupting the flow of customers at the service counter.

Portion and cost control

Great care needs to be taken here and all staff should be made aware of the necessity for good portion control in relation to serving equipment and pre-portioned foods as this ultimately affects profit margins.

With this form of service, portion control equipment is used to ensure standardisation of the portion size served. Such equipment includes scoops, ladles, bowls, milk dispensers and cold beverage dispensers. Pre-portioned foods such as butter, sugars, jams, cream, cheeses and biscuits may also be used.

Carvery-type operations

This is a style of operation that demands good liaison and understanding between both the food service and food preparation staff. This is essential to ensure the guest receives the best possible service. Thus the preparation for service must be adequate both in the room and at the carvery point and the equipment sufficient in relation to the number of covers it is anticipated will be served. The setting-up of the room would follow the principles and methods set out for table service.

The carvery

On the carvery point itself the servers and carvers must ensure there is sufficient crockery (main course plates) for the service and as back-up stock. These will be kept in the hot cupboard or plate lowerators. Small paper napkins should be at hand for the customers to be able to hold the hot main course plates.

To avoid delays and congestion around the carvery point, it is important to ensure there is sufficient back-up of both equipment and food. The carvers should have available suitable carving equipment for the joints to be carved, together with service and portion control equipment such as slices, ladles, scoops and draining spoons, all in readiness for the food items to be served.

Buffet preparation

The main types of buffet are knife and fork, fork and finger buffets. The requirements of a particular occasion and the host's wishes will determine the exact format in setting up the room. Whatever the nature of the occasion there are certain basic principles to follow.

Factors to consider

- The buffet should be set up in a prominent position in the room – the buffet may be one complete display or split into several separate displays around a room, e.g. starters and main courses, desserts, hot beverages and bar service.
- There should be ample space on the buffet for display and presentation.
- The buffet should be within easy access of the stillroom and wash-up so that replenishment of the buffet and the clearing of dirty items may be carried out without disturbing the customers.
- There must be ample space for customer circulation – buffets can be positioned and set up so that customers can access one or both sides of the buffet at once.
- Provision should be made for sufficient occasional tables and chairs within the room.
- The total presentation of the room should be attractive and promote a good atmosphere that is appropriate for the occasion.

Setting up the buffet

The exact equipment required when setting up the room will be determined by the occasion, such as a finger buffet for a prize-giving, a fork buffet for a retirement party or a knife and fork buffet for a wedding party.

The buffet should be covered with suitable cloths (buffet), making sure that:

- the drop of the cloth is within 1.25 cm (approx ½ in) from the ground, all the way around the front and sides of the buffet

- if more than one cloth is used, the creases should be lined up
- where the cloths overlap one another the overlap should be facing away from the entrance to the room
- the ends of the buffet should be box pleated, thereby giving a better overall presentation of the buffet.

To achieve a neat, crisp finish, the following procedure needs to be carried out with as little handling as possible. This may be achieved by taking the following steps:

1. With assistance, open the screen folded buffet cloth along the length of the buffet table (see Figure 13.17(a)).
2. With a person at either end unfold the cloth, following the procedure shown in Figure 13.5(a)–(d), so that the front and sides of the buffet table are covered and the cloth is no more than 1.25 cm (½ in.) from the ground.
3. Stand in front of the table and from the edge place your thumb on the front corner and take the far side of the cloth, lift and bring it back towards you in a semi-circle motion (see Figure 13.17(b)). This will bring the side of the cloth horizontal with the ground.
4. The fold on top of the table will now resemble a triangle (see Figure 13.17(c)). This should be folded back towards the side of the table, ensuring that the folded edge is in line with the side of the table (see Figure 13.17(d)).
5. Use the back of your hand to flatten the fold.
6. Repeat the procedure at the other end of the table.

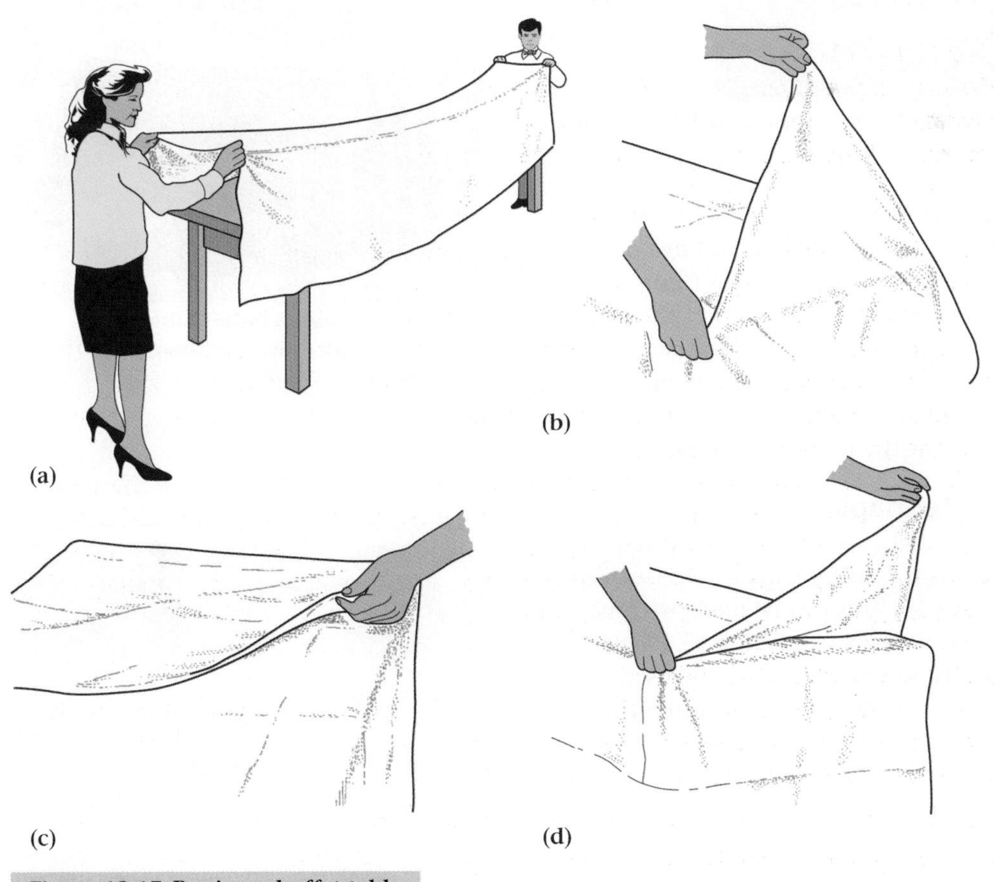

Figure 13.17 Boxing a buffet table

Should more than one buffet cloth be used to cloth up the length of the buffet, the clothing-up procedure should be repeated. All creases should be in line and slip cloths (white or coloured) may be used to enhance and finish the top of the buffet table.

Buffet displays may be further enhanced by the introduction of a box that has been box-clothed. This can be placed on the buffet table to give extra height and to provide display space for special features.

Table skirting

Alternative methods of dressing a buffet table may include the use of table skirting (see Figure 13.18(b)). Although the initial outlay for such skirting may be high, the ease and simplicity of use makes it very popular for buffet and table decoration. One other feature of skirting is that it is made up of separate panels so that it is comfortable when customers are seated at a table.

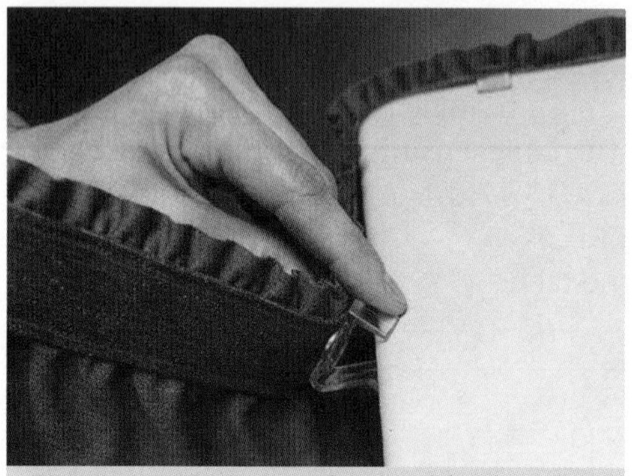

Figure 13.18(a) Attaching table skirting to a table edge

Figure 13.18(b) A buffet table with table skirting attached (images courtesy of Snap-Drape Europe Limited)

A table will be clothed up and then the skirting is attached to the edge of the table by a plastic clip (see Figure 13.18(a)), which is fitted to the top of the skirting. The skirting is attached to the table by sliding the clip into place over the lip of the table. The plastic clips are removable to allow the fabric to be cleaned.

Buffet napkin fold

For buffets, a commonly used napkin fold is the buffet napkin fold (see Figure 13.19(a)). This can be made with paper or linen napkins (see Figure 13.19(b)). It is especially useful as it can be used to hold cutlery so that customers can either help themselves to this at the buffet or it can be given out by staff as customers collect their food from the buffet.

Figure 13.19(a) Buffet napkin fold

1 Open out the napkin and fold into four, ensuring the four loose edges are at A.

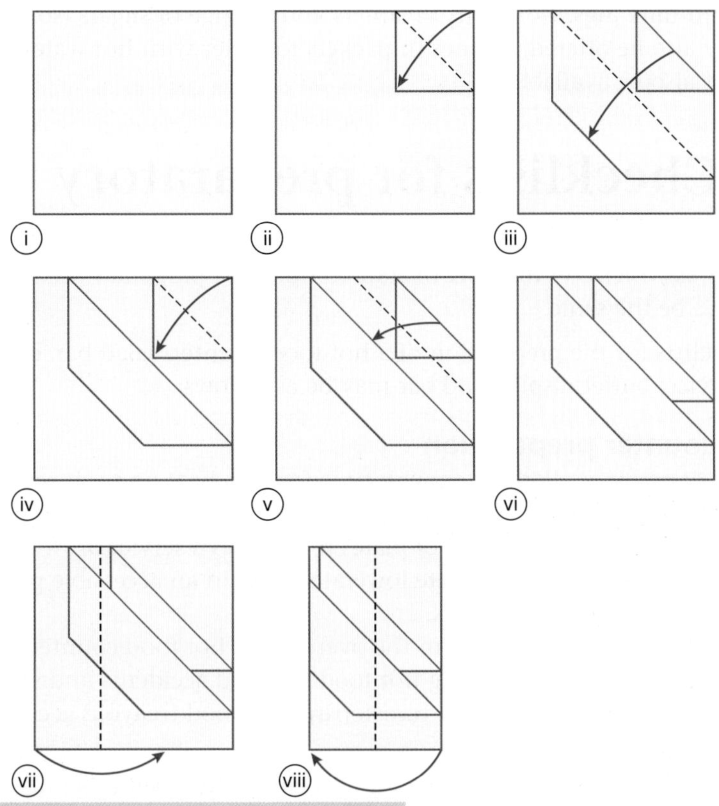

Figure 13.19(b) Making the buffet napkin fold

2 Fold down top flap as indicated.
3 Fold the top flap again along dotted line.
4 Fold down second flap.
5 Fold second flap again along dotted line.
6 Tuck second fold under first fold.
7 Fold napkin along dotted line putting the folded part underneath.
8 Fold napkin along dotted line.
9 Finished fold.

Setting up the buffet for a reception or buffet tea

When setting up the buffet it is necessary to ensure there is ample space for customer circulation and that a number of occasional tables and chairs are placed round the room. These occasional tables may be covered with clean, well-starched linen cloths, and have a small vase of flowers on them.

A raised floral centrepiece on the buffet display can be the focal point around which the dishes of food are placed. Cake stands may also be used for presentation and display purposes.

The afternoon tea tableware, crockery and napkins should be laid along the front of the buffet in groups with the teacups, saucers and teaspoons concentrated in one or more tea service points as required. Sugar bowls may be placed on the buffet or on the occasional tables that are spread round the room.

The tea may be served from urns, which should be kept hot, or pump-dispense insulated jugs, at the separate tea service points along the buffet. Fresh milk should be available in milk jugs. Non-dairy creamers and a range of sugars (sometimes in packets) may also be offered. Tisanes in packets together with hot water and slices of lemon might also be available.

13.6 Checklists for preparatory tasks

Checklists are essential to ensure continuity in work method and to maintain standards. Thus whichever member of staff completes a particular task, the outcome should always be the same.

Typical checklists for the preparation of a hot food counter, salad bar, dining area, takeaway service, buffet display and bar may be as follows:

Hot food counter preparation

1. Turn on hot counter, allowing enough time for it to heat up to the correct temperature.
2. Ensure that an adequate number of plates for the day's service are available on the hot food service counter or in plate lowerators and in an accessible place near the hot food counter as back-up stock.
3. Transfer regenerated hot food from the oven to the hot food counter. Important:
   - use oven cloths when handling hot food to avoid accidents and spillages
   - if appropriate, use a tray when transferring hot food to avoid accidents and spillages.
4. Check hot food menu items for the day and ensure that before service begins there is one dish of each menu item on the hot food counter.
5. Ensure that all hot food is properly covered to prevent any heat loss and deterioration in quality.
6. Have cleaning materials available to wipe any spills.
7. Ensure that for each dish on the hot food counter there is an appropriate service implement. The implements will depend on the dish but are likely to include:
   - large spoons for dishes such as vegetarian lasagne
   - perforated large spoons for dishes such as boiled vegetables (to drain off excess water)
   - ladles for dishes such as seafood mornay, soups and sauces
   - food tongs for dishes such as fried plantain and Caribbean chicken
   - fish slices for dishes such as pizza.
8. When service implements are not in use, remember to return each one to its designated position on the hot food service counter. This prevents any confusion during a busy service period, which may otherwise arise if service implements have been misplaced.

Salad bar counter preparation

1. Turn on the salad bar, allowing enough time for it to chill to the correct temperature.
2. Ensure an adequate number of required salad bowls and plates are available for the day's service of salads, pâtés, cold meats, cold quiches and flans, cold pies, cheeses and items such as taramasalata, humous and tsatsiki. Remember:
   - bowls are for salads only
   - plates should be used for the other cold items detailed above.

At any one time there should be enough salad bowls and plates on the cold counter for customer service, plus a back-up stock beneath the salad bar.

3 Ensure that service utensils are ready and situated in their designated places for service, including:
   - salad tongs for dry salads such as freshly prepared green salad
   - large spoons for wet salads such as *champignons à la grecque*
   - fish slices for pâté, cold meats, cold quiches or flans and cold pies
   - large spoons for taramasalata, humous and tsatsiki
   - tongs for sliced French sticks and granary rolls.
4 Transfer prepared salad items from the kitchen to the chilled salad bar.
5 Cover all food prior to service.
6 Have cleaning materials ready to maintain appearance and cleanliness.

Preparing dining area for cafeteria/counter service

1 Arrange tables and chairs, making sure they are all clean.
2 Wipe each table.
3 Ensure adequate and clean cutlery provisions for the day's service are in place.
4 Ensure trays are clean and there is an adequate supply in the tray stack, ready for the customers' use.
5 Ensure all salt and pepper cruets are filled and that there is one pair on each table. If using sachets of salt and pepper ensure that there are two bowls, containing salt and pepper respectively, at the counter near the payment point. Other sauces should be immediately available, e.g. sachets of tomato sauce, brown sauce, mayonnaise and tartare sauce. Sachets of white and brown sugars and alternatives must also be on hand to accompany hot beverages.
6 Fill drinking water jugs and place them in their designated place or make sure the water dispenser is in working order.
7 Ensure the napkin dispenser is filled up.
8 Ensure the clearing-up trolley and lined bins for different kinds of waste are in position.
9 Have cleaning materials ready to wipe clean tables and used trays during service.

Takeaway service preparation

Below is an example checklist for the setting up of a takeaway area prior to service.

Ensure all equipment is functioning correctly and switched on.

1 Check all temperature-controlled equipment is at the correct temperature.
2 Make sure adequate supplies of packaging, napkins and plates are available.
3 Ensure that the takeaway menu and prices are clearly displayed.
4 Ensure that sufficient supplies of ready-prepared food items and beverages are to hand to ensure minimum delay on receipt of orders.
5 Prepare foods using the 'batch cooking' approach to ensure the quality and freshness of the product at all times.
6 Ensure that the necessary uniforms, such as hats, overalls and aprons, are worn in all preparation areas.
7 For safety reasons, have available such items as oven cloths, tea towels and trays.

8 Have available and on show sales literature to assist in projecting the image of the establishment.
9 Make sure all serving utensils are available and to hand.
10 Ensure that everything is in its place and therefore easily found as required. This will assist in an efficient work method.
11 Check that waste bins for the different types of waste are available with clean plastic sacks in them.
12 Ensure that all working/serving surfaces are clean and have been wiped down prior to service with the appropriate cleaning materials.
13 Have cleaning materials available for wiping down and in case of spillages.

Note: In a takeaway service, care must be taken to ensure the quality of the product, hygiene, packaging and labelling, and temperature control.

Buffet preparation

Duties may include:

- The preparation of the buffet table to the supervisor's instructions.
- The display of:
  - accompaniments
  - food items
  - underplates for large dishes
  - service spoons and forks and other serving utensils, including carving knives if required
  - water jugs and joint knives for pâtés or mousses
  - crockery, glassware and cutlery as required
  - beverage items as required
  - floral decorations
  - placement of chafing dishes (see Figure 13.20).

Figure 13.20 Chafing dishes used for buffets (image courtesy of Steelite International)

Bar preparation

For information on bar preparation please refer to bar equipment in Chapter 3, Section 3.5, page 51 and Section 13.2, page 221).

CHAPTER 14

Order of service and taking customer orders

This chapter will help you to learn about:

1. The order of table service
2. The order of self-service, assisted service and single-point service
3. Personal or positive selling
4. Methods of taking food and beverage orders
5. Special checks
6. Variations in order-taking methods
7. Additional considerations when taking food and beverage orders

14.1 The order of table service

Table service is offered for main meals including luncheon, dinner and also breakfast and afternoon teas.

Pre-service tasks

Food and beverage service staff should be on duty with sufficient time before the service is due to commence to:

- check the sideboards/workstations have all the equipment necessary for service
- check that tables are laid correctly
- check the menu and have a full understanding of the dishes, methods of cooking, garnishes, the correct covers, accompaniments and mode of service
- ascertain the allocation of stations/work areas and other duties, if these are not already known
- allow the headwaiter/supervisor to check that all staff are dressed correctly in a clean and well-presented uniform of the establishment.

Procedure for plated or silver service of a meal

In the example for the order of service given below, customers are having a starter, main course and sweet, to be accompanied by aperitifs, wine with the meal and liqueurs.

1. Greet customers at the entrance to the restaurant. Check to see if they have a reservation. If not, allocate a table if available. Assist with the customers' coats if required.
2. Ask customers if they would like an aperitif in the lounge or reception area, or prefer to have one at the table.
3. Assuming they are to have the aperitif at their table, the customers are led to the allocated table and introduced to the server who will be looking after them.

4 The customers are then helped to be seated and each customer's napkin is placed over his or her lap.
5 The order for any aperitifs is taken and the order is then served.
6 Menus are presented to each customer, open. Guests first and host last. Bread is offered, butter and alternatives are placed on the table and any chilled water ordered is poured.

Note: At this point all the customers at the table will have something to read, drink and eat, so they can be left for a while to allow them time to make their selection.

7 Explanations and advice of specific menu items are given on request. The food order is then taken from the host. Once taken it will be read back to the host to confirm all the items ordered together with degrees of cooking and sauces ordered.
8 Immediately after the food order has been taken and dispatched to the kitchen, the server or the sommelier will check with the host to see if wine is required to accompany the meal. Again, the order is taken from the host and advice as to suitable wines to accompany certain dishes is given on request. The glassware will also be adjusted for the wine to be served. Sometimes the food and wine orders will be taken at the same time.
9 The covers will be adjusted or laid for the first course. In more casual establishments the covers are laid for the first and main course at the beginning of the meal.
10 The wine ordered will be presented to the host to confirm that the correct bottle of wine is about to be opened.
11 The wine or other beverages are always served before the food. The wine will be opened, decanted if necessary, and the host will be asked to taste the wine to assess the quality of the contents and that the serving temperature is correct. (The host may taste the wine or designate another customer to taste the wine. In either case the person tasting the wine always has their glass topped up last.)
12 The plated first course(s) will now be served, cold before hot, and the accompaniments offered. Once all plates are on the table, explanations of the dishes are given to the customers. For silver service the first course plates will be laid in front of each customer, the dishes to be served will be presented to the table and an explanation of the dishes given. The first course(s) will be silver served to the customers from their left-hand side and any accompaniments will be offered.
13 The server will now check the table to ensure everything is satisfactory and the customers have all they require.
14 Wine and water glasses will be topped up as necessary. Used or empty glasses will be removed from the table.
15 When all the customers have finished their first courses, clear the first course plates using the correct stacking techniques and remove any accompaniments.
16 If a different wine is to be served with the main course, the correct glasses should be placed on the table and the wine then served before the food in the same way as the previous wine. If a bottle of the same wine is to be served then this is normally offered with a clean glass for tasting the new wine.

17 If necessary the covers should be laid for the main course.
18 The server will now check that the correct main course covers are set on the table, any accompaniments required are to hand and any other drinks ordered have been served.
19 Empty or used glasses will be removed from the table.
20 The plated main course(s) will now be brought to the table and served from the right-hand side of the customer, cold before hot, and the accompaniments offered. Once all plates are on the table, explanations of the dishes are given to the customers. For silver service the main course plates will be laid in front of each customer, the dishes to be served will be presented to the table and an explanation of the dishes given. The main course(s) will be silver served to the customers from their left-hand side, and any accompaniments will be offered.
21 The server will now check the table to ensure everything is satisfactory and the customers have all they require.
22 Wine and water glasses will be topped up as necessary.
23 When customers have finished eating their main courses, the main course plates and cutlery are cleared. Side plates and side knives, all accompaniments, butter dish and the cruet set are also cleared using the correct clearing techniques.
24 The table is then crumbed down.
25 Present the sweet menu. Give customers time to make their choice. Explanations and advice of specific menu items are given on request. The food order for the sweet will then be taken through the host. Once taken it will be read back to the host to confirm all the items ordered.
26 Covers for the sweet course are laid.
27 Empty or used wine glasses and bottles are cleared away.
28 If wine is to be served with the sweet course, the correct glasses should be placed on the table and the wine then served before the food in the same way as for the previous wines.
29 The plated sweet course(s) will now be brought to the table and served from the right-hand side of the customer, cold before hot, and the accompaniments offered. Once all plates are on the table, explanations of the dishes are given to the customers. For silver service the sweet course plates will be laid in front of each customer. The dishes to be served will be presented to the table and an explanation of the dishes given. The sweet course(s) will be silver served to the customers from their left-hand side.
30 Offer any appropriate accompaniments such as caster sugar, custard or cream with the sweet course.
31 Clear the sweet course and remove accompaniments.
32 The server will now take the hot beverage order for tea, coffee or other beverages.
33 While the hot beverages are being prepared, a drink order for digestifs, such as liqueurs, brandy or port, will be taken.
34 The beverage order will then be served.
35 Tea and coffee or other beverages will be served.
36 If petits fours/friandises are to be served then these are offered to the customers or the tray placed on the table.
37 When required, the bill will be presented to the host. The server will receive payment from the host. (For billing see Chapter 18, Section 18.8, page 310.)
38 The server will see the customers out, assisting with their coats if required.
39 The table is cleared down and then relaid if required.

Removal of spare covers

Figure 14.1 **Traditional restaurant ready for service (Le Columbier Restaurant, London)**

In many instances the number of customers in a party is less than the table is laid for. The waiter must then remove the spare cover(s) laid on the table. Judgement must be used as to which cover is removed – this may depend on the actual position of the table. General considerations are that customers, where possible, should face into the room. The cover should be removed using a service plate or a service salver. When this has been done the position of the other covers should be adjusted if necessary and the table accompaniments repositioned. The spare chair should also be removed.

Where there is an uneven number of customers each side of a table, the covers should be positioned so that the full length of the table is used for both sides, by spacing the covers out on each side. This ensures that one customer is not left facing a space on the other side of the table.

Relaying of tables

In a busy restaurant or dining room, tables often have to be relaid in order to cope with the inflow of customers. Where this is the case the table should first be completely cleared of all items of equipment and then crumbed down. At this stage, if the tablecloth is a little soiled or grubby a slip cloth should be placed over it, or if necessary the tablecloth may be changed. The table may then be relaid, following the procedures given in Chapter 13, Section 13.4, page 231.

14.2 The order of self-service, assisted service and single-point service

The three groups of service methods discussed in this section are:

1. **Self-service:** where the customer is required to help him or herself from a counter or buffet.
2. **Assisted service:** where the customer is served part of the meal at a table and is required to obtain part through self-service from some form of display or buffet.
3. **Single-point service:** where the customer orders, pays and receives the food and beverages at one point.

For these three groups of service methods, the customer comes to where the food and beverage service is offered and the service is provided in areas primarily designed for that purpose. In these groups of service methods, the customers can be involved in:

- viewing the menu and beverages on offer
- making a selection
- being served with the food and beverage items selected/ordered
- paying for the items

- collecting ancillary items (cutlery, seasonings, sauces, napkins) as required
- selecting a table where their food and beverage order may be consumed or leaving the establishment if the order is for takeaway
- disposing of dirties as appropriate.

The customer processes for these three groups of service methods are summarised, together with the other two groups of service methods, in Chapter 2, Section 2.3 (page 35). For the full identification of the five groups of service methods, see Table 2.5 (page 37).

Pre-service tasks

Members of staff must be on duty in sufficient time before the service is due to commence to allow them to:

- check that all work areas have the required equipment in readiness for the service to commence
- check that the dining area is set up correctly
- ensure that they have a complete knowledge of all beverages and food dishes being offered, including ingredients, accompaniments, vegetarian dishes and those dishes not suitable for allergy sufferers
- determine the availability of back-up food and in what quantities
- determine the amount of back-up crockery on hand, should it be required
- check all temperature-controlled equipment is functioning at the required temperatures
- ensure that they themselves are presented correctly, with the recognised uniforms and service cloths for use with the hot equipment and crockery.

Self-service

The main form of self-service is found in cafeterias. In this form of service customers collect a tray from the beginning of the service counter, move along the counter to select their meal, pay and then collect the required cutlery for their meal, together with any ancillary items. Some 'call order' (cooked to order) food production may be included in cafeterias.

Menus should be prominently displayed at the entrance to the cafeteria or foodservice area so that customers may decide as far as possible what meal they will purchase before arriving at the service points. This saves time later and ensures that the customer turnover is as quick as possible.

Cafeterias often have a **straight-line counter** where customers queue in line formation past a service counter and choose their menu requirements in stages before loading them onto a tray and proceeding to a payment point at the end of the counter. The layout of the counter may include a **carousel** – a revolving stacked counter, in order to save display space.

Where customer turnover is particularly high in a very narrow period of time, and when space is limited, then a variation on the cafeteria straight-line counter type service may operate. Examples of these are:

- **Free-flow:** Selection as in counter (above) but in a food service area where customers move at will to random service points; customers usually exit area via a payment point.
- **Echelon:** Series of counters at angles to the customer flow within a free-flow area, thus saving space.
- **Supermarket/shopping mall:** Island service points within a free-flow area.

Each of the service points may offer a different main course dish, together with the potatoes, vegetable dishes, sauces and accompaniments as appropriate. Other service points offer hot and cold sweets, beverages, sandwiches, pastries, confectionery items and miscellaneous foods. On entering the foodservice area, the customer can check the menu to see what they require and then go immediately to the appropriate service point. The advantage of this system is those selecting a full meal do not hold up a customer who requires just a sandwich and a hot drink.

Order of service

The following list indicates a customer's progress from their entry into the eating area through to the conclusion of the meal:

1. The customer enters the eating area.
2. Views the menus and dishes available.
3. Collects a tray from the tray stack, which may be sited at the entrance to the service area or at the beginning of the service counter, or at each separate service point.
4. Proceeds to the service counter (straight line), or single/staggered service point (echelon), or island service point (shopping mall) to view the display of food and drink available and to make their choices and place them on the tray.
5. At the end of the counter completes the payment required.
6. Proceeds to the cutlery stand and selects their requirements.
7. Also selects napkins, seasonings and sauces.
8. Chooses a table and consumes the meal.
9. At the conclusion of the meal takes the tray of dirties to the nearest tray stand. Disposable items are placed in the correct waste bins provided (according to type of waste for recycling).
10. Table cleaners/clearers clear anything remaining and wipe down tabletops in readiness for the next customers.

Figure 14.2 Free-flow cafeteria area (image courtesy of FCSI UK)

Assisted service

The main form of assisted service is found in carvery-type operations. The customer is served part of the meal at a table and is required to obtain part through self-service from some form of display or buffet. Customers are able to help themselves to joints and other dishes but usually with the assistance of a carver or server at the buffet.

This form of service is also used for breakfast service, afternoon tea service and for events.

Assisted service involves the customer in two methods of food service, namely table service and self-service. Here the server is also usually responsible for the service of both food (starters, desserts and hot beverages) and alcoholic beverages on their allocated tables and they will be assisted by chefs/carvers at the carvery for the service of the main course.

The order of service for a meal in a carvery-type operation will proceed in almost exactly the same way as for table service (see Section 14.1, page 247). The main difference here is that the main course is not served at the table; instead the customer approaches the carvery point to receive this course. This is now the assisted/self-service part of the carvery service. Customers may also, should they wish, return to the carvery point to replenish their plates.

Service of food at the carvery display

- All food items served onto plates should be attractively presented and arranged.
- If food has not already been pre-plated, it should be served onto plates using a service spoon in one hand and a service fork in the other, and should be placed neatly onto the customer's plate.
- Alternative service equipment might be used and this will be determined by the nature of the dishes displayed on the buffet (carvery), e.g. scoops, sauce ladles, soup ladles, slices, serving spoons and knives.
- Care must be taken to ensure stocks of crockery and food on the buffet have adequate back-up stock and food items should be re-ordered before they run out.

Note: For food safety reasons prepared foods must be held at specific temperatures. Chilled foods must be kept at or below 8°C (26.4°F). Foods being kept hot should remain at or above 63°C (145.4°F). Food may be left at room temperature for limited periods during service or when on display. However, these flexibilities can be used only once for each batch of food. The temperature of chilled foods can only exceed 8°C for a maximum of four hours. The temperature of hot foods can only fall below 63°C for a maximum of two hours.

Service from buffets

Depending on the nature of the occasion and the style of buffet on offer, the customers may queue at the buffet to receive their food or they may be called up to the buffet, table by table. The customers will take a tray or be given a plate and then proceed along the buffet to make their selection. The main principles for service here follow those for counter/cafeteria service and carvery service.

Buffet or American breakfast

The buffet can be used for any type of breakfast, with the most extensive often called American Buffet Breakfast. For the service of this style of breakfast meal customers are presented with the breakfast menu when they sit down and from that they make their choice of either the full breakfast or other types of breakfast. With the buffet breakfast all items are self-served from the buffet, with perhaps the exception of any egg dishes or other cooked-to-order items, and also the beverages required.

Reception or buffet tea

A reception or buffet tea is offered for special functions and private parties only and, as the name implies, the food and beverage are served from a buffet table and not at individual tables.

During the reception some of the staff must be positioned behind the buffet for the service and replenishment of the dishes of food and beverages. Other members of staff should circulate the room with the food and to clear away any dirty items. As the dishes on the buffet become depleted, they should be quickly replenished or cleared away so that the buffet looks clean and tidy at all times.

Checklists

Typical checklists for staff to follow in performance of service standards and related to a buffet or counter, salad bar and dining areas are given below.

Hot and cold counters

- Do not leave the hot food service counter unattended once service begins, as this will cause congestion in the flow of service.
- Arrange for someone to take your place if you have to leave the service area for any reason.
- Wipe up any spillages immediately. Spillages left on a hot counter for too long will harden and create problems later with cleaning.
- When serving, it is important to adhere to portion control specifications.
- When a dish of hot food is only one-third full, inform the kitchen that more will be needed. Do not allow food items to run out during service. If the end of service time is approaching, check with the supervisor before requesting more.
- Ensure plates are kept well stocked. If running low on plates on the service counter, replenish immediately from back-up stock.
- Hot food items left too long in the hot food service counter, prior to service, may deteriorate. The time factor here is important. Allow minimum time between placing in/on the hot food service counter and serving. This will help to ensure that the food item, when requested, is served in prime condition.
- Ensure the correct holding temperature is set for the hot counter and cold temperatures for cold counters. This will mean all foods are served at the correct temperatures and will retain their quality as menu items.

Salad bar

- Keep a constant eye on food levels in the salad bar.
- Never refill bowls or replenish plates at the counter. Take a bowl or plate to the kitchen and fill or replenish it there.
- Replace service spoons, slices, etc., to their respective bowls, dishes and plates, if misplaced by customers.
- Wipe up any spillages immediately.
- Keep the salad bar tidy, well arranged and well presented at all times.

- Keep a constant eye on the supply of bowls and plates for the salad counter service.
- Remember: do not wait for a supply of salad bowls and plates to run out before replenishing from the back-up supply (beneath the cold counter). During a busy service period this will inevitably hinder the flow of service.

Dining areas

- Ensure the clearing station is ready and in place and that the following items are available:
  - lined bin
  - bin liners
  - clearing trolley
  - wiping cloths
  - recommended cleaning materials.
- Keep a constant eye on tables and make sure they are clean and tidy at all times. Change table covers regularly, as and when required. An untidy and messy table is not pleasant for the customer.
- The dining area should be self-clearing, i.e. customers are requested to return their trays containing used plates and cutlery to the clearing station. Failing this, promptly clear tables of any trays.
- At the clearing station:
  - empty the tray of used plates and cutlery, etc., and stack ready for the dishwasher
  - empty disposable contents of a tray into a lined standing bin
  - wipe the tray clean with recommended cleaning materials.
- Return the stack of cleaned trays to the tray stack, lining each tray with a paper liner (if used) before putting into place.
- Ensure there is always enough water in the drinking water jugs.
- Ensure there are enough napkins in the napkin dispenser.
- Check cutlery containers are adequately stocked.

Note: During service always ensure that at any one time there is an adequate supply of trays in the tray rack, ready for the customers' use.

Single-point service

The main forms of single-point service are found in:

- **Takeaways:** Where the customer orders and is served from a single point, at a counter, hatch or snack stand; the customer consumes off the premises; some takeaway establishments provide dining areas. This also includes drive-thrus, where the customer drives their vehicle past the order, payment and collection points.
- **Food courts:** Series of autonomous counters where customers may either order and eat or buy from a number of counters and eat in a separate eating area, or takeaway.
- **Kiosk:** Outstation used to provide service for peak demand or in a specific location; may be open for customers to order and be served, or used for dispensing to staff only.
- **Vending:** Provision of food service and beverage service by means of automatic retailing.
- **Bar:** Order, service and payment point and consumption area in licensed premises.

Figure 14.3 Bar and seating area (image courtesy of Gleneagles Hotel, Scotland)

Bar service

The service of food and beverages in bars may be to customers at the bar or alternatively to customers seated at tables. If customers are to be served at tables then the procedures for this are based on table service as described in Section 14.1, page 247. Customers at the bar will have their order taken and served at the bar, with payment usually taken at the same time.

For information on bar preparation refer to bar equipment in Chapter 3, Section 3.5, page 51 and bar preparation in Chapter 13, Section 13.2, page 221. For information on the service of alcoholic drinks and non-alcoholic drinks refer to Chapter 16.

14.3 Personal or positive selling

Ability in personal selling is necessary for all aspects of successful food and beverage service. The contribution of service staff to the meal experience is vital. The service staff contribute to the customers' perception of value for money, hygiene and cleanliness, the level of service and the perception of atmosphere that the customer experiences. Good food and beverage service staff therefore must have a detailed knowledge of the food and beverages on offer, be technically competent, have well-developed interpersonal skills and be able to work as part of a team.

All service staff should have good personal selling techniques. Personal selling refers specifically to the ability of the staff in a food and beverage operation to contribute to the promotion of sales. Sometimes this is also referred to as 'up selling' but more usually 'using positive selling techniques'.

Within the context of personal selling, the service staff should be able to:

- describe the food, wines and drinks on offer in an informative and appealing way, that makes the product sound interesting and desirable
- use the opportunity to promote specific items or deals when seeking orders from the customer
- apply positive selling techniques to seek information from the customer in a way that promotes sales, e.g. rather than asking *if* a sweet is required, ask *which* sweet is required

- use opportunities for the use of positive selling techniques to promote the sales of additional items such as extra garnishes, special sauces or accompanying drinks, such as a dessert wine with a sweet course
- provide a competent service of the items for sale and seek customers' views on the acceptability of the food, drinks and the service.

Positive selling is especially important where there are specific promotions being undertaken. The promise of a particular type of menu or drink, a special deal or the availability of a particular service can often be devalued by the inability of the staff to fulfil the requirements as promised. It is therefore important to involve service staff in the formulation of particular offers and to ensure that briefing and training are given so that the customer can actually experience what has been promised.

What the server needs to know

Members of staff will feel more confident about selling if they have information about the products on offer – if staff can tell well they can then sell well. Examples of the type of information staff will need to know include:

- a description of what the item is (food, wine or other drink) and an explanation of how it is prepared and served
- where the produce comes from
- what the local animals are fed on
- where the fish are caught
- where the local fruit and vegetables are grown
- how the produce is delivered
- where and how the local drinks are made
- what the specialities of the establishment are and their origin.

There are various ways of enhancing the product knowledge of staff, such as:

- arranging for staff visits to suppliers
- arranging visits to other establishments that use local produce
- seeking out supplier information
- allowing staff to taste products
- arranging for staff to visit local trade fairs
- organising training and briefing sessions for staff.

14.4 Methods of taking food and beverage orders

Essentially there are four main methods of taking food and beverage orders from customers. These are summarised in Table 14.1.

Table 14.1 Main methods of taking food and beverage orders

Method	Description
Triplicate	Order is taken; top copy goes to the supply point; second copy is sent to the cashier for billing; third copy is retained by the server as a means of reference during service
Duplicate	Order is taken; top copy goes to the supply point; second copy is retained for service and billing purposes

Method	Description
Service with order	Order is taken; customer is served and payment received according to that order, e.g. bar service or takeaway methods
Pre-ordered	(a) Individually, e.g. room service breakfast (b) Hospital tray system (c) Events

All order-taking methods are based upon these four basic concepts. Even the most sophisticated electronic system is based upon either the triplicate or duplicate method. Checks can be written on check pads or keyed in on handheld terminals. The order is then communicated by hand or electronically to visual display units (VDUs) or printout terminals in the food production or beverage provision areas (see Figure 14.4). The main systems used are described in Chapter 18, Section 18.6, page 309.

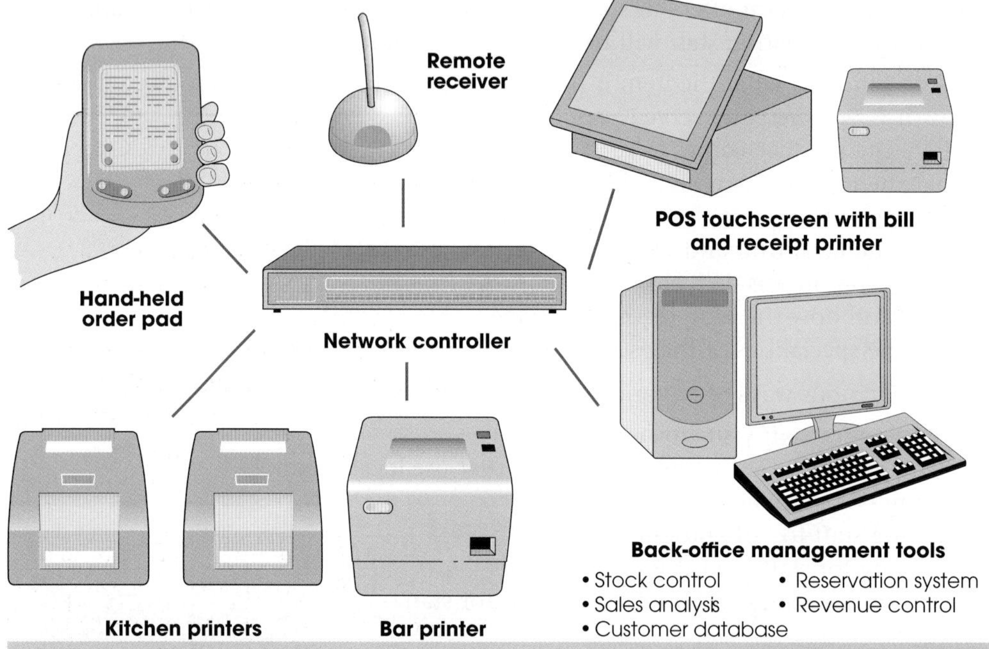

Figure 14.4 Radio-controlled electronic system for order-taking and communication to food production and bar areas

Triplicate checking method

This is an order-taking method used in the majority of medium and large first-class establishments. As the name implies, the food check consists of three copies. To ensure efficient control the server must fill in the following information in the four corners of the check:

- table number or room number
- number of covers
- date
- signature of server taking the order.

Writing the order

On taking the food order it is written from top to bottom of the food check. Where only a table d'hôte menu is in operation the customers would initially only order their first and main courses. A second new food check is written out for the sweet course, this being taken after the main course is finished. A third new check will be completed if any beverages such as coffee, tea or tisanes are required. The operation for an à la carte menu is similar, although customers may order course by course according to their requirements.

All checks should be legible. Abbreviations may be used when taking the order as long as everyone understands them and they are not misinterpreted by the kitchen or beverage dispense, as the wrong order may be prepared.

When taking orders a note should be taken of who is having what order. This ensures that specific orders are identified and that they are served to the correct customer. A system for ensuring that the right customer receives the correct food is to identify on the order which customer is having which dish. A check pad design that might be used for this is shown in Figure 14.5. An electronic handheld order-taking system is show in Figure 14.6.

The triplicate food check

- The top copy of the food order goes to the kitchen and is handed to the aboyeur at the hotplate.
- The duplicate goes to the cashier who makes out the customer's bill.
- The flimsy, or third copy, is retained by the waiter at his or her workstation for reference.
- Any checks or bills that have to be cancelled should have the signature of either the headwaiter or supervisor on them, as should checks and bills which have alterations made on them.

IN3603WP WAITRPAD® www.nationalchecking.com

Table	Guests	Server	/ /
			082205

DRINKS STARTERS MAINS SIDES DESSERT

Figure 14.5 Check pad design enabling the waiter to identify specific orders (image courtesy of National Checking Co)

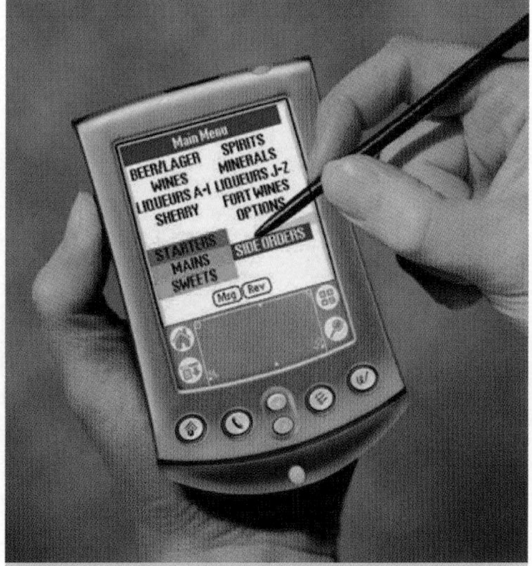

Figure 14.6 Handheld electronic pad for order-taking (image courtesy of Uniwell Systems (UK) Ltd/Palm TEQ UK)

Duplicate checking method

This is a control system that is more likely to be found in the smaller hotel, popular-price restaurant and cafés and department store catering. It is generally used where a table d'hôte menu is in operation and sometimes a very limited à la carte menu. It is often also used for beverage orders.

As the name implies, there are two copies of each of these food checks, each set being serial numbered. A check pad, or bill pad as it is sometimes termed, usually contains a set of 50 or 100 food checks. The top copy of the food check is usually carbon-backed, but if not a sheet of carbon must be placed between the top and duplicate copy every time a fresh order is taken.

For control purposes the top copy may have printed on it a server's number or letter. This should be the number or letter given to a waiter on joining the staff. The control and accounts department should be informed of the person to whom the number applies, and he or she retains it throughout their employment. On each set of food checks there should also be printed a serial number.

Beverage orders

For beverage orders an efficient system must operate here to ensure that:

- the correct wine and other drinks are served at the right table
- the service rendered is charged to the correct bill
- a record is kept of all wine and other drinks issued from the bar
- management is able to assess sales over a financial period and make comparisons.

The usual system of control is a duplicate check pad. The colour of the check pad may be pink or white, but is generally pink or some other colour to distinguish it from a food check. This acts as an aid to the cashier and the control and accounts department in differentiating quickly between food (white) and drink (pink) checks (see Figure 14.7).

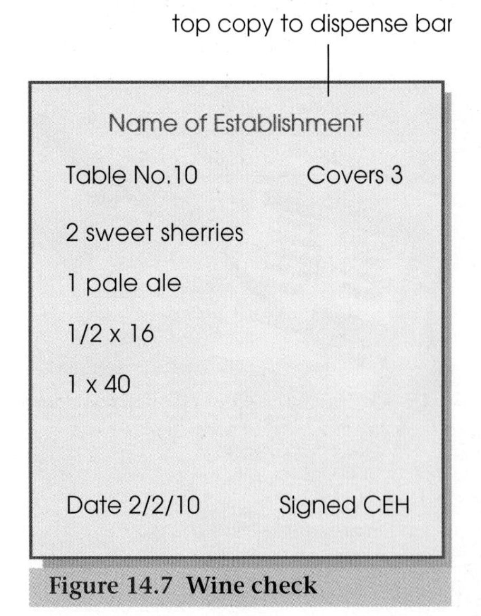

Figure 14.7 Wine check

Taking the beverage order

When the beverage order is taken the service staff must remember to fill in the four items of information required, one in each corner of the check. These are as follows:

- table number or room number
- number of covers
- date
- signature.

Abbreviations are allowed when writing the order as long as they are understood by the bar staff and the cashier. When wines are ordered only the bin number, together with the number of bottles required, should be written down. The bin number is an aid to the bar staff and cellar staff in finding, without delay, the wine required by a customer. Each wine in the wine list will have a bin number printed against it.

On taking the order the staff should hand both copies to the bar staff, who retain the top copy, put up the order and leave the duplicate copy with the order. This enables the staff to see which their order is when they come to collect their wines and drinks. After serving the wines and drinks the duplicate copy is handed to the cashier.

Perforated checks

Sometimes the top copy of the set of food and drink checks is made up of a number of perforated slips, usually 4–5 in number. There is a section at the bottom of the food and drink check for the table number to be entered. The top copy sometimes has a cash column for entering the price of a meal or the dishes ordered, but if this is not the case, the waiter must enter them independently on the duplicate copy against the particular dishes ordered.

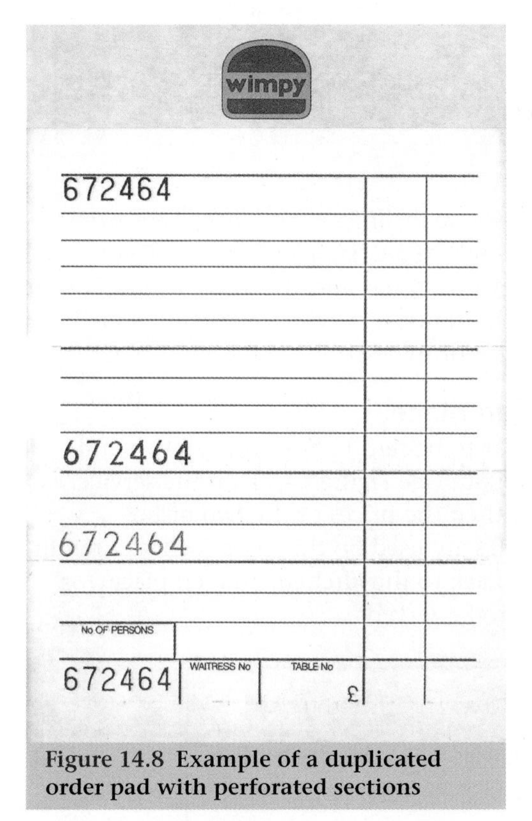
wimpy
672464
672464
672464
No OF PERSONS
672464 | WAITRESS No | TABLE No | £

Figure 14.8 Example of a duplicated order pad with perforated sections

When writing out a customer's order a different perforated slip should be used for each course or beverage. The server must remember to write out the number of covers and the order on each slip. Before sending each slip to the hotplate, check that the details are entered correctly on the duplicate copy.

As soon as the first course is served (and allowing time for this course to be consumed), the second perforated slip showing the next course or beverage order is taken to the hotplate or bar area by the waiter. Similar procedures as with the first course are followed and this dish will then be collected when required. This same procedure is carried on throughout the meal. When there are insufficient perforated slips, a supplementary check pad is used.

14.5 Special checks

In certain instances it is necessary to write out special checks. These are described below.

To follow/suivant

This is used where it is necessary to write out more than one food check for a meal, for instance, where a sweet check is written out after the first and main courses have been cleared. At the head of this check should be written the word 'suivant' which means 'follow on' and shows that one check has already been written out for that particular table (see Figure 14.9).

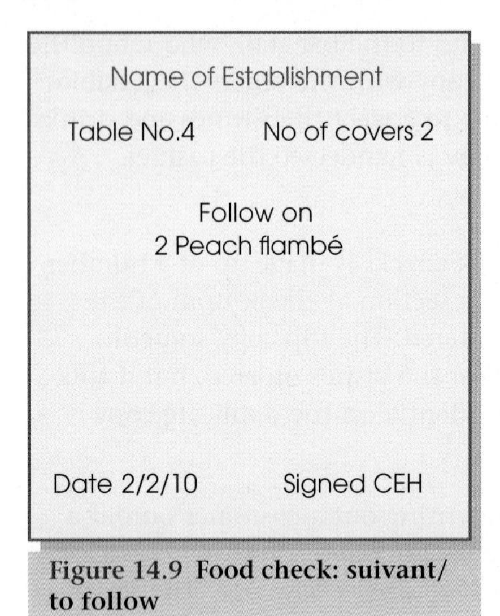

Figure 14.9 Food check: suivant/ to follow

Figure 14.10 Food check: supplement

Supplement

When an extra portion of food is required because insufficient has been sent from the kitchen, a special check must be written out headed 'supplement' (see Figure 14.10). This means the food is a supplement to what has already been previously sent and this check should be signed by the headwaiter or supervisor. Normally there is no charge (n/c), but this depends on the policy of the establishment concerned.

Return and in its place/retour and en place

Where a wrong dish has been ordered and has to be sent back to the kitchen and replaced, a special check must again be made out (see Figure 14.11). If the service being carried out is from an à la carte menu then the prices of the two dishes concerned must be shown. Two main headings are used on this special check, 'retour' (or 'return') and the name of the dish going back to the kitchen, and 'en place' (or 'in its place') and the name of the new dish to be served.

Figure 14.11 Food check: return/ in its place

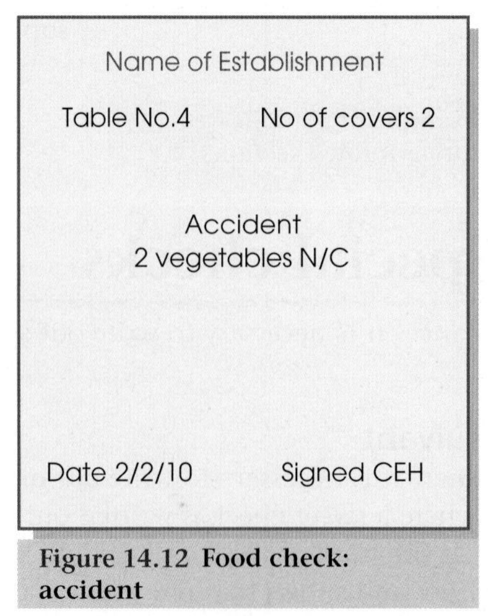

Figure 14.12 Food check: accident

Accident

It occasionally happens that the waiter may have an accident in the room and perhaps some vegetables are dropped. These must be replaced without any extra charge to the customer. Here a check must be completed headed 'accident' (see Figure 14.11). It will show the number of portions of vegetables required and should be signed by the headwaiter or supervisor in charge. No charge (n/c) is stated on the check to ensure that no charge is made to the customer.

14.6 Variations in order-taking methods

Menu order and customer bill

This shows the menu order and customer's bill combined on one sheet and would be allocated to each party of customers. When the order is taken, each customer's requirements would be written down in the column next to the price column. Thus, if a party of two customers requested two cream soups, one mushroom omelette and chips and one fried cod and chips, it would be noted down as shown in Figure 14.13.

Single order sheet

A further simple form of checking is used in cafés, quick turnover restaurants and department stores. It is a simple form of ordering that may be used, or adapted for use, in various forms of operation.

The menu is normally very limited. The server takes the order and marks down the customer's requirements, calls for the order verbally over the hotplate and, when the customer requests the bill, prices the order sheet and hands it to him/her. The customer then hands it to the cashier on leaving and pays the required amount. There is only one copy of this order and bill combined, and the cashier retains this for control purposes, after the customer has made the necessary payment.

Soup		
Cream soup	2.60	2
Hot dishes		
Omelette served with chips and salad		
Plain		
Cheese		
Ham		
Mushroom	4.50	1
Tomato		
Fried cod and chips	4.75	1

Figure 14.13 Quick service menu order and customer bill

Customer self-complete order

A more modern trend is to ask customers to take their own food and drink order. This method is often found in bar operations and it allows staff to concentrate on the service of food (plate service) and beverages, and to accept payments. The customer order form may take the format shown in Figure 14.14.

Please note down your table number and choice of meals on this slip. Take it with you and place your order and pay at the food till

TABLE NUMBER

Starters

Children's meals

Main meals

Side orders

Drinks

Desserts, coffees and teas may be ordered at the food till at the end of your meal

Figure 14.14 Example of customer self-complete order sheet (not full size)

The order for the food and drink requirements, once complete, is taken by the customer to the food till and sent electronically by a member of staff to the kitchen where a printed copy is processed for the kitchen staff to produce the dishes required.

After submitting the initial food and beverage order at the food till, an account will be opened using the table number and by processing the customer's credit card. This is so any additional items such as sweets, coffee or alcoholic beverages may be added to the bill. The customer may then pay the total bill at the conclusion of their meal. These additional items required may be ordered at the food till or at the customer's table.

14.7 Additional considerations when taking food and beverage orders

Taking children's orders

Staff should pay special attention when taking orders for children. Staff need to be aware of:

- the availability and choice of children's meals
- what the children's meals consist of
- portion size, e.g. the number of sausages
- the cost per head
- the need to make a special note of any specific requests, such as no baked beans
- the need to serve young/small children first as they often become agitated when everyone else has been served and their meal is still to come
- the importance of not overfilling cups, bowls or glasses
- the need to always ensure children's plates are warm rather than hot to avoid mishaps
- providing children with the establishment 'give aways' in order to keep them occupied, e.g. a placemat to be coloured in. This can also encourage sales.

Customers with additional needs

Customers with additional needs may require particular attention. These are customers who may be hearing impaired, blind or partially sighted. In these instances consider the following:

- Where applicable, when taking the order, face the customer so they see you full face.
- Speak normally but distinctly.

- Keep descriptions to a minimum.
- Indicate precisely any modifiers that are available with a specific dish, e.g. a choice of dips being available with a starter, or the different degrees of cooking available for a grilled steak.
- Read back the order given for confirmation.

Other additional needs may relate to vegetarians, those with particular religious or cultural restrictions and those with special dietary needs (see Chapter 8, Section 8.3, page 127).

CHAPTER 15

Food service skills

This chapter will help you to develop your skills in:

1 Restaurant service
2 Function/banquet service
3 Room service
4 Lounge service
5 Service enhancements

15.1 Restaurant service

The six basic technical skills that are used in food and beverage service are described in Chapter 12. The service of food and beverages is also governed by a set of service conventions (also described in Chapter 12, page 208). This chapter now explains the application of the basic technical skills and service conventions for various service requirements.

Service of soup

Soup may be served pre-plated, from a tureen at the sideboard or on the gueridon, or silver served from an individual tureen as shown in Figure 15.1. The waiter ensures that the soup is poured away from the customer to avoid 'splashes' onto the customer's clothing. The underflat acts as a drip plate to prevent any spillage from going on the tablecloth.

Figure 15.1(a) Silver service of soup from an individual tureen

Figure 15.1(b) Silver service of soup from an individual tureen

Consommé is traditionally served in a consommé cup on a consommé saucer with a fishplate underneath. It is traditional for this type of soup to be eaten with a sweet spoon. This is because consommé was originally taken before going home, after a function, as a warming beverage. It was originally drunk from a large cup. The garnish was eaten with the sweet spoon. The tradition of the sweet spoon has continued, but a soup spoon would also be acceptable.

Silver service from flats (meat/fish)

- The correct cover is laid prior to the food item ordered being served.
- The service cloth is folded neatly and placed on the palm of the hand as a protection against heat from the serving dish.
- The fold of the cloth should be on the tips of the fingers.
- The dish is presented to the customer so they may see the complete dish as it has come from the kitchen. This is to show off the chef's artistry in presentation.
- The serving dish should be held a little above the hot joint plate with the front edge slightly overlapping the rim of the hot joint plate.
- The portion of food is placed in the 6 o'clock position (i.e. nearest to the customer) on the hot joint plate.
- When moving to serve the second portion, the flat should be rotated on the service cloth so the next meat portion to be served will be nearest the hot main course plate.
- Note that the portion of food served, on the plate nearest to the customer, allows ample room on the plate to serve and present the potatoes and other vegetables attractively.
- If vegetables are being served onto separate plates, then the main food item (meat or fish) is placed in the middle of the hot main course plate.

Silver service of potatoes and vegetables

- The general rule is for potatoes to be served before vegetables.
- When serving either potatoes or vegetables, the vegetable dish itself should always be placed on an underflat with a napkin on it. This is for presentation purposes.
- The purpose of the napkin is also to prevent the vegetable dish slipping about on the underflat while the service is being carried out.

- A separate service spoon and fork should be used for each different type of potato and vegetable dish to be served.
- Note again the use of the service cloth as protection against heat and to allow the easier rotation of the vegetable dish on its underflat. This ensures the items to be served are nearest the hot main course plate.
- With the serving dish in its correct position the potato dish nearest the hot joint plate should be served.
- The potato dish served is placed on the hot joint plate on the far side in the 2 o'clock position, allowing the server to work towards themselves as they serve the remaining food items ordered and making it easier to present the food attractively. Any vegetables to be served are therefore placed on the hot joint plate nearer to the server and in the 10 o'clock position.
- Creamed potato is served by placing the service fork into the service spoon and then taking a scoop of the creamed potato from the vegetable dish. This is then carried to the hot main course plate and the fork moved slightly. The potato should then fall off onto the plate.

Figure 15.2 Silver service of potato and vegetables

Note: Figure 15.2 shows the use of an underflat under the potato and vegetable dishes. It also indicates:

- how a variety of potatoes and vegetables can be served at one time by using a large underflat
- the use of a service cloth for protection from heat and to prevent the underflat from slipping
- the correct handling of the service spoon and fork
- the separate service spoon and fork for each different potato and vegetable dish to be served
- service from the left-hand side of the customer.

Service of accompanying sauces

- The sauce should be presented in a sauceboat on an underplate, with a sauce ladle.
- A ladleful of sauce should be lifted clear of the sauceboat.
- The underside of the sauce ladle should then be run over the edge of the sauceboat to avoid any drips falling on the tablecloth or over the edge of the customer's plate.
- The sauce should be napped over the portion of meat already served or at the side of the meat, depending on the customer's preference.

15.2 Function/banquet service

Traditional service

For formal events it is normal practice that the top table service staff always commences to serve/clear first.

- The banqueting/events headwaiter will organise their staff so that, at a given signal, the top table service staff can commence to serve, immediately followed by all the other service staff.
- The banqueting/events headwaiter will not give any signal to clear a course until all guests have finished eating.
- All staff should leave and enter the room led by the top table staff and followed by the other service staff in a predetermined order.
- This predetermined order generally means that those staff with stations furthest from the service doors should be nearer the top table service staff in the line-up.
- Theoretically this means that, when entering the room, all service staff reach their stations at more or less the same time.
- Each member of staff then serves their own table using the predetermined service method – either full silver service or a combination of plated and silver service.
- When deciding on the predetermined order, another factor that should influence the final decision is that of safety. As far as it is possible, any cross-flow of staff and bottlenecks in their movement to and from the room should be avoided.

Wave service

- Wave service can be used mainly when meals are plated, although some establishments also use this style of service organisation for silver service and other forms of service. It is a way of saving on staffing for conventional service and/or speeding up service for plated systems.
- The term 'wave' comes from the approach where tables are not served together but are served over a period of time, with guests on some tables being served quickly at one time before the service on other tables is started. There are two basic approaches to this:

1. For both plated service and traditional silver service the staff from two tables next to each other will work together as a team. This happens throughout the room. The pair work together to serve one of the tables completely and then will assist each other to completely serve the other table.
2. The alternative is for a larger group of staff to work as a team, serving one table completely at a time before going on to the next. This is especially useful when plated service is being used for the food.

The resulting effect of adopting these approaches is that tables are served throughout the room, over a period, but with each individual table's service being completed quickly.

Wave service may also be used for events where guests are seated on a top table and sprigs. In this case, sections of the banquet tables are served before moving to another section of the table layout.

For plated service, one of the difficulties is ensuring that the food is hot when being served. The speed of the transfer of the plate from the kitchen can ensure that the food is hot when reaching the table, assuming of course that the food has always been first presented onto hot plates.

Carlton Club service

Carlton Club service (named after the members' club in St James', London, where it was first used) is an enhancement of plated service. This is used for both restaurant table service and for functions.

- Members of the service staff carry two plates from the kitchen, one in each hand, with the hands crossed (which makes for steady carrying). On reaching the table one member of staff stands between each two guests.
- When a signal is given, all members of staff bend forward, uncross their arms and place the two plates simultaneously in front of two guests, one plate to the left and one to the right.
- Care is also taken to ensure that the plated foods are placed so that the food items are consistently in the same position for all guests.

15.3 Room service

Depending upon the type of establishment the service offered here may vary from only a tray service for continental breakfast to the service of all meals and beverages (table service) in the room, over a 24-hour day. Staff should have a wide and varied knowledge of the service of all types of meals and beverages and the technical skills involved.

Tray service

The laying up of a tray involves the same procedure, with a few exceptions, as laying up a table in the restaurant. As most orders for the service in the room are known in advance, the tray may be laid according to the order. The main differences between laying a tray and a table for the service in a restaurant are:

- a tray cloth replaces the tablecloth
- underplates are usually left out because of lack of space and to reduce the weight of the tray.

With standard orders for service in the rooms, the trays are often laid up in advance and kept in the pantry and covered with a clean cloth.

The positioning of the items on the tray is important:

- items should be placed so that everything is to hand for the guest, e.g. a beverage and the cup, saucer and teaspoon should be placed to the top centre-right of the tray, as this is in the correct position for pouring and helps balance the tray
- any bottled proprietary sauce required should be laid flat to avoid accidents when carrying the tray

- the spouts of hot beverage pots or jugs should face inwards, to avoid spillages, which may cause scalding to the server or slippages on wet floors.

The service procedure:

- On arriving at the door of the room, the member of staff should knock loudly, wait for a reply, and then enter, placing the tray on a table and then adjusting the items on the tray as appropriate.
- If there are two or more people taking a meal in the guest room, it may be necessary to lay up a table or trolley (see Figure 15.3(a)–(c)) and to serve the breakfast in the same way as in the restaurant. After approximately 45 minutes the floor service staff should return to the room, knock and wait for a reply, enter and ask if it is convenient to clear the breakfast tray away.

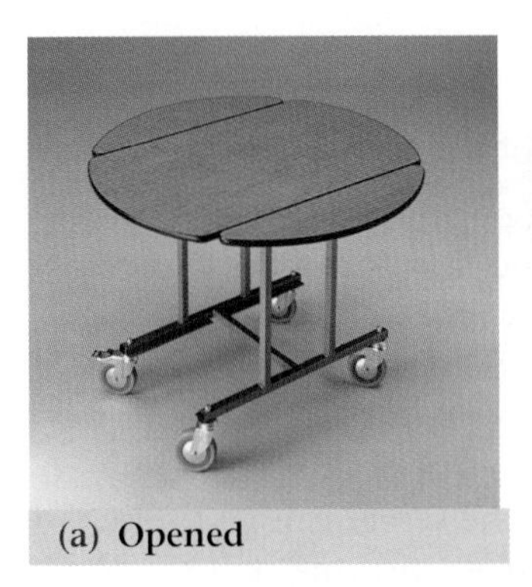

(a) Opened

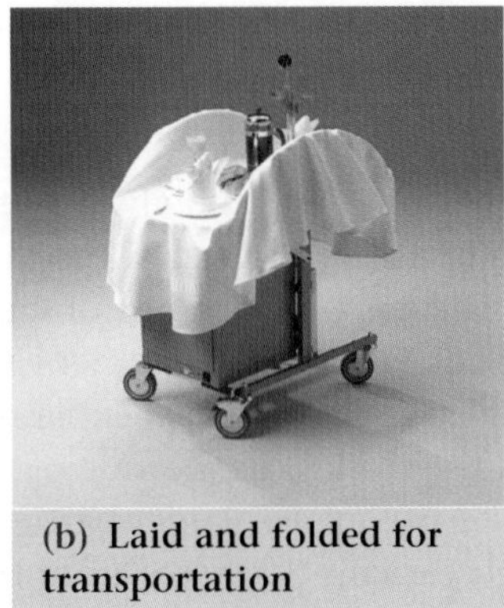

(b) Laid and folded for transportation

(c) Laid and opened for service, with hot cupboard fitted

Figure 15.3 Room service tables (images courtesy of Burgess Furniture Ltd, London, UK)

15.4 Lounge service

The lounge is very often the front window of the establishment, so the standards of service should be high to reflect overall standards. This responsibility rests with the lounge staff and they must therefore be of smart appearance, efficient and attentive to the hotel guests or other customers.

They should have a good knowledge of food and beverage service, especially the licensing laws, and of the technical skills required to provide a competent service. Throughout the day the lounge staff must ensure that the areas are presentable at all times.

The lounge staff must be prepared for the following types of service in the lounge:

- various breakfast foods
- morning coffee
- aperitifs and cocktails
- main meals
- coffee, liqueurs and brandy
- afternoon tea
- aperitifs and cocktails before dinner
- service of late-night beverages, both alcoholic and non-alcoholic
- other snacks throughout the day, depending on the type of establishment.

Chance customers usually pay for the service at the time. Resident hotel guests may not wish to pay in the lounge and staff must then ensure that the hotel guest signs the check to confirm the services received. The check must show the correct room number. The amount should then be charged to the guest's hotel account.

15.5 Service enhancements

Service enhancements include service from trolleys. These can include cheese, sweet, carving or drinks trolleys and also gueridon service. The various trolleys provide opportunities to use them as selling aids as they display the items on offer to the customers. These service enhancements (sometimes referred to as 'restaurant theatre') are, however, more costly to provide as they:

- take longer than plated or silver service
- require a higher level of service skills
- use more expensive and elaborate equipment
- require larger service areas to allow for the movement of the trolleys.

When serving from a trolley, the trolley should always be positioned between the staff and customer as if it were in a shop. Sweet, cheese and drinks trolleys should be attractively presented from the customer's point of view and well laid out from behind for the server. Plates for dirty service equipment should therefore be to the back of the trolley nearest the server. Staff should explain food or beverage items to customers, either from behind the trolley, to the side of the trolley or standing by the table, but not in front of the trolley. For larger parties the server can go to the customers at the table and then explain the items from there, ensuring that the customers can see the trolley.

Note: When working at trolleys food is not usually served by the spoon and fork technique. Instead, service is with one implement in one hand and another in the other hand with the service on to plates on the trolley. This is more accurate and quicker.

Sweet and cheese trolleys

When the customer makes a selection from the sweet or cheese trolley, a plate should be positioned near the item to be served. Then, using the service equipment (one in each hand) the food should be portioned and transferred neatly to the plate. The plate should then be placed in front of the customer from the right. For larger parties, two people will be required – one to take the orders and place the plate with food in front of the customer, the other to stand at the trolley and portion and plate the foods.

Some sweet and cheese trolleys have a plate-holding ring within their design. In this instance the dish holding the food item ordered must be placed next to this holding ring. Thus, when the food item is portioned it may be transferred easily and safely onto the customer's plate, there being minimum distance between the dish holding the food item ordered and the customer's plate. For temperature control purposes many sweet trolleys now come with ice pack compartments, which should be replenished before each service.

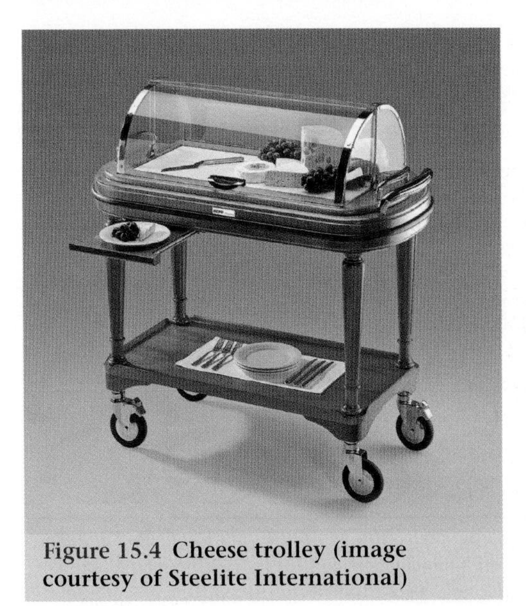

Figure 15.4 Cheese trolley (image courtesy of Steelite International)

For notes on the accompaniments to be offered with sweets see Chapter 9, Section 9.10 (page 161) and for cheese see Chapter 9, Section 9.9 (page 157).

Note: Always remember to push trolleys and not to pull them. This enables a trolley to be controlled when steering and ensures it is moved safely to avoid accidents.

Gueridon service

Gueridon service is an enhanced form of table service. It is normally found in establishments with an à la carte menu and higher levels of service. The definition of the term 'gueridon' is a movable service table, or trolley, from which food may be served. In effect, the gueridon is a movable sideboard or service station carrying sufficient equipment for the service requirements, together with any spare equipment that may be necessary.

Gueridon service usually indicates serving foods onto the customers' plates at the gueridon. Gueridon service is also often used to refer to other enhanced service techniques such as service using a drinks trolley, carving trolley, cheese trolley or a sweet trolley.

Further enhancements to the basic gueridon service include:

- preparing and serving foods in the service area such as salads and dressings
- carving, jointing or filleting foods in a service area
- flambage (the preparation and finishing, or cooking, of foods in the restaurant, which are also flambéed).

Approaches to gueridon service

For gueridon service the taking of food orders is similar to that detailed in Chapter 14, Section 14.4 (page 257). When gueridon service is being undertaken, all dishes must be presented to the customers at the table before the actual service of the food and especially before any portioning, filleting, jointing, carving or service of any dish. This is so that the customers can see the dishes as the kitchen has presented them before the dishes are to be served. Customers can also confirm that the orders are correct.

Mise-en-place for gueridon service

In many establishments where gueridon service is carried out, the basic layout is standardised. This is to ensure that the required standards of service are met and that safety is a prime consideration of all the service staff. There are many designs of gueridon available on the market today, but the basic format for the lay-up of the top of the gueridon may be as shown in Figure 15.5.

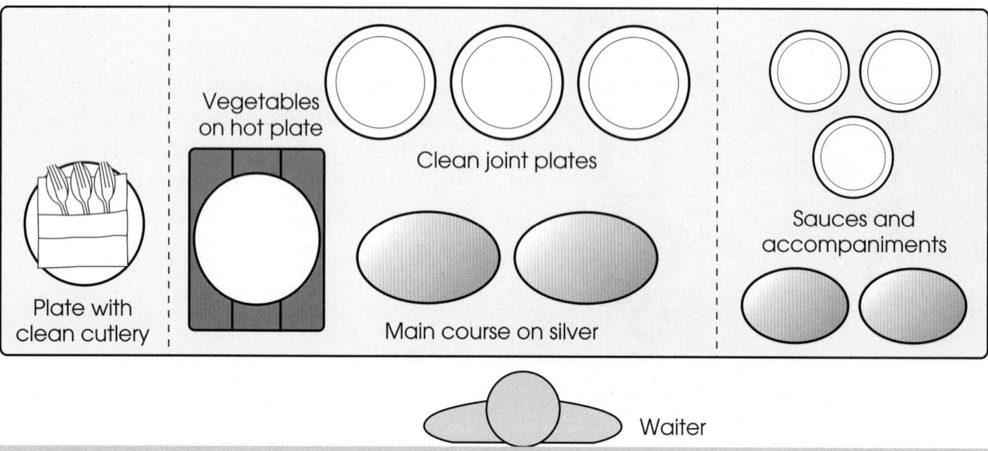

Figure 15.5 Example of a basic gueridon lay-up

If hotplates or food warmers are used then these are placed on the left-hand side on the top of the gueridon. These heaters may be gas, electric or methylated spirit.

Procedure for gueridon service

- Guéridon service is essentially a waiter and commis service. There must therefore be complete liaison and teamwork between them and the other members of the team.
- Always push the gueridon, never pull it. This helps to control and steer the gueridon in the right direction and avoid accidents.
- The gueridon should be kept in one position for the service of a complete course and not moved from customer to customer.
- Unlike silver service, where the spoon and fork are used together in one hand, gueridon service requires that the spoon and fork are used one in each hand. This gives more control and makes the service quicker.
- The dish is first presented to the customer and the name of the dish is stated for example, 'Your Dover sole, madam'. The dish is then returned to the gueridon.
- Hot serving plates are placed on the side of the trolley, with the dish for the food to be served placed onto the hotplate.
- The food dishes are then served onto the customers' plates. This may also include portioning, carving, jointing or filleting if necessary.
- When transferring foods and liquids from the service flats and dishes to the plate, always run the fork along the underside of the spoon to avoid drips marking the plate.
- The waiter may then serve the potatoes and vegetables onto the plate while the plates are still on the gueridon. The waiter also serves the sauces onto the plates. The plates are then placed in front of the customers.
- Alternatively, where more than two covers are being served from the gueridon, only the main dish of each customer would be served from the gueridon, with potatoes and vegetables, sauces and accompaniments being served to the customer once the main food items have been served onto the customers' plates and put in front of the customers.

- The commis must always keep the gueridon clear of dirties.
- When the service is finished at one table, wipe down the gueridon and move on to the next table immediately. It will then be ready for the commis coming from the kitchen with a loaded tray.

Note: Never carve on silver or stainless steel flats or dishes as a knife can ruin them. Use either a carving board or a hot joint plate.

Some service considerations for a variety of different foods are shown in Table 15.1.

Table 15.1 Service considerations for different foods

Hors d'oeuvre or other appetisers	These are served in the usual way except for various speciality dishes (see also Section 9.2, page 150).
Soups	Always served from the gueridon, whether in individual soup tureens or in larger soup tureens requiring a ladle.
Egg dishes	Unless there is any special treatment required these are served straight to the table.
Pasta and rice dishes	Served onto the customers' plates at the gueridon. The pasta is served by lifting the pasta high from the serving dish using a service spoon and fork, and then moving this over to the customer's plate and lowering the pasta onto the plate. Accompaniments are offered at the table.
Fish dishes	Served from the presentation dishes or flats onto the customers' plates. Some fish dishes may be presented for filleting or carving at the gueridon and this is carried out, served and presented onto the customer's plate at the gueridon.
Meats	Served from the presentation dishes or flats onto the customer's plates. Some meat dishes may be presented for carving or jointing at the gueridon and this is then carried out but always on a carving board. The dish is then served directly onto the customer's plate at the gueridon.
Potatoes and vegetables	Either served onto the customer's plate at the gueridon, or served as in silver service, after the main courses have been put onto the customer's plate and placed in front of them. Sauces and accompaniments are served at the table.
Cheese	May be served plated or often served from a cheese trolley, but may also be served from a cheese presentation (such as a cheese board), which is presented on a gueridon.
Sweet	Unless pre-plated, or served from a cold sweet trolley, sweet dishes are served from the presentation dishes or flats onto the customer's plate at the gueridon. Some sweet dishes may be presented for portioning at the gueridon and this is then carried out and then served directly onto the customer's plate at the gueridon.
Savoury	Unless pre-plated these are served onto the customer's plate at the gueridon.
Coffee and tea	Usual service is at the table unless speciality coffees are required.

Introduction to carving, jointing and filleting

Carving techniques are craft skills of real value to the foodservice trade. They will be required in those restaurants using a carving trolley, in carvery-type operations, for serving at a buffet and for special occasions. In some establishments these tasks are carried out by service staff as part of their usual service duties, especially for gueridon service. In other establishments there may be a specialist carver (trancheur). Carving, filleting and jointing skills are also necessary for counter or buffet assistants.

All customers have their likes and dislikes – the meat to be medium or well done, some with fat or very little fat, a portion carved from the end of the joint, sliced thinly or thickly, white meat only, a mix of white and brown meat, and so on. The service staff must acknowledge all of these requests while remaining organised and efficient. They must have all the correct equipment to hand for the foods to be served, together with the appropriate accompaniments and sauces.

Carving, jointing and filleting skills

Carving, jointing and filleting are skilled arts only perfected by continual practice. General considerations are as follows:

- Always use a very sharp knife, making sure it is sharpened beforehand and not in front of the customer. Remember you are going to carve a joint, not cut it to pieces.
- Carving is best achieved by pulling the knife back towards you and not by pushing the knife forwards.
- Use the whole length of the knife so as to let the knife cut the food properly.
- Cut economically and correctly to maximise the portions obtained and to keep wastage to a minimum.
- Work quickly and efficiently to avoid hold-ups in the room.
- Meat is carved across the grain, with the exception of saddle of mutton or lamb, which is sometimes cut at right angles to the ribs.
- The carving fork must hold the joint firmly to prevent accidents. For smaller joints use the fork with the prongs pointed down to hold the food. For larger joints use the fork to pierce the meat to hold it steady while carving.
- Practise as much as possible to acquire expertise in the art of carving and to develop confidence in front of the customer.

Selection of tools

- For most joints a knife with a blade 25–30 cm (10–12 in) long and about 2.5 cm (1 in) wide is required.
- For poultry or game a knife with a blade 20 cm (8 in) long is more suitable.
- For ham a carving knife with a long flexible blade is preferred. This is often referred to as a ham knife.
- Serrated knives do not always cut better than the plain-bladed knife, with the latter giving a cleaner cut.
- A carving fork is needed to hold the joint firmly in position when carving.
- Carve on a board, either wooden or plastic. Avoid carving on china plates or metal. Apart from the damage this can cause (especially with silver) small splinters of metal can become attached to the meat slices.

Cleanliness and hygiene

The standard of cleanliness of the carver and their equipment during the practical application of the craft are of the utmost importance. Good service practices are listed below.

- Always wear spotlessly clean protective clothing. Remember customers are watching a demonstration of the craft.
- Ensure that personal cleanliness is given priority as you are working in the vicinity of your customers as well as handling food.
- Always pre-check work areas and equipment to ensure good hygiene practices.
- Do not move meat, poultry or game excessively when on a board for carving or jointing.

- Carve as required and do not pre-carve too much or too early.
- Keep all meat, poultry or game under cover, be it hot or cold, and at the correct serving temperature.
- Be constantly vigilant for any sign of deterioration in the food being offered.
- At the conclusion of each service ensure all equipment is thoroughly cleaned and well rinsed.

Methods of carving, jointing and filleting

The carving of all hot food must be performed quickly so that there is minimum heat loss. General guidance on carving, jointing and filleting is given in Table 15.2. More detailed information is given in the various sections in the remainder of this chapter.

Table 15.2 General guidance on carving, filleting and jointing

Beef and ham	Always cut very thinly
Rib of beef	May either be carved on the bone or by being first removed from the bone and then sliced
Steaks	Chateaubriand or entrecôte double are sliced at angles, either in half or into more slices, depending on the customer's preference
Lamb, mutton, pork, tongue and veal	Carved at double the thickness of beef and ham
Saddle of lamb	Carved along the loin in long, fairly thick slices
Shoulder of lamb	This has an awkward bone formation. Starting from the top, cut down to the bone, then work from top to bottom, then turn the piece over and work gradually round
Lamb best ends	These are sliced into individual culets by carving between the cutlet bones; best ends can also be double-cut by cutting close to each side of the bone
Boiled beef and pressed meats	Generally carved slightly thicker than roast meats and each portion will include some fat. Boiled beef should be carved with the grain to avoid the meat shredding
Cold ham	Carved onto the bone from top to bottom in very thin slices
Whole chicken	A medium-sized bird is often dissected into eight pieces, making up four portions
Poussin and small feathered game	May be offered whole or split into two portions
Duckling	May be carved into four/six portions, two legs, two wings and the breast cut into long strips
Turkey and other large birds	Often portioned into legs, wings and breast and then carved into slices separately. Make up portions with white meat from the wings or breast together with a slice of brown meat off the leg and a share of the stuffing. Alternatively, the bird may be left whole with the joints separated from the main carcase so as to allow for carving without jointing first
Poached salmon	This is first skinned whether it is hot or cold. It is then served in fillets, one from each side of the bone. Cut slices up to 10 cm (4 in) long and 2.5 cm (1 in) thick
Lobster and crayfish	Hold firmly. Pierce vertically with a strong knife and cut with a levering motion towards tail and head. Hold shell down with a spoon on a dish, slowly lifting out the meat with a fork. Slice the meat diagonally
Sole	First remove the bones along either edge. Then draw the fillets apart with the aid of two large forks. Serve a top and bottom fillet per portion

Carving trolley

During service staff must be salespeople and be able to sell the dishes on the menu by brief and accurate description. The carving trolley supplements this by being a visual aid to selling and should be at the table as the waiter takes orders so that they may suggest and show particular items to the customer.

Figure 15.6 Carving trolley (image courtesy of Euroservice UK)

Presentation of the trolley

- The carver must always ensure that the carving trolley is correctly laid up before it is taken to the table.
- The plate rest for the hot joint plates should be extended and the two containers for gravy and sauces should be already filled. These two containers should always be placed at the end nearest the plate rest. This is for ease of service and also provides the shortest space between the containers and the plates.
- When being used the carving trolley should be placed next to the customer's table, in between the customer and the carver. This ensures that the customer can see every operation performed by the carver and appreciate the skills involved.
- The trolley should be positioned to ensure that the safety valve is on the side away from the carver. This is to ensure that the carver will not be scalded when using the trolley.
- The trolley should be positioned in such a way that the lid is drawn back from the trolley towards the carver so as to reveal the foods to the customer.

Care and maintenance of equipment

It is the visual display of preparing food at the table that is attractive to many customers. All actions must therefore meet the highest hygiene and safety standards, and good planning and organisation can achieve this. The hygiene and safety factors relating to gueridon service are described below.

- Hygiene and appearance of staff should be of the highest standard (see Section 4.2, page 69).
- All equipment should be spotlessly clean and polished daily.
- Food should not be handled with bare hands.
- Trolleys should be wiped down between each use.
- The hotplate or lamp should never be placed outside of the trolley legs.
- The trolley should not be positioned for use close to curtains or soft furnishings.
- Spirits and other alcoholic liquors should never be left near heated trolleys or naked flames.
- Spirits and other alcoholic liquors should be handled carefully when flaming dishes.
- The trolley should not be moved around the restaurant with food or equipment on it.
- Lamps should be checked on a daily basis to ensure they are in good working order.

A daily safety inspection and cleaning programme should be enforced through the use of a cleaning rota or schedule. The food service personnel should carry out this work as part of the normal mise-en-place period and under the supervision of a senior member of the team.

CHAPTER 16

Beverage service skills

This chapter will help you to learn about serving:

1 Popular bar drinks
2 Cocktails
3 Wines
4 Beers and ciders
5 Liqueurs
6 Non-alcoholic bar beverages – cold
7 Tea and coffee
8 Chocolate

16.1 Popular bar drinks

The service of examples of popular bar drinks is shown in Table 16.1 below.

Table 16.1 Service of bar drinks

Aerated waters (e.g. cola)	Served chilled or with ice and a slice of lemon/lime or orange. Sometimes served with cordials
Baileys	Either chilled or with crushed ice as frappé
Brandy	No additions to good brandies. Popular mixers for lesser brandies are lemonade or peppermint, together with ice
Campari	Soda water or lemonade together with ice and a slice of orange
Dark rum	Lemonade or cola with ice and slice of lemon/lime or with blackcurrant and no ice
Fruit juices	Served chilled or served with lemonade, tonic water or sparkling mineral water. Also served with ice and a slice of lemon, orange or other fruit
Gin	Angostura bitters and ice (Pink Gin) or with tonic water or bitter lemon together with ice and a slice of lemon/lime
Liqueurs	May be served naturally or on crushed ice as frappé
Mineral water	Properly served chilled only, but can be with ice and lemon/lime at the request of the guest. Sometimes served with cordials or fruit juices
Pernod	Water and with ice offered and sometimes with cordials or lemonade
Pimm's	Lemonade, ice and slice of lemon, cucumber, apple, orange and a sprig of mint. Sometimes also topped up with ginger ale, soda or tonic water
Port (ruby)	Good port served naturally. Lesser port either by itself or with lemonade and ice
Port (white)	Serve chilled, sometimes with ice and a slice of lemon/lime

Sambuca	Coffee bean and set alight (for safety reasons this should be done at the table and the flame extinguished as soon as the oil from the bean is released into the drink)
Sherries	Served chilled
Vermouths	With ice and a slice of lemon/lime or sometimes with lemonade. Dry vermouths may alternatively be served with an olive; sweeter vermouths with a cocktail cherry
Vodka	Tonic water, lemonade, ice and a slice of lemon/lime; orange cordial, ice and a slice of orange; lime cordial, ice and a slice of lemon/lime; a range of fresh juices with ice and slice of lemon/lime
Whisk(e)y	Natural or with water (often still mineral water), with ice offered or with dry ginger or Canada Dry or soda water and with ice offered
White rum	Natural with ice or with cola, ice and a slice of lemon/lime
Wine	By the glass and sometimes, for white wine, with soda water or sparkling mineral water or lemonade, as spritzer

Many establishments serve bar drinks on to a glass coaster (often paper) at the point of sale. When serving in a lounge or restaurant, drinks should always be carried to the customer on a service salver.

Each establishment has their own range of glassware for the service of drinks. Examples of glasses for the service of drinks are shown in Figure 16.1.

16.2 Cocktails

Cocktails should always be served well chilled in an appropriately sized glass with the correct garnish, straw and umbrella, according to the policy of the establishment. Many cocktails are served in the traditional V-shaped cocktail glass (often called a Martini glass) but, if the cocktail is a long drink, then a larger glass such as a Slim Jim or Highball will be better suited. The key consideration here should be the presentation of the cocktail as seen visually by the customer.

Points to note in making cocktails

- Ice should always be clear and clean.
- Do not overfill the cocktail shaker.
- Effervescent drinks should never be shaken.
- To avoid spillage, do not fill glasses to brim.
- When egg white or yolk is an ingredient, first break the egg into separate containers before use.
- Serve cocktails in chilled glasses.
- To shake, use short and snappy actions.
- Always place ice in the shaker or mixing glass first, followed by non-alcoholic and then alcoholic beverages.
- To stir, stir briskly until blend is cold.
- As a general rule the mixing glass is used for those cocktails based on liqueurs or wines (clear liquids).
- Shakers are used for cocktails that might include fruit juices, cream, sugar and similar ingredients.
- When egg white or yolk is an ingredient then the Boston shaker should normally be used.

Figure 16.1 Examples of drinking glasses and their uses

- Always add the garnish after the cocktail has been made and to the glass in which the cocktail is to be served.
- Always measure out ingredients; inaccurate amounts spoil the balance of the blend and taste.
- Never use the same ice twice.

A list of cocktail and mixed drink ingredients and methods is given in Annex A, pages 319–26.

Note: Examples of bar equipment are shown in Chapter 3, Section 3.5 (page 51).

16.3 Wines

The sommelier or wine waiter must be able to advise and suggest wines to the host as required. This means that the wine waiter must have a good knowledge of the wines contained within the wine list and be able to identify examples of wines that will pair well with the menu dishes. Immediately the food order has been taken the wine list should again be presented to the host so that he or she may order wine to accompany the meals that the guests have ordered.

There are seven key aspects to be taken into account when serving wines.

1. The wine waiter must be able to describe the wines and their characteristics honestly – bluffing should be avoided.
2. Always serve the wine before the food. Avoid any delay in serving the food once the wine has been served.
3. Serve wine at the correct temperature – it is better to tell the customer that the wine is not at the right temperature for service, rather than resorting to quick heating or cooling methods as these can damage the wine.
4. Treat wine with respect and demonstrate a high level of technical skill, supported by the use of high-quality service equipment. As the customer is paying for the wine and the service they have the right to expect their chosen wine to be treated with care.
5. When pouring wine, the neck of the bottle should be over the glass but not resting on the rim in case of an accident. Care should be taken to avoid splashing the wine and when pouring is complete, the bottle should be twisted and raised as it is taken away. This prevents drops of wine falling on the tablecloth or on the customer's clothes. Any drops on the rim of the bottle should be wiped away with a clean service cloth or napkin.
6. Do not overfill glasses. Fill glasses to the right level, usually to the widest part of the bowl or two-thirds full, whichever is the lesser. Sparkling wine served in a flute is usually filled to about two-thirds to three-quarters of the glass. Doing so helps the wine to be better appreciated and looks better too.
7. Avoid unnecessary topping up – it does not sell more wine and it often irritates customers. Another reason for being cautious about topping up wine glasses is that the customer may be driving. If wine is constantly topped up the customer may not notice how much they are consuming. In general, it is preferable to ask the customer about topping up their wine.

Serving temperatures for wines

- *Red wines*: 15.5–18°C (60–65°F). Some young red wines may also be drunk cool at about 12.5–15.5°C (55–60°F).
- *White wines*: 10–12.5°C (50–55°F).
- *Dessert wines, champagne and other sparkling white wines*: 4.5–10°C (40–50°F).

Wine glasses

Wines may be served in the types of glasses indicated below:

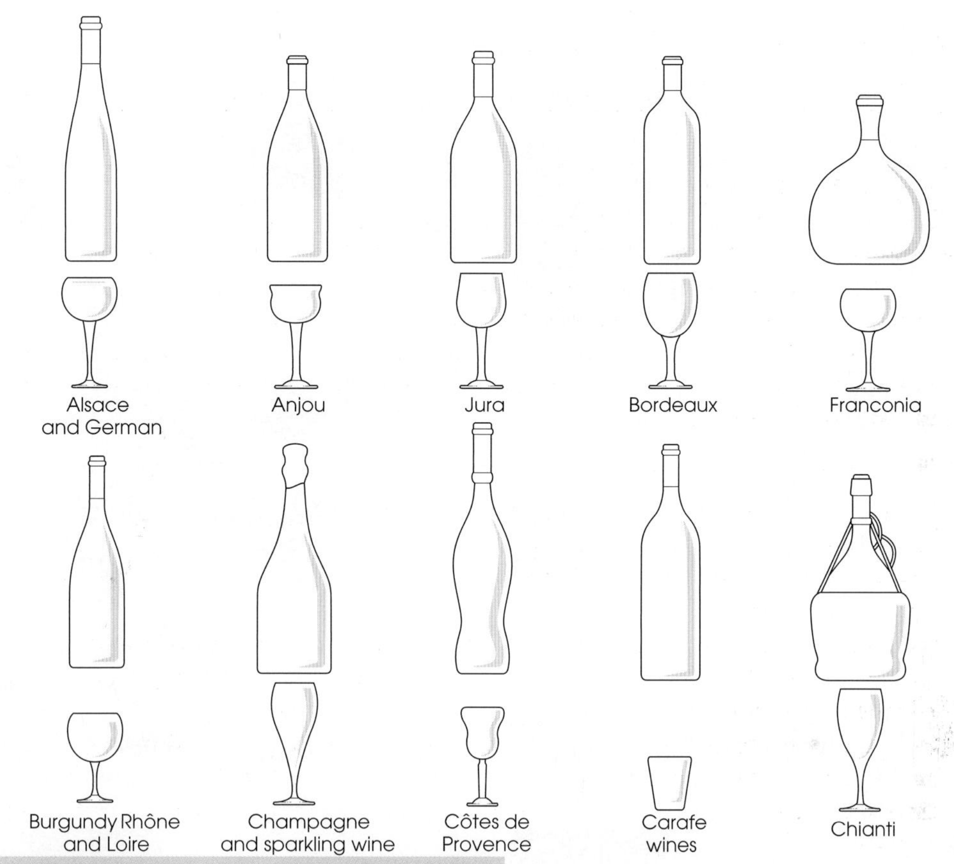

Figure 16.2 Bottle types and glasses for wine

- *Champagne and other sparkling wines*: flute or tulip-shaped glass.
- *German and Alsace wines*: traditionally a long-stemmed German wine glass but nowadays a medium-sized wine glass.
- *White wines*: medium-sized wine glass.
- *Rosé wines*: flute or medium-sized wine glass.
- *Red wines*: large wine glass.

Examples of wine bottle types and glasses for wine are shown in Figure 16.2.

Service of white wines

1. Obtain the wine from the bar or storage area. Check that the order is correct and that the wine is clear and properly temperatured.
2. Take to the table in an ice bucket and place the ice bucket in a stand.
3. Present the bottle to the host with the label showing – this allows him or her to check that the correct wine is to be served (see Figure 16.3(a)).
4. Ensure the correct glasses are placed on the table for the wine to be served.
5. Make sure a clean napkin is tied to the handle of the ice bucket – this is used to wipe away condensation and water from the outside of the bottle before pouring the wine.

6 Using a wine knife, cut the foil all the way round, below or above the bottle rim at the top of the bottle (some bottles have small caps rather than foils). The top of the foil only is then removed and the top of the cork is wiped with the napkin (see Figure 16.3(b)).

Figure 16.3(a) Service of white wine – presenting the bottle

Figure 16.3(b) Removing the foil

Figure 16.3(c) Removing the cork

Figure 16.3(d) Pouring the wine

7 Remove the cork using a wine knife (see Figure 16.3(c)). Smell the cork in case the wine is 'corked'.
8 Place the cork in the ice bucket. If the wine is a high-quality vintage wine then the cork would generally be placed on a side plate at the head of the host's cover. This cork should have the name and year of the wine printed on it.
9 Wipe the inside of the neck of the bottle with the napkin.
10 Wipe the bottle dry.
11 Hold the bottle for pouring so that the label may be seen. Use the waiter's cloth in the other hand, folded, to catch any drips from the neck of the bottle (see Figure 16.3(d)).
12 Give a taste of the wine to the host, pouring from the right-hand side. He or she should acknowledge that the wine is suitable, i.e. that it has the correct taste, bouquet and temperature.
13 Serve ladies first, then gentlemen and the host last, always commencing from the host's right. However, nowadays service often follows from one customer to the next, anti-clockwise.
14 Fill each glass two-thirds full or to the widest part of the bowl – whichever is the lower. This leaves room for an appreciation of the bouquet.
15 Replace the remaining wine in the wine bucket and refill the glasses when necessary.
16 If a fresh bottle is required, then fresh glasses should be placed upon the table, and the host asked to taste the new wine before it is served.
17 On finishing pouring a glass of wine, twist the neck of the bottle and raise it at the same time to prevent drops from falling on the tablecloth.

Note: For bottles with screw caps, the opening procedure is to hold the whole length of the seal in the opening hand and to hold the base of the bottle in the other hand. The closure is held firmly in the opening hand with more pressure, from the thumb and first finger, around the cap itself. The bottle is then sharply twisted using the hand holding the base. There will be a click and then the upper part of the screw top can be removed.

Service of red wine

The basic procedure for the opening and serving of red wines is the same as for white wines described above. If the red wine to be opened is young the bottle may stand on an underplate or coaster on the table and be opened from this position. This adds to the overall presentation of the bottle and may prevent drips of red wine from staining the tablecloth. Although there is no technical reason why red wine should be served with the bottle in a wine basket or wine cradle, these are used in a number of establishments for display/presentation purposes. They also assist in retaining the sediment, found in some older red wines, in the base of the bottle.

The cork should be removed from the bottle of red wine as early as possible so that the wine may attain room temperature naturally. If the wine is of age and/or is likely to have a heavy sediment, then the wine should be decanted (see Figure 16.4(a)–(d)). It should be placed in a wine basket and first presented to the customer. Placing the bottle in a wine basket helps to keep the bottle as horizontal as possible, comparable to its storage position in the cellar, in order to prevent the sediment from being shaken up. The wine should then be decanted. Alternatively, if the wine is ordered in advance it can be left standing for a few days before opening.

There is a trend nowadays to decant younger red wines, simply because exposure to air improves the bouquet and softens and mellows the wine. Decanting also enhances the appearance of the wine, especially when presented in a fine wine decanter. However, the permission of the host should always be sought before decanting a wine in the restaurant.

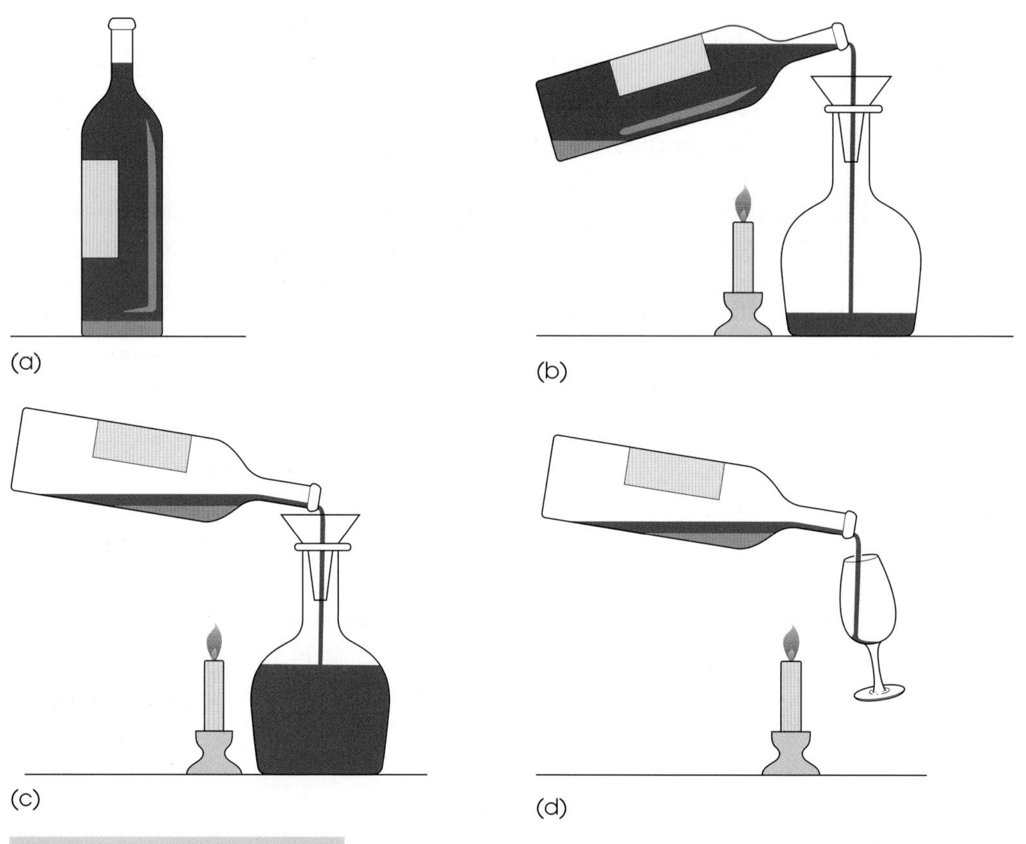

Figure 16.4 Decanting wine

Decanting is the movement of wine from its original container to a fresh glass receptacle, leaving the sediment behind.

1 Extract the cork carefully. The cork may disintegrate because of long contact with alcohol, so be careful.
2 Place a single point light behind the shoulder of the bottle, a candle if you are decanting in front of customers, but a torch, light bulb or any light source will do (see Figure 16.4(b)).
3 Carefully pour the wine into an absolutely clean decanter. The light will reveal the first sign of sediment entering the neck of the bottle (see Figure 16.4(c)).
4 As soon as sediment is seen, stop pouring into the decanter but continue pouring into a glass (see Figure 16.4(d)). The latter wine, when it settles, can be used as a taster or for sauces in the kitchen.
5 The wine should always be checked to make sure that it is clear before being presented at the table for service.

6 If the wine is not clear after decanting then it should be decanted again into a fresh decanter, but this time using a wine funnel which has a piece of fine muslin in the mouth of the funnel. If the wine is still not clear it should not be served and a new bottle of the wine selected. It is more common now for a wine funnel to be used as part of the decanting process generally, as shown in Figure 16.4(a) and (c).

Very old red wine can break up with too much exposure to air. Such wines can be left to stand for a few days to allow the sediment to settle in the bottom of the bottle. The bottle is then opened before the meal is served and the wine is poured very carefully straight into the glass, with the bottle held in the pouring position as each glass is approached. This prevents the wine slopping back to disturb the sediment. Sufficient glasses should be available to finish the bottle, thereby ensuring that the wine does not re-mingle with its sediment during the pouring process.

Service of champagne and sparkling wine

The same method is used for opening all sparkling wines. The wine should be served well chilled in order to obtain the full effect of the secondary fermentation in the bottle, namely, effervescence and bouquet. The pressure in a champagne bottle, due to its maturing and secondary fermentation, will be about 5 kg per cm^2 (about 70 lb per sq in). Great care must therefore be taken not to shake the bottle otherwise the pressure will build up and could cause an accident.

1 After presenting the bottle to the host the wine is ready for opening.
2 The neck of the bottle should be kept pointed towards a safe area in the restaurant during the opening process, in order to avoid any accidents to customers should the cork be released suddenly.
3 The thumb should be held over the cork with the remainder of the hand holding the neck of the bottle.
4 The foil around the top of the cork is separated from the foil around the neck of the bottle by pulling on the tab on the foil, or by using a wine knife to cut it. The foil is not removed.
5 The wine cage is carefully loosened, but not removed.
6 Then, holding the cork and the cage in one hand, the bottom of the bottle should be twisted with the other hand to slowly release the cork.

Sparkling wine should be served in flutes or tulip-shaped glasses, from the right-hand side of each customer. It is also worth considering lifting the glass from the table so as to pour the wine more easily and quickly, and to reduce the frothing of the wine.

Service of wine by the glass

Many establishments offer a range of wines for sale by the glass. Wines are mostly offered in 125 ml or 175 ml measures. With the exception of sparkling wines, it is often better to serve the wine in a glass larger than the measure. This allows the aroma to develop in the glass and the wine to be better appreciated. Many establishments now also pour a measure of wine into a small carafe for the service of wine by the glass. This then allows the customer to pour into their glass the wine as required.

Storage of open wine

Once a bottle is opened the wine can deteriorate quite quickly as it reacts with the air and oxidises. There are various methods of keeping wines once they have been opened. Some work by creating a vacuum within the bottle and then sealing the bottle with a removable closure, either manually or mechanically. Another system involves putting a layer of carbon dioxide gas (CO_2) on the surface of the wine, thus preventing air getting to it.

16.4 Beers and ciders

Beer and ciders should be served at a temperature of 12.5–15.5°C (55–60°F), with lagers generally cooler than other beers at 8.0–10.5°C (48–51°F). Many different varieties of bottled beers are also served chilled. Draught beer and cider, on its route from the keg/cask to the pump, often passes through a chilling unit.

Types of beer and cider glasses

All glasses used should be spotlessly clean with no finger marks, grease or lipstick on them. Pouring beer into a dirty glass will cause it to go flat very quickly. The main types of beer and cider glasses are:

- half pint/pint tankards for draught beer
- pint tumblers for draught beer
- tumblers for any bottled beer
- short-stemmed 34.08 cl (12 fl oz) beer glass for Bass/Worthington/Guinness
- lager glass for lager
- wine goblets in various sizes including 22.72, 28.40, 34.08 cl (8, 10, 12 fl oz) for brown/pale/strong ales.

Increasing sales of beers to be consumed with restaurant meals has encouraged changes in styles of glassware used. Generally these beer glasses, although often based on the listing above, are more elegant in style and made of higher-quality glass.

Pouring beers and ciders

Draft or bottled beer and cider should be poured slowly down the inside of the glass, with the glass held at a slight angle. This is especially important where a beer may produce a large head if it is not poured slowly and carefully, for example, Guinness or stouts.

Draught beers should have a small head on them, and the bar person should ensure that he or she serves the correct quantity of beer with a small head, and not a large head to make up the quantity required. A beer in a good condition will have the head, or froth of the beer, clinging to the inside of the glass as the beer is drunk. This is sometimes called 'lace' on the glass.

For bottled beers and ciders, the neck of the bottle should not be placed in the beer when pouring, especially where two bottles are being held and poured from the same hand. If a bottled beer has a sediment, a little beer must be left in the base of the bottle to ensure that the sediment does not go into the poured beer.

16.5 Liqueurs

Liqueurs (sweetened and flavoured spirits) may be served by the glass, or in a restaurant they may also be served from a liqueur trolley at the table.

If a customer asks for a liqueur to be served frappé, for example, crème de menthe frappé, it is served on crushed ice and a larger glass will be needed. The glass should be two-thirds filled with crushed ice and then the measure of liqueur poured over the ice. Two short drinking straws should be placed into the glass before the liqueur is served.

If a liqueur is requested with cream, for example, Tia Maria with cream, then the cream is slowly poured over the back of a teaspoon to settle on the top of the selected liqueur.

Basic equipment required on a liqueur trolley:

- assorted liqueurs
- assorted glasses – liqueur/brandy/port
- draining stand
- 25 and 50 ml measures
- service salver
- jug of double cream
- teaspoons
- drinking straws (short stemmed)
- cigars – according to house policy
- matches
- cigar cutter
- wine list and check pad.

Other beverages served from the liqueur trolley include brandies and fortified (liqueur) wines such as Port or Madeira.

Figure 16.5 Bar trolley for the service of liqueurs (image courtesy of Euroservice UK)

16.6 Non-alcoholic bar beverages – cold

Non-alcoholic bar beverages are categorised into five main groups:

- aerated waters
- natural spring water or mineral waters
- squashes
- juices
- syrups.

Aerated waters

Aerated waters may be served on their own, chilled, in either Slim Jim tumblers, wine goblets, Highball glasses or 34.08 cl (12 fl oz) short-stemmed beer glasses, depending on the requirements of the customer and the policy of the establishment. They may also accompany other drinks as mixers, for example:

- whisky and dry ginger
- gin and tonic
- vodka and bitter lemon
- rum and cola.

Natural spring waters/mineral waters

Natural spring or mineral waters are normally drunk on their own for medicinal purposes. However, as has been previously mentioned, some mineral waters may be mixed with alcoholic beverages to form an appetising drink. In all cases they should be drunk well chilled, at approximately 7–10°C (42–48°F). If drunk on their own, they should be served in an 18.93 cl (6⅔ fl oz) Paris goblet or a Slim Jim tumbler. Examples include Apollinaris, Buxton, Malvern, Perrier, Saint Galmier and Aix-la-Chapelle.

Squashes

- **Service from the bar:** A measure of squash should be poured into a tumbler or 34.08 cl (12 fl oz) short-stemmed beer glass containing ice. This is topped up with iced water or the soda syphon. The edge of the glass should be decorated with a slice of fruit where applicable and drinking straws added.
- **Service from the lounge or restaurant:** The wine butler or lounge waiter must take all the items required, to give efficient service, on a service salver to the customer. Such items will include:
  - a measure of squash in a tumbler or 34.08 cl (12 fl oz) short-stemmed beer glass
  - straws
  - jug of iced water (on an underplate to prevent the condensation running onto the table)
  - small ice bucket and tongs (on an underplate because of condensation)
  - soda syphon
  - a coaster on which to place the glass in the lounge.

The coaster should be placed on the side table in the lounge and the glass containing the measure of squash placed on the coaster. The waiter should then add the ice and enquire whether the customer wishes iced water or soda to be added. The drinking straws should be placed in the glass at the last moment if required. It may be necessary to leave the iced water and ice bucket on the side table for the customer. If this is the case they should be left on underplates.

Juices

All juices should be served chilled in a 14.20 cl (5 fl oz) goblet or alternative glass.

- **Tomato juice:** Should be served chilled in a 14.20 cl (5 fl oz) goblet or other glass, on a doily on an underplate with a teaspoon. The Worcestershire sauce should be shaken, the top removed, placed on an underplate and offered as an accompaniment. The goblet may have a slice of lemon placed over the edge as additional presentation.

- **Fresh fruit juice:** If fresh fruit juice is to be served in the lounge, then the service should be similar to the service of squash described above, except that a small bowl of caster sugar on an underplate with a teaspoon should be taken to the table.

Syrups

Syrups are never served as drinks in their own right but generally as flavourings in such items as cocktails, fruit cups, long drinks and milkshakes.

16.7 Tea and coffee

Tray service

The following equipment is required for the tray service of coffee or tea:

Coffee tray

- tray or salver
- tray cloth/napkin
- teacup and saucer
- teaspoon
- sugar basin and tongs or a teaspoon according to the type of sugar offered
- coffee pot
- jug of cream or hot milk
- stands for the coffee pot and hot milk jug

Tea tray

- tray or salver
- tray cloth/napkin
- teapot
- hot water jug
- jug of cold milk
- slop basin
- tea strainer
- stands for teapot and hot water jug
- sugar basin and tongs
- teacup and saucer
- teaspoon

Variations of this basic equipment will depend on the type of coffee or tea that is being served. General points to note in laying up a coffee or tea tray are given below:

- Position the items to ensure an evenly balanced tray for carrying.
- Position the items for the convenience of the customer: beverage on the right with spouts facing inwards, and handles outwards and towards the customer for ease of access.
- Ensure the beverage is placed on the tray at the last moment so that it is served hot.

For the various types of tea and their service see Chapter 10, Section 10.1, page 166.

For a list of modern by-the-cup coffee styles see Chapter 10, Section 10.2, page 175.

Service of tea and coffee for table and assisted service

Tea is not usually served but the teapot is placed on the table, on a stand, and to the right-hand side of the person who ordered. The customers will then help themselves. The cold milk and sugars (and alternatives) are also placed onto the table.

Coffee may be silver served at the table from a service salver. However, this traditional method of serving coffee is not so common today. Generally, other speedier methods are used, such as placing the cafetière on the table together with milk and sugars (and alternatives) for customers to help themselves.

Other methods of serving tea and coffee are:

- Service from a pot of tea or a pot of hot black coffee held on the sideboard on a hotplate. Cold milk, hot milk or cream and sugars are placed on the table.
- Service of both cold milk and hot milk or cream together with the tea and coffee from pots, one held in each of the waiter's hands. Sugars are placed on the table for customers to help themselves.
- In event catering where larger numbers often have to be served, the cold milk, hot milk or cream and sugars are often placed on the table for customers to help themselves. The tea and coffee is then served from a one-litre plus capacity vacuum flask, which may be kept on the waiters' sideboard in readiness for replenishment should the customers require it. This method of holding and serving tea and coffee ensures that it remains hot at all times. (For examples of vacuum jugs for tea or coffee see Figure 10.4, page 173.)

Note: When serving tea and coffee from multi-portion pots/urns it is usual to remove the tea leaves, coffee grounds or tea/coffee bags once the beverage has brewed, so that the tea and coffee does not become stewed.

Placement of tea and coffee cups from a tray

- Figure 16.6(a) shows the beverage equipment required, positioned on the service salver, and assuming a table of four customers is to be served. Using this method the server only has to make one journey from the sideboard/workstation to the restaurant or lounge table.
- Note the beverage service for each customer is made up of a teacup on its saucer, with a teaspoon resting in the saucer and at right angles under the handle of the cup.
- The beverage service is placed on the table from the customer's right-hand side, as the beverage ordered will be served from the right.
- The beverage service is positioned on the right-hand side of the customer with the handle to the right and the teaspoon set at right angles under the handle of the cup.
- While moving to the right-hand side of the second customer, the server will place a teacup upon the tea saucer and the teaspoon in the saucer and at right angles under the handle of the cup. This beverage service is then ready to place on the right-hand side of the second customer (see Figure 16.6(b)).
- This procedure is then repeated until all the beverage services have been placed on the table for those customers requiring tea or coffee.

Note: When coffee is served after lunch or dinner, teacups are more commonly used. The use of the small coffee cups (demi-tasse) has declined for conventional coffee service although they are still sometimes used in event catering. These cups are also used for espresso.

Figure 16.6(a) Service salver before service

Figure 16.6(b) Service salver by the time the second customer is reached

16.8 Chocolate

Hot chocolate is most often served individually in special (heat-resistant) glasses that fit into a special holder with a handle. It can also be served in a mug. Hot chocolate may also be presented in a pot or jug for the customer to pour into a teacup. Usually white sugar and sweeteners are also offered for the customer to add, so the glasses or mugs are usually presented on side plates or saucers together with a teaspoon. Teacups are presented on saucers together with a teaspoon. The placement and service of teacups from a tray is the same procedure shown in Figure 16.6 (see above). For more information on chocolate see Chapter 10, Section 10.3 (page 176).

CHAPTER 17

Clearing during and after service

This chapter will help you to learn about:

1 The importance of clearing techniques
2 Clearing for table service and assisted service
3 Clearing for self-service and single-point service
4 General after-service duties
5 Specific after-service duties

17.1 The importance of clearing techniques

Developing good clearing techniques helps to:

- ensure speed and efficiency around the table and service areas
- avoid the possibility of accidents
- create minimum inconvenience to customers
- allow more to be cleared, in less time and in fewer journeys
- provide the opportunity for plates, cutlery, glassware and linen paper and food waste items to be separated according to the needs of the establishment
- allow for dirties to be collected and stacked neatly and correctly on the sideboard/ workstations or trolleys.

17.2 Clearing for table service and assisted service

The main method of clearing in a plated and table service operation, and with customers in the room, is described below.

Clearing techniques

All clearing techniques stem from the two main hand positions shown in Chapter 12, Figure 12.3(a)–(b) (page 211).

Expertise comes with practice, therefore practise regularly.

- Dirties should always be cleared from the right-hand side of the customer.
- The server should position himself or herself, taking up a sideways stance at the table.

Clearing soup plates

- The server, having positioned himself or herself correctly, will then pick up the first dirty soup plate on its underplate. This stance allows the waiter to pass the dirty soup service from the clearing hand to the holding hand.
- Using this procedure ensures the dirty plates are held away from the table and customers, reducing the likelihood of accidents.
- Figure 17.1(a) shows one of the two main hand positions previously mentioned, and the first dirty soup plate cleared.
- This dirty soup plate should be held firmly on its underplate with the latter pushed up firmly between the thumb and the first and second fingers.
- It is important that this first dirty soup plate is held firmly as succeeding dirties are built up on this one, meaning there is a considerable weight to be held.

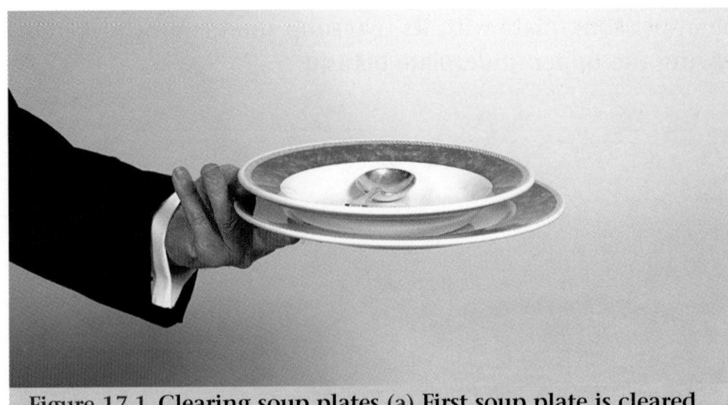

Figure 17.1 Clearing soup plates (a) First soup plate is cleared

- Figure 17.1(b) shows the second dirty soup plate on its underplate cleared and positioned on the holding hand.

Figure 17.1(b) First stage of clearing the second soup plate

- Figure 17.1(c) shows the position of the second dirty soup plate on the holding hand. The soup spoon is taken from the lower soup plate to be placed in the upper soup plate.

Figure 17.1(c) **Second stage of clearing the second soup plate**

- Figure 17.1(d) shows the upper soup plate with its two soup spoons now placed in the lower soup plate, leaving the upper underplate behind.

Figure 17.1(d) **Second soup plate is cleared in preparation for the next dirty soup plate**

- The third dirty soup plate with its underplate is now cleared from the right and placed on the upper underplate on the holding hand. The above procedure is then repeated each time a dirty soup plate on its underplate is cleared.

Clearing joint plates

- Figure 17.2(a) shows one of the two main hand positions previously shown in Figure 12.3 (page 211), and the first dirty joint plate cleared.
- The dirty joint plate should be held firmly pushed up to the joint between the thumb and the first and second finger.
- Note the position of the cutlery: the fork held firmly with the thumb over the end of its handle and the blade of the joint knife placed under the arch in the handle of the fork.
- Any debris or crumbs will be pushed into the triangle formed by the handles of the joint knife and joint fork and the rim of the plate. This is nearest the holding hand.
- Figure 17.2(b) shows the second dirty joint plate cleared and positioned on the holding hand.

Figure 17.2 Clearing joint plates (a) **First joint plate is cleared**

Figure 17.2(b) **Second joint plate is cleared**

- Figure 17.2(c) shows the second dirty joint knife positioned correctly and debris being cleared from the upper joint plate onto the lower joint plate using the second dirty joint fork cleared. This procedure is carried out as the waiter moves on to his next position in readiness to clear the third dirty joint plate.

Figure 17.2(c) **Clearing debris from the upper plate**

- Figure 17.2(d) shows the holding hand with the already cleared items held correctly and ready to receive the next dirty joint plate to be cleared.

Figure 17.2(d) **Preparing to clear the next dirty plate**

- Figure 17.3 shows the dirty joint plates and cutlery correctly stacked, and with the side plates and side knives also being cleared in one journey to the table. This is an alternative to clearing the joint plates and then the side plates in two phases.

Figure 17.3 **Clearing joint and side plates in one journey**

Clearing side plates

- Side plates are cleared using a service salver or service plate. The reason for this is to allow a larger working surface on which to clear the dirty side knives and any debris remaining.
- Figure 17.4(a) illustrates the method of clearing debris from the upper dirty side plate and on to the service salver/plate.

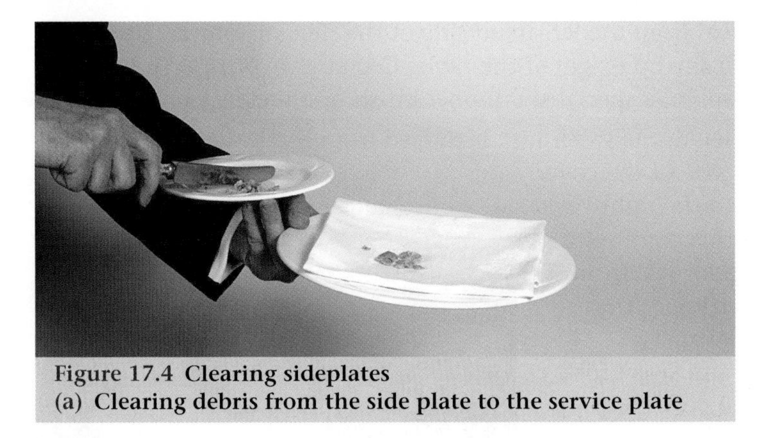

Figure 17.4 Clearing sideplates
(a) Clearing debris from the side plate to the service plate

- Figure 17.4(b) shows the holding hand having cleared four place settings with the dirty items and debris stacked correctly and safely.

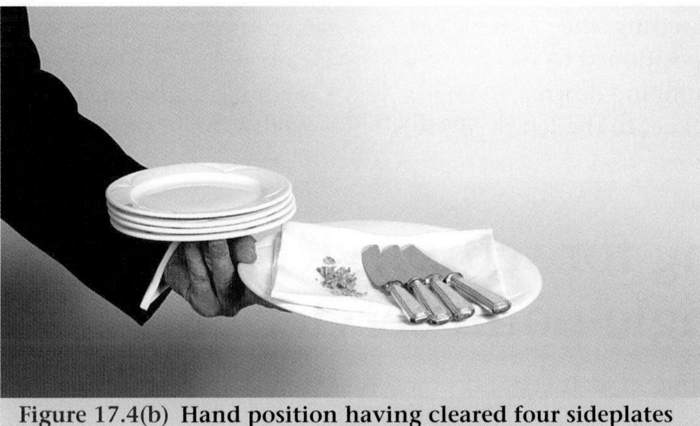

Figure 17.4(b) Hand position having cleared four sideplates

- This method generally allows the waiter to clear more dirty side plates and side knives in one journey between sideboard/workstation and table and is especially useful when working in banqueting.

Crumbing down

The process of crumbing down usually takes place after the main course has been cleared and before the sweet order is taken and served. The purpose is to remove any crumbs or debris left on the tablecloth at this stage of the meal.

The items of equipment used to crumb down are:

- a service plate (a joint plate with a napkin on it)
- the waiter's cloth or service cloth or a metal crumber or crumber brush and pan.

If a table d'hôte cover has previously been laid, the sweet spoon and fork, prior to crumbing down, should normally be positioned at the head of the cover. However, if an à la carte cover has initially been laid, then, after the main course has been cleared, there should be no tableware on the table prior to crumbing down.

Crumbing down commences from the left-hand side of the first customer. The service plate is placed just beneath the lip (edge) of the table. Crumbs are brushed towards the plate using a folded napkin, a specialist crumber brush or a metal crumber.

- This having been completed, the sweet fork is moved from the head of the place setting to the left-hand side of the cover.
- The waiter now moves to the right-hand side of the same customer and completes the crumbing down of this place setting.
- The sweet spoon is then moved from the head of the place setting to the right-hand side of the cover.
- While the sweet spoon and sweet fork are being moved to their correct positions, the service cloth is held under the service plate by the fingers of the holding hand.
- Having completed the crumbing down procedure for one place setting, the waiter is now correctly positioned to commence again the crumbing down of the next place setting, i.e. to the left of the next customer.

Figure 17.5 Crumbing down (note the neatly folded service cloth)

17.3 Clearing for self-service and single-point service

The main methods for clearing in foodservice operations are summarised in Table 17.1.

Table 17.1 Clearing methods

System	Description
Manual	The collection and sorting to trolleys by operators for transportation to the wash-up area
Semi-self-clear	The placing of soiled ware by customers on strategically placed trolleys within the dining area for removal by operators
Self-clear	The placing of soiled ware by customers on a conveyor or conveyor belt tray collecting system for mechanical transportation to the dish wash area
Self-clear and strip	The placing of soiled ware into conveyor belt dish wash baskets by customers for direct entry of the baskets through the dishwashing machines

(*Source*: Croner's Catering)

In all cases food waste and disposable items are usually put directly into the waste bins provided, which are often separated into different recyclable types such as food, paper, plastics and cans.

Clearing tables in the dining areas

As tables are vacated and customers remain in the room the procedures described below may be followed.

- The basic clearing techniques described in Section 17.2 (page 294) can be employed as appropriate.
- Once plates are cleared from the table, the debris (food wastage) would be scraped from plates into a plastic bowl. These bowls of food wastage would be cleared on a regular basis from the workstations for hygiene reasons and to avoid smells affecting the dining area.
- Used cutlery is often initially placed into a plastic bowl containing hot water and a soap liquid detergent. This loosens grease and oil from the cutlery prior to it being placed into the dishwasher for washing, rinsing and sterilisation. Alternatively, dirty cutlery may be placed into cutlery stands at the workstation or on the clearing trolley in readiness for transportation to the wash-up area, where they would be placed into the dishwasher.
- Stack same-sized plates together on a tray and never mix sizes as this can cause a safety hazard resulting in accidents to staff or customers. Spread the weight load on a tray evenly to make it easier to carry. Further information on carrying trays may be found in Chapter 12, Section 12.7 (page 214).
- Glassware should be cleared onto separate trays from crockery and cutlery. This way it is less likely for accidents to occur. Dirty glassware will be taken to the workstation and can be put into glass racks for transportation to the wash-up area.
- Immediately customers vacate their tables the dining area staff should clear any remaining items from the table onto trays and return them to the workstation. The tables should be wiped down with antibacterial cleaning agents and any table accompaniments normally set on the table as part of the lay-up should be replenished.

17.4 General after-service duties

At the end of service a range of duties needs to be completed. These duties are carried out with or without customers in the service/dining areas. Depending on the type of establishment these duties may be carried out at the conclusion of a meal period or towards the end of the working day or continue throughout the day.

The general duties that may be carried out at the end of service, and without customers in the service areas, are:

- Clear the cold buffet to the larder. Collect and wash all carving knives and assist generally in clearing the food service areas.
- Collect all linen, both clean and dirty, and check that the correct quantities of each item of linen are returned. Used napkins should be tied in bundles of ten. All linen should be placed in the linen basket and returned with the linen list to the linen room or according to the establishment policy.
- Switch off the hotplate. Clear away any service silver or other service dishes remaining and restock the hotplate with clean crockery.
- Return cutlery, glassware, crockery, tableware and trolleys to their designated storage areas.
- Collect all cruets and accompaniments and return them to their correct storage place. Where appropriate, return sauces, etc., to their original containers.
- Check all the sideboards/workstations are completely empty.
- Clear down the bar top, put all the equipment away and wash and polish used glasses. These should be put away in their correct storage place. Remove all empty

bottles, etc. Complete consumption and stock sheets. Bar shutters and doors should be made secure.
- Restock the bar from the cellar.
- Empty all beverage service equipment, wash and put away. All perishable materials should be put away in their correct storage places. Still sets and milk urns should be emptied, washed out and then left standing with cold water in them. Other beverage-making equipment to be cleaned according to the manufacturer's instructions.
- Empty and clean all trolleys and return them to their storage places. Any unused food items from the trolleys should be returned to the appropriate department. Any service equipment used on the trolleys should be cleaned and returned to storage areas.
- Reset duties should be completed in readiness for the next service period. This might include both table lay-ups and sideboard/workstation lay-ups.
- As appropriate all dining area tables and chairs should be wiped down with antibacterial cleaning agent.
- Replenish napkin holders, sugar sachets, sauce sachets, cutlery trays and tray stacks as appropriate.
- At all times consideration should be given to sustainability issues, including the recycling of used items, the management of waste and the control of energy.

17.5 Specific after-service duties

After service certain duties will need to be carried out by the food and beverage service staff. The allocation of specific responsibilities helps to ensure that all areas are left safe, clean and restocked in readiness for the next service. Examples of these specific duties are shown below.

Headwaiter/supervisor

1. Ensure gas and electrical appliances are switched off and plugs removed from sockets.
2. Return any special equipment to the appropriate work/storage area.
3. Secure all windows and check fire exits.
4. Check that all tasks are completed in a satisfactory manner prior to staff completing their shift.

Station waiter/server/dining area attendant

1. Replace all equipment in the sideboard/workstations according to the equipment listing checklists.
2. Wipe down the sideboard and trolleys, clearing all dirty equipment to the wash-up area.
3. Clear down tables and crumb down. Relay tablecloths and slip cloths as appropriate.
4. Reset tables and sideboards/workstation if required.
5. Switch off and clean sideboard hotplates.
6. Return special equipment to work/storage areas.
7. Return to store cupboards any surplus crockery and silver.
8. Remove plugs, having switched off all electrical sockets.
9. Mop, vacuum and sweep floors as appropriate.

Bar staff

1 All working surfaces to be wiped down.
2 Ensure that all equipment is washed, dried and put away in its correct place for future use.
3 Make sure all glassware is washed, rinsed, dried and then stored correctly.
4 Empty the bottle trolley and waste bin. Replace the bin liner in the waste bin.
5 Place surplus orange/lemon slices onto plates and cover with cling film. Store in the chilling unit or fridge.
6 Sweep and mop the floor.
7 Return the liqueur trolley to the bar.
8 Drain the glass-washing machine.
9 Turn off the chiller lights.
10 Complete the control system.
11 Replenish bar stock.
12 Make the bar secure.
13 Check area of responsibility with headwaiter/supervisor.

Still room staff

1 Ensure the correct storage of such food items as bread, butter, milk, teabags and ground coffee.
2 Wipe down all working surfaces.
3 Clean and tidy the still room fridge and check its working temperature.
4 Check that all equipment is left clean and stored in its correct place.
5 Leftover foods to be placed into clean containers and stored correctly.
6 All surplus accompaniments to be stored correctly in proprietary jars and their lids to be wiped down.
7 Switch off applicable electrical appliances.
8 Make sure all carrying trays are wiped down and stacked correctly.
9 All surplus teapots/coffee pots, etc., to be stored in the appropriate storage area.
10 Check area of responsibility with the head waiter/supervisor, or the person taking over the area, prior to leaving.

Buffet/counter staff

1 Turn off the electricity supply to the hot food and cold food counter.
2 Clear the hot food counter and cold food counters and return all leftover food to the kitchen.
3 Turn off the power supply to the oven at the wall.
4 Clear the oven of any remaining food.
5 Important: write down on the day sheet the number of portions of each type of regenerated meal that is left over as waste. This exercise is essential for portion control monitoring and gives an indication of the popularity or otherwise of any one particular dish. Hand in the daily sheet to the supervisor who will then prepare a consumption sheet (see Chapter 18, Section 18.10, page 314) to show what was taken out and what is now left. This will then be entered into the sales analysis book.

Figure 17.6 **Still room area cleared at the end of service**

6 Clean all service utensils such as serving spoons, ladles, fish slices, knives and trays that have been used during the course of the day in hot food preparation and service. Wipe them dry.
7 Return all cleaned and dried service utensils to the appropriate storage places ready for the next day's use.
8 Check the stock of plates needed for the next day's service of food.
9 Check area of responsibility with supervisor.

Figure 17.7 **Counter service unit cleaned and ready for the next service**

CHAPTER 18

Bookings, billing and revenue control

This chapter will help you to learn about:

1 Taking bookings
2 The booking sheet
3 The procedure for taking bookings
4 Larger party bookings
5 Purpose of a revenue control system
6 Systems for revenue control
7 The role of the cashier
8 Billing methods
9 Payment methods
10 Sales summary sheets
11 Examples of performance measures

18.1 Taking bookings

The procedure for booking a table is often the first contact that a potential customer has with the establishment. It is therefore of the utmost importance that the right impression is given. This will be reflected in your tone of voice, appearance, attitude to the customer and the knowledge you show in asking the right questions in order to gain the correct information to enter on your booking sheet. The right approach will immediately put the customer at ease and allow them to respond more clearly and accurately. They will feel that you wish to assist them in every way you can. It may also encourage future sales due to your pleasant and knowledgeable response.

Bookings may be taken:

- by post
- by email
- by telephone
- via the internet (using online systems)
- from customers coming to the establishment in person.

18.2 The booking sheet

The basic information required is the same regardless of how the bookings are taken.

Most establishments use some form of booking sheet, either manual or electronic.

An example of the information that might be required on a booking sheet is given in Figure 18.1. This includes:

- day and date
- name of the customer
- customer's telephone number
- number of covers required
- time of the event – arrival
- any special requirements, e.g. vegetarian or children's meals
- signature of the person taking the booking in case of any queries

This form also shows the maximum number of covers to be booked for a service period and enables a running total of pre-booked covers to be kept. Depending on the policy of the establishment and the total number of covers requested when a booking is being made, written confirmation may be required and/or credit card details taken in order to secure a deposit.

Other information that might be sought includes:

- whether the occasion of the meal is for a special event, such as an anniversary or birthday
- customer preferences about the size, shape and location of a table
- special requests such as requirements for a birthday/anniversary cake and other information, such as customers with allergies.

Should party bookings require special menus, the booking should be referred to the supervisor. Procedures similar to large party bookings (see Section 18.4) will then be adopted.

Restaurant............		Day.............		Date............	Maximum covers.............	
Name	Tel. no.	Covers	Arrival time	Running total	Special requirements	Signature

Figure 18.1 Example of a booking sheet

18.3 The procedure for taking bookings

When taking bookings extreme care needs to be taken to ensure all booking details are correct. Should any error be made or the information not be clear it can result in:

- poor customer and establishment relations
- loss of sales
- tension among the staff resulting in a lowering of standards in the workplace
- problems relating to seating, space available and the provision for those customers with additional needs
- disturbance to other customers.

Bookings by telephone

When taking a booking by telephone the procedure shown below might be used.

- When the telephone rings, lift the receiver and say: 'Good morning (state the name of the establishment). May I help you?'
- If the customer is making the booking in person then say 'Good morning, sir/ madam, how may I help you?'
- When taking the booking the essential information required is as listed previously.
- When you have received this information from the customer and made your notes, the full details of the booking should be repeated back to the customer to check that you have understood the customer's requirements properly and to give the customer the opportunity to confirm the details.
- At the end of a telephone call for a booking one should say: 'Thank you for your booking, we shall look forward to seeing you on...'

Other bookings

The procedures for taking a booking in person are similar to those for taking a booking via the telephone. When dealing with bookings by post or email the information required is the same as that described above.

Confirmation of a booking is normally sent back to the customer by the same method as the booking was received, for example, by post or email.

Internet bookings are often automatically confirmed to the customer at the time the booking is made. The details of the booking are then forwarded to the establishment for inclusion on the booking sheet.

Cancellations

When a cancellation is received, the cancellation details are confirmed back to the customer by repeating his/her request over the telephone. It is also good practice to then ask if you can take a booking for any other occasion in place of the cancellation.

18.4 Larger party bookings

There will often be different procedures in an establishment for dealing with bookings for larger parties, for example, for parties of six covers or more. When a customer is ready to make a booking a file is opened. This can be handwritten or computerised depending on the establishment. The file will contain the client's details and will be used to hold all the requirements for the particular event, as well as all correspondence sent and received. The basic information that is recorded is as listed previously. There will also be additional specific information required according to the nature of the occasion. This may include:

- date and time of event (including access and clear down times)
- type of event – such as birthday celebration, wedding, conference, cocktail party or exhibition
- food and beverage requirements
- service methods (including wines and drinks being inclusive or cash)
- table plan
- price being charged (for the party as a whole or charged as the price per head) and the inclusion or otherwise of service charges

- additional charges that will be made
- provision for customers with additional needs
- deadline for confirmation of final numbers
- contractual requirements (deposit payments, payment in advance, etc.)
- car parking requirements.

18.5 Purpose of a revenue control system

In order to make maximum profit for an establishment a control system covering the sale of all food and beverages in a foodservice operation is essential. The type of control system used will vary from one operation to another.

In large establishments a control and accounts department will be in overall charge of the efficient running and working of the control systems used. In a smaller establishment this may be managed by an assistant manager, who will personally carry out the necessary daily and weekly checks. To make it easier for food and beverage service staff to operate, control systems should be kept as simple as possible.

A control system essentially monitors areas where selling takes place.

- There must be efficient control of all food and beverage items issued from the various departments.
- The system should reduce any pilfering and keep wastage to a minimum.
- Management should be provided with any information they require for costing purposes and so that they may estimate accurately for the coming financial period.
- The cashier should be able to make out the customer's bill correctly so that the customer is neither overcharged nor undercharged.
- The system should show a breakdown of sales and income received in order that adjustments and improvements may be made.

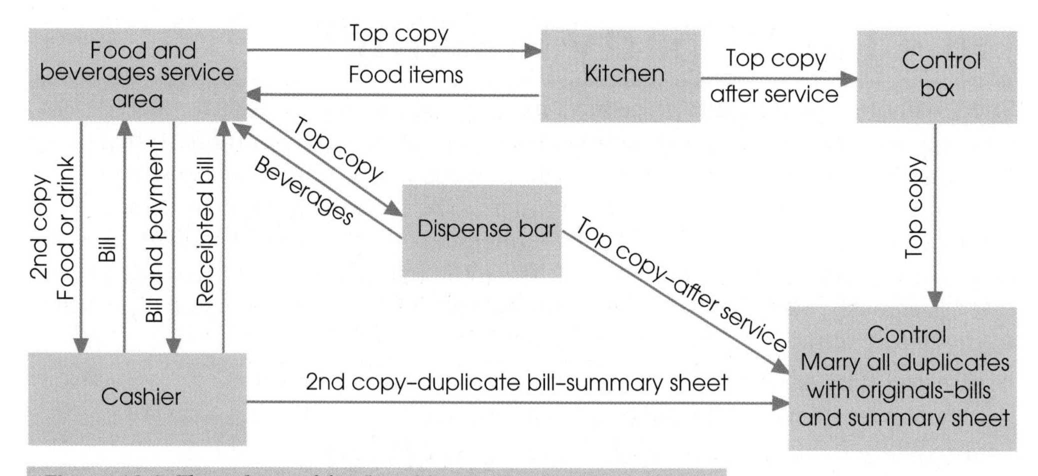

Figure 18.2 Flow chart of food and beverage checking system

The main control methods in use in foodservice establishments are:

- Order-taking methods (see Chapter 14, Section 14.4, page 257).
- Billing methods (see Section 18.8, page 310).

- Sales summary sheets (see Section 18.10, page 314).
- Performance measures (see Section 18.11, page 315).

The process of food and beverage revenue control is summarised in Figure 18.2. This chart is based upon the triplicate method for food and the duplicate method for the dispense bar. The chart indicates that all top copies go to the dispense points (bar, kitchen) and follows the flow of information through until top and second copies are matched up by control.

18.6 Systems for revenue control

The systems that are used to support the various order-taking and billing methods are summarised in Table 18.1.

Table 18.1 Order-taking and billing method control systems

Method	Description
Manual systems	Handwritten duplicate or triplicate checks for ordering from kitchen and bar and for informing the cashier. Often used with a cash till or cash register. Found in high-class restaurants and in popular catering
Pre-checking system	Orders entered directly onto a keyboard; each order check is printed with a duplicate and retains a record of all transactions. Keyboard may be preset or pre-priced. Found in many full-service restaurants and in popular catering
Electronic cash registers	Allows for a wider range of functions including sales analysis. Installed as standalone or linked systems. Found in store restaurants, cafeterias and bars
Electronic point of sale (EPOS) control systems	Separate keyboard terminals in the various service areas, linked to remote printers or visual display units (VDUs) in the kitchen, bar, etc. Terminals can be fixed or set in docking stations for hand-held use. In hotels this equipment may also be linked to the hotel accounting systems. The more sophisticated of the systems (point-of-sale, computerised and satellite) provide for increasingly efficient service at the point of sale, as well as improving the flow and quality of information to management for control purposes (For an illustration of an electronic hand-held control system, see Figure 14.6, page 292)
Computerised systems	Enables a number of serving terminals, intelligent tills and remote printers to be controlled by a master unit compatible with standard computer hardware. Functions may also include a variety of performance measures such as planning and costing, sales analysis, gross profit reporting, stock control, re-ordering and forecasting, VAT returns, payroll, staff scheduling and account information. Often found in hotels, fast-food and chain restaurants
Satellite stations	Remote terminals linked by telephone to a central processor to enable sales performance to be analysed (usually overnight) and reported back. These systems are found in fast-food and chain restaurant operations

18.7 The role of the cashier

Before the start of service the cashier should have made all relevant checks and have the required materials to hand. Each establishment will have its own procedure but will generally include the following:

- Check the float: if it is incorrect follow the company procedure.

- Ensure the cash drawer is properly organised with notes and coins in the relevant compartments.
- Ensure there are enough till rolls, promotional items, bill folders, stapler or paper clips and pens, etc.

The cashier's duties for table and assisted service may be summarised as follows:

- issuing and recording of check books
- maintaining cash floats
- preparation of customer bills
- maintaining copies of the food and wine orders together with the bills in case of server or customer queries
- counter-signing spoilt checks
- receiving payments (which may include cash, credit card and cheque payments as well as luncheon vouchers or other forms of prepaid voucher)
- receiving all unused checks back
- ensuring payments are balanced with manual or electronic sales summaries
- delivering the reports and payment to the control department.

In some operations the individual servers may take payments. Cashiers on cafeteria checkouts may have similar duties but excluding the tasks involving checks.

Where services are provided to residents in hotel lounges and in room service, payment might not be taken at the same time. Therefore, all bills must be signed by the resident concerned to show he or she has received a particular service. When a resident signs a bill the waiter must ensure the correct room number is obtained so that the charge can be made on the right bill. These bills should then be immediately passed to the control and accounts department. It is their job to ensure that the bills are posted onto the guest's account. In this way all residents' bills are kept up to date and all services provided are charged for.

18.8 Billing methods

The seven basic billing methods are described in Table 18.2.

Table 18.2 **Billing methods**

Method	Description
Bill as check	Second copy of order used as bill
Separate bill	Bill made up from duplicate check and presented to customer
Bill with order	Service to order and billing at same time, e.g. bar or takeaway service methods
Prepaid	Customer purchases ticket or card in advance, either for specific meal or specific value
Voucher	Customer has credit issued by third party for either specific meal or specific value, e.g. a luncheon voucher or tourist agency voucher
No charge	Customer not paying – credit transaction
Deferred	Refers to, e.g. event catering where the bill is to be paid by the organiser, or customers who have an account

> **Note:** All billing methods are based upon these seven concepts. The main systems used to support these methods and the different payment methods are described in Section 18.9 (page 311).

Figure 18.3 **Electronic point of sale billing and payment system**

PALM COURT RESTAURANT & LOUNGE
THE LANGHAM, LONDON
VAT: 672331741
703 Yavuz 2

PALM COURT
1/1 1289 GST 2
NOV30'09 6:48PM

1	Smoked Salmon	16.00
1	Prawn Cocktail	16.00
1	225g Sirloin	25.00
1	225g Rib Eye	24.00
1	HB 656 Sancerre	21.00
1	425 Ch la Croix	35.00
1	Voss Sparkling	5.50
1	Capuccino	4.50
2	Americano	9.00
	Food	94.50
	Wine	56.00
	Non Alc	5.50
	12.5% SERV CHG	19.50
	PAYMENT	175.50

PALM COURT

31
09334000067
American Express 175.50
----23 CLOSED NOV30 8:57PM-----

Figure 18.4 **Example of a bill**

18.9 Payment methods

There are various ways of making payment for goods or services received. The main methods of payment are described below.

Cash

When accepting cash the amount of cash received by the operator should always be checked in front of the customer and when change is given it should be counted back to the customer. Any notes received by the operator should be checked to ensure they are not forgeries. An itemised and receipted bill should always accompany the change.

Cheque

A cheque guarantee card should always accompany payment by cheque. The operator receiving the cheque should make sure:

- it is dated correctly
- it is made payable to the correct firm or company
- the correct amount is filled in
- it is signed by the person indicated on the cheque

- the signature on the cheque is the same as that on the cheque guarantee card
- the bank sort code is the same as on the cheque card
- the cheque guarantee card is valid – it has not expired in relation to the dates indicated.

The cheque guarantee card indicates that the bank concerned will meet the cheque payment (up to the limit indicated on the back of the card). This will be the case even if the person writing the cheque has insufficient monies in his or her account. Some credit and debit cards also act as cheque guarantee cards. An example of this is a Barclaycard.

Note: The use of cheques is currently being phased out or being limited to payment for amounts over, for example £15. Check with the policy of the establishment.

Credit cards/debit cards/charge cards

- *Credit cards*: allow customers to spend up to a predetermined limit. The customer receives a statement of payments at the end of each month, which he can then pay off in full or in part. Interest is charged on any remaining balance.
- *Debit cards*: used in a similar way to a credit card but the amount due is immediately deducted from the customer's bank account. Examples include the Visa debit, Maestro and Connect cards.
- *Charge cards*: these work in a similar way to credit cards but the customer is invoiced once a month. The account must then be paid up in full. Examples include the American Express and Diners Club cards.

On receipt of a credit, debit or charge card the operator should check that it is still valid by looking at the dates on the card. There are now two systems for accepting payments with these types of cards: signature verified and chip and PIN.

Signature verified

This is a manual system in which the validity of the card is checked, often through an online or dial-up connection to the card issuer, by passing it through an electronic card reader. Once verified, the details of the transaction are printed in the form of an itemised bill, which the customer is then asked to sign. A copy of this itemised bill is given as a receipt. Some establishments also make out a sales voucher. The customer is then requested to sign the voucher after which the operator should check the signature with that on the card. The customer receives a copy of the voucher as a receipt.

Chip and PIN

Chip and PIN means that the customer enters their PIN (personal identification number) into a keypad when they use a credit, debit or charge card for face-to-face transactions in shops, hotels or restaurants.

- The POS (point of sale) terminals provide the step-by-step instructions on how to complete a transaction.
- Customers *must* enter their own PIN – it is not secure for a member of staff to do it and customers are required not to reveal their PIN to anyone.
- The prompts on the POS terminal screen are followed and the payment is processed.

- The card is then removed from the card reader.
- The receipt is issued and the receipt and the card are returned to the customer.

For payments in restaurants there are two ways of dealing with payments:

- The customer may be asked to come to the cash desk or workstation to complete the payment transaction there – some customers may prefer this.
- A hand-held self-powered terminal is taken to the customer at their table.

Figure 18.5 Example of a hand-held credit/debit card payment terminal with printer

Locked PIN

If the customer enters the wrong PIN three times in a row, the card will become temporarily unusable. Customers can unlock their PIN by contacting their card issuer. Contact numbers are on the back of most cards or on statements, and/ or at most cash machines which have an unlock PIN facility.

People with disabilities

The procedures for taking payment are generally the same as described above. However, some additional considerations are given below.

- Offer to assist when needed and, most importantly, exercise patience to ensure that a customer has enough time to complete a stress-free transaction.
- Make sure all customers, including those who use wheelchairs, can easily reach the desk or table to sign the bill or to access the PIN pad.
- Follow the terminal prompts – some cardholders may have chip and signature cards instead of chip and PIN cards. Chip and PIN terminals will recognise this type of card and automatically ask for a signature.
- Encourage, or help, the customer to pick up the PIN pad from the cradle if appropriate.
- Suggest that the customer shields the PIN pad from other customers as they enter their PIN.

Declined transactions

Procedures for declined transactions are the same for any credit card/debit card/ charge card payments, whether signature verified or chip and PIN. Where the card is declined, always ask for an alternative method of payment.

Traveller's cheques

These may be issued in sterling, US dollars, euros and other currencies. The traveller's cheque must be signed once when issued and again when used to pay for something or when exchanging for cash. The rate of exchange will be that at the time of the transaction. All traveller's cheques come in different values and this value is guaranteed as long as the two signatures match. When a payment is made by traveller's cheque the customer must:

- date the cheque or cheques required
- make them payable to the establishment concerned
- sign the cheque or cheques for a second time in the appropriate place.

The cashier will then:

- match the two signatures
- ask for other identification to check the two signatures against, e.g. the customer's passport
- give change where needed, most often in the local currency.

Vouchers and tokens

Vouchers, such as luncheon vouchers, may be offered in exchange for food in those establishments that accept them. The vouchers have an expiry date. Should food be purchased above the value of the voucher, the difference must be paid for in cash.

Tokens might be exchanged for specific meals or for certain values. If food purchased is more than the value of the token then the difference is again paid in cash. No change can be given for purchases valued at less than the token being exchanged.

Dealing with discrepancies

When dealing with cash, do not allow anyone to interrupt you during the transaction or get involved with the counting of money as this will only lead to confusion.

- Always double-check cash received before placing it in the till, and any change before giving it out.
- If you make a mistake always apologise and remain polite. If you feel you cannot deal with a situation ask for assistance from your supervisor or manager.
- Banknotes should be checked for forgeries and if found to be fake, they must not be accepted. You should explain why you cannot accept them, advising the customer to take the note to the police station.
- If credit card fraud is suspected the credit card company may request that the card is retained. Suggest to the customer that they contact the company to discuss the matter. You may wish to offer the use of a telephone with some privacy.

18.10 Sales summary sheets

Sales summary sheets are also known as restaurant analysis sheets, bill summaries or records of restaurant sales. They provide for:

- the reconciliation of items with different gross profits
- sales mix information
- records of popular/unpopular items
- records for stock control.

There are many different formats for sales summaries which are often electronically produced. Depending on the needs of the establishment, the information may include:

- date
- address of food and beverage outlet (if more than one exists)
- period of service
- bill numbers
- table numbers
- number of covers per table
- bill totals

- analysis of sales, e.g. food, beverages, or more detailed, such as menu and wine and drink list items
- various performance measures (see below)
- cashier's name.

They may also include individual staff or till sales breakdowns.

Consumption control

In food and beverage service areas there may be food and beverage items displayed on:

- cold tables
- buffets
- carving trolleys
- sweet trolleys
- liqueur trolleys
- food and beverage counters.

A consumption control method is used for these services that identify the number of portions or measures issued to the area (see Table 18.3). Following service, returns are deducted and the final total equals the consumption. The consumption is then checked with actual sales to identify shortages/surpluses. This method of control is also found in room and lounge service.

Table 18.3 Example of a completed consumption control sheet

Consumption control sheet		Date: 22/06/2010		Service period: Luncheon		
Item	*Portions issued*	*Portions returned*	*Portions consumed*	*Billed portions*	*Difference*	
					+	–
Fruit salad	24	6	18	15		3
Gateau	20	5	15	14		1
Flan	30	10	20	16		4

18.11 Examples of performance measures

There is a range of information that is collected during the revenue control phase. This information is often given automatically on the sales summaries and control sheets. This can include performance measures such as sales mix, gross profit, cost percentages, seat turnover, sales per seat and sales per area. This section provides notes on these various performance measures.

The relationship between revenue, costs and profits

For a foodservice operation there is a relationship between the costs of running the operation, the revenue that is received and the profit that is made. In foodservice operations there are three elements of cost:

1. **Food or beverage costs:** often called cost of sales.
2. **Labour:** wages, salaries, staff feeding, uniforms.
3. **Overheads:** rent, rates, advertising, fuel.

There are also two types of profit:

1. **Gross profit:** Total revenue *less* cost of sales.
2. **Net profit:** Gross profit *less* labour costs and overhead costs.

In foodservice operations, sales or revenue is always equal to 100 per cent. Therefore, the relationship between the elements of costs and profits in foodservice operations may be seen as shown in Figure 18.6.

All elements of cost and profits in a foodservice operation are therefore always calculated as a percentage of the total sales figures. In many retail operations, the cost of sales figures are taken as 100 per cent so the gross profit percentage is worked out as a percentage of the cost price.

Note: In kitchen operations gross profit is sometimes called kitchen percentage or kitchen profit.

Sales mix

Sales mix figures may be taken from a sales summary sheet (see page 314) and shown in a simple report as in Table 18.4, and with an application of percentages as shown in Table 18.5.

Food and drink sales may be broken down further to provide sales mix data. This not only reconciles sales of items with differing gross profits but also provides information on:

- popular/unpopular items on the menu/drinks lists
- records for stock control, e.g. to help predict future demand
- changes in customers' interests
- where profits/losses are being made.

Food and beverage costs	Cost of sales
Labour costs Overhead costs Net profit	} Gross profit
Total sales £	**Revenue 100%**

Figure 18.6 Summary of the relationship between revenue, costs and profits in foodservice operations

Table 18.4 Simple sales report

Service	Total	Food	Liquor
	£	£	£
Lunches	90	60	30
Dinners	80	50	30
Snacks	15	15	–
Daily total	185	125	60

Table 18.5 Application of percentages

Service	Total		Food		Liquor	
	£	%	£	%	£	%
Lunches	90	49	60	67	30	33
Dinners	80	43	50	62	30	38
Snacks	15	8	15	100	–	–
Daily total	185	100	125	68	60	32

Cost percentages

All costs such as cost of sales, labour or overheads can be classified in relation to sales. For example, the cost of labour would be as follows:

$$\text{Labour costs as a percentage of total wages cost} = \frac{\text{Department labour cost}}{\text{Total wage cost}} \times 100$$

$$\text{Labour costs as a percentage of sales} = \frac{\text{Labour cost}}{\text{Revenue}} \times 100$$

These calculations of labour costs are summarised in Table 18.6.

Table 18.6 Labour cost percentages

Sales		**Direct labour costs**	**% of total labour costs**	**% of department sales**
Food	£125	£35	78%	28%
Liquor	£60	£10	22%	17%
Total	£185	£45	100%	24%

By using a similar approach, all costs (food, drink, labour or overheads) can be attributed to a return in revenue.

Seat turnover

Seat turnover is a pointer to efficiency. It shows how many times a seat is being used during a service period. An example of a report can be seen in Table 18.7. Seat turnover is calculated by dividing the number of covers served by the actual number of seats available per service period. Therefore:

- in a snack bar the seat turnover might be four to five times per service period
- in an expensive restaurant the seat turnover might be once per service period.

In operations where customers do not occupy specific seats (such as in cafeterias or takeaway operations) the customer throughput is calculated by the number of till transactions per service period (e.g. lunch) or time period (e.g. per hour).

Table 18.7 Example of seat turnover calculation

Service period	No. of covers served	No. of seats available	Seat turnover
Lunch	60	80	0.75 times
Dinner	85	80	1.06 times

Average spend per head/average check

The average spend per head is a calculation of the average amount spent per person during a service period. It is calculated by dividing the total sales by the number of people or covers served. This performance measure is useful in restaurants where the total number of customers (covers) is known.

The average check is a calculation of the average spend per order taken, during a service period. It is calculated by dividing the total sales by the number of orders taken. This performance measure is useful in bars or takeaway operations where the actual number of customers is not known. An example of both of these calculations is shown in Table 18.8.

Table 18.8 Example of average check and average spend per head calculations

	Total revenue	No. of orders taken	Average check	No. of covers served	Average spend per head
	£				£
Food	490	16	30.62	48	10.20
Beverages	280	13	21.54	39	7.18
Overall	770	29	26.55	87	8.85

This data can also be used to calculate the average number of customers in a group. This is calculated by dividing the number of covers served by the number of orders taken. Using the data for food sales in Table 18.8, this would be:

48 covers served, divided by 16 orders taken = an average of 3 persons in each group.

Sales per seat available

Sales per seat available shows the sales value that can be earned by each seat in a restaurant, coffee shop, etc. It is used for comparison of different types of operation as well as a record of earnings per seat over a period of time. It is calculated by dividing the sales figures by the number of seats available in the dining area for specific service periods.

Sales per square metre

An alternative method of comparison between establishments is to calculate the sales per square metre or per foot. This is particularly useful in bars or takeaway operations where earnings per seat cannot be calculated. It is calculated by dividing the total sales by the square meterage of the service area, for a specific service period.

Stock turnover

The rate of stock turnover gives the number of times that the average level of stock has turned over in a given period. It is calculated as follows:

$$\text{Rate of stock turnover} = \frac{\text{Cost of food or beverage consumed in specific period}}{\text{Average stockholding (food or beverage) at cost}}$$

The average stockholding is calculated by taking the opening stock value, adding the closing stock value and dividing by two. High stock turnover should be expected in a restaurant using predominantly fresh foods. Low stock turnover indicates usage of convenience food. Too high a turnover indicates potential problems through panic buying and lack of forecasting. Too low a turnover indicates that capital is being tied up in unused stocks.

The calculation of stock turnover can also be used for items such as glassware, crockery, cutlery, tableware, linen, etc. It can be calculated on the costs of the equipment for calculated for individual units, for example, number of plates.

ANNEX A

Cocktails and mixed drinks recipes

The list of cocktails and mixed drinks below is drawn from various sources including previous editions of this book, the official listings of the International Bartenders Guild and the United Kingdom Bartenders Guild.

When making cocktails and mixed drinks it is important to check the definition for permitted alcoholic liquor measures for your country, including any licensing restrictions on sales to minors.

Examples of glasses for the service of cocktails are shown in Figure 16.1 (page 281).

Alcoholic cocktails

Name	Ingredients	Method
Americano	3.0 cl Campari 3.0 cl red vermouth Soda water	Place the Campari and sweet vermouth over ice into a Highball glass. Stir well to chill. Top up with the soda water to taste. Garnish with half a slice of orange and lemon peel.
B&B	3.0 cl Cognac 3.0 cl Bénédictine	Stir well on ice in the bar mixing glass and strain into a liqueur glass (or brandy balloon).
B52	2.0 cl Kahlúa 2.0 cl Baileys Irish Cream 2.0 cl Grand Marnier	Build all ingredients over ice into a medium shot glass. Serve with stirrer.
Bacardi	4.5 cl Bacardi white rum 2.0 cl fresh lemon or lime juice 0.5 cl grenadine syrup	Place all ingredients on ice into a cocktail shaker. Shake well. Strain into a cocktail glass.
Bellini	10 cl well-chilled dry champagne 5.0 cl fresh peach purée	Prepare in champagne flute by pouring in the fresh peach purée first and then topping up with the well-chilled champagne or sparkling wine. Garnish with a slice of fresh peach. Peaches can be minced to make a smoother juice.
Between the Sheets	1.5 cl Cognac 1.5 cl Cointreau 1.5 cl white rum ½ fresh lemon juice	Shake all ingredients well on ice and strain into an Old Fashioned glass.
Black Russian	5.0 cl vodka 2.0 cl coffee liqueur	Pour all ingredients into an Old Fashioned glass filled with ice cubes. Stir gently.
Black Velvet	Guinness Chilled dry champagne	Top up the Guinness with the chilled dry champagne. Sometimes served in silver tankards.

Name	Ingredients	Method
Bloody Mary	4.5 cl vodka 9.0 cl tomato juice (or as required) 1.5 cl lemon juice	Place ingredients in the cocktail shaker and shake well on ice. Season and serve in a Highball glass.
	Variations: To make tomato juice spicier, add salt, pepper and Worcestershire sauce to taste. Any of the following may also be added to enhance flavour: dash of Tabasco, fresh lemon juice, pepper from the peppermill or cayenne pepper. Garnish may also be varied by the use of a stick of celery, carrot stick or a wedge of lemon. A *Virgin Mary* excludes the vodka.	
Blue Lady	1.5 cl Cognac 1.5 cl blue Curaçao 1.5 cl lemon juice 1 egg white	Put all the ingredients together into a cocktail shaker with ice. Shake vigorously. Strain into a cocktail glass.
Bramble	5cl gin Fresh lime or lemon juice 1 teaspoon caster sugar or use gomme syrup 1 cl crème de mûre (blackberry) liqueur Soda water Crushed ice	Fill a Highball glass with crushed ice, gin, lemon or lime juice and sugar or sugar syrup and stir. Top up with more soda and then lace drink with crème de mûre by slowly pouring over. Serve with two short straws and often garnished with a lemon slice and a blackberry.
Brandy Alexander	2.0 cl Cognac 2.0 cl fresh cream 2.0 cl brown crème de cacao	Put all ingredients into a cocktail shaker with ice and shake well. Strain into a chilled cocktail glass. Sprinkle the surface with fresh ground nutmeg.
Brandy Cosmopolitan	5cl cognac 1.5cl Cointreau 1.5cl fresh lemon juice 2 cl cranberry juice	Pour all ingredients into a shaker with ice and shake. Strain into a cocktail glass. Garnish with a wedge of lime.
Bucks Fizz	5.0 cl well-chilled champagne 10 cl fresh orange juice	Prepare in champagne flute by first pouring in the fresh orange and then top up with the well-chilled champagne. Decorate with a curl/twist of orange peel.
Caipirinha	5.0 cl cachaça (Brazilian spirit distilled from fermented sugarcane) 1 small fresh lime 1½ teaspoons caster sugar	Wash the lime and slice off the top and bottom and cut into small segments from top to bottom. Add the lime segments and the sugar to an Old Fashioned glass. Crush the lime to make juice, and muddle to make sure the sugar has dissolved. Add ice cubes and the cachaça and stir. Serve with a stirrer and an optional straw.

Name	Ingredients	Method
Champagne Cocktail	½ sugar cube 2 dashes Angostura bitters 5.0 cl champagne (well chilled) or sparkling wine 0.5 cl brandy	Place the sugar cube soaked in Angostura into a champagne flute. Pour over the well-chilled champagne and float the brandy on the surface by pouring over the back of a teaspoon. Garnish with a slice of orange and a maraschino cherry.
	Note: This cocktail may be made with any sparkling wine but should then be called by the name of the wine used and not *Champagne Cocktail* as the name champagne is protected.	
Cosmopolitan	4.0 cl vodka 1.5 cl Cointreau 1.5 cl fresh lime juice 3.0 cl cranberry juice	Place all ingredients into cocktail shaker filled with ice. Shake well and strain into large cocktail glass. Garnish with lime slice.
Cuba Libre	5.0 cl white rum 10 cl cola	Pour the white rum and into a Collins glass with ice. Garnish with a lemon/lime wedge. Top up with cola to taste.
Daiquiri	4.5 cl Daiquiri white rum 2.0 cl fresh lemon/lime juice 0.5 cl gomme syrup	Place all ingredients on ice into a cocktail shaker. Shake well. Strain into a cocktail glass.
	Variation: *Frozen Daiquiri*: ingredients as for above with the addition of one scoop of vanilla ice cream. Pour all ingredients into blender with crushed ice. Blend until slushy and smooth and pour into chilled goblet.	
Gin Fizz	4.5 cl gin 3.0 cl fresh lemon juice 1.0 cl gomme syrup 8.0 cl soda water	Shake all ingredients except soda water with ice cubes in a cocktail shaker. Strain into a Highball glass. Garnish with lemon and add straws.
	Variations: Make with Sloe Gin; *Golden Fizz* – same as Gin Fizz plus egg yolk; *Royal Fizz* – same as Gin Fizz plus whole egg; *Silver Fizz* – same as Gin Fizz plus egg white only.	
Golden Dream	2.0 cl Galliano 2.0 cl Cointreau 2.0 cl fresh orange juice 2.0 cl single cream	Shake all ingredients vigorously over ice in the cocktail shaker. Strain into a chilled cocktail glass.
Grasshopper	2.0 cl crème de menthe 2.0 cl white crème de cacao 2.0 cl single cream	Place all ingredients over ice in the cocktail shaker. Shake thoroughly. Strain into a chilled cocktail glass.
Harvey Wallbanger	4.5 cl vodka 9.0 cl orange juice 1.5 cl Galliano	Pour the vodka and orange juice directly into a Highball glass containing ice. Float the Galliano on top by pouring over the back of a teaspoon. Garnish with a slice of orange and a maraschino cherry.
Highball	5.0 cl whisky Dry ginger ale	Place ice in a Highball glass. Add the whisky and stir to chill well. Add the dry ginger ale to taste. Decorate with a twist of lemon peel.

Name	Ingredients	Method
John Collins	4.5 cl gin 3.0 cl fresh lemon juice 1.5 cl gomme syrup 6.0 cl soda water	Pour all ingredients directly into a Highball filled with ice. Stir gently. Garnish with lemon slice and maraschino cherry. Add dash of Angostura bitter. (Note: Use 'Old Tom' gin for a Tom Collins.)
Kamikaze	3.0 cl vodka 3.0 cl Cointreau 3.0 cl lemon juice	Add all ingredients into cocktail glass shaker filled with ice. Shake well and strain into cocktail glass. Garnish with a lime wedge and stirrer.
Kir	1.0 cl crème de cassis 9.0 cl white wine (dry white Burgundy)	Place the crème de cassis in a chilled wine glass. Add the well-chilled white wine. Stir thoroughly.
Kir Royale	9.0 cl dry champagne 1.0 cl crème de cassis	Place the crème de cassis in a chilled champagne flute. Add the well-chilled champagne. Do not stir.
Mai-Tai	3.0 cl white rum 3.0 cl dark rum 1.5 cl orange Curacao 1.5 cl orgeat syrup (almond) 0.5 cl rock candy syrup 1.0 cl fresh lime juice	Add all ingredients except dark rum into cocktail shaker filled with ice. Shake well and strain into Highball glass. Float dark rum over the back of a spoon on top, garnish with pineapple spear and lime peel. Serve with a straw.
Manhattan	5.0 cl American rye whiskey 2.0 cl sweet vermouth 1 dash of Angostura bitters	Pour ingredients into mixing glass and stir until well chilled. Strain into a cocktail glass. Garnish with a maraschino cherry.
	Variation: *Dry Manhattan* – substitute sweet vermouth with 2.0 cl dry vermouth. Garnish with a thin twist of lemon or an olive.	
Margarita	5.0 cl tequila 5.0 cl fresh lemon juice 2.5 cl Cointreau or triple sec	Place all ingredients on ice into a cocktail shaker. Shake well. Strain into a cocktail glass rimmed with salt.
Martini	5.5 cl gin 1.5 cl dry vermouth	Pour the gin and vermouth into the bar mixing glass filled with ice cubes. Stir. Strain into a chilled Martini cocktail glass. For a *Dry Martini* squeeze oil from lemon peel onto the drink and garnish with either an olive on a cocktail stick or a twist of lemon.
	Variations: *Sweet Martini* – basic method as for *Dry Martini* but using red (sweet) vermouth instead of dry and garnish with a maraschino cherry. For *Vodka Martini* replace gin with vodka.	
Mint Julep	3.0 cl Bourbon whiskey Soda water to moisten Caster sugar Mint leaves Crushed ice	Place mint leaves and sugar into a Highball glass. Moisten with soda water and muddle the mixture to dissolve the caster sugar. Add the Bourbon whiskey and fill the highball glass with the crushed ice. Stir and decorate with mint. Serve with straws.

Name	Ingredients	Method
Mojito	4.0 cl white rum 3.0 cl fresh lime juice 3 sprigs of mint 2 teaspoons sugar Soda water	Muddle mint sprigs with sugar and lime juice in a Highball glass. Add rum and top with soda water. Garnish with sprig of mint leaves. Serve with a straw.
Moscow Mule	4.5 cl vodka 3.0 cl fresh lemon juice Ginger beer to taste	Fill a Highball glass with ice. Add the vodka and fresh lemon juice. Stir well to blend and chill. Top with ginger beer to taste. Decorate with a twist of lemon/lime.
Mulled Wine (Serves 20)	2 bottles of Burgundy or Rhône red wine ¼ bottle dark rum ½ bottle Dubonnet ½ bottle drinking water Whole orange studded with cloves (clouted) 2 cinnamon sticks 25 g (1 oz) sultanas 2 lemon halves 5 g (¼ oz) mixed spice 1 x 400 g (1 lb) jar of clear honey	Heat the clouted orange for 10 minutes in the oven to bring out the flavour. Tie the mixed spices in a muslin bag to prevent clouding the wine. Place all of the ingredients with the exception of the rum into a large pot. Hold some of the honey back so as to be able to adjust the flavour later. Place the pot on a low heat and stir occasionally. Bring the mixture to boiling point but do not allow it to boil. When ready to serve add the rest of the honey to taste. Finish with the rum just before serving into small Paris goblets or similar. Sprinkle a little grated nutmeg onto the top of each drink.
Negroni	3.0 cl gin 3.0 cl sweet vermouth 3.0 cl Campari Dash of soda water	Stir all ingredients over ice in the bar mixing glass. Strain into a Collins glass filled with crushed ice. Add the soda water to taste. Garnish with a slice of lemon.
Old Fashioned	4.0 cl Bourbon, Scotch or rye whiskey 2 dashes Angostura bitters 1 sugar cube 1 splash soda water	In an Old Fashioned glass saturate one lump of sugar (or one heaped teaspoon of caster sugar) with Angostura and add a dash of water. Gently shake to dissolve caster sugar and then add whiskey. Fill glass with ice, stir and garnish with a slice of orange and two maraschino cherries.
Pimm's	5.0 cl Pimm's No 1 cup 9.0 cl lemonade/tonic water	Pour Pimm's into a Worthington or Highball glass. Add ice and top up with lemonade or alternatives. Decorate with slice of apple, orange, lemon, lime and a twist of cucumber peel. Alternatively just use mint leaves. Stirrer and straws are optional.
Pina Colada	3.0 cl white rum 3.0 cl coconut cream 9.0 cl pineapple juice	Shake or blend all ingredients vigorously on ice until smooth. Strain into a chilled Highball glass. Garnish with fresh pineapple wedge and a maraschino cherry. Add straws.

Name	Ingredients	Method
Pink Gin	5.0 cl gin 2 or 3 drops of Angostura bitters to taste	Fill a Paris goblet or Rocks glass with crushed ice to chill it. Remove the ice and place the Angostura bitters in and swill around. Tip out the excess and pour in gin.
Red Snapper	1 cl Canadian rye whisky 1 cl amaretto 2 cl cranberry juice	Pour all the ingredients into a cocktail shaker with ice cubes. Shake well and strain into a chilled cocktail glass.
Round the World	3.0 cl banana liqueur 3.0 cl Scotch whisky 0.5 cl Cointreau 0.5 cl orange cordial Orange slice	Put the banana liqueur and whisky into a shaker with plenty of ice. Add Cointreau and undiluted orange cordial. Shake and strain into a cocktail glass. Add orange to garnish and serve.
Rusty Nail (or Kilt Lifter)	4.5 cl Scotch whisky 2.5 cl Drambuie	Pour all ingredients directly into an Old Fashioned glass filled with ice. Stir gently. Garnish with a lemon twist.
Salty Dog	4.0 cl vodka 10.0 cl grapefruit juice	Shake vodka and grapefruit juice in cocktail shaker. Strain into a salt-rimmed Highball glass filled with ice.
Sazerac	5 cl Bourbon 1 cl Pernod Dash Peychaud bitters Dash Angostura bitters 1 white sugar cube Dash soda water	Place a sugar cube in an Old Fashioned glass and soak with the Angostura and Peychaud bitters. Add enough soda to cover the sugar and crush it with the back of a bar spoon. Add the Bourbon. Stir. Float the Pernod over the top. Garnish with a twist of lemon.
Screwdriver	5.0 cl vodka 10 cl fresh orange juice	Place all ingredients on ice into a Highball glass. Stir gently. Decorate with a slice/twist of fresh orange.
Sea Breeze	4.0 cl vodka 12.0 cl cranberry juice 3.0 cl grapefruit juice	Build all ingredients in a Highball glass filled with ice. Garnish with lime wedge.
Sex on the Beach	4.0 cl vodka 2.0 cl peach schnapps 4.0 cl orange juice 4.0 cl cranberry juice	Pour all ingredients into cocktail shaker. Shake and pour into a Highball glass filled with ice. Garnish with orange slice.
Sherry Cup	5.0 cl dry sherry 9.0 cl medium cider Fresh sliced unpeeled cucumber	Use very chilled ingredients. Put sherry into a Highball or Worthington glass and top up with cider. Garnish with freshly-cut cucumber slices.
Sidecar	3.0 cl Cognac 3.0 cl Cointreau 3.0 cl fresh lemon juice	Shake all ingredients well on ice and strain into a Highball glass partially filled with crushed ice.

Name	Ingredients	Method
Singapore Sling	4.0 cl gin 2.0 cl cherry brandy 0.5 cl Cointreau 0.5 cl Bénédictine D.O.M. 1.0 cl grenadine 8.0 cl pineapple juice 3.0 cl fresh lemon juice 1 dash Angostura bitters	Pour all ingredients into a cocktail shaker filled with ice cubes. Shake well. Strain into a Highball glass. Garnish with a pineapple slice and a maraschino cherry.
Tequila Sunrise	4.5 cl tequila 1.5 cl grenadine 9.0 cl orange juice	Place the tequila and fresh orange juice on ice in a Collins glass. Stir well to chill and blend. Add grenadine. Do not stir again. Garnish with an orange slice, maraschino cherry, straws and a stirrer.
Whiskey Collins	3.0 cl American rye whiskey 2 teaspoons caster sugar 3.0 cl lemon juice Soda water	Collins is a sour served on the rocks in a Collins (or Highball) glass and topped with soda water. Garnish as a sour but add straws.
Whiskey Sour	4.5 cl Bourbon whiskey 3.0 cl fresh lemon juice 1 dash of egg white 1.5 cl gomme syrup	Pour all ingredients into a cocktail shaker filled with ice. Shake well. Strain into a Sour (or Rocks) glass. Garnish with a slice of orange and a maraschino cherry.
	Variations: Gin Sour, Bourbon Sour, Rum Sour (dark rum), *Scotch Sour, Daquiri Sour* (light rum).	
White Lady	3.0 cl gin 1.5 cl Cointreau 1.5 cl fresh lemon juice Dash of egg white	Place all ingredients on ice into a cocktail shaker. Shake well and strain into a cocktail glass. Decorate with a twist of lemon.

Non-alcoholic cocktails

Name	Ingredients	Methods
Fruit Cup	3.0 cl orange juice 3.0 cl grapefruit juice 3.0 cl apple juice Lemonade/soda water	Pour all ingredients, with the exception of the lemonade/soda, onto ice in a glass jug. Stir well to blend and chill. Add sliced fruit garnish. Top up with lemonade or soda water. Serve well chilled in Highball or Worthington glasses.
Pussyfoot	2.0 cl orange juice 1.0 cl fresh lemon juice 1.0 cl lime cordial 0.5 cl grenadine 1 egg yolk Soda water	Place all ingredients with the exception of the soda water on ice into a cocktail shaker. Shake vigorously to blend well together. Strain over crushed ice into a Collins glass. Top up with the soda water. Add straws.
Saint Clements	4.5 cl orange juice 4.5 cl bitter lemon	Mix the orange juice and bitter lemon on ice in a Worthington or Highball glass. Stir well to blend. Garnish with a slice of orange and lemon.

Name	Ingredients	Methods
Shirley Temple/Roy Rogers	9.0 cl ginger ale 0.5 cl grenadine	Place ice in a Highball glass and add grenadine. Pour in the chilled ginger ale. Decorate with full fruit garnish and add straws.
	Variations: Ginger ale and fresh lime juice, or ginger ale and lime cordial to taste.	
Tropicana	4.5 cl pineapple juice 4.5 cl orange juice	Mix the well-chilled ingredients on crushed ice in a Slim Jim glass and serve with straws.
Virgin Mary	Made as for a Bloody Mary (see above) but without any alcohol.	

Index